Houghton Mifflin Harcourt

Texas GO Math!

Volume 2

Texas GO Math!

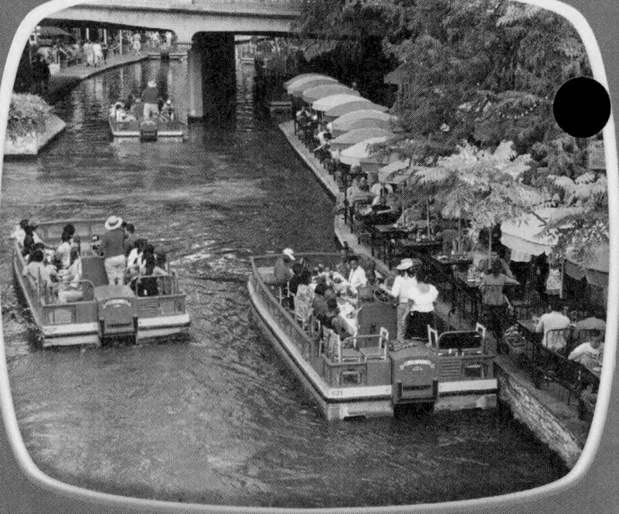

Printed in the U.S.A.

ISBN 978-0-544-08683-8

10 0928 22 21 20 19

4500743247 C D E F G

Cover Image Credits: (The Alamo) ©Michael DeFreitas/Getty Images; (refinery) ©Lynn Johnson/Getty Images; (landscape) ©David Hensley/Getty Images; (turtle) ©Kristina Vackova/ Shutterstock.

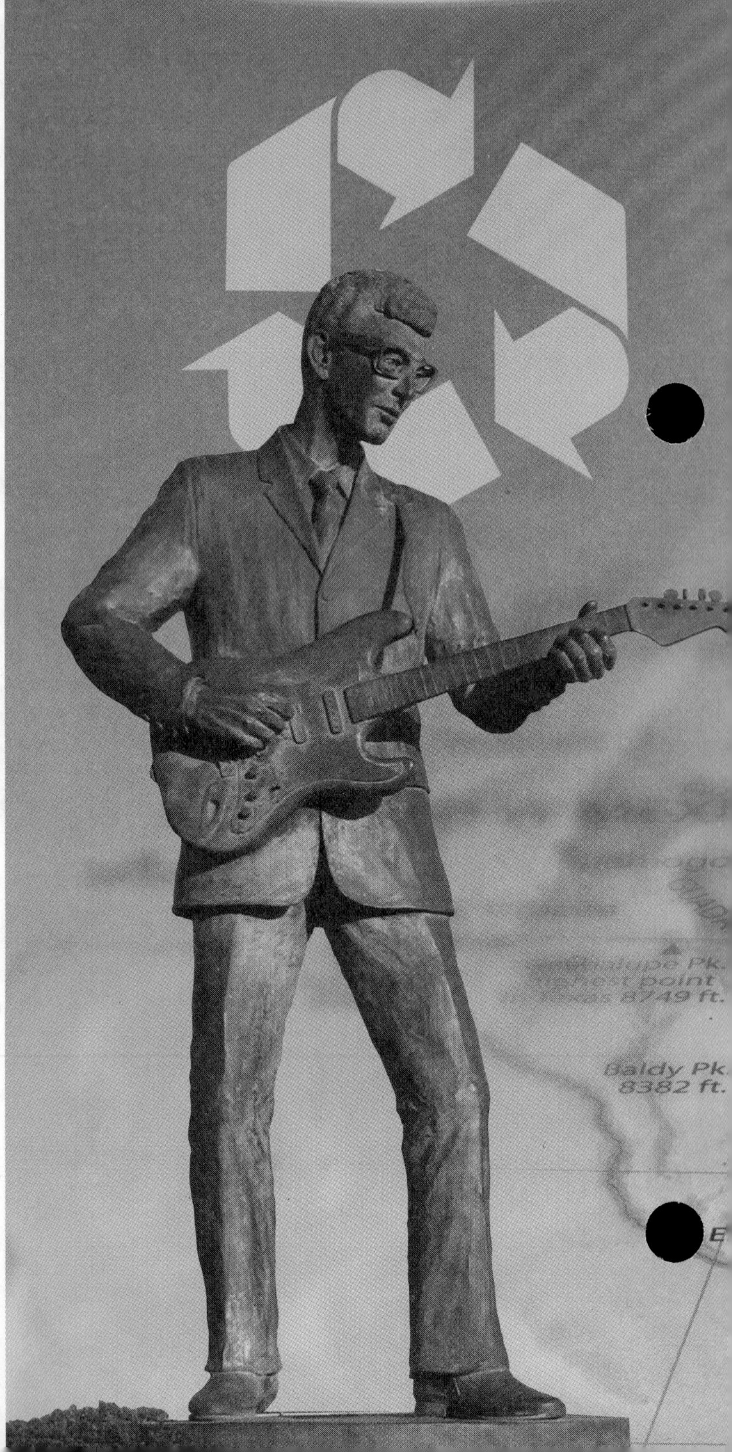

Dear Students and Families,

Welcome to **Texas Go Math!**, Grade 4! In this exciting mathematics program, there are hands-on activities to do and real-world problems to solve. Best of all, you will write your ideas and answers right in your book. In **Texas Go Math!**, writing and drawing on the pages helps you think deeply about what you are learning, and you will really understand math!

By the way, all of the pages in your **Texas Go Math!** book are made using recycled paper. We wanted you to know that you can Go Green with **Texas Go Math!**

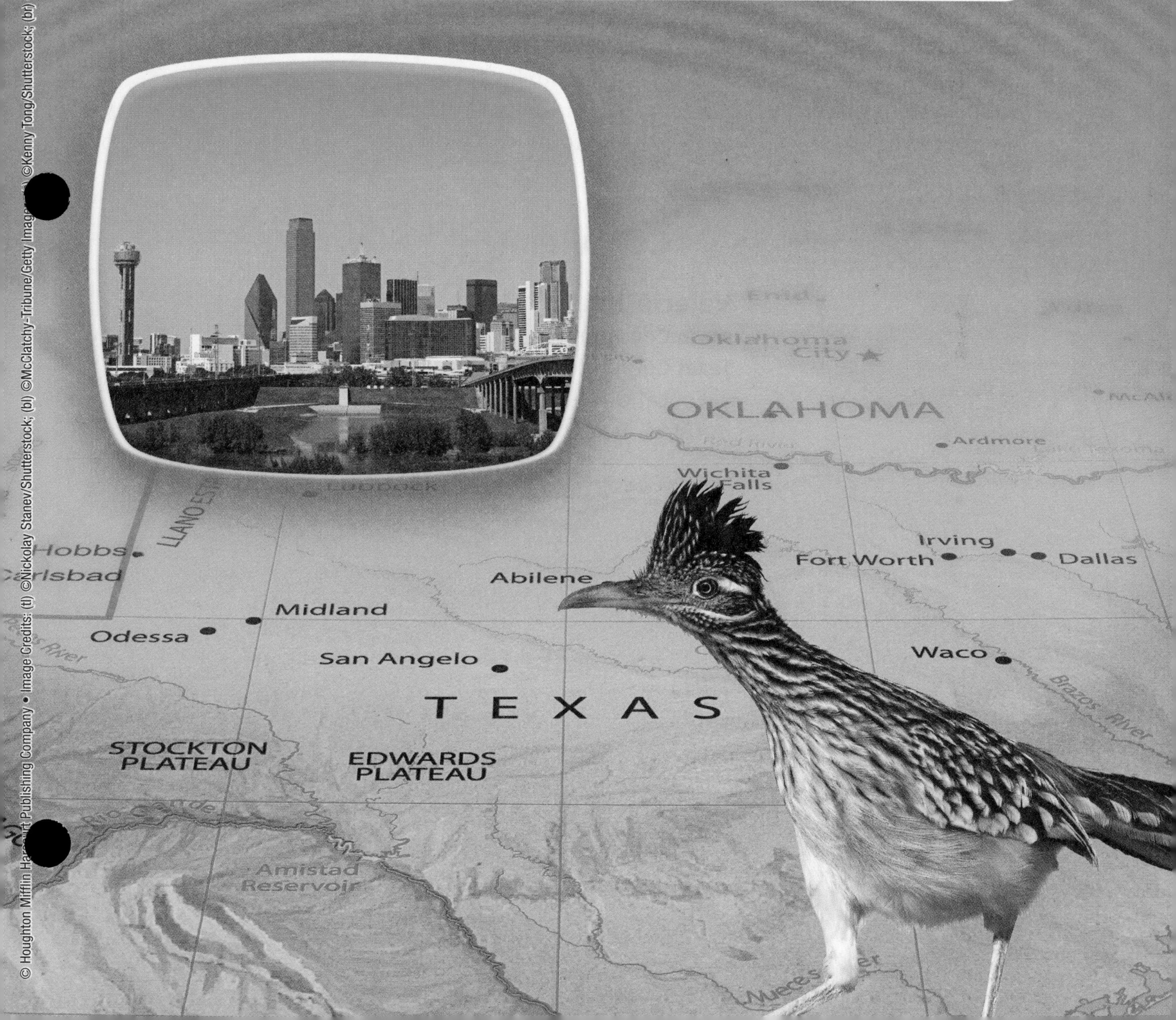

Sincerely,

The Authors

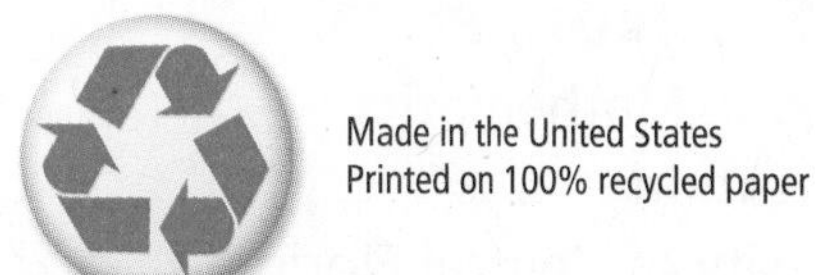

Texas GO Math!

Authors

Juli K. Dixon, Ph.D.
Professor, Mathematics Education
University of Central Florida
Orlando, Florida

Edward B. Burger, Ph.D.
President
Southwestern University
Georgetown, Texas

Matthew R. Larson, Ph.D.
K-12 Curriculum Specialist for Mathematics
Lincoln Public Schools
Lincoln, Nebraska

Martha E. Sandoval-Martinez
Math Instructor
El Camino College
Torrance, California

Consultant

Valerie Johse
Math Consultant
Texas Council for Economic Education
Houston, Texas

Volume 1

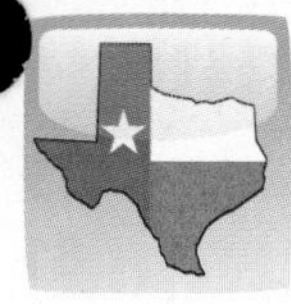

Unit 1 • Number and Operations: Place Value, Fraction Concepts, and Operations

Module 1 Whole Number Place Value

Module 2 Decimal Place Value

Look for these:

H.O.T. Problems
Higher Order Thinking
Multi-Step Problems

Homework and Practice

Homework and TEKS Practice in every lesson.

GO DIGITAL Resources

DIGITAL RESOURCES
Go online for the Interactive Student Edition with Math on the Spot Videos. Use *i*Tools, the Multimedia *e*Glossary, and more.

Module 3 Fraction Concepts

Module 4 Compare Fractions

Module 5 Add and Subtract Fractions

Look for these:

H.O.T. Problems
Higher Order Thinking
Multi-Step Problems

GO DIGITAL Resources

DIGITAL RESOURCES
Go online for the Interactive Student Edition with Math on the Spot Videos. Use *i*Tools, the Multimedia *e*Glossary, and more.

Volume 1

Unit 2 • Number and Operations: Whole Number and Decimal Operations

H.O.T. Problems
Higher Order Thinking
Multi-Step Problems

Module 6 Add and Subtract Whole Numbers and Decimals

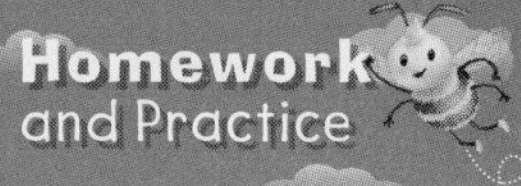

Homework and TEKS Practice in every lesson.

Module 7 Multiply by 1-Digit Numbers

Look for these:

H.O.T. Problems
Higher Order Thinking
Multi-Step Problems

Module 8 Multiply 2-Digit Numbers

Module 9 Division Strategies

Module 10 Divide by 1-Digit Numbers

GO DIGITAL Resources

DIGITAL RESOURCES
Go online for the Interactive Student Edition with Math on the Spot Videos. Use *i*Tools, the Multimedia *e*Glossary, and more.

Volume 2

Unit 3 • Algebraic Reasoning

Module 11 Algebra: Multi-Step Problems

Module 12 Number Patterns, Perimeter, and Area

Look for these:

H.O.T. Problems
Higher Order Thinking
Multi-Step Problems

Homework and Practice

Homework and TEKS Practice in every lesson.

Volume 2

Unit 4 • Geometry and Measurement

Module 13 Geometry Concepts

Module 14 Measure Angles

Look for these:

Real World

H.O.T. Problems
Higher Order Thinking
Multi-Step Problems

GO DIGITAL Resources

DIGITAL RESOURCES
Go online for the Interactive Student Edition with Math on the Spot Videos. Use *i*Tools, the Multimedia *e*Glossary, and more.

Module 15 Customary and Metric Measures

Module 16 Time and Money

Volume 2

Unit 5 • Data Analysis

Module 17 Represent and Interpret Data

Look for these:

H.O.T. Problems
Higher Order Thinking
Multi-Step Problems

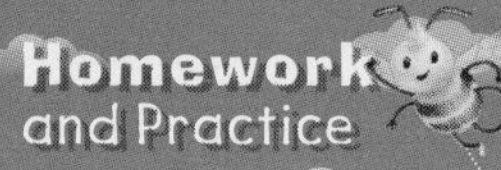

Homework and TEKS Practice in every lesson.

Look for these:

H.O.T. Problems
Higher Order Thinking
Multi-Step Problems

Volume 2

Unit 6 • Personal Financial Literacy

Module 18 Financial Literacy

GO DIGITAL Resources

DIGITAL RESOURCES
Go online for the Interactive Student Edition with Math on the Spot Videos. Use *i*Tools, the Multimedia *e*Glossary, and more.

Unit 3

Algebraic Reasoning

Show What You Know

Check your understanding of important skills.

Name ______________________________

▶ Missing Factors Find the missing factor.

1. 

_____ × 6 = 24

2. 3 × _____ = 27

▶ Find Perimeter Add to find the perimeter.

3. 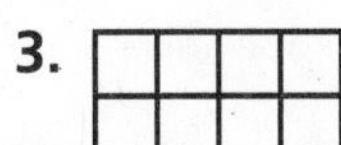

Perimeter = _____

4. Perimeter = _____

5. 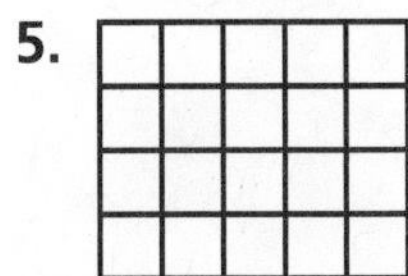

Perimeter = _____

6. 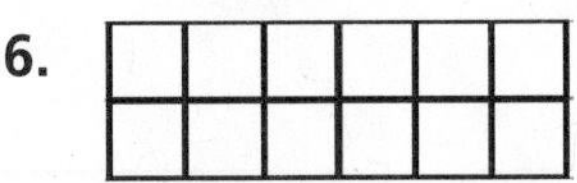

Perimeter = _____

▶ Find Area of Rectangles Find the area.

7. 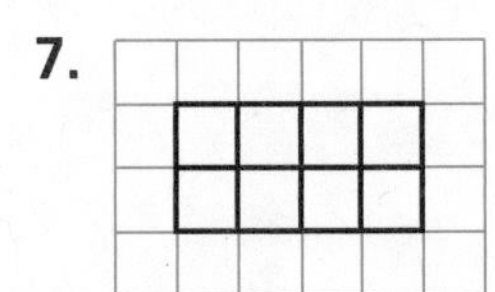

Area = _____ square units

8. 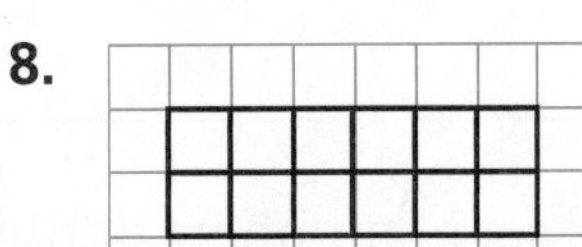

Area = _____ square units

GO DIGITAL Assessment Options: Soar to Success

Vocabulary Builder

▶ Visualize It

Place the checked words in the appropriate columns of the table. Words may be used more than once.

the carpet covering the floor of a rectangular room	the base board around the edge of the floor of a rectangular room

Review Words

✓ unit

Preview Words

✓ area
✓ formula
✓ length
pattern
✓ perimeter
✓ square unit
term
✓ width

▶ Understand Vocabulary

Write the word or term that answers the riddle.

1. I am the number of unit squares needed to cover a flat surface.

____

2. I am the distance around a figure.

____

3. I am a unit of area that measures 1 unit by 1 unit.

____

4. I am a set of symbols that expresses a mathematical rule.

____

5. I am an ordered set of numbers or objects.

____

GO DIGITAL • Interactive Student Edition • Multimedia eGlossary

Reading & Writing Math

Name ___________________________

Reading In reading, thinking about what you already know helps you to understand a new topic. You already know a lot about geometry and measurement. You can use what you know to move ahead.

Before beginning a lesson on perimeter and area, Lili lists five things she already knows.

Topic: Perimeter and Area

What do I already know?

1. Perimeter is the distance around a shape.
2. You can use an inch ruler to measure perimeter.
3. You can use a centimeter ruler to measure perimeter.
4. Area is the number of square units needed to cover a flat surface.
5. You use grid paper to find area.

Writing Think about what you know about perimeter and area. Use grid paper. Draw a rectangle. Find its perimeter. Find its area.

Think
I remember finding the perimeter of a rectangle. I added the lengths of its sides.

Get Ready Game

Find the Area

Object of the Game Practice finding the area of different sized rectangles.

Materials

- Inch Rulers
- Rectangle Cards (2 sets)

Set Up

Each player gets an inch ruler. Players shuffle the Rectangle Cards and place them face down in a stack.

Number of Players 2

How to Play

1. Players take turns drawing a card from the stack until each player has four cards.
2. Players use an inch ruler to measure the length and width of each rectangle to the nearest inch.
3. Players find the area for each rectangle and add the areas together.
4. The player with the largest sum scores a point.
5. Return all the cards to the stack and shuffle. Repeat steps 1–4. The first player to score a total of 3 points is the winner.

Name ______________________________

Multi-Step Addition Problems

Essential Question How can you represent and solve multi-step addition problems using strip diagrams?

Unlock the Problem (Real World)

Sami scored 3,489 points in the first round of a new computer game. He scored 7,415 more points in the second round than he did in the first round. How many points did Sami score in the two rounds?

Example 1

Remember

A variable is a letter or symbol that stands for a number. An equation is a number sentence which shows that two quantities are equal.

STEP 1 Find how many points Sami scored in the second round.

First round points | 7,415 more points

3,489

Second round ______

p ← Let p represent the total number of points scored in the second round.

______ + ______ $= p$ Write an equation.

______ $= p$ Solve.

STEP 2 Find how many total points were scored.

First round points | Second round points

3,489 | 10,904

n ← Let n represent the number of points scored in the two rounds.

______ + ______ $= n$ Write an equation.

______ $= n$ Solve.

So, Sami scored ______ points in the game.

Kylie and her grandfather collect stamps. Kylie has 1,342 stamps. Her grandfather has 2,887 more stamps than she does. How many stamps do Kylie and her grandfather have combined?

Example 2

STEP 1 Find how many stamps Kylie's grandfather has.

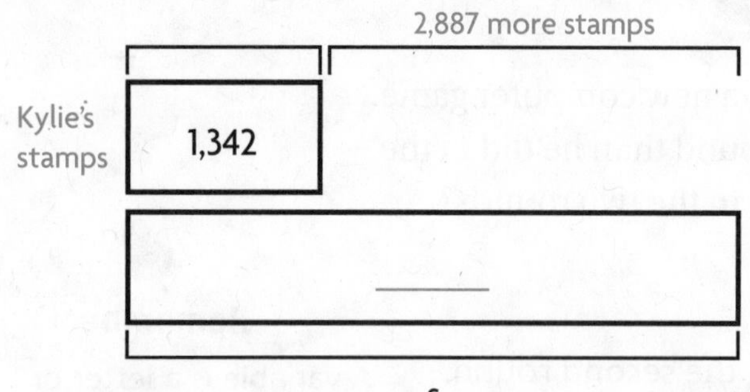

s ← Number of stamps Kylie's grandfather has.

1,342 + ________ = s Write an equation.

________ = s Solve.

STEP 2 Find how many stamps Kylie and her grandfather have combined.

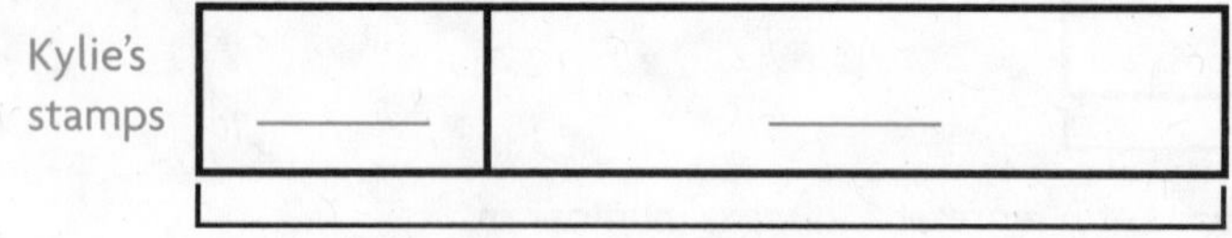

t ← Number of stamps combined.

________ + ________ = t Write an equation.

________ = t Solve.

So, Kylie and her grandfather have ________ stamps combined.

Math Talk Mathematical Processes

Explain how the strip diagram helps you represent the problem.

Share and Show

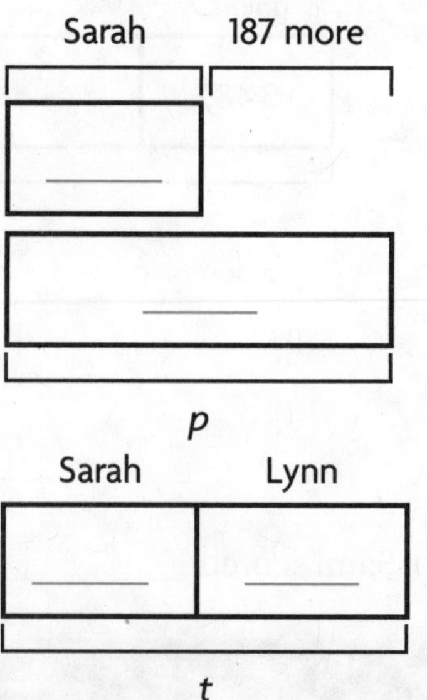

1. Sarah has 345 pennies in her coin bank. Her sister Lynn has 187 more pennies than Sarah. How many pennies do they have together?

   a. **First,** find how many pennies Lynn has. **Think:** $345 + 187 = p$

   So, Lynn has ________ pennies.

   b. **Next,** find the total number of pennies. **Think:** $345 + 532 = t$

   So, Sarah and Lynn have ________ pennies.

Name ______________________________

Problem Solving Real World

For Problems 2–3, use the table.

Phones Sold at Phone Hut	
Week 1	432
Week 2	641
Week 3	870
Week 4	1,157

2. Phone Hut had a sale on phones for five weeks. During week 5, they sold 787 more phones than they did during week 4. How many phones did Phone Hut sell during weeks 4 and 5?

____

3. H.O.T. **Analyze** **What if** the number of phones sold during week 5 was 1,798 more phones than week 1. How many phones were sold during weeks 1 and 5?

____

____

4. H.O.T. **Multi-Step** The We Like Animals Zoo had 1,453 visitors on Saturday. On Sunday, they had 239 more visitors than they did on Saturday. How many total visitors did the zoo get on Saturday and Sunday?

____

5. H.O.T. **What's the Error** Kyle drove 476 miles on Wednesday and 121 more miles on Thursday than on Wednesday. Kyle said he drove 597 miles on Wednesday and Thursday. Is he correct? **Explain.**

____

____

____

____

Write Math ▸ **Show Your Work**

Daily Assessment Task

Fill in the bubble completely to show your answer.

6. The outer edge of Saturn's Ring E is about 308,000 km away from Ring G. Ring G is 108,100 km away from Ring D. How far would you travel from Ring E through Ring G to Ring D and back to Ring E?

Ⓐ 832,200 km
Ⓒ 416,100 km
Ⓑ 399,800 km
Ⓓ 804,200 km

7. Sarah plays a video game and scores 56,432 points in the first round. She scores 1,823 more points in the second round than she did in the first. How many points does Sarah score in both rounds?

Ⓐ 54,609 points
Ⓒ 58,255 points
Ⓑ 103,687 points
Ⓓ 114,687 points

8. **Multi-Step** A movie makes $243,102 in ticket sales in its first weekend. It makes $123,463 more in its second weekend than in its first weekend. How much does the movie make during the two weekends?

Ⓐ $454,473
Ⓒ $609,667
Ⓑ $278,657
Ⓓ $697,575

TEXAS Test Prep

9. During the first day of basketball practice, Bradley shot 130 free throws. During the second day of practice, he shot 45 more free throws than he did the first day of practice. How many total free throws did Bradley shoot during the two days of practice?

Ⓐ 305
Ⓑ 95
Ⓒ 85
Ⓓ 295

TEKS Algebraic Reasoning—4.5.A
MATHEMATICAL PROCESSES 4.1.C, 4.1.D, 4.1.E

Name ______________________

11.1 Multi-Step Addition Problems

1. On Friday, 1,860 people attended the computer fair. On Saturday, 3,207 more people attended the fair than did on Friday. How many people attended the computer fair on the two days?

a. Find the number of people who attended the fair on Saturday.

Number who attended Friday

3,207 more people

_____ + 3,207 = f

_____ = f

b. Find the number of people who attended the fair on the two days.

Number who attended Friday

Number who attended Saturday

_____ + 5,067 = p

p = _____ people attended on the 2 days

Problem Solving Real World

2. The birding club counted 344 seagulls on their last visit to the ocean. The club saw 215 more seagulls today than they did on their last visit. How many seagulls did the club see on the two visits to the ocean?

____

3. On Friday, 2,364 cars parked in the parking garage at the mall. On Saturday, 2,455 more cars parked in the garage than on Friday. How many cars parked in the garage during the two days?

____

4. Today, 4,715 more people read Hank's blog than read it yesterday. Yesterday, 8,291 people read the blog. How many people read the blog during the two days?

____

5. A fishing crew caught 439 pounds of fish on Tuesday. On Wednesday they caught 211 more pounds than they did on Tuesday. The captain says they caught 1,089 pounds of fish on the two days. Is he correct? **Explain.**

____

Lesson Check

TEXAS Test Prep

Fill in the bubble completely to show your answer.

6. **Multi-Step** A nursery sold 4,721 plants last month. This month they sold 1,250 more plants than last month. How many plants did they sell during both months?

   Ⓐ 5,971
   Ⓑ 10,692
   Ⓒ 7,221
   Ⓓ 9,692

7. **Multi-Step** Randy has 386 hockey cards. He has 165 more baseball cards than hockey cards. How many cards does he have in all?

   Ⓐ 1,102
   Ⓑ 937
   Ⓒ 551
   Ⓓ 716

8. **Multi-Step** The population of Brook Valley is 10,680 more than the population of Lone Hill. The population of Lone Hill is 56,318. What is the total population of the two places?

   Ⓐ 66,998
   Ⓑ 77,678
   Ⓒ 123,316
   Ⓓ 112,206

9. **Multi-Step** Nora drove 520 miles farther this week than last week. Last week she drove 216 miles. How many miles did she drive in the two weeks?

   Ⓐ 1,256 miles
   Ⓑ 736 miles
   Ⓒ 952 miles
   Ⓓ 1,472 miles

10. **Multi-Step** A shipping company shipped 693 packages on Monday. They shipped 207 more packages on Tuesday than on Monday. How many packages did they ship on the two days?

    Ⓐ 900
    Ⓑ 1,593
    Ⓒ 1,107
    Ⓓ 1,590

11. **Multi-Step** On Friday, 536 boats left Warm Harbor. On Saturday, 275 more boats left the harbor than did on Friday. How many boats left the harbor during the two days?

    Ⓐ 1,622
    Ⓑ 1,086
    Ⓒ 811
    Ⓓ 1,347

Name ___________________________

11.2 Multi-Step Subtraction Problems

Essential Question How can you represent and solve multi-step subtraction problems using strip diagrams?

Unlock the Problem (Real World)

During the harvest, 13,485 apples were picked. Week one, 4,589 apples were sold. Week two, 2,113 apples were sold. How many apples are left after two weeks?

Example 1

STEP 1 Find how many apples were left after week 1.

Apples sold during week 1	4,589	a	← Apples left after 1 week
	13,485		← Apples picked

_______ − _______ = a Write an equation.

_______ = a Solve.

STEP 2 Find how many apples were left after week 2.

Apples sold during week 2	2,113	t	← Apples left after 2 weeks
	8,896		← Apples left after 1 week

_______ − _______ = t Write an equation.

_______ = t Solve.

So, the Yummy Apple Orchard had _______ apples left after two weeks.

- How does Step 1 differ from Step 2? ___________________________

____

Greg and his family are driving 4 days to visit his grandparents. They live 2,415 miles from Greg. The first 2 days they drove 1,141 miles. The third day they drove 612 miles. How many more miles do they have to drive on the fourth day?

Example 2

STEP 1 Find how many miles are left after 2 days of driving.

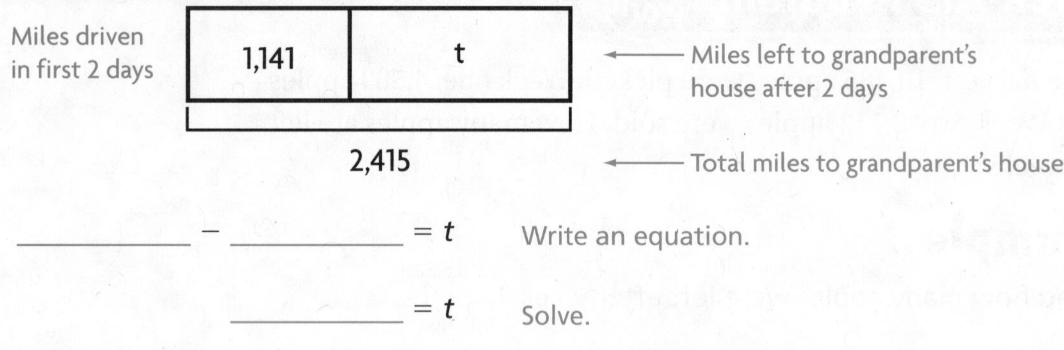

______ – ______ = t Write an equation.

______ = t Solve.

STEP 2 Find how many more miles they have to drive on the fourth day.

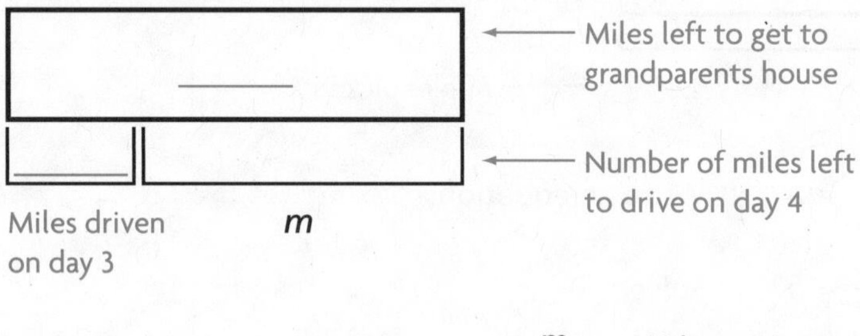

______ – ______ = m Write an equation.

______ = m Solve.

So, Greg's family drove ______ more miles on the fourth day.

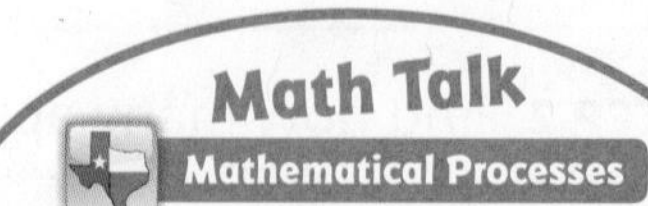

Explain why it takes more than one step to solve the problem in Example 2.

Share and Show

1. During a school wide vote, 632 students voted for Hat Friday. Pajama Friday received 187 fewer votes than Hat Friday. How many students voted?

Hat Friday

Pajama Friday

v

a. **First,** find how many students voted for Pajama Friday.

So, ______ students voted for Pajama Friday.

$v =$ ______

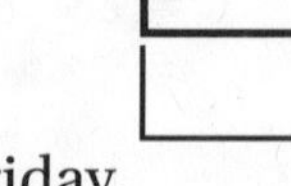

Hat Friday

Pajama Friday

f

b. **Next,** find the total number of students who voted.

Think: $632 + 445 = f$

So, ______ students voted.

$f =$ ______

Name ___________________________

Problem Solving Real World

For Problems 2–3, use the chart.

Cans of Soup Sold at the Kind Supermarket	
January	1,432
February	893
March	870
April	574

2. The Kind Supermarket had 5,213 cans of soup at the beginning of January. How many cans of soup did the Kind Supermarket have after February?

____

3. If the Kind Supermarket sold 189 less cans of soup in May than in April, how many cans of soup did they sell during April and May?

____

Write Math ▶ Show Your Work

4. H.O.T. Apply **Multi-Step** During the first week of a game's launch, an electronic store sold 275 copies of the game. During the second week, they sold 295 copies of the game. They sold some copies of the game during the third week. After the first three weeks, the electronic store sold 984 copies of the game. How many copies of the game did they sell during week 3?

____

5. H.O.T. **What's the Error?** Ken went to the Planters Nursery to buy some trees for his backyard. He wanted to spend no more than $300 for the trees. The first tree he bought was $175. The second tree he bought was $25 less than the first tree. Those were the only two items that Ken bought. Ken said that he spent less than he wanted to. Is he correct? **Explain** his error.

____

____

____

Daily Assessment Task

Fill in the bubble completely to show your answer.

6. The snack vendors have 500,000 bottles of water to sell during the parade. They sell 128,520 bottles during the first half of the parade. During the second half of the parade, they sell 205,000 more bottles than they sold during the first half. How many unsold bottles are left at the end of the parade?

   Ⓐ 166,480 bottles
   Ⓑ 37,960 bottles
   Ⓒ 371,480 bottles
   Ⓓ 379,600 bottles

7. The flag company makes 750,000 flags. They sell 405,200 flags for Memorial Day and 125,475 flags for Flag Day. How many flags do they have left to sell for the Fourth of July?

   Ⓐ 470,275 flags
   Ⓑ 230,475 flags
   Ⓒ 219,325 flags
   Ⓓ 220,435 flags

8. **Multi-Step** Katie buys 125,000 beads. She uses 108,246 to make bracelets. She goes back to the store and buys 100,000 more beads than she bought the first time. How many beads does Katie have now to make bracelets?

   Ⓐ 241,754 beads
   Ⓑ 208,246 beads
   Ⓒ 116,754 beads
   Ⓓ 6,754 beads

TEXAS Test Prep

9. Melinda saved 456 pennies one week, 374 pennies the second week, and some more pennies during the third week. Together Melinda saved 1,245 pennies during those three weeks. How many pennies did Melinda save during the third week?

   Ⓐ 615
   Ⓑ 415
   Ⓒ 2,075
   Ⓓ 525

Name ________________

11.2 Multi-Step Subtraction Problems

1. Louis bought a package of 500 paper plates. He used 341 of them at a family reunion. He used 39 for a picnic. How many paper plates does he have left?

a. Find the number of paper plates that were left after the reunion.

number of plates left | b | ______ | number of plates used at family reunion

500 ← total number of plates.

$500 - \_\_\_\_\_\_ = b$

$b =$ ______ plates left after reunion

b. Find the number of plates that were left after the picnic.

number of plates used at picnic | ______ | p | number of plates left

______ ← number of plates left after family reunion

$159 - \_\_\_\_\_\_ = p$

$p =$ ______ plates left after the picnic

Problem Solving Real World

Use the chart for problems 2–4.

Bundles of Campfire Wood Sold at Nature's Campground	
June	482
July	1,286
August	1,527

2. At the beginning of June, Nature's Campground had 3,450 bundles of campfire wood. How many bundles were left at the end of July?

______

3. How many bundles of firewood were left at the end of August?

______

4. For next year, the campground director wants to make 4,000 new bundles of wood. The crew made 1,238 bundles in September and 1,141 bundles in October. How many more bundles do they need to make?

______

Lesson Check

Fill in the bubble completely to show your answer.

5. **Multi-Step** It is 1,262 miles from Webster's house to his aunt's house. He drove 416 miles yesterday. The hotel he will stay in tonight is 380 miles from his aunt's house. How far will he drive today?

   Ⓐ 846 miles

   Ⓑ 466 miles

   Ⓒ 380 miles

   Ⓓ 576 miles

6. **Multi-Step** Eric bought 600 flower bulbs. He bought 280 iris bulbs, 75 tulip bulbs, and the rest are lilies. How many lily bulbs did Eric buy?

   Ⓐ 320

   Ⓑ 355

   Ⓒ 205

   Ⓓ 245

7. **Multi-Step** There were 10,647 tickets sold for a football game. Of those tickets, 872 were box seats and 4,366 were end zone tickets. The rest were sideline tickets. How many sideline tickets were sold?

   Ⓐ 5,506

   Ⓑ 6,281

   Ⓒ 5,409

   Ⓓ 6,509

8. **Multi-Step** Mindy needs to score 500,000 points or more in three games to move to the next level in her computer game. She scored 173,211 points the first game and 155,963 points the second game. What is the fewest points she can score in the third game to go on to the next level?

   Ⓐ 170,826

   Ⓑ 326,789

   Ⓒ 171,826

   Ⓓ 271,826

9. **Multi-Step** The glee club is going to have a float in the parade. They made 437 paper flowers for the float last week. They made 322 more this week than last week. They need 1,250 flowers. How many more do they need to make?

   Ⓐ 759

   Ⓑ 169

   Ⓒ 54

   Ⓓ 491

10. **Multi-Step** Last week Sandra spent $247 of her savings on a new DVD player. Today, she put $562 into her savings account. Now she has $951 in the account. How much money did she have in the account before she bought the DVD player?

   Ⓐ $636

   Ⓑ $142

   Ⓒ $1,266

   Ⓓ $746

Name ______________________________

11.3 Solve Multi-Step Problems Using Equations

Essential Question How can you represent and solve multi-step problems using equations?

Unlock the Problem (Real World)

Chris's computer has 3 hard drives with 64 gigabytes of space each, and 2 hard drives with 16 gigabytes of space each. The files on her computer use 78 gigabytes of space. How much hard drive space does her computer have left?

- Underline the important information.

One Way Use multiple single-step equations.

STEP 1 Find how much hard drive space is on 3 hard drives with 64 gigabytes of space each.

64	64	64

← 3 hard drives with 64 gigabytes.

n ← Total space on 3 hard drives with 64 gigabytes.

$3 \times 64 = n$

_____ $= n$

STEP 2 Find how much hard drive space is on 2 hard drives with 16 gigabytes of space.

16	16

← 2 hard drives with 16 gigabytes.

p ← Total space on 2 hard drives with 16 gigabytes.

$2 \times 16 = p$

_____ $= p$

STEP 3 Find the total hard drive space on the computer.

Total space on 64-gigabyte hard drives. ↓ Total space on 16-gigabyte hard drives. ↓

192	32

a ← Total hard drive space on computer.

$192 + 32 = a$

_____ $= a$

STEP 4 The files use 78 gigabytes of space. Find how much hard drive space the computer has left.

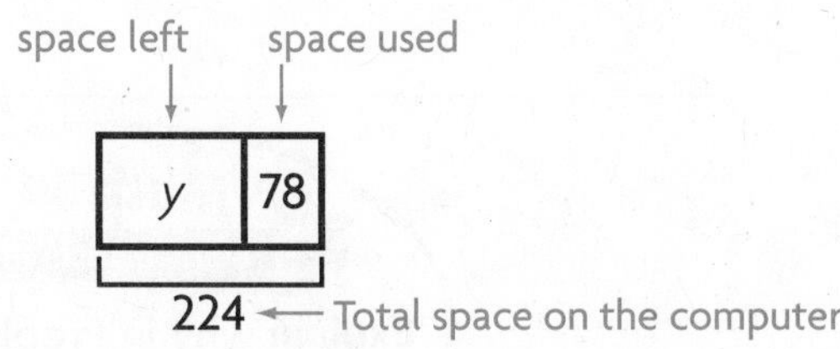

$224 - 78 = y$

_____ $= y$

So, Chris has _____ gigabytes of hard drive space left on her computer.

Share and Show

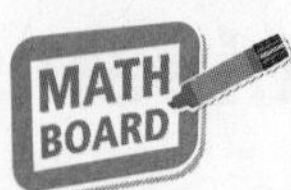

1. Carnie and Doug bake cookies to sell at a bake sale. Carnie makes 3 batches of 17 cookies each and Doug makes 3 batches of 20 cookies each. After ten minutes at the bake sale, they sold 32 cookies. How many cookies do Carnie and Doug have left to sell?

17	17	17

p

$3 \times 17 = p$; $51 = p$ ← First, multiply 3×17. Let p represent the number of cookies Carnie makes.

20	20	20

a

$3 \times 20 = a$; $60 = a$ ← Next, multiply 3×20. Let a represent the number of cookies Doug makes.

51	60

y

$51 + 60 = y$; $111 = y$ ← Then, add the two products. Let y represent the number of cookies Carnie and Doug make.

$111 - 32 = n$; $79 = n$ ← Finally, subtract to find the number of cookies Carnie and Doug have left to sell.

2. Tammy buys 3 bags of lollipops, with 12 lollipops in each bag. She also buys 4 bags of gum, with 11 pieces in each bag. How many lollipops and pieces of gum does Tammy have?

3. Maddox has 4 boxes with 32 marbles in each box. He has 7 boxes with 18 shells in each box. If he gets 20 marbles from a friend, how many marbles and shells does he have?

Problem Solving

4. Mario drove 60 miles to work each day for 5 days. Then he drove 54 miles on both Saturday and Sunday. How many miles did Mario drive during those seven days?

5. H.O.T. **Apply** Maggie has 3 binders with 25 stamps in each binder. She has 5 binders with 24 baseball cards in each binder. If she gives 35 stamps to a friend, how many stamps and cards does she have left?

Math Talk

Mathematical Processes

Explain why in Problem 1 you added during step 3 instead of multiplied.

Name ______________________________

What's the Error?

6. **Multi-Step** Dominic has 5 books with 12 postcards in each book. He has 4 boxes with 20 coins in each box. If he gives 15 postcards to a friend, how many postcards and coins does he have?

Dominic drew this model.

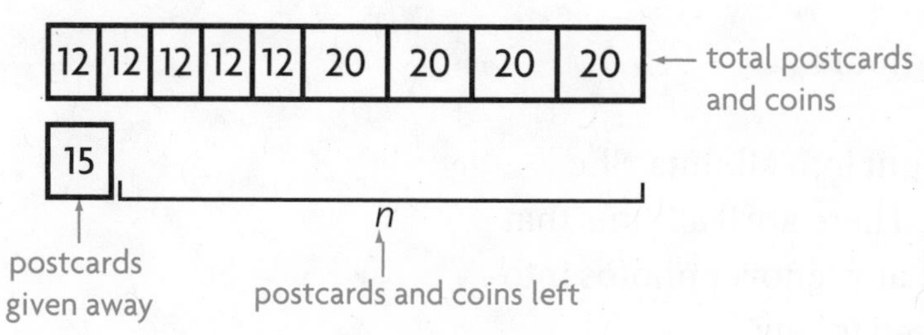

Dominic used these steps to solve.

$5 + 12 = p$

$4 + 20 = c$

$17 + 24 = y$

$41 - 15 = n$

$26 = n$

Look at the steps Dominic used to solve this problem. Find and describe his error.

____

____

____

Use the correct steps to solve the problem.

____

____

____

____

____

So, there are ______ postcards and coins left.

Daily Assessment Task

Fill in the bubble completely to show your answer.

7. Eric is getting his mountain climbing certificate. There are 63 days that Eric climbs for 2 hours, there are 97 days that he climbs for 1 hour, and there are 22 days that he climbs for 3 hours. How many more hours does Eric need to climb until he earns a certificate for climbing 500 hours?

   Ⓐ 289 hours
   Ⓑ 318 hours
   Ⓒ 321 hours
   Ⓓ 211 hours

8. Teresa has 315 photos that she wants to put into albums. She buys 4 albums that hold 24 photos each. There are 3 albums that hold 72 photos each. Teresa plans to put any leftover photos into frames. How many frames will Teresa need to buy?

   Ⓐ 3 frames
   Ⓑ 13 frames
   Ⓒ 0 frames
   Ⓓ 5 frames

9. **Multi-Step** The soccer team sells 54 bagels with cream cheese for $2 each and 36 muffins for $1 each during a bake sale. The coach uses the bake sale money to buy socks for the 14 players at $6 a pair. How much money does the coach have left to buy soccer balls?

   Ⓐ $138
   Ⓑ $60
   Ⓒ $0
   Ⓓ $27

TEXAS Test Prep

10. Trina has 2 bags with 14 pinecones in each bag. She has 7 boxes with 15 acorns in each box. If she trades 5 pinecones for 10 acorns, how many pinecones and acorns does she have?

    Ⓐ 28
    Ⓑ 105
    Ⓒ 133
    Ⓓ 138

Homework and Practice

TEKS Algebraic Reasoning—4.5.A
MATHEMATICAL PROCESSES 4.1.A, 4.1.C, 4.1.F

Name ______________________

11.3 Solve Multi-Step Problems Using Equations

Problem Solving Real World

1. Rebecca bought a flat of 144 pansies. She planted 3 rows of 16 pansies each. She planted 4 rows of 14 pansies each. How many pansies does she have left to plant?

16	16	16	14	14	14	14	p

144

$16 \times 3 =$ ______ $14 \times 4 =$ ______

$p = 144 -$ ______ $-$ ______

$p =$ ______

2. Julie packed 18 DVDs in each of 4 boxes. She packed 15 DVDs in each of 5 boxes. She has 8 DVDs left over. How many DVDs does Julie have?

____

3. Monty buys 2 adult dinner tickets for \$22 each, 2 senior tickets for \$18 each and 3 child tickets for \$12 each. How much change will he get from \$120?

____

4. John has 4 shelves with 22 dinosaur models on each shelf. He has 3 shelves with 20 dragon models on each shelf. How many more dinosaur models than dragon models does John have?

____

5. Alexis needs 280 screws to finish her deck. She bought 3 boxes of screws with 40 screws in a box. She had 168 screws. How many screws will she have left over when she finishes the deck?

____

Lesson Check

TEXAS Test Prep

Fill in the bubble completely to show your answer.

6. **Multi-Step** Erika baked 7 trays of 12 muffins each. Simon baked 5 trays of 18 muffins each. They agreed to make 200 muffins for the school bake sale. How many more muffins do they need to make?

   Ⓐ 26
   Ⓑ 38
   Ⓒ 36
   Ⓓ 52

7. **Multi-Step** Victoria is buying stickers. She bought 3 packages of stars with 24 in each package. She bought 2 packages of rainbows with 16 in each package. She bought 4 packages of hearts with 10 in each package. She used 82 of the stickers to make cards. How many stickers does Victoria have left?

   Ⓐ 72
   Ⓑ 62
   Ⓒ 144
   Ⓓ 96

8. **Multi-Step** Willie bagged his potatoes in 18 ten-pound bags, 16 five-pound bags, and 4 twenty-five pound bags. He has 2 pounds of potatoes left over. How many pounds of potatoes does Willie have?

   Ⓐ 358 pounds
   Ⓑ 262 pounds
   Ⓒ 352 pounds
   Ⓓ 362 pounds

9. **Multi-Step** Matt bought 6 hats for $14 each and 3 belts for $33 each. How much change did he get from $200?

   Ⓐ $7
   Ⓑ $17
   Ⓒ $58
   Ⓓ $27

10. **Multi-Step** Carla bought four 64-ounce bottles of juice and three 32-ounce bottles of juice. She used 320 ounces of juice to make punch. How many ounces of juice does Carla have left?

    Ⓐ 42 ounces
    Ⓑ 52 ounces
    Ⓒ 32 ounces
    Ⓓ 22 ounces

11. **Multi-Step** Alden has 6 bags of balloons with 10 in each bag, 2 bags with 25 in each bag, 1 bag of 50 balloons, and 14 balloons that are already blown up. How many balloons does Alden have in all?

    Ⓐ 160
    Ⓑ 146
    Ⓒ 174
    Ⓓ 107

Name ____________________

PROBLEM SOLVING • Multi-Step Division Problems

TEKS Algebraic Reasoning—4.5.A
MATHEMATICAL PROCESSES 4.1.B, 4.1.F

Essential Question How can you use the strategy *draw a diagram* to solve multi-step division problems?

Unlock the Problem (Real World)

Lucia and her dad will prepare corn for a community picnic. There are 3 bags of corn. Each bag holds 32 ears of corn. When the corn is cooked, they want to divide the corn equally among 8 serving plates. How many ears of corn should they put on each of 8 serving plates?

Read

What do I need to find?

I need to find the number of ________ that will go on each plate.

What information am I given?

_____ bags with _____ ears in each bag. The total ears are divided equally into _____ groups.

Plan

What is my plan or strategy?

I will make a strip diagram for each step and use equations. Then I will ________ to find the total and ________ to find the number for each plate.

Solve

I can draw strip diagrams and use equations and then decide how to find how many ears of corn should go on a plate.

First, I will find the total number of ears of corn.

32	32	32

$32 \times$ _____ $= e$

_____ $= e$

Then I will find how many ears of corn should go on each plate.

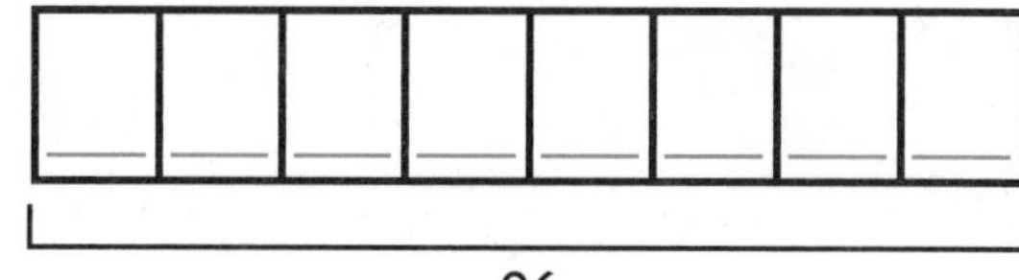

$96 \div$ _____ $= c$

_____ $= c$

1. How many ears of corn should go on each plate? ____________________

2. How can you check your answer? ____________________

Try Another Problem

There are 8 dinner rolls in a package. How many packages will be needed to feed 64 people if each person has 2 dinner rolls?

Read	Solve
What do I need to find?	
What information am I given?	
Plan	
What is my plan or strategy?	

3. How many packages of rolls will be needed? ___________

4. How did drawing a strip diagram help you solve the problem?

____

____

____

Math Talk

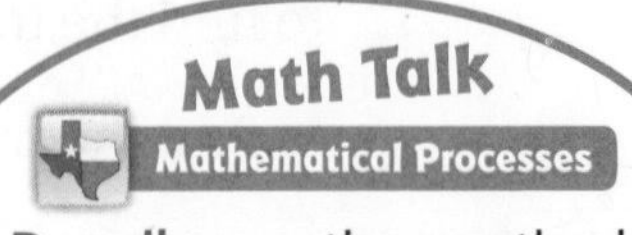

Describe another method you could have used to solve the problem.

Name ___________________________

Share and Show

Tips

- ✓ Use the Problem Solving MathBoard.
- ✓ Underline important facts.
- ✓ Choose a strategy you know.

Math Talk
Mathematical Processes
Explain how you could check that your answer is correct.

✓ 1. A firehouse pantry has 52 cans of vegetables and 74 cans of soup. Each shelf holds 9 cans. What is the least number of shelves needed for all the cans?

First, draw a strip diagram for the total number of cans.

Next, add to find the total number of cans.

Then, draw a strip diagram to show the number of shelves needed.

Finally, divide to find the number of shelves needed.

So, ______ shelves are needed to hold all of the cans.

✓ 2. **H.O.T.** **Multi-Step** **What if** 18 cans fit on a shelf? What is the least number of shelves needed? **Describe** how your answer would be different.

____

____

____

Problem Solving

3. **H.O.T.** **Multi-Step** Ms. Johnson bought 6 bags of balloons. Each bag has 25 balloons. She fills all the balloons and puts 5 balloons in each bunch. How many bunches can she make?

____

Mathematical Processes
Model • Reason • Communicate

Daily Assessment Task

Fill in the bubble completely to show your answer.

4. Basketball jerseys are shipped in packages of 6. How many packages of jerseys are needed for 12 players if each player gets 4 jerseys?

Ⓐ 3 packages

Ⓑ 2 packages

Ⓒ 8 packages

Ⓓ 48 packages

5. Robin and her grandmother bake muffins. Each batch of batter makes 36 mini muffins. They make 4 batches. They divide the muffins equally into bags of 3 muffins for a bake sale. How many bags of 3 muffins do they have?

Ⓐ 9 bags

Ⓑ 48 bags

Ⓒ 12 bags

Ⓓ 3 bags

6. H.O.T. Multi-Step The fourth graders at Sunshine School go to the Museum of Nature and Science. The school pays $671 for the trip. The adult tickets are $10 each and the student tickets are $7 each. There are 9 adults going on the trip. How many students go on the trip?

Ⓐ 74 students

Ⓑ 86 students

Ⓒ 95 students

Ⓓ 83 students

TEXAS Test Prep

7. Ben collected 43 cans and some bottles. He received 5¢ for each can or bottle. If Ben received a total of $4.95, how many bottles did he collect?

Ⓐ 56

Ⓑ 99

Ⓒ 560

Ⓓ 990

Name ______________________

11.4 PROBLEM SOLVING • Multi-Step Division Problems

Problem Solving Real World

1. Marco bought 2 bottles of juice. Each bottle is 48 ounces. How many 8-ounce glasses of juice can Marco pour from the two bottles?

a. Draw a strip diagram for the number of ounces of juice in the two bottles.

b. Write an equation to find the total number of ounces of juice in the two bottles.

c. Draw a strip diagram to show the number of 8-ounce glasses of juice that can be poured.

d. Write an equation to find the number of glasses of juice.

Marco can pour ______ glasses of juice.

2. Describe another method you could have used to solve the problem.

____

____

3. What if Marco poured 10-ounce glasses of juice? What is the greatest number of full glasses of juice he could have poured? **Explain.**

____

____

Lesson Check

TEXAS Test Prep

Fill in the bubble completely to show your answer.

4. **Multi-Step** Orlando has a bag of 37 apples and a bag of 29 apples. He can bake 6 apples in a pan. How many pans of apples can Orlando make?

   Ⓐ 66

   Ⓑ 33

   Ⓒ 11

   Ⓓ 22

5. **Multi-Step** Anna has 5 bunches of flowers with 12 flowers in each bunch. She has 4 bunches of flowers with 10 flowers in each bunch. How many vases can Anna fill if she puts 10 flowers in each vase?

   Ⓐ 10

   Ⓑ 100

   Ⓒ 9

   Ⓓ 15

6. **Multi-Step** Five friends are going to share the cost of two gifts. One gift costs $39 and the other gift costs $26. What is each person's share of the cost?

   Ⓐ $7

   Ⓑ $15

   Ⓒ $18

   Ⓓ $13

7. **Multi-Step** There are 14 chairs in each of 6 rows. There are 18 chairs in each of 4 rows. How many rows of 13 chairs can be made from all of the chairs?

   Ⓐ 13

   Ⓑ 12

   Ⓒ 14

   Ⓓ 18

8. **Multi-Step** Justin collected 26 shells, Amy collected 31 shells. Jose collected 21 shells. If they share all of the shells equally, how many shells will each person get?

   Ⓐ 24

   Ⓑ 78

   Ⓒ 26

   Ⓓ 19

9. **Multi-Step** Taylor has 2 packages of 36 tacks each and 16 tacks. How many garage sale posters can she put up if she uses 4 tacks for each poster?

   Ⓐ 13

   Ⓑ 22

   Ⓒ 17

   Ⓓ 21

Name ___

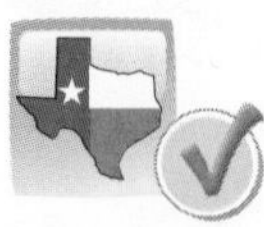

Module 11 Assessment

Concepts and Skills

Find the sum. TEKS 4.5.A

1. 4,348 + 2,047

2. 35,041 + 27,595

3. 728,625 + 211,582

Find the value of *n*. TEKS 4.5.A

4. $264,185 + 38,642 = n$

   ___ $= n$

5. $238,375 + 29,558 = n$

   ___ $= n$

6. $342,205 + 127,539 = n$

   ___ $= n$

Find the difference. TEKS 4.5.A

7. 5,417 − 2,238

8. 46,347 − 18,619

9. 527,624 − 241,302

Find the value of *n*. TEKS 4.5.A

10. $162,712 - 24,729 = n$

    ___ $= n$

11. $483,700 - 26,308 = n$

    ___ $= n$

12. $400,000 - 128,803 = n$

    ___ $= n$

Find the product. TEKS 4.5.A

13. 32 × 4

14. 45 × 6

15. 468 × 5

16. 2,270 × 8

Find the value of *n*. TEKS 4.5.A

17. $24 \times 10 = n$

    ___ $= n$

18. $100 \times 36 = n$

    ___ $= n$

19. $45 \times 23 = n$

    ___ $= n$

Find the value of *n*. TEKS 4.5.A

20. $65 \div 5 = n$

    ___ $= n$

21. $516 \div 3 = n$

    ___ $= n$

22. $620 \div 4 = n$

    ___ $= n$

23. $1,026 \div 9 = n$

    ___ $= n$

Fill in the bubble completely to show your answer.
Use strip diagrams or equations to help you solve.

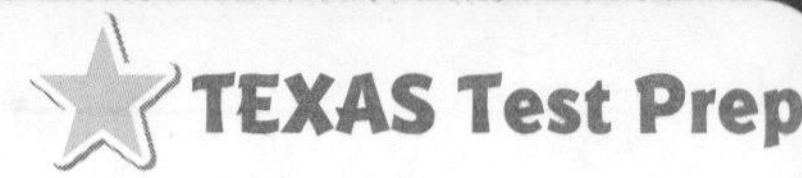

24. During October, Joe's ice cream shop had 11,094 customers and Tatum's yogurt shop had 10,237 customers. Matt's yogurt shop had 3,810 more customers than Tatum's shop. How many customers did all three shops have during October? TEKS 4.5.A

Ⓐ 14,047

Ⓑ 5,640

Ⓒ 35,378

Ⓓ 22,331

25. The town of Summerville has a population of 40,285 during the summer, a population of 18,463 during the winter, and a population of 38,709 during the fall. How many more people spend time in Summerville during the winter and fall combined than during the summer? TEKS 4.5.A

Ⓐ 20,246 Ⓒ 7,501

Ⓑ 57,172 Ⓓ 16,887

26. The Davis family are on a ten day road trip. They travel 10 hours each day for 3 days. They travel 8 hours each day for 7 days. How many hours does the Davis family travel during their road trip? TEKS 4.5.A

Ⓐ 86 Ⓒ 26

Ⓑ 56 Ⓓ 30

27. The garden warehouse delivered 1,550 pounds of topsoil in 5-pound bags to the garden shop. The garden shop sold half of the bags the same day they were delivered. How many bags does the garden shop have left to sell? TEKS 4.5.A

Record your answer and fill in the bubbles on the grid. Be sure to use the correct place value.

			.		
⓪	⓪	⓪		⓪	⓪
①	①	①		①	①
②	②	②		②	②
③	③	③		③	③
④	④	④		④	④
⑤	⑤	⑤		⑤	⑤
⑥	⑥	⑥		⑥	⑥
⑦	⑦	⑦		⑦	⑦
⑧	⑧	⑧		⑧	⑧
⑨	⑨	⑨		⑨	⑨

Name ______________________________

12.1 Number Patterns

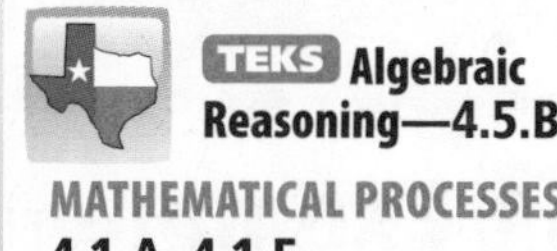

Essential Question

How can you make and describe patterns?

Unlock the Problem (Real World)

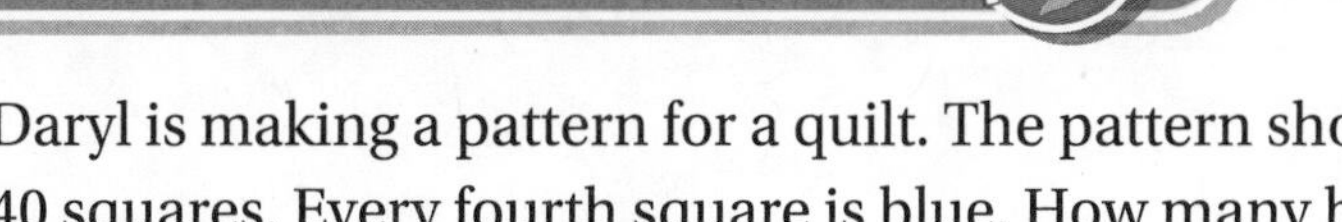

Daryl is making a pattern for a quilt. The pattern shows 40 squares. Every fourth square is blue. How many blue squares are in the pattern?

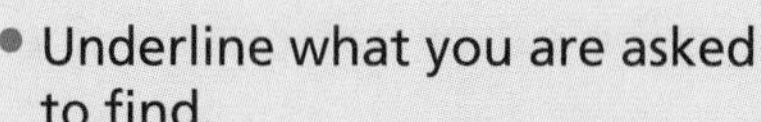

- Underline what you are asked to find.
- Circle what you need to use.

A **pattern** is an ordered set of numbers or objects. Each number or object in the pattern is called a **term**.

Activity Find a pattern.

Materials ■ color pencils

Shade the squares that are blue.

1	2	3	4	5	6	7	8	9	10
11	12	13	14	15	16	17	18	19	20
21	22	23	24	25	26	27	28	29	30
31	32	33	34	35	36	37	38	39	40

Math Talk — Mathematical Processes

Describe another number pattern in Daryl's quilt.

Which squares are blue? ______________________________

So, there are ______ blue squares in the pattern.

1. What patterns do you see in the arrangement of the blue squares?

____

____

2. What patterns do you see in the numbers of the blue squares?

____

____

Example Find and describe a pattern.

The rule for the pattern is *add* 5. The first term in the pattern is 5.

A **Use the rule to write the numbers in the pattern.**

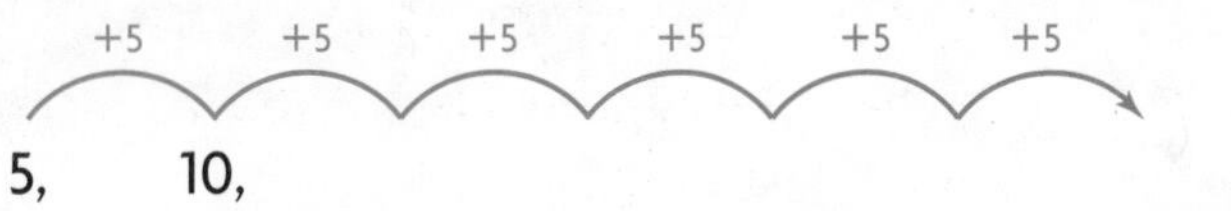

5, 10, ____, ____, ____, ____, ____, ...

B **Describe other patterns in the numbers.**

What do you notice about the digits in the ones place?

____

Describe the pattern using the words *odd* and *even*.

____

Share and Show

Use the rule to write the numbers in the pattern.

1. Rule: Subtract 10. First term: 100

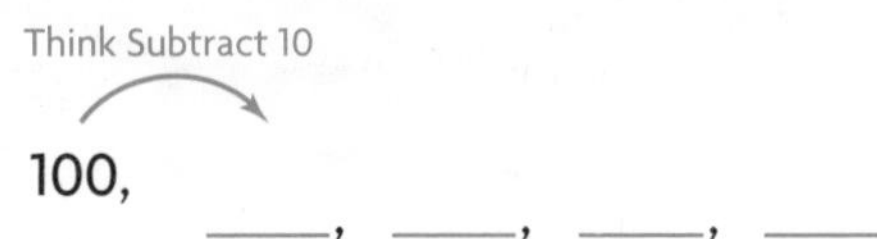

100, ____, ____, ____, ____, ...

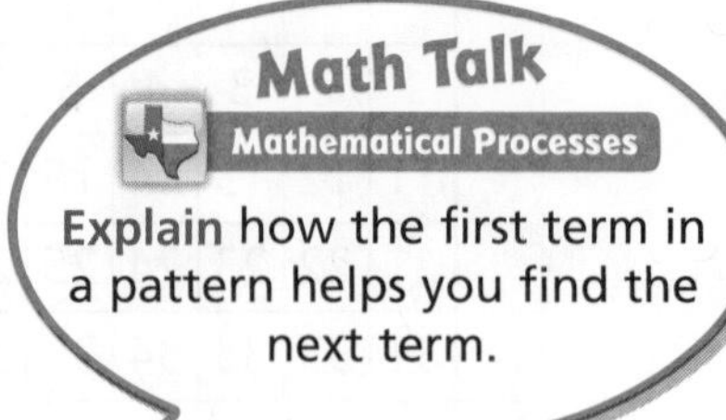

Use the rule to write the numbers in the pattern.
Describe another pattern in the numbers.

2. Rule: Multiply by 2. First term: 4

4, ____, ____, ____, ____, ...

____

3. Rule: Skip-count by 6. First term: 12

12, ____, ____, ____, ____, ...

____

4. Rule: add 3. First term: 6

6, ____, ____, ____, ____, ...

____

Name ____________________

Problem Solving 

5. **Analyze** The odd- and even-numbered hotel rooms are on different sides of the hall. Room 231 is between which two rooms?

6. H.O.T. **Multi-Step** John is saving for his trip to see the Alamo. He started with $24 in his savings account. Every week he earns $15 for baby-sitting. Out of that, he spends $8 and saves the rest. John uses the rule *add 7* to find out how much money he has at the end of each week. What are the first 8 numbers in the pattern?

Math on the Spot

7. H.O.T. **Multi-Step** **Pose a Problem** An activity at the Math Fair shows two charts.

Numbers
2
3
5
6
10

Operations
addition
subtraction
multiplication

Use at least two of the numbers and an operation from the charts to write a pattern problem. Include the first five terms of your pattern in the solution to your problem.

Pose a problem.	Solve your problem.

- **Describe** other patterns in the terms you wrote.

Mathematical Processes
Model • Reason • Communicate

Daily Assessment Task

Fill in the bubble completely to show your answer.

8. Which pattern follows the rule *add 3?*

Ⓐ 60, 63, 60, 63, ...

Ⓑ 3, 1, 4, 2, ...

Ⓒ 60, 63, 62, 65, ...

Ⓓ 60, 63, 66, 69, ...

9. The rule for a pattern is *add* 5. The first term in the pattern is 6. Which shows the numbers in the pattern?

Ⓐ 6, 11, 9, 14, 12, ...

Ⓑ 6, 11, 16, 21, 26, ...

Ⓒ 5, 10, 8, 13, 11, ...

Ⓓ 5, 2, 10, 8, 15, ...

10. **Multi-Step** Sandy lives on the side of a street where all the house numbers are even. The house to the left of hers is number 356. The house to the right side of hers is 360. What is Sandy's house number?

Ⓐ 354 Ⓒ 362

Ⓑ 358 Ⓓ 357

TEXAS Test Prep

11. Some groups of cicadas appear once every 13 years. Darla is 5 when she hears her first group of cicadas. Which pattern shows her ages the next 4 times that a group of cicadas appears?

Ⓐ 13, 26, 39, 52

Ⓑ 13, 18, 23, 28

Ⓒ 18, 31, 44, 57

Ⓓ 18, 23, 28, 33

Name ______________________

12.1 Number Patterns

Use the rule to write the numbers in the pattern.

1. Rule: Subtract 5. First term: 50

50, ______, ______, ______, ______, ...

2. Rule: Multiply by 3. First term: 2

2, ______, ______, ______, ______, ...

Use the rule to write the numbers in the pattern. Describe another pattern in the numbers.

3. Rule: Skip-count by 4. First term: 8

8, ______, ______, ______, ______, ...

____

4. Rule: Add 3 First term: 2

2, ______, ______, ______, ______, ______,...

____

Problem Solving

5. Kate's hair is currently 10 inches long. She read that her hair grows about 6 inches per year. Kate uses the rule *add* 6 to find out how long her hair would be in 4 years if she does not cut it. What are the first 5 numbers in the pattern?

____

6. After not raining for weeks, John measured 2 inches of rainfall in his rain gauge on Monday. On Tuesday, 2 more inches fell. John uses the rule *add* 2 to find out how many inches of rainfall he will measure if the pattern continues. What are the first 4 numbers in the pattern?

____

Lesson Check

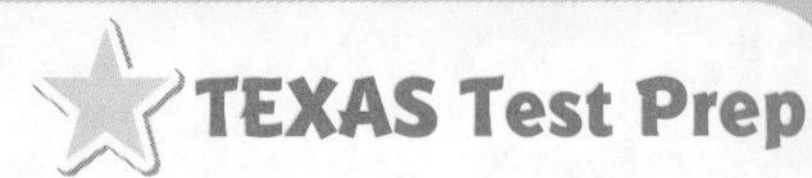

Fill in the bubble completely to show your answer.

7. The rule for a pattern is *add* 4. The first term in the pattern is 4. Which shows the numbers in the pattern?

Ⓐ 4, 8, 12, 16, 20

Ⓑ 4, 1, 5, 2, 6

Ⓒ 5, 20, 80, 160, 640

Ⓓ 5, 9, 13, 17, 21

8. Cassie's family has a reunion every 3 years. Cassie was 4 at her first family reunion. Which pattern shows Cassies age for the next 5 family reunions?

Ⓐ 7, 10, 13, 16, 19

Ⓑ 9, 14, 19, 24, 29

Ⓒ 8, 12, 16, 20, 24

Ⓓ 9, 12, 15, 18, 21

9. Which pattern shows the rule *multiply by* 4?

Ⓐ 4, 8, 12, 16 . . .

Ⓑ 1, 4, 16, 64 . . .

Ⓒ 4, 12, 36, 108 . . .

Ⓓ 10, 14, 18, 22 . . .

10. Rahul has saved $86 from his summer job. When school begins, he plans to spend $5 each week. Which pattern shows how much money Rahul will have after 4 weeks?

Ⓐ $82, $78, $74, $70

Ⓑ $81, $77, $72, $68

Ⓒ $82, $77, $72, $67

Ⓓ $81, $76, $71, $66

11. **Multi-Step** Paul earns $7 each week walking his neighbor's dog. Each week, he subtracts $3 from his earnings to spend and saves the rest. Which pattern shows the amount that Paul will have in his savings after 6 weeks?

Ⓐ $4, $8, $12, $16, $20, $24

Ⓑ $7, $14, $21, $28, $35, $42

Ⓒ $4, $7, $11, $18, $22, $26

Ⓓ $7, $10, $13, $16, $19, $22

12. **Multi-Step** Marcie likes to collect stickers, but she also likes to give them away. Currently, Marcie has 87 stickers in her collection. If Marcie collects 5 new stickers each week and gives away 3 stickers each week, which of the following patterns shows how many stickers Marcie will have in her collection after 5 weeks?

Ⓐ 87, 84, 81, 78, 75, 72

Ⓑ 87, 89, 91, 93, 95, 97

Ⓒ 87, 92, 97, 102, 107, 112

Ⓓ 87, 95, 103, 111, 119, 127

Name ______________________________

12.2 Find a Rule

TEKS Algebraic Reasoning—4.5.B

MATHEMATICAL PROCESSES 4.1.E, 4.1.F

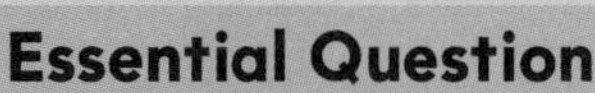

Essential Question

How can you write a rule for a function?

Unlock the Problem

A server at a restaurant is setting up tables for a large group. One table has 4 chairs. Two tables have 8 chairs. Three tables have 12 chairs. Four tables have 16 chairs, and so on. How many chairs are at 5 tables?

- Underline the information you will use.
- Circle the numbers of chairs.

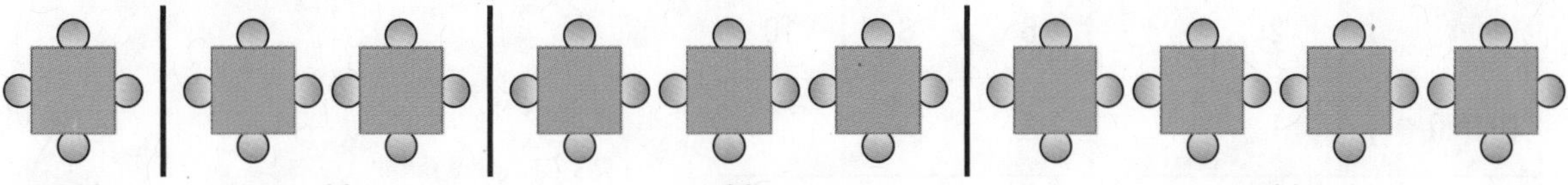

You can use an **input/output table** to show a pattern. A pattern is called a function when one quantity depends on the other. The number of chairs that can be used depends on the number of tables used. You can write a rule to describe the relationship between the inputs and outputs of a function.

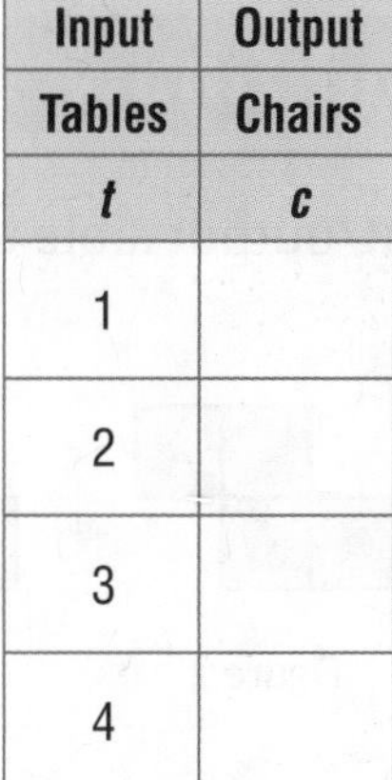

Input	Output
Tables	Chairs
t	c
1	
2	
3	
4	

Use a table to write a rule.

STEP 1 Complete the input/output table.

STEP 2 Describe the relationship between tables and chairs.

Think: $1 \times 4 = 4$ 1 table × 4 = 4 chairs
$2 \times 4 = 8$ 2 tables × 4 = 8 chairs
$3 \times 4 = 12$ 3 tables × 4 = 12 chairs
$4 \times 4 = 16$ 4 tables × 4 = 16 chairs

The number of chairs is ______ times the number of tables.

STEP 3 Find a rule. Use an expression to write your rule.

Think: Use t for the number of tables.

Rule: The number of chairs is ______ × ______.

STEP 4 Use the rule to find the number of chairs at 5 tables.

The number of chairs at 5 tables is 5 × ______.

So, there are ______ chairs at 5 tables.

ERROR Alert

A rule must work for each pair of numbers in the function table. Be sure to test your rule for each pair of numbers.

Math Talk

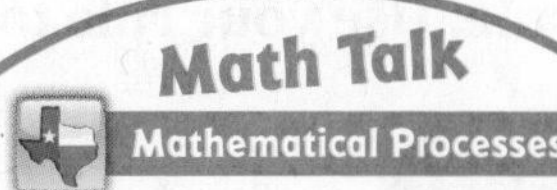

Explain how you can use the rule to find the number of chairs at 8 tables.

Examples

A **Find a rule. Use your rule to write an expression.**

The output is ______ more than the input.

Use ______ for the input.

Rule: The output is ______ + ______.

Think:

2 + ______ = 5

4 + ______ = 7

6 + ______ = 9

8 + ______ = 11

Input	Output
b	*c*
2	5
4	7
6	9
8	11

B **Use the rule to complete the input/output table.**

Rule: The output is $n \div 2$.

Think: $4 \div 2$ $8 \div 2$ $10 \div 2$

Input	*n*	2	4	6	8	10
Output	*p*	1		3		

Share and Show

1. Use the input/output table to show the pattern. Find a rule.

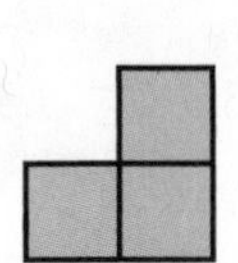
Figure 1

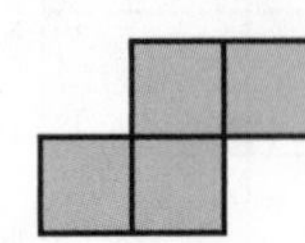
Figure 2

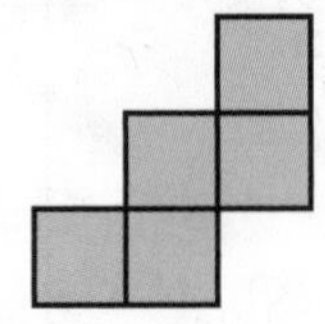
Figure 3

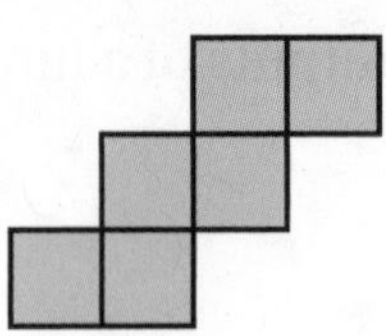
Figure 4

Input	Output
Figures	Squares
f	*s*
1	
2	
3	
4	

Rule: The number of squares is ______ + ______.

Use the rule to complete the input/output table.

2. **Rule:** The output is $n - 5$.

Input	*n*	10	20	30	40
Output	*p*	5			

Math Talk Mathematical Processes

Explain how you can find a rule.

Find a rule. Use your rule to write an expression.

3.

Input	*y*	1	2	3	4
Output	*z*	5	6	7	8

Rule: ______________________

4.

Input	*b*	1	2	3	4
Output	*c*	2	4	6	8

Rule: ______________________

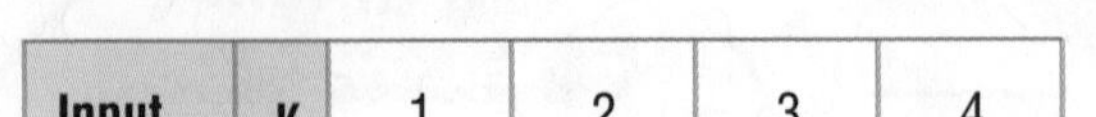

Name ___

Problem Solving Real World

5. **Record** Use the food pyramid to complete the input/output table below. Find a rule that tells how many cups of milk a child should drink in *d* days.

Grains	Vegetables	Fruits	Milk	Meat & Beans
6 ounces	$2\frac{1}{2}$ cups	$1\frac{1}{2}$ cups	3 cups	5 ounces

Input	*d*	2	3	4	5
Output	*c*				

___

6. One gallon of water is equivalent to 4 quarts of water. You can write a rule to show this.

Let *g* represent the number of gallons of water, the input, and let *q* represent the total number of quarts of water, the output.

Rule: The number of quarts is $g \times 4$.

Use the rule to complete the input/output table.

Input	Gallons	*g*	1	2	4	6
Output	Quarts	*q*				

Write Math Show Your Work

7. H.O.T. **Analyze** One gallon of water equals 4 quarts of water and 1 quart of water equals 2 pints of water. How many pints of water equal 1 gallon of water? **Explain.**

___

___

___

___

8. H.O.T. Look back at Problem 6. **What if** there are 36 quarts of water?

How many gallons of water are there? ___

Mathematical Processes
Model • Reason • Communicate

Daily Assessment Task

Fill in the bubble completely to show your answer.

9. Tanya is waiting in line at a skate park. There are 4 people in front of her. The input/output table shows the relationship between the number of people (p) in line and the length of time (t) she will wait in line. Which could be a rule for the input/output table?

Input	p	1	2	3	4
Output	t	4	8	12	16

Ⓐ The output is $p + 3$.
Ⓑ The output is $p \times 4$.
Ⓒ The output is $t - 3$.
Ⓓ The output is $p \times 2$.

10. Use the rule to find the missing number. What is the missing number?

Rule: The output is $n - 7$.					
Input	n	12	14	16	18
Output	z	5		9	11

Ⓐ 21
Ⓑ 8
Ⓒ 7
Ⓓ 2

11. **Multi-Step** In a photo album, one page holds 4 photographs. Two pages hold 8 photographs. Three pages hold 12 photographs. Four pages hold 16 photographs, and so on. How many photographs do 5 pages hold?

Input	Number of Pages	a	1	2	3	4
Output	Number of Photographs	p				

Ⓐ 5
Ⓑ 18
Ⓒ 24
Ⓓ 20

TEXAS Test Prep

12. Maggie runs the same distance every week. She made the input/output table to show how many miles (m) she will run in w weeks. Which rule works for the input/output table?

Input	w	3	4	6	8
Output	m	9	12	18	24

Ⓐ The output is $w + 6$.
Ⓑ The output is $w \div 2$.
Ⓒ The output is $w \times 3$.
Ⓓ The output is $w \div 3$.

Homework and Practice

Name ______________________

12.2 Find a Rule

Use the rule to complete the input/output table.

1. **Rule:** The output is $n + 3$.

Input	n	1	2	3	4
Output	p	4	7	10	13

2. **Rule:** The output is $y \times 5$.

Input	y	2	3	4	5
Output	z	10	15	20	25

3. **Rule:** The output is $f - 4$.

Input	f	10	20	30	40
Output	s	6	2	-8	-4

4. **Rule:** The output is $x \div 10$.

Input	x	100	200	300	400
Output	y	10	20	30	40

Find a rule. Use your rule to write an expression.

5.

Input	y	1	2	3	4
Output	Z	6	7	8	9

Rule: +5

6.

Input	b	1	2	3	4
Output	c	3	6	9	12

Rule: X3

Problem Solving (Real World)

7. One gallon of water is equal to 8 pints of water. Find a rule that tells how many pints of water are in g gallons.

Rule: ______________________.

Input	gallons	g	1	2	3	4
Output	pints	p	8	16	24	32

8. One quart of water is equal to 4 cups of water. Find a rule that tells how many cups of water are in q quarts.

Rule: ______________________.

Input	quarts	q	1	2	3	4
Output	cups	c	4	8	12	16

Lesson Check

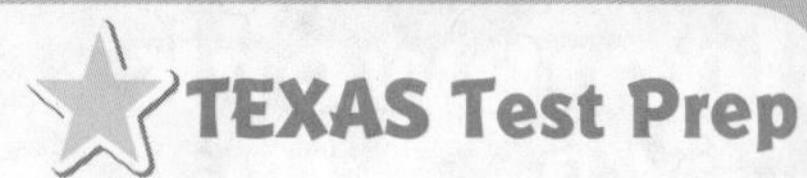

Fill in the bubble completely to show your answer.

9. Use the rule to find the missing number. What is the missing number?

Rule: The output is $x - 6$.					
Input	x	10	12	14	16
Output	y	4	6		10

Ⓐ 20
Ⓑ 2
Ⓒ 8
Ⓓ 5

10. Which rule could be used for the table?

Input	n	10	15	20	25
Output	p	20	30	40	50

Ⓐ The output is $n + 10$.
Ⓑ The output is $n \times 2$.
Ⓒ The output is $n - 2$.
Ⓓ The output is $n - 10$.

11. Nikki is making necklaces. The input/output table shows the relationship between the number of necklaces (n) and the number of beads (b) used.

Input	n	2	4	6	8
Output	b	16	32	48	64

Which could be a rule for the table?

Ⓐ The output is $n \times 8$.
Ⓑ The output is $n + 14$.
Ⓒ The output is $n + 8$.
Ⓓ The output is $n - 14$.

12. Ken works the same number of hours each week. He made the input/output table to show how many hours (h) he will work in d days.

Input	d	5	6	7	8
Output	h	35	42	49	56

Which could be a rule for the table?

Ⓐ The output is $d - 30$.
Ⓑ The output is $d \div 7$.
Ⓒ The output is $d \times 7$.
Ⓓ The output is $d + 30$.

13. **Multi-Step** A baker packs cupcakes in boxes to sell. One box holds 6 cupcakes. Two boxes hold 12 cupcakes, and so on. How many cupcakes (c) will the baker need for 4 boxes (b)?

Input	b	1	2	3	4
Output	c				

Ⓐ 6
Ⓑ 24
Ⓒ 18
Ⓓ 12

14 **Multi-Step** Students in a gym class will be divided into 2 teams to play games. For 30 students there will be 15 on each team. For 28 students, there will be 14 on each team, and so on. How many students (t) will be on each team if there are 22 students (s)?

Input	s	30	28	24	22
Output	t				

Ⓐ 11 Ⓑ 12 Ⓒ 10 Ⓓ 8

Name ______________________

12.3 Model Perimeter Formulas

TEKS Algebraic Reasoning—4.5.C, 4.5.D
MATHEMATICAL PROCESSES 4.1.A, 4.1.F

Essential Question

How can you use a formula to find the perimeter of a rectangle?

Unlock the Problem (Real World)

Julio is putting a stone border around his rectangular garden. The length of the garden is 7 feet. The width of the garden is 5 feet. How many feet of stone border does Julio need?

- Circle the numbers you will use.
- What are you asked to find?

____

____

Perimeter is the distance around a figure.

To find how many feet of stone border Julio needs, find the perimeter of the garden.

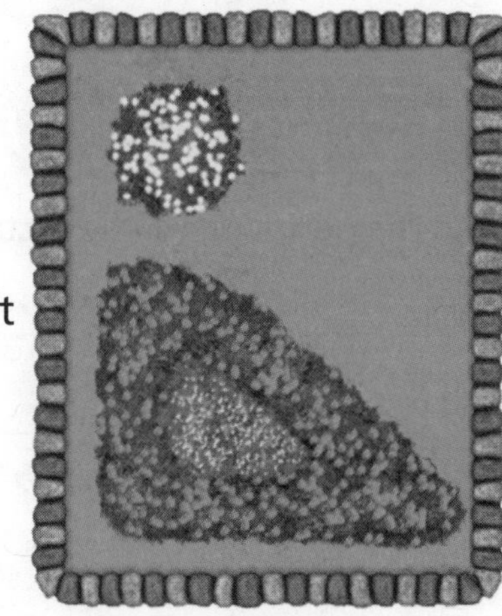

Use addition.

Perimeter of a Rectangle = length + width + length + width

$7 + 5 + 7 + 5 =$ ______

The perimeter is ______ feet.

So, Julio needs ______ feet of stone border.

Use multiplication.

A Find Perimeter of a Rectangle

Perimeter = (2 × length) + (2 × width), or $2l + 2w$

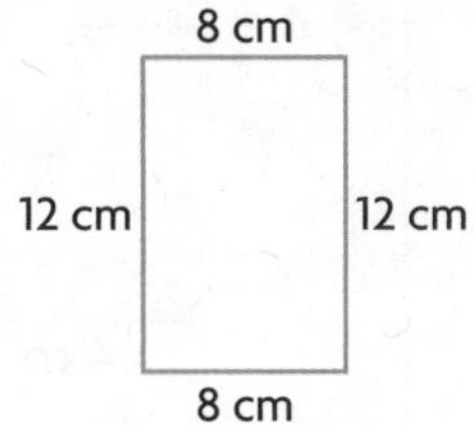

Perimeter = $(2 \times 12) + (2 \times 8)$

$= 24 + 16$

$=$ ______

So, the perimeter is ______ centimeters.

B Find Perimeter of a Square

Perimeter = 4 × one side, or $4 \times s$

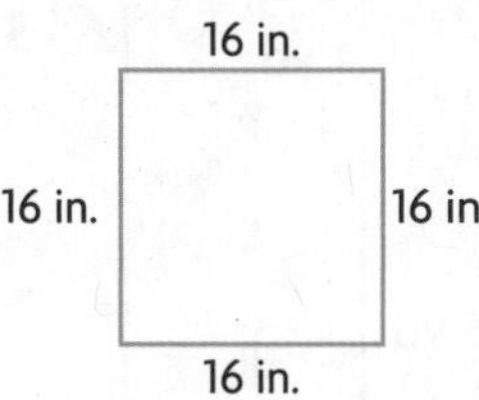

Perimeter = 4×16

$=$ ______

So, the perimeter is ______ inches.

Use a Formula A **formula** is a mathematical rule. You can use a formula to find perimeter.

$$P = (2 \times l) + (2 \times w)$$

P ↑ perimeter; l ↑ length; w ↑ width

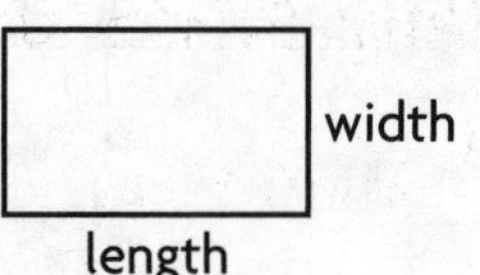

Example Find the perimeter of the rectangle.

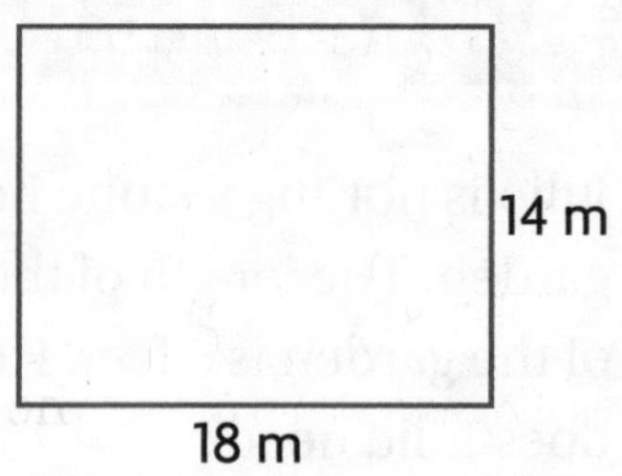

$P = (2 \times l) + (2 \times w)$

$= (2 \times$ ______ $) + (2 \times$ ______ $)$ Think: Write the measures you know.

$=$ ______ $+$ ______ Think: Do what is in parentheses first.

$=$ ______

The perimeter of the rectangle is ____________.

Share and Show

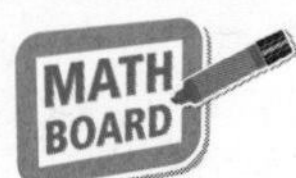

1. Find the perimeter of the rectangle.

$P = ($ ______ $\times$ ______ $) + ($ ______ $\times$ ______ $)$

$= ($ ______ $\times$ ______ $) + ($ ______ $\times$ ______ $)$

$=$ ______ $+$ ______

$=$ ______

8 ft
4 ft

The perimeter is ______ feet.

Formulas for Perimeter

Rectangle:

$P = (2 \times l) + (2 \times w)$ or

$P = 2l + 2w$

Square:

$P = 4 \times s$, or $P = 4s$

Find the perimeter of the rectangle or square.

2.

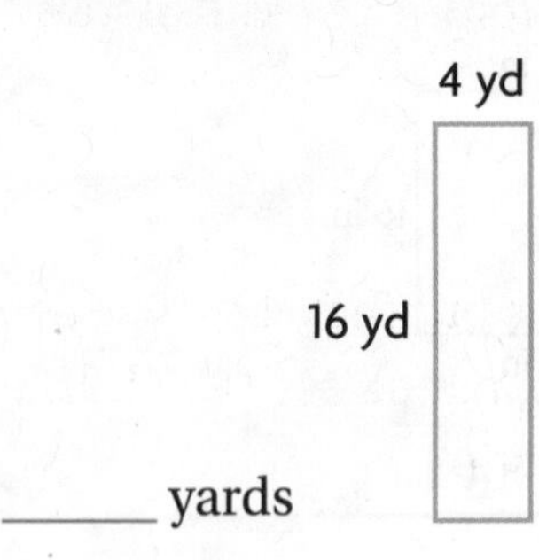

______ yards

3.

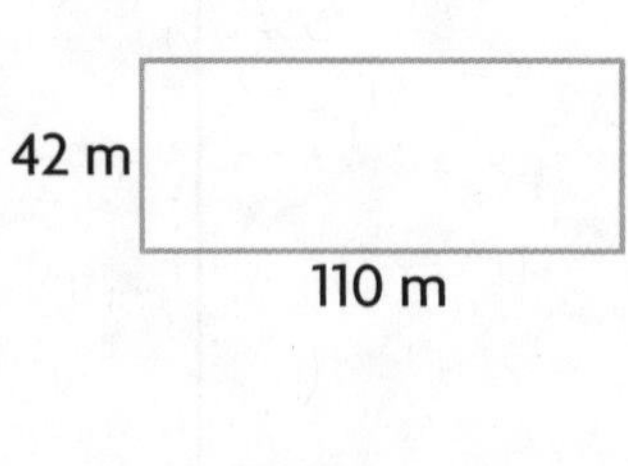

______ meters

4.

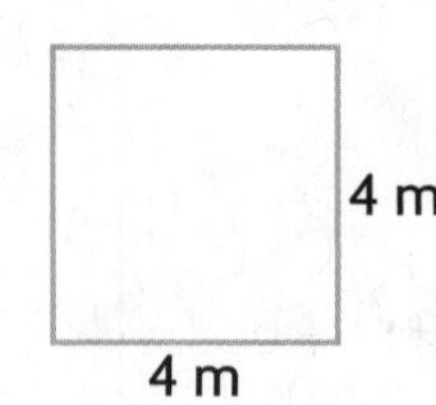

______ meters

Math Talk

Mathematical Processes

Can you use the formula $P = (2 \times l) + (2 \times w)$ to find the perimeter of a square? **Explain.**

Name ________________________________

Unlock the Problem

Real World

5.  **Multi-Step** Alejandra plans to sew fringe on a scarf. The scarf is shaped like a rectangle. The length of the scarf is 48 inches. The width is one half the length. How much fringe does Alejandra need?

Ⓐ 72 inches
Ⓑ 96 inches
Ⓒ 120 inches
Ⓓ 144 inches

a. Draw a picture of the scarf, and label the given measurements on your drawing.

b. What do you need to find?

____

c. What formula will you use?

____

d. Show the steps you use to solve the problem.

e. Complete.

The length of the scarf is ______ inches.

The width is one half the length

or ______ ÷ 2.

The width is ______ inches.

So, the perimeter is (______ × ______) +

(______ × ______) = ______ inches.

Fill in the bubble for the correct answer choice above.

6. H.O.T. **Reasoning** What is the side length of a square with a perimeter of 44 centimeters?

Ⓐ 4 centimeters
Ⓑ 11 centimeters
Ⓒ 22 centimeters
Ⓓ 176 centimeters

7. **Apply** Mr. Wong is putting a brick edge around his rectangular patio. What is the perimeter of the patio?

18 ft

10 ft

Ⓐ 28 ft Ⓑ 38 ft Ⓒ 56 ft Ⓓ 66 ft

Daily Assessment Task

Fill in the bubble completely to show your answer.

8. A rectangular swimming pool is 24 feet long and 12 feet wide. What is the perimeter of the swimming pool?

   Ⓐ 288 ft　　Ⓒ 60 ft

   Ⓑ 36 ft　　Ⓓ 72 ft

9. Todd is putting a fence around a square shaped section of his backyard. The square section is 102 m on each side. How many meters of fence does Todd need in all?

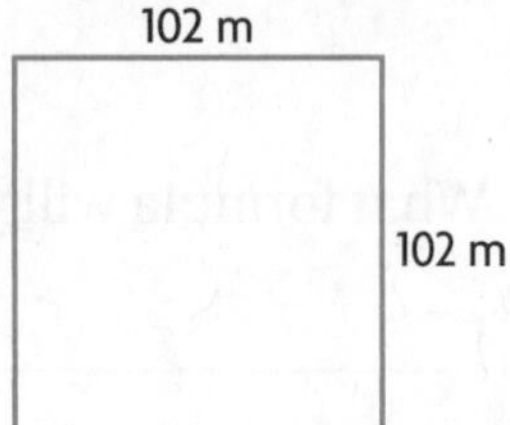

   Ⓐ 408 m　　Ⓒ 800 m

   Ⓑ 104 m　　Ⓓ 204 m

10. **Multi-Step** Joe is putting pavers around his rectangular patio. The width of the patio is 14 feet. The length is three times the width. How many feet of pavers does he need?

   Ⓐ 34 ft　　Ⓒ 112 ft

   Ⓑ 588 ft　　Ⓓ 168 ft

TEXAS Test Prep

11. Lola is putting a border on the quilt she is making. The quilt is shaped like a rectangle. The width of the quilt is 48 inches and its length is twice its width. How much border does Lola need?

   Ⓐ 96 inches

   Ⓑ 288 inches

   Ⓒ 144 inches

   Ⓓ 192 inches

Name ______________________

12.3 Model Perimeter Formulas

Find the perimeter of the rectangle or square.

1.

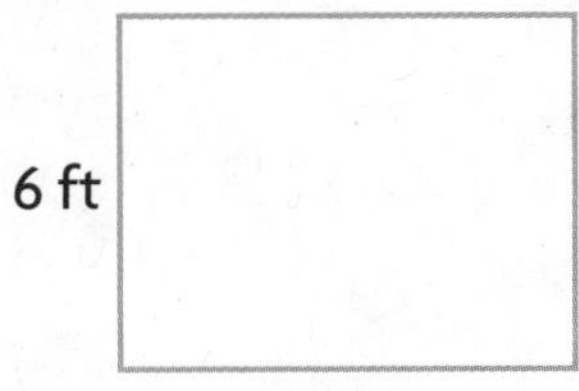

__________ feet

2.

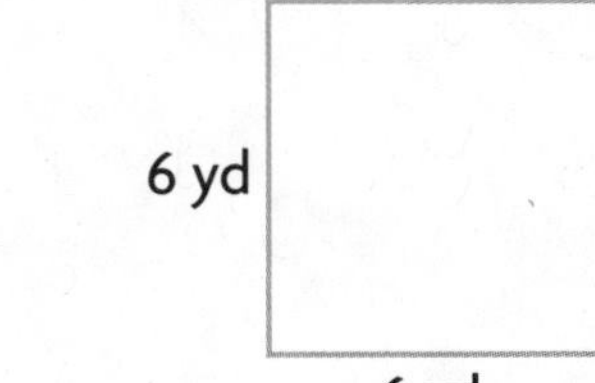

__________ yards

3.

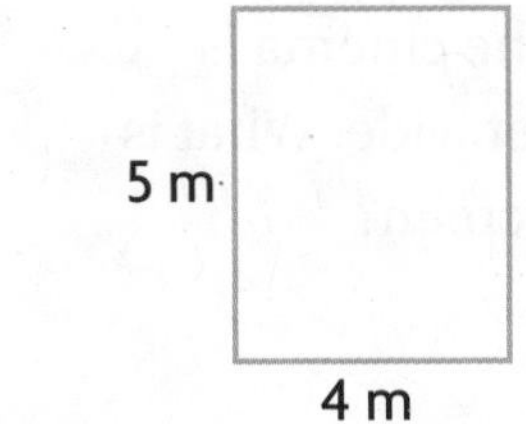

__________ meters

4.

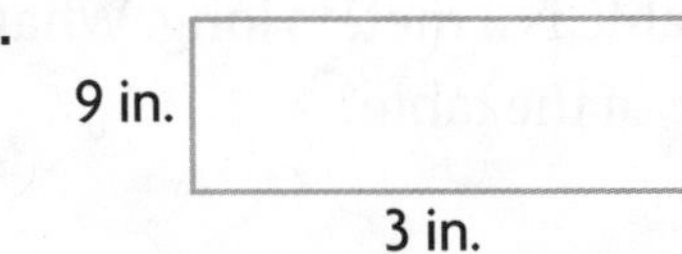

__________ inches

5.

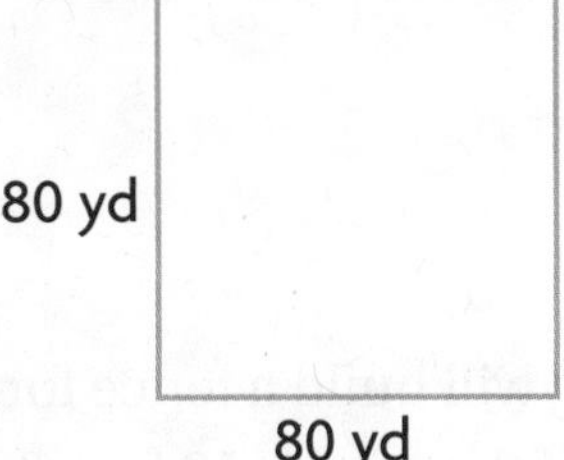

__________ yards

6.

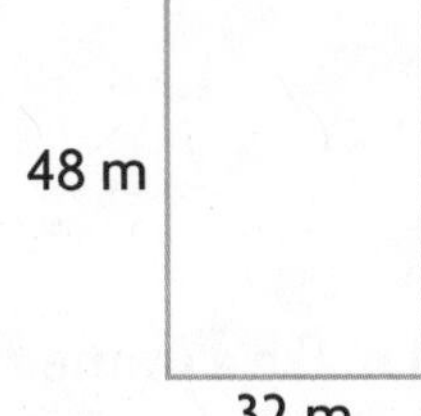

__________ meters

Problem Solving

7. Mrs. Sanders will put a border around a bulletin board that is 52 inches long and 30 inches wide. How many inches of border will she need?

____

8. A rectangular room is 10 meters wide and 14 meters long. What is its perimeter?

____

Lesson Check

TEXAS Test Prep

Fill in the bubble completely to show your answer.

9. What is the side length of a square with a perimeter of 60 meters?

Ⓐ 240 meters

Ⓑ 30 meters

Ⓒ 4 meters

Ⓓ 15 meters

10. Robert wants to put lights around the edge of his yard. The yard is 40 feet long and 25 feet wide. How many feet of lights does he need?

Ⓐ 1000 feet

Ⓑ 130 feet

Ⓒ 100 feet

Ⓓ 160 feet

11. Each side of a table is 3 meters long. What is the perimeter of the table?

Ⓐ 30 meters

Ⓑ 9 meters

Ⓒ 6 meters

Ⓓ 12 meters

12. The movie screen at the cinema is 70 feet long and 30 feet wide. What is the perimeter of the screen?

Ⓐ 200 feet

Ⓑ 140 feet

Ⓒ 60 feet

Ⓓ 2100 feet

13. **Multi-Step** Marcia will make a frame for her picture. The length of the picture is 15 inches. The width is one third of the length. How much wood does Marcia need for the frame?

Ⓐ 18 inches

Ⓑ 40 inches

Ⓒ 30 inches

Ⓓ 45 inches

14. **Multi-Step** Greg will build a fence for his yard. The width of the yard is 12 feet. The length of the yard is twice its width. How much fencing will Greg need for his yard?

Ⓐ 60 feet

Ⓑ 48 feet

Ⓒ 24 feet

Ⓓ 72 feet

Name ________________________________

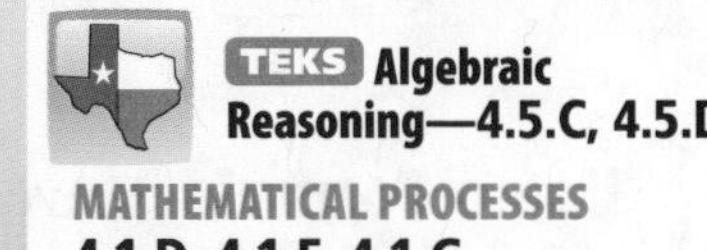

TEKS Algebraic Reasoning—4.5.C, 4.5.D
MATHEMATICAL PROCESSES
4.1.D, 4.1.F, 4.1.G

12.4 Model Area Formulas

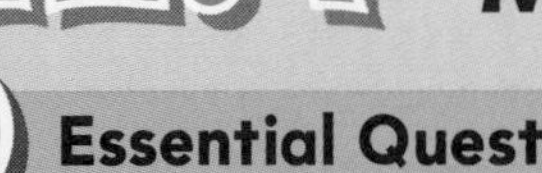

Essential Question How can you use a formula to find the area of a rectangle?

Unlock the Problem

The length, *l*, of a rectangle, can be the measure of any side. The width, *w*, is the measure of a side perpendicular to the side used as the length.

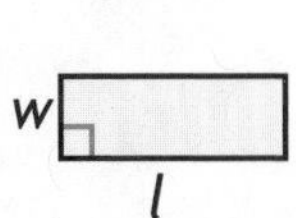

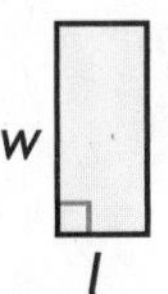

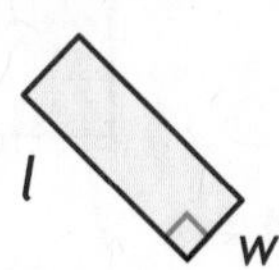

Remember

Perpendicular lines and perpendicular line segments form right angles.

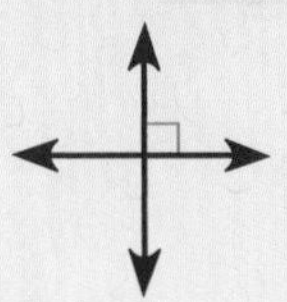

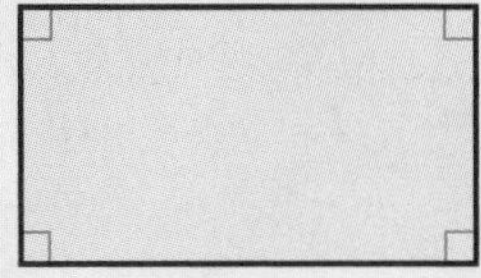

A **unit square** is a square that is 1 unit long and 1 unit wide. **Area** is the number of unit squares needed to cover a flat surface without any gaps or overlaps. The area of a unit square is 1 **square unit**. To find the area of a figure, count the number of unit squares inside the figure. The area is expressed in square units.

1 unit
1 unit 1 unit
1 unit

How are the length, width, and area of a rectangle related?

Complete the table to find the area.

Figure	Length	Width	Area
	5 units		

- What relationship do you see among the length, the width, and the area? Write a formula for the area of a rectangle. Use the letter *A* for area, the letter *l* for length, and the letter *w* for width.

____

____

Use a Formula You can use a formula to find the area.

$A = l \times w$

↑ area ↑ length ↑ width

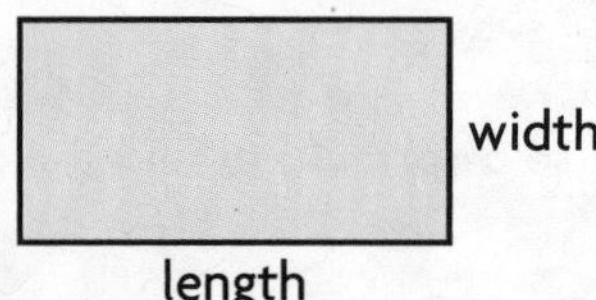

 **Examples** **Use a formula to find the area of a rectangle and a square.**

A

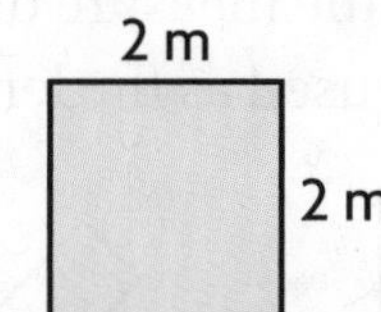

$A = l \times w$

$= \_\_\_\_ \times \_\_\_\_ = \_\_\_\_$

The area is ________________.

B

$A = l \times w$

$= \_\_\_\_ \times \_\_\_\_ = \_\_\_\_$

The area is ________________.

Share and Show

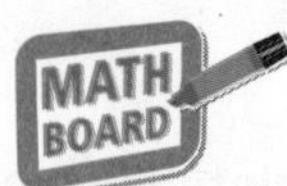

1. Find the area of the rectangle.

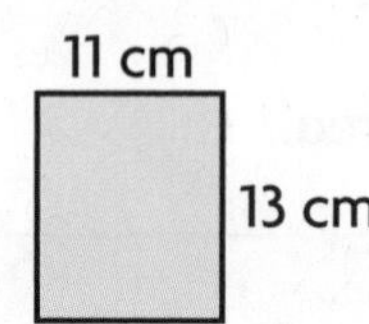

$A = l \times \_\_\_\_$

$= \_\_\_\_ \times \_\_\_\_ = \_\_\_\_\_\_$

Find the area of the rectangle or square.

2.

____

3.

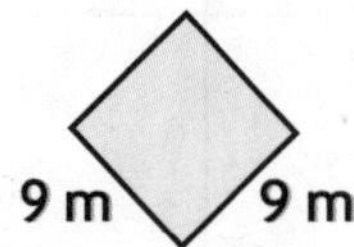

____

4.

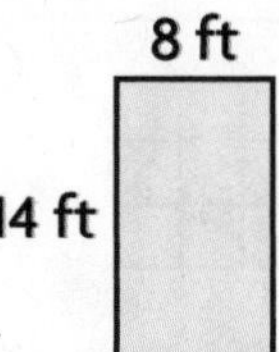

____

Practice: Copy and Solve **Find the area of the rectangle.**

5. length: 16 feet
width: 6 feet

____

6. length: 9 yards
width: 17 yards

____

7. length: 14 centimeters
width: 11 centimeters

____

Name ____________________________

Problem Solving Real World

8. **H.O.T.** **Multi-Step** Nancy and Luke are drawing plans for rectangular flower gardens. In Nancy's plan, the garden is 18 feet by 12 feet. In Luke's plan, the garden is 15 feet by 15 feet. Who drew the garden plan with the greater area? What is the area?

Ⓐ Luke; 205 square feet
Ⓑ Nancy; 206 square feet
Ⓒ Nancy; 216 square feet
Ⓓ Luke; 225 square feet

a. What do you need to find? ____________________

____

b. What formula will you use? ____________________

c. What units will you use to write the answer? ____________________

d. Show the steps to solve the problem.

e. Complete the sentences.

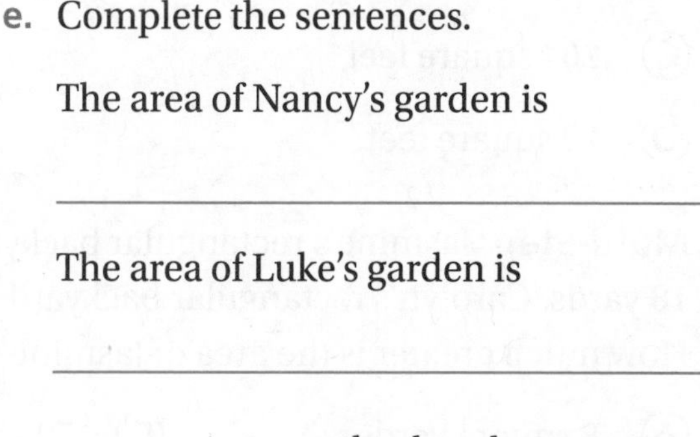

The area of Nancy's garden is

____________________.

The area of Luke's garden is

____________________.

__________ garden has the greater area.

f. **Record** Fill in the bubble for the correct answer choice above.

9. **H.O.T.** **Use Diagrams** Find the area of the rectangle.

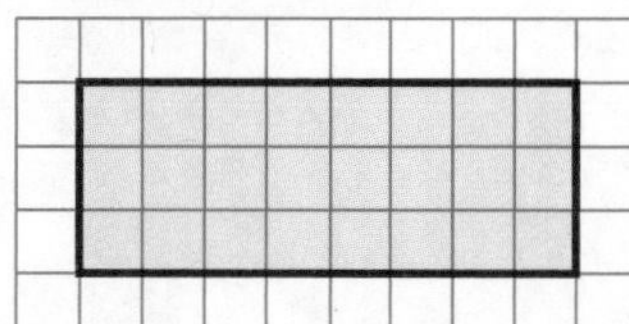

The length of one small square is 4 feet.

Ⓐ 32 square feet
Ⓑ 88 square feet
Ⓒ 336 square feet
Ⓓ 384 square feet

10. **Evaluate** Sonia is buying carpet for the dining room, which measures 15 feet by 12 feet. How many square feet of carpet does Sonia need to cover the dining room?

Ⓐ 45 square feet
Ⓑ 54 square feet
Ⓒ 170 square feet
Ⓓ 180 square feet

Daily Assessment Task

Fill in the bubble completely to show your answer.

11. The shape of Denzel's bedroom floor is shown below. What is the area of the floor?

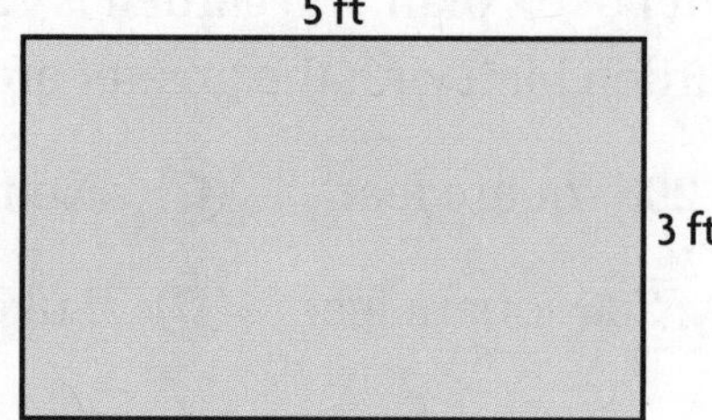

Ⓐ 15 square feet

Ⓑ 8 square feet

Ⓒ 2 square feet

Ⓓ 16 square feet

12. Ms. Jenkins is buying tile for her kitchen floor, which measures 17 feet by 12 feet. How many square feet of tile does Ms. Jenkins need to cover the kitchen floor?

Ⓐ 58 square feet

Ⓑ 194 square feet

Ⓒ 204 square feet

Ⓓ 29 square feet

13. **Multi-Step** Jasmine's rectangular backyard is 15 yards by 18 yards. Carolyn's rectangular backyard is 20 yards by 9 yards. How much greater is the area of Jasmine's yard than Carolyn's?

Ⓐ 8 square yards

Ⓑ 4 square yards

Ⓒ 50 square yards

Ⓓ 90 square yards

TEXAS Test Prep

14. Barry is building a dog house. He wants to put linoleum on the floor. The floor of the dog house is a rectangle that is 56 inches long. The width is half its length. How many square inches of linoleum does Barry need for his dog house?

Ⓐ 6,272 square inches

Ⓑ 336 square inches

Ⓒ 168 square inches

Ⓓ 1,568 square inches

Name ______________________

12.4 Model Area Formulas

Find the area of the square or rectangle.

1. 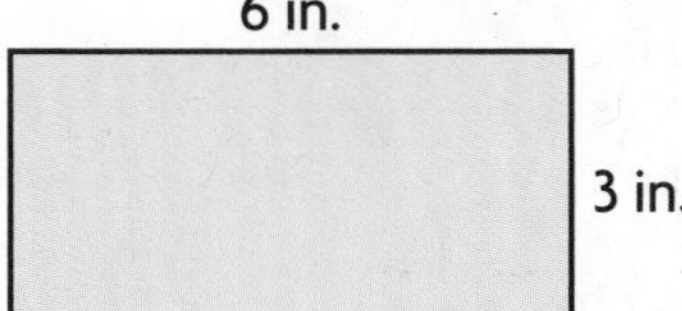

____

2. 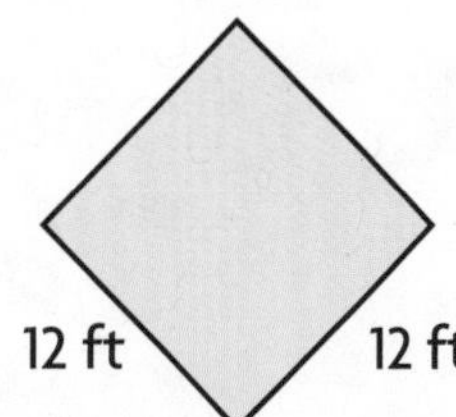

____

3. 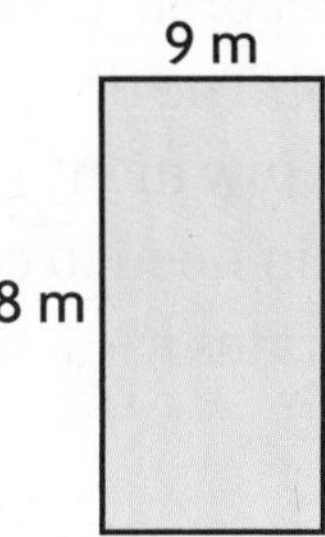

____

4. 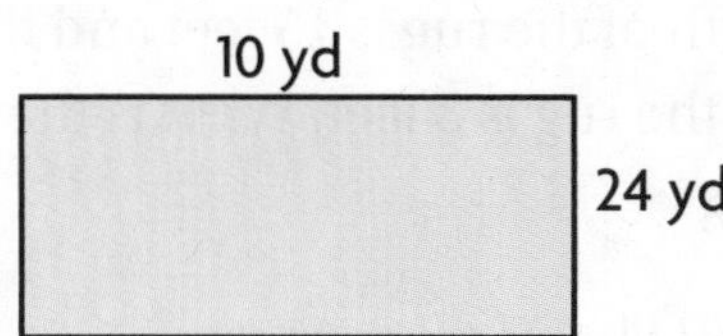

____

Find the area of the rectangle.

5. length: 25 centimeters
   width: 10 centimeters

____

6. length: 8 feet
   width: 4 feet

____

7. length: 12 yards
   width: 10 yards

____

8. length: 22 inches
   width: 5 inches

____

Problem Solving

9. JoAnn will cover a bulletin board with paper. The board measures 6 feet by 4 feet. How many square feet of paper does JoAnn need to cover the board?

____

10. Frank will paint a wall that measures 10 feet by 14 feet. What is the area of the wall that Frank will paint?

____

Lesson Check

★ TEXAS Test Prep

Fill in the bubble completely to show your answer.

11. The length of a basketball court is 94 feet. The width of the court is 50 feet. What is the area of the court?

Ⓐ 4,700 sq ft

Ⓑ 288 sq ft

Ⓒ 470 sq ft

Ⓓ 2,880 sq ft

12. Carmen sewed a baby quilt that measures 36 inches on each side. What is the area of the quilt?

Ⓐ 1,266 sq in.

Ⓑ 324 sq in.

Ⓒ 144 sq in.

Ⓓ 1,296 sq in.

13. Amy bought a new rug for her hallway. The length of the rug is 15 feet and the width of the rug is 3 feet. What is the area of the rug?

Ⓐ 90 sq ft

Ⓑ 45 sq ft

Ⓒ 225 sq ft

Ⓓ 36 sq ft

14. Mr. Crain wants to decorate his door for the first day of school. The door is 7 feet tall and 3 feet wide. How many square feet of paper will Mr. Crain need to cover the door before he decorates it?

Ⓐ 28 sq ft

Ⓑ 20 sq ft

Ⓒ 21 sq ft

Ⓓ 49 sq ft

15. **Multi-Step** Xavier wants to buy fertilizer for his yard. The yard measures 35 feet by 55 feet. The directions on the bag of fertilizer say that one bag will cover 1,250 sq ft. How many bags of fertilizer should Xavier buy?

Ⓐ 2

Ⓑ 4

Ⓒ 3

Ⓓ 1

16. **Multi-Step** Jean will cover the front and back of a folder with craft paper. The folder measures 29 centimeters by 24 centimeters. How many square centimeters of craft paper will Jean use?

Ⓐ 696 sq cm

Ⓑ 212 sq cm

Ⓒ 576 sq cm

Ⓓ 1,392 sq cm

Name ____________________

12.5 PROBLEM SOLVING • Find the Perimeter and Area

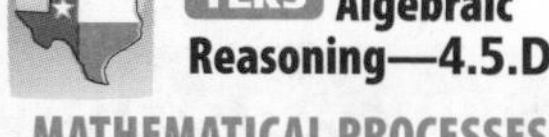

TEKS Algebraic Reasoning—4.5.D

MATHEMATICAL PROCESSES 4.1.A, 4.1.B, 4.1.D

Essential Question How can you use the strategy *solve a simpler problem* to solve perimeter and area problems?

Unlock the Problem (Real World)

A landscaper is laying turf for a rectangular playground. The turf will cover the whole playground except for a square sandbox. How many square yards of turf will the landscaper use?

25 yd
Playground
Sandbox
6 yd
15 yd

Read

What do I need to find?

I need to find how many ____________ the landscaper will use.

What information am I given?

The turf will cover the ____________.

The turf will not cover the ____________.

The length and width of the playground are ____________ and ____________.

The side length of the square sandbox is ____________.

Plan

What is my plan or strategy?

I can solve simpler problems.

Find the area of the ____________.

Find the area of the ____________.

Then ________ the area of the ________ from the area of the ____________.

Solve

First, find the area of the playground.

$A = l \times w$

$= \_\_\_\_ \times \_\_\_\_$

$= \_\_\_\_$ square yards

Next, find the area of the sandbox.

$A = s \times s$

$= \_\_\_\_ \times \_\_\_\_$

$= \_\_\_\_$ square yards

Last, subtract the area of the sandbox from the area of the playground.

$$\begin{array}{r} 375 \\ -\ 36 \\ \hline \square \end{array}$$ square yards

So, the landscaper will use ____________ ____________ of turf to cover the playground.

Try Another Problem

Zach is planting a garden for a new museum. A fence will be around the sides of the garden, as shown in the diagram. How many meters of fence does Zach need?

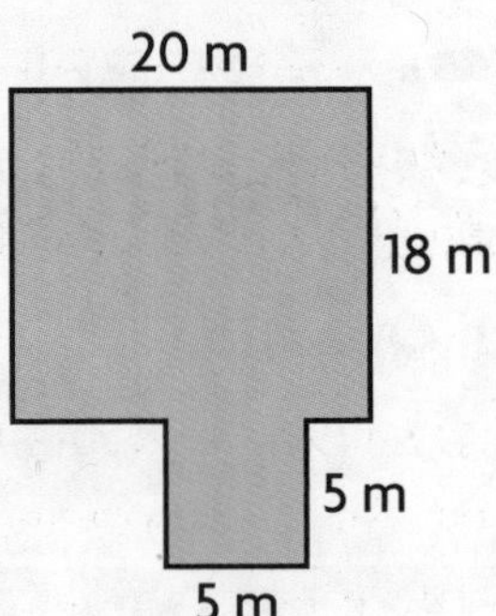

Read	Solve
What do I need to find?	
What information am I given?	
Plan	
What is my plan or strategy?	

- How many meters of fence does Zach need? **Explain.**

Name ___________________________

Share and Show

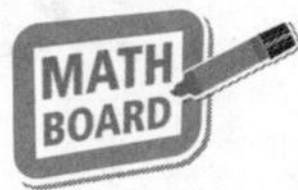

Unlock the Problem Tips

- ✓ Use the Problem Solving MathBoard.
- ✓ Underline important facts.
- ✓ Choose a strategy you know.

1. Lila is wallpapering one wall of her bedroom, as shown in the diagram. She will cover the whole wall except for the doorway. How many square feet of wallpaper does Lila need?

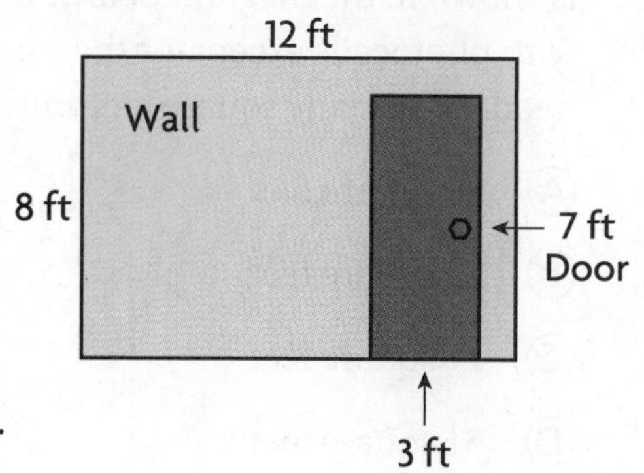

First, find the area of the wall.

$A = l \times w =$ _____ $\times$ _____ $=$ _____ square feet

Next, find the area of the door.

$A = l \times w =$ _____ $\times$ _____ $=$ _____ square feet

Last, subtract the area of the door from the area of the wall.

_____ $-$ _____ $=$ _____ square feet

So, Lila needs _______________ of wallpaper.

2. Ed is building a model of a house with a flat roof, as shown in the diagram. There is a chimney through the roof. Ed will cover the roof with square tiles. If the area of each tile is 1 square inch, how many tiles will he need? **Explain.**

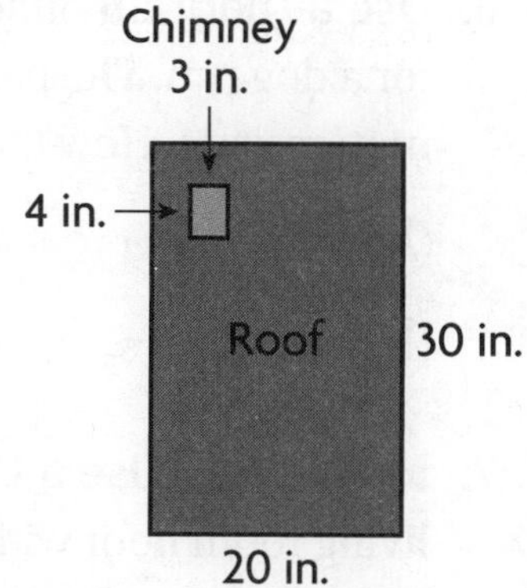

____

____

Problem Solving

3. H.O.T. **Multi-Step** Mr. Foster is framing two pictures. One is 6 inches by 4 inches and the other is 5 inches by 5 inches. Does he need the same amount of framing for each picture? **Explain.**

____

____

____

4. H.O.T. **Multi-Step** Mr. Foster is covering two pictures with glass. One is 6 inches by 4 inches and the other one is 5 inches by 5 inches. Does he need the same number of square inches of glass for each picture? **Explain.**

____

____

____

Daily Assessment Task

Fill in the bubble completely to show your answer.

5. **Multi-Step** Flynn builds a solar-powered car. The top of the car is shown in the diagram below. He will cover the rectangular top with photocells except for the square that is cut out for the driver's head. How many square feet will be covered with photocells?

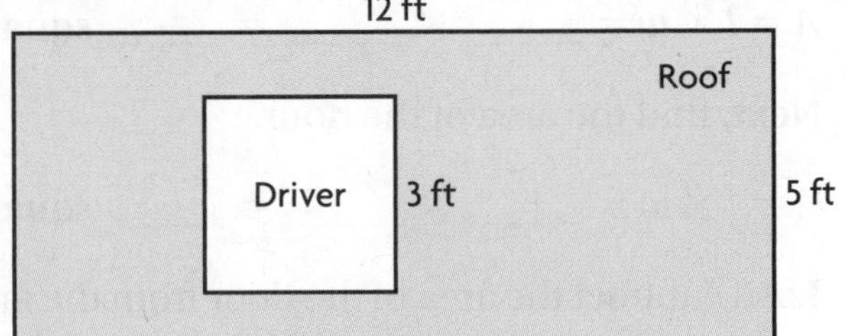

Ⓐ 60 square feet

Ⓑ 22 square feet

Ⓒ 11 square feet

Ⓓ 51 square feet

6. **Use a Diagram** Julie is putting a fence around part of her yard for a dog run. The part she wants to fence is 25 meters long and 16 meters wide. How many meters of fencing will Julie need?

Ⓐ 400 meters

Ⓑ 82 meters

Ⓒ 380 meters

Ⓓ 64 meters

7. **Multi-Step Use a Diagram** Connor is covering his living room floor with square tiles that are each 1 square foot. There is a fireplace on one side of the room that won't be tiled. How many tiles does Connor need for the floor?

15 ft
2 ft
3 ft
Floor
10 ft
Fireplace

Ⓐ 144 tiles

Ⓑ 20 tiles

Ⓒ 44 tiles

Ⓓ 35 tiles

TEXAS Test Prep

8. A rectangular floor is 12 feet long and 11 feet wide. A rug that is 9 feet long and 7 feet wide covers part of the floor. How many square feet of the floor are NOT covered by the rug?

Ⓐ 63 square feet

Ⓑ 69 square feet

Ⓒ 132 square feet

Ⓓ 195 square feet

Homework and Practice

TEKS Algebraic Reasoning—4.5.D
MATHEMATICAL PROCESSES 4.1.A, 4.1.B, 4.1.D

Name ________________

12.5 PROBLEM SOLVING • Find the Perimeter and Area

Problem Solving (Real World)

1. Volunteers are fencing a part of City Park for toddlers. The diagram shows the area of a park that will be fenced. How many feet of fencing will be used?

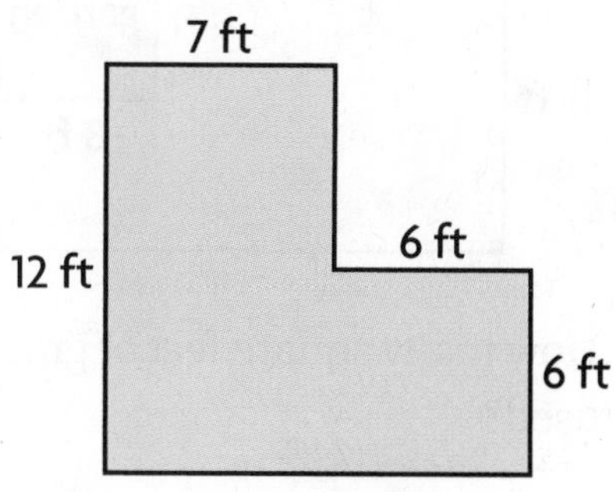

____

2. Sam is carpeting a room. The size of the room is shown in the diagram. How many square feet of carpet does Sam need?

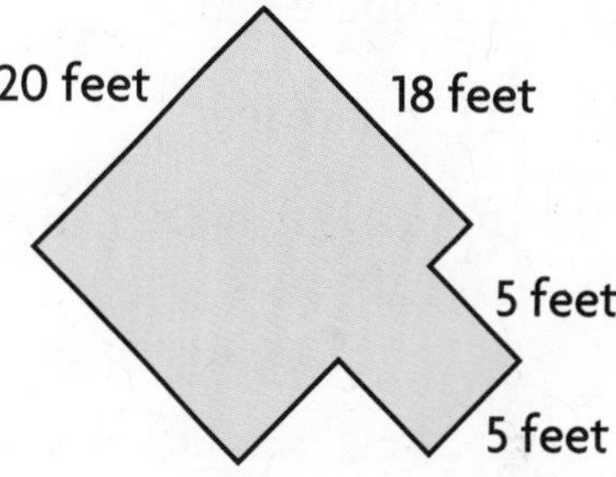

____

3. Grace is helping her teacher cover the classroom door with paper, as shown in the diagram. She will cover the whole door except for the window. How many square feet of paper does Grace need?

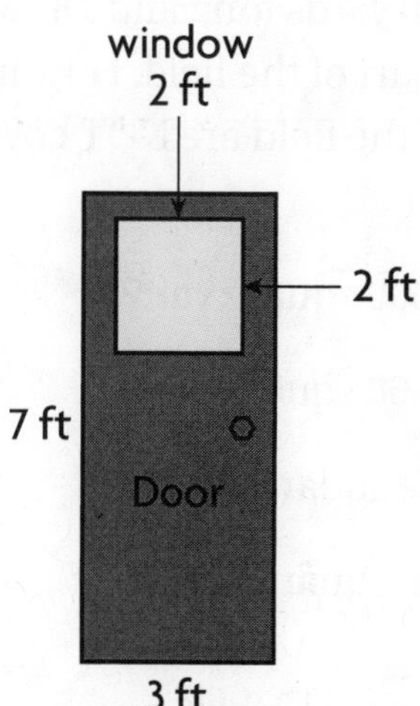

____

Lesson Check

★ TEXAS Test Prep

Fill in the bubble completely to show your answer.

4. Mr. Floyd is laying grass squares in his back yard. He will cover the entire yard except for the vegetable garden.

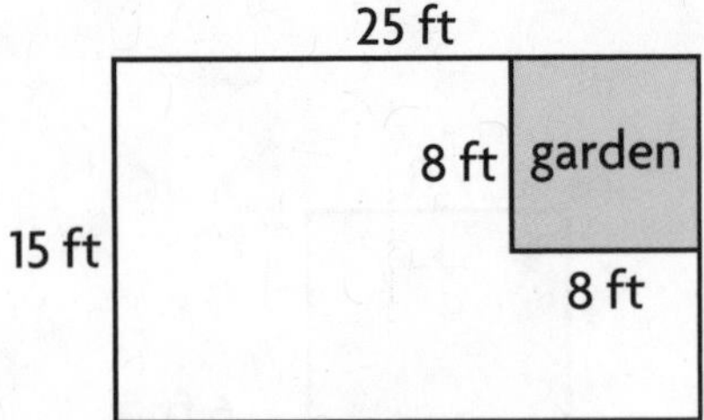

How many square feet of grass will be used?

Ⓐ 439 square feet

Ⓑ 112 square feet

Ⓒ 375 square feet

Ⓓ 311 square feet

5. Builders are covering a wall that is 4 meters tall and 7 meters wide with bricks. They will cover the entire wall except for a square window that measures 2 meters on all sides.

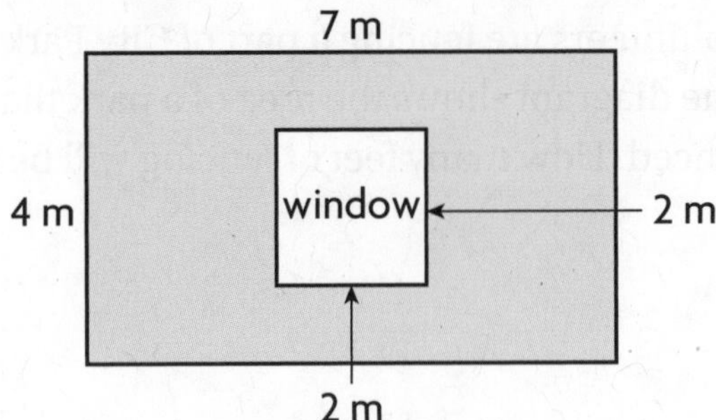

How many square meters of the wall will be covered in bricks?

Ⓐ 28 square meters

Ⓑ 32 square meters

Ⓒ 24 square meters

Ⓓ 25 square meters

6. **Multi-Step** A rectangular field is 120 yards long and 53 yards wide. A tent that is 20 yards long and 18 yards wide covers part of the field. How many square yards of the field are NOT covered by the tent?

Ⓐ 6,000 square yards

Ⓑ 6,360 square yards

Ⓒ 422 square yards

Ⓓ 706 square yards

7. **Multi-Step** Jason is adding a baseboard trim around the edge of his floor. The room is 14 feet wide and 20 feet long. There is a door opening that is 3 feet wide. How many feet of trim will Jason need?

Ⓐ 68 feet

Ⓑ 65 feet

Ⓒ 277 feet

Ⓓ 280 feet

Name ______________________________

Module 12 Assessment

Vocabulary

Vocabulary
area
pattern
formula
perimeter
square unit (sq un)

Choose the best term from the box.

1. A ______________ is an ordered set of numbers or objects. (p. 409)
2. A set of symbols that expresses a mathematical rule is called a ______________. (p. 422)
3. The ______________ is the distance around a figure. (p. 421)

Concepts and Skills

Use the rule to write the first six terms in the pattern. Describe another pattern in the numbers. TEKS 4.5.B

4. Rule: Add 10. First term: 11

____

____

Use the rule to complete the input/output table. TEKS 4.5.B

5. **Rule:** The output is $t - 3$.

Input	t	17	20	22	24
Output	r				

6. **Rule:** The output is $a + 7$.

Input	a	18	21	23	24
Output	b				

Find the perimeter and area of the rectangle or square. TEKS 4.5.D

7. 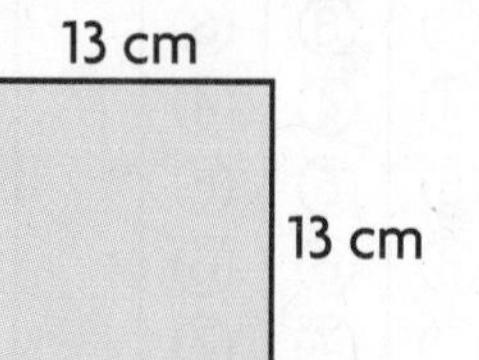

____

8. 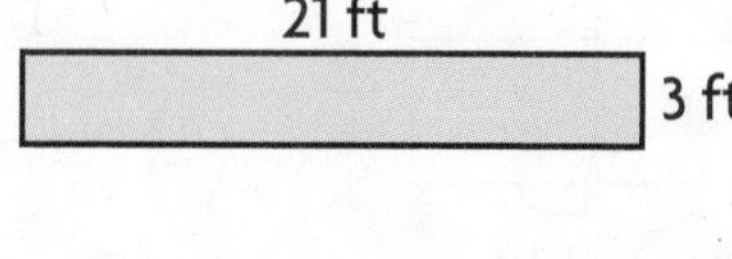

____

9. 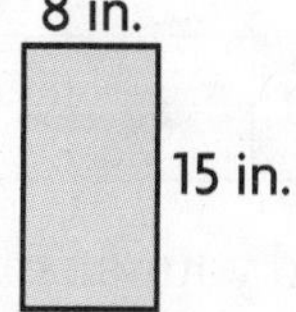

____

Fill in the bubble completely to show your answer.

10. Erica knits 18 squares on Monday. She knits 7 more squares each day for the rest of the week. How many squares does Erica have after Friday? TEKS 4.5.B

Ⓐ 39

Ⓑ 90

Ⓒ 53

Ⓓ 46

11. Darren wants to use a formula to find the perimeter of the figure below. Which formula should Darren use? TEKS 4.5.C

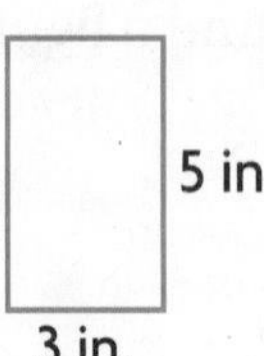

Ⓐ $P = l + w$

Ⓑ $P = l + w + l + w$

Ⓒ $P = l \times w$

Ⓓ $P = 2 + w + 2 + w$

12. Carol wants to find the area of her rectangular garden below so she will know how much mulch to buy. Which formula should she use to find the area? TEKS 4.5.C

13 cm

6 cm

Ⓐ $A = l + w$

Ⓑ $A = 2 \times w$

Ⓒ $A = l \times w + l \times w$

Ⓓ $A = l \times w$

13. The input-output table below shows the number of boxes, b, and the number of pillows, p, Jason is packing in the boxes. Using the rule $b \times 4$, how many pillows would Jason pack in 7 boxes?

Input	b	3	4	6	7
Output	p	12			

Record your answer and fill in the bubbles on the grid. Be sure to use the correct place value. TEKS 4.5.B

Name ________________________________

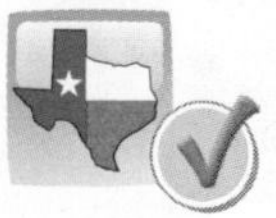

Unit 3 Assessment

Vocabulary

Choose the best term from the box.

Vocabulary
perimeter
area
formula
pattern
square unit (sq un)

1. A set of symbols that expresses a mathematical rule is called a ____________. (p. 422)
2. The ____________ is the distance around a figure. (p. 421)
3. A ____________ is an ordered set of numbers or objects. (p. 409)

Concepts and Skills

Use the rule to write the first ten terms in the pattern. Describe another pattern in the numbers. TEKS 4.5.B

4. Rule: Add 8. First term: 7

____

____

5. Find a rule. Use your rule to write an expression. TEKS 4.5.B

Input	*t*	5	6	7	8
Output	*r*	11	12	13	14

Rule: ____________________

6. Use the rule to complete the input/output table. TEKS 4.5.B

Rule: The output is $a \times 5$.

Input	*a*	2	3	4	5
Output	*b*	10			

Find the perimeter and area of the rectangle or square. TEKS 4.5.D

7.
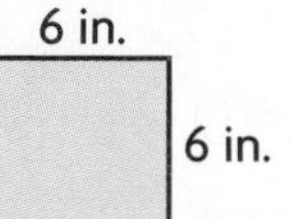

____

8.
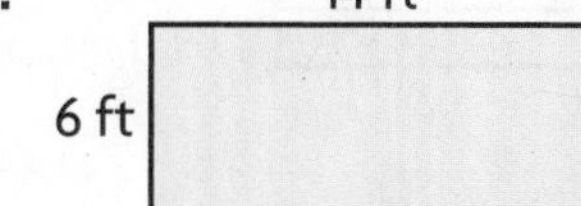

____

9. 12 mm, 18 mm

____

Fill in the bubble completely to show your answer.

10. Melissa wants to use a formula to find the perimeter of the figure below. Which formula should Melissa use? TEKS 4.5.C

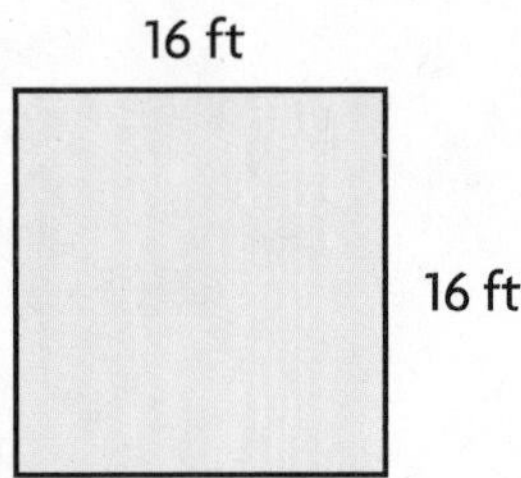

Ⓐ $P = 2 + w + 2 + l$
Ⓑ $P = l + w$
Ⓒ $P = l \times w + l \times w$
Ⓓ $P = 4s$

11. Martin buys four packs of baseball cards. Each pack has 12 cards in it. He then buys 3 more packs of cards with 8 cards in each pack. How many baseball cards did Martin buy? Use strip diagrams or equations to help you solve. TEKS 4.5.A

Ⓐ 96
Ⓑ 72
Ⓒ 27
Ⓓ 66

12. Greg drew the sketch of his garden below. What is the area of Greg's garden? TEKS 4.5.C

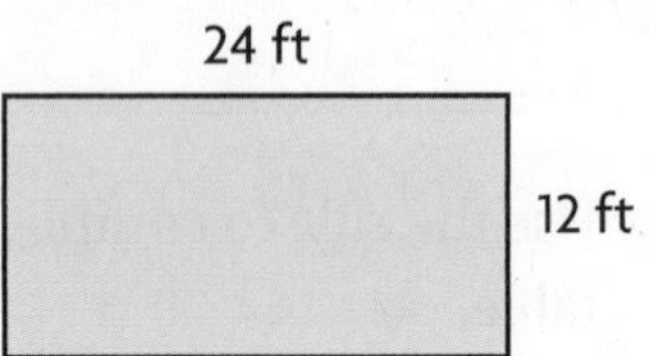

Ⓐ 36 square feet
Ⓑ 200 square feet
Ⓒ 288 square feet
Ⓓ 72 square feet

13. Pablo is using this strip diagram to solve a problem. Which equation is shown by the strip diagram? TEKS 4.5.A

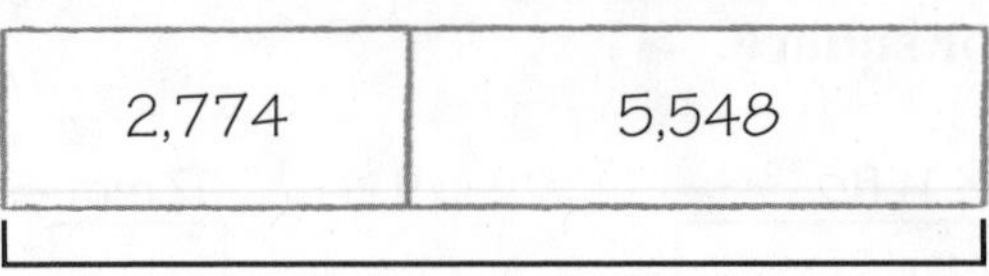

Ⓐ $5{,}548 - 2{,}774 = p$
Ⓑ $5{,}548 - p = 2{,}774$
Ⓒ $2{,}774 + 5{,}548 = p$
Ⓓ $2{,}774 + p = 5{,}548$

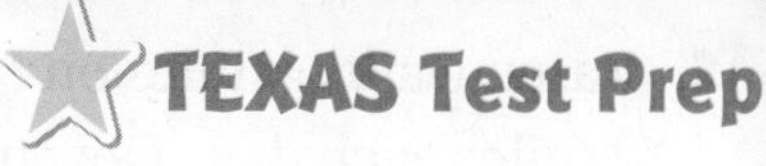

14. Marcel had 72 stickers. He gave 14 of his stickers to his sister. Then he gave 27 stickers to his brother. How many stickers does Marcel have left? Use strip diagrams or equations to help you solve. TEKS 4.5.A

Ⓐ 58

Ⓑ 31

Ⓒ 45

Ⓓ 113

15. Gabby wants to put a fence around the perimeter of her backyard. She drew a sketch of her backyard to determine the perimeter. What is the perimeter of Gabby's backyard? TEKS 4.5.D

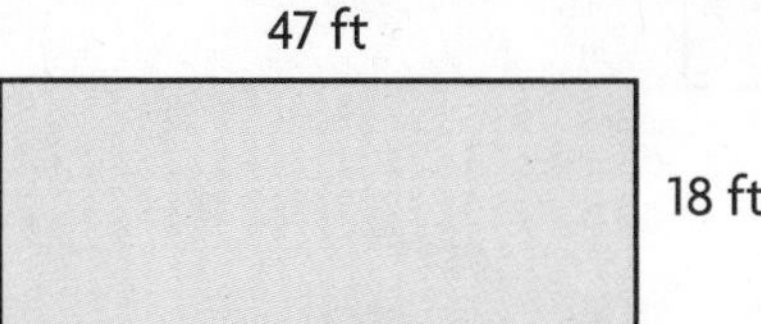

Ⓐ 130 ft

Ⓑ 611 ft

Ⓒ 112 ft

Ⓓ 83 ft

16. Dan wants to find the area of his rectangular room so he will know how much carpet to buy. Which formula should he use to find the area of his room? TEKS 4.5.C

Ⓐ $A = l + w$

Ⓑ $A = l \times w$

Ⓒ $A = (l \times w) + (l \times w)$

Ⓓ $A = (2 \times w) + (2 \times l)$

17. Erica has 144 lollipops. She wants to put the lollipops into 8 different bags, with each bag having the same number of lollipops. Once Erica has all the lollipops in the 8 bags, she takes 2 lollipops out of each bag. How many lollipops are in each of the 8 bags? Use strip diagrams or equations to help you solve. TEKS 4.5.A

Ⓐ 12

Ⓑ 16

Ⓒ 20

Ⓓ 18

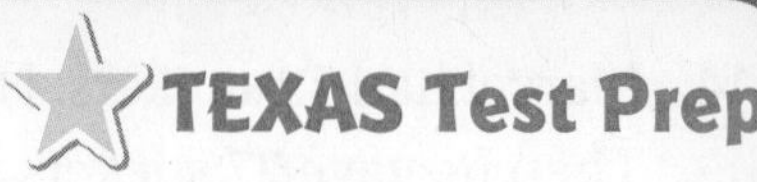

18. Karen walks 4 miles on Monday. For the next 7 days, she walks 2 miles each day. How many miles total does Karen walk during the 8 days? TEKS 4.5.B

Ⓐ 18 miles
Ⓑ 14 miles
Ⓒ 34 miles
Ⓓ Not here

19. During recess, Gretchen walked around the perimeter of the playground. When she got home, she drew a sketch of the playground to help her determine how far she walked during recess. What is the perimeter of the playground? TEKS 4.5.D

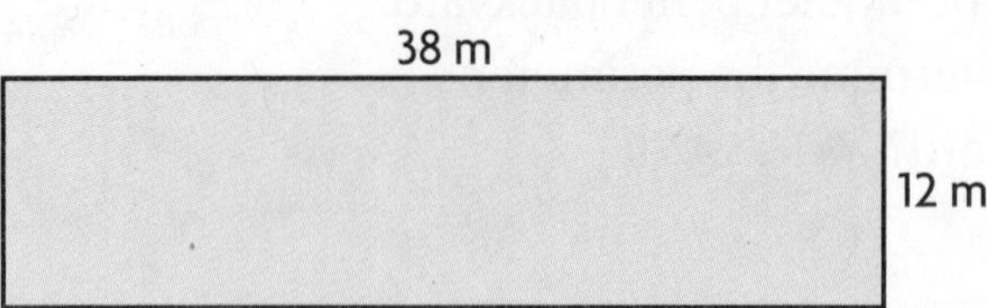

Ⓐ 50 m
Ⓑ 88 m
Ⓒ 62 m
Ⓓ 100 m

20. Van is buying new tires for some cars at his store. The input-output table below shows the number of cars, *c*, and the number of tires, *t*, on each car. Using the rule $c \times 4$, how many tires does Van have to buy to replace all the tires on 6 cars? TEKS 4.5.B

Input	Cars, *c*	1	2	3	4	5	6
Output	Tires, *t*	4	8				

Ⓐ 12
Ⓑ 16
Ⓒ 24
Ⓓ 20

21. An art museum adds 3 new pieces of art each month. If the museum starts with 75 pieces and the pattern continues, write the numbers in the pattern for the next 8 months. Describe another pattern in the numbers. TEKS 4.5.B

Unit 4

Geometry and Measurement

Show What You Know

Check your understanding of important skills.

Name ______________________________

▶ Identify Two-Dimensional Shapes Write the number of sides and vertices.

1. 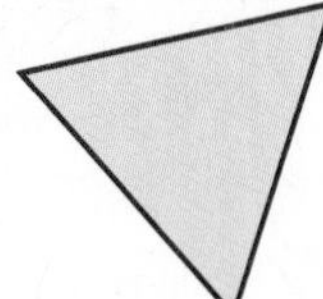

_____ sides

_____ vertices

__________ name

2. 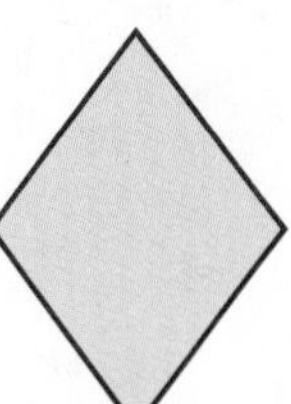

_____ sides

_____ vertices

__________ name

▶ Classify Angles Classify the angle. Write *acute, right,* or *obtuse.*

3. 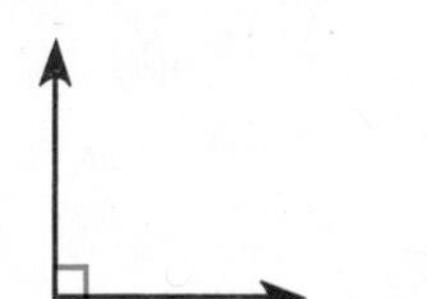

____

4. 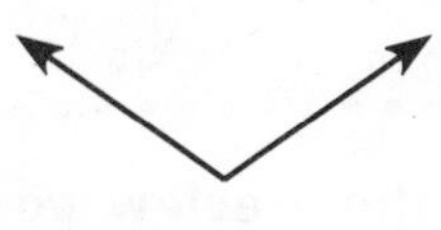

____

5. 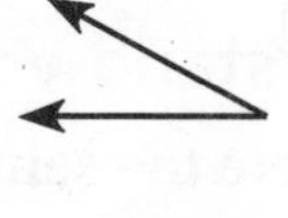

____

▶ Time to the Half Hour Read the clock. Write the time.

6. 

____

7. 

____

8. 

____

GO DIGITAL Assessment Options: Soar to Success Math

Vocabulary Builder

▶ Visualize It

Sort words with a ✓ using the Venn diagram.

Measurement

Customary

Metric

Preview Words

acute angle
acute triangle
✓ cups
✓ decimeters
✓ gallons
✓ kilometer
line
✓ mile
✓ milliliter
✓ millimeter
obtuse angle
obtuse triangle
parallel lines
perpendicular lines
point
✓ pound
protractor
ray
rectangle
right triangle
✓ second
square
✓ tons

▶ Understand Vocabulary

Complete the sentences by using the preview words.

1. An angle less than 90° is called an ________________.

2. A triangle with one 90° angle is called a ________________.

3. A quadrilateral with two pairs of parallel sides, four sides of equal length, and four right angles is called a ________________.

4. A pair of lines in the same plane which never cross and are always the same distance apart are called ________________.

5. A pair of lines that intersect in four right angles are called ________________.

GO DIGITAL
• Interactive Student Edition
• Multimedia eGlossary

Name ______________________________

Reading Vocabulary is important in everyday language. Mathematics also has its own set of words that you need to learn.

1. **Math words have precise meanings.** The figures shown below are all quadrilaterals. As the word *quadrilateral* suggests, each has 4 (*quadri-*) sides (*lateral*). Which three of the figures are also parallelograms? How can you tell?

2. **You need to know the language of math in order to keep learning.** In mathematics, you learn something new in every grade. You learn something new in every module and lesson. In mathematics, you always build on what you know.

Think

I keep a log of all the math words I learn.

Writing Preview Module 13. Make a list of words that are highlighted or in boldface type. Write "Yes" next to each word you know. Write "No" next to those that are new. Keep the list handy as you work on the lessons. Turn every "No" into a "Yes"!

WORD LOG—Module 13

	Word	Already Know?	Meaning
Lesson 1	acute angle	no	
	angle	yes	
	line		
	line segment		

Get Ready **Game**

What's the Measure?

Object of the Game Compare angles to right angles to earn more points than the other player.

Materials
- Angle Cards

Set Up
Cut out the angle cards and place them face down in a stack.

Number of Players 2

How to Play

1. Player 1 picks a card from the stack and decides if the angle shown is a right angle, is less than a right angle, or is greater than a right angle.
   - If the angle is less than a right angle, Player 1 gets one point.
   - If the angle is a right angle, Player 1 gets two points.
   - If the angle is greater than a right angle, Player 1 gets three points.
2. Player 2 repeats Step 1. If a player incorrectly classifies an angle, the points go to the other player.
3. When all cards have been used, players add up their points.
4. The player with more points wins.

Name ____________________

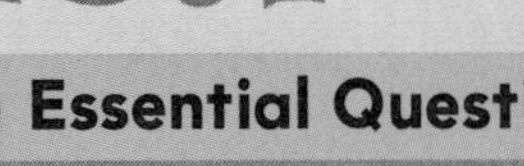

13.1 Lines, Rays, and Angles

TEKS Geometry and Measurement—4.6.A
MATHEMATICAL PROCESSES
4.1.D, 4.1.E

Essential Question How can you identify and draw points, lines, line segments, rays, and angles?

Unlock the Problem (Real World)

Everyday things can model geometric figures. For example, the period at the end of this sentence models a point. A solid painted stripe in the middle of a straight road models a line.

Term and Definition	Draw It	Read It	Write It	Example
A **point** is an exact location in space.	A •	point *A*	point *A*	
A **line** is a straight path of points that continues without end in both directions.	line through B and C with arrows at both ends	line *BC* line *CB*	$\overleftrightarrow{BC}$ $\overleftrightarrow{CB}$	
A **line segment** is part of a line between two endpoints.	segment with endpoints D and E	line segment *DE* line segment *ED*	$\overline{DE}$ $\overline{ED}$	YIELD
A **ray** is a part of a line that has one endpoint and continues without end in one direction.	ray from F through G	ray *FG*	$\overrightarrow{FG}$	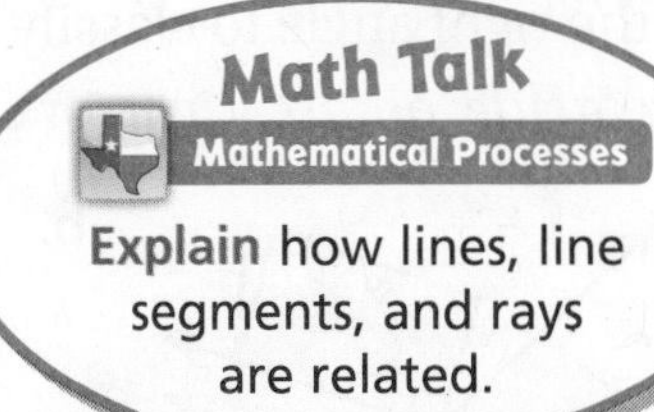

Activity 1 Draw and label $\overline{JK}$.

____

Math Talk Mathematical Processes

Explain how lines, line segments, and rays are related.

- Is there another way to name $\overline{JK}$? **Explain.**

____

Angles

Term and Definition	Draw It	Read It	Write It	Example
An **angle** is formed by two rays or line segments that have the same endpoint. The shared endpoint is called the vertex.	P Q R	angle *PQR* angle *RQP* angle *Q*	$\angle PQR$ $\angle RQP$ $\angle Q$	

You can name an angle by the vertex. When you name an angle using 3 points, the vertex is always the point in the middle.

Angles are classified by the size of the opening between the rays.

A **right angle** forms a square corner.	A **straight angle** forms a line.	An **acute angle** is less than a right angle.	An **obtuse angle** is greater than a right angle and less than a straight angle.

Activity 2 Classify an angle.

Materials ■ paper

To classify an angle, you can compare it to a right angle.

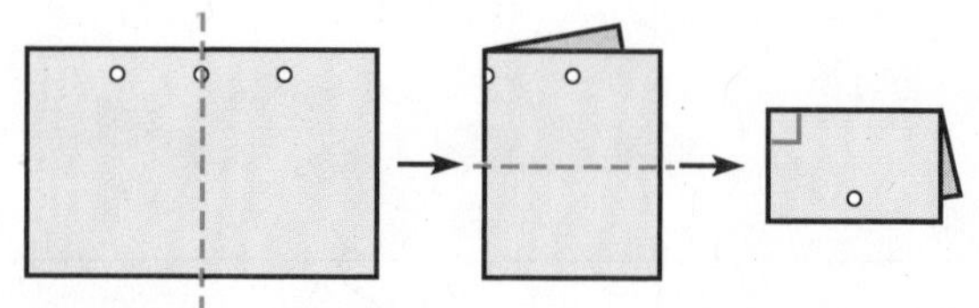

Make a right angle by using a sheet of paper. Fold the paper twice evenly to model a right angle. Use the right angle to classify the angles below. Write *acute, obtuse, right,* or *straight.*

a. 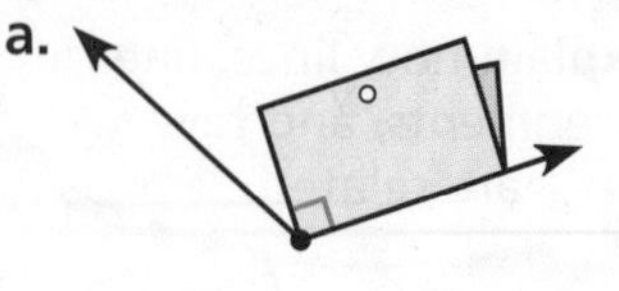 _______________

b. 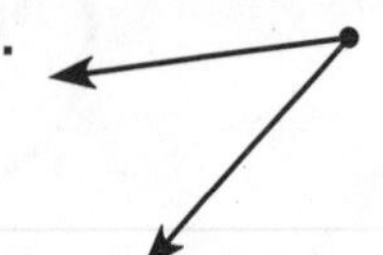 _______________

c. 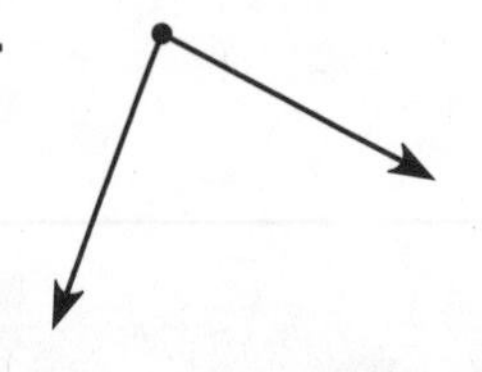 _______________

d. 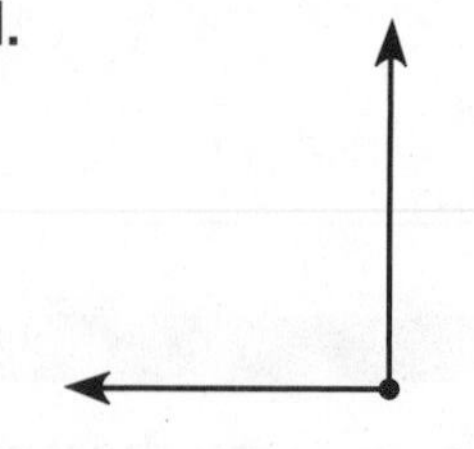 _______________

Name ______________________

Share and Show

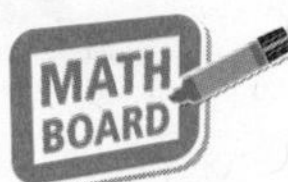

1. Draw and label $\overline{AB}$ in the space at the right.

   $\overline{AB}$ is a ______________.

Draw and label an example of the figure.

2. $\overleftrightarrow{XY}$

3. obtuse $\angle K$

4. right $\angle CDE$

Use Figure *M* for 5 and 6.

5. Name a line segment.

   ____

6. Name a right angle.

   ____

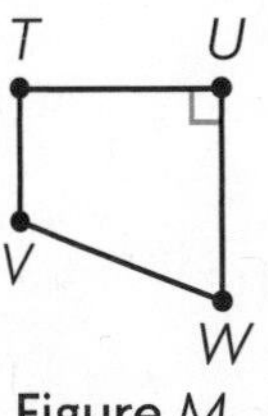

Figure *M*

Problem Solving

Use the picture of the bridge for 7 and 8.

7. Classify $\angle A$.

   ____

8. Which angle appears to be obtuse?

   ____

9. H.O.T. **Use Diagrams** How many different angles are in Figure *X*? List them.

   ____

   ____

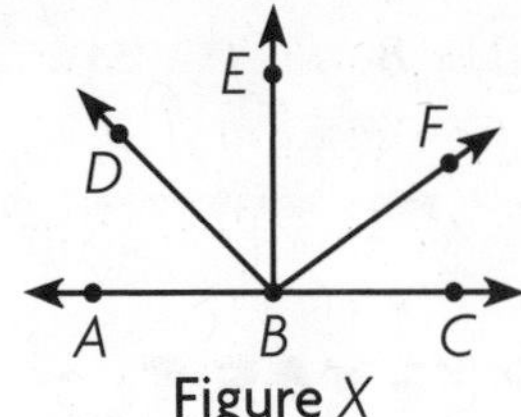

Figure *X*

10. H.O.T. **Multi-Step What's the Error?** Vanessa drew the angle at the right and named it $\angle TRS$. Explain why Vanessa's name for the angle is incorrect. Write a correct name for the angle.

    ____

    ____

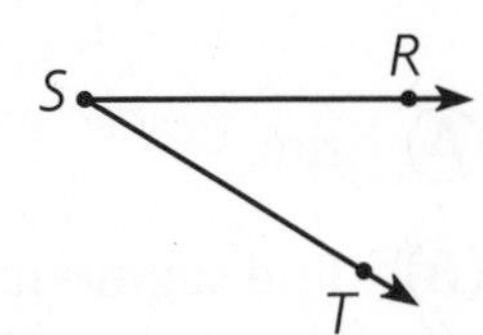

Mathematical Processes
Model • Reason • Communicate

Daily Assessment Task

Fill in the bubble completely to show your answer.

11. What type of angle is ∠*ABC*?

Ⓐ acute
Ⓑ right
Ⓒ obtuse
Ⓓ straight

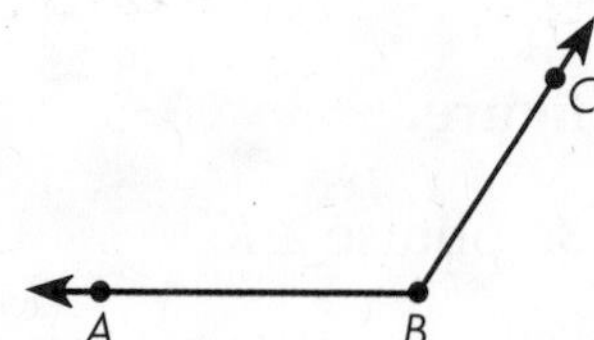

12. Which names a straight angle in the figure below?

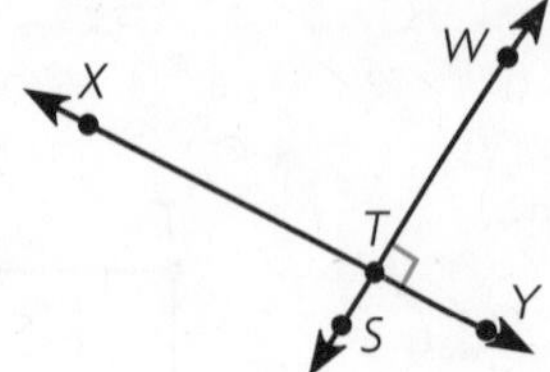

Ⓐ ∠*XTW*
Ⓑ ∠*STX*
Ⓒ ∠*STY*
Ⓓ ∠*WTS*

13. Multi-Step What is the total number of acute angles in the figures shown below?

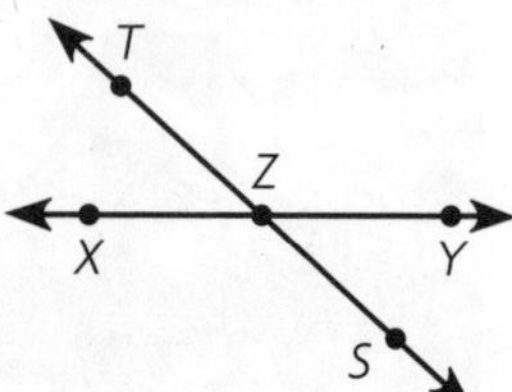

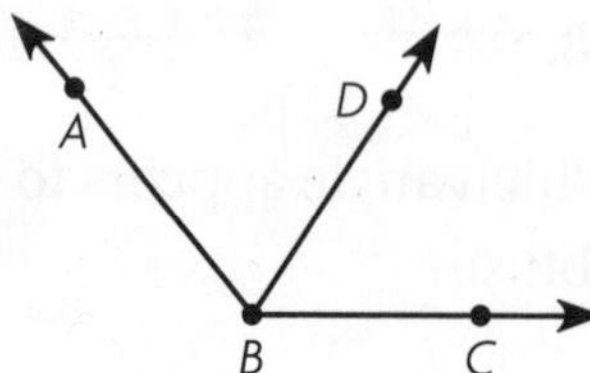

Ⓐ 2
Ⓑ 8
Ⓒ 4
Ⓓ 6

TEXAS Test Prep

14. Which of the following terms best describes the figure below?

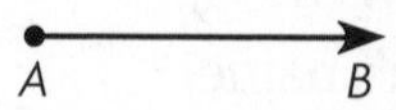

Ⓐ ray
Ⓑ line segment
Ⓒ line
Ⓓ angle

Name ______________________

13.1 Lines, Rays, and Angles

Draw and label an example of the figure.

1. $\overrightarrow{AB}$

2. acute $\angle J$

3. right $\angle ABC$

4. $\overleftrightarrow{JK}$

5. obtuse $\angle XYZ$

6. $\overline{PQ}$

Use figure *A* for 7 and 8.

7. Name an acute angle. ______________________

8. Name an obtuse angle. ______________________

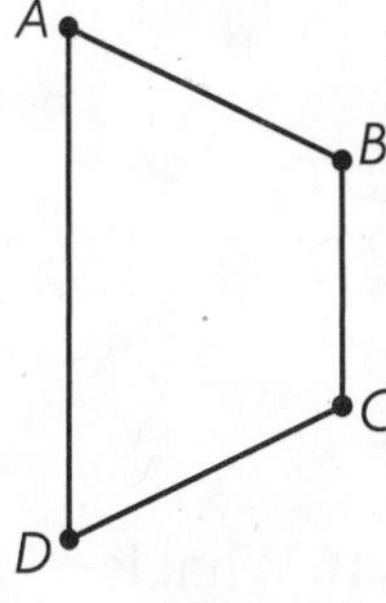

Figure *A*

Problem Solving Real World

Use the bridge drawing for 9 and 10.

9. Classify $\angle B$ ______________________

10. Jenny thinks that $\angle C$ is a right angle. **Explain** why Jenny's name for the angle is incorrect. Write a correct name for the angle.

____

____

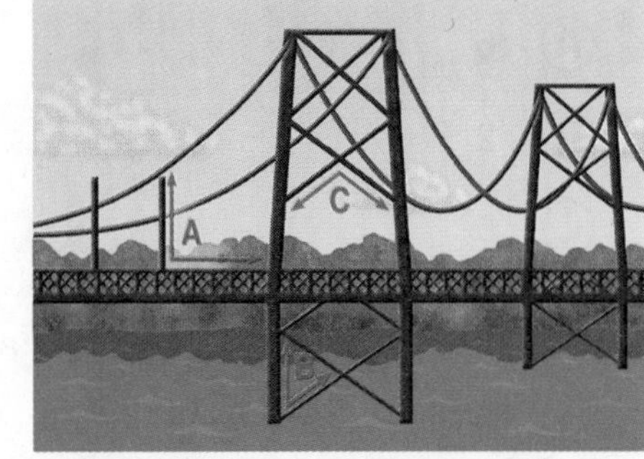

Lesson Check

Fill in the bubble completely to show your answer.

11. What type of angle is $\angle XYZ$?

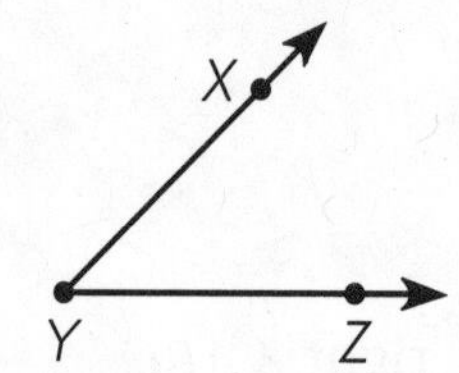

Ⓐ right

Ⓑ acute

Ⓒ straight

Ⓓ obtuse

12. Which names an obtuse angle in the figure below?

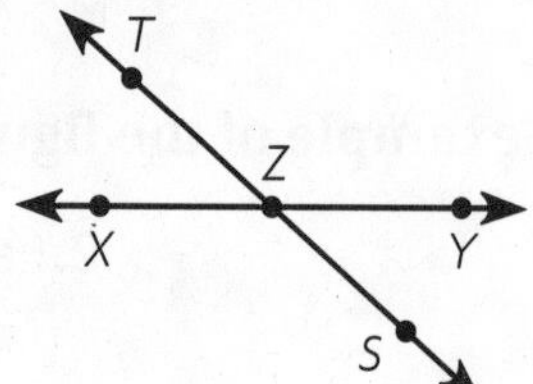

Ⓐ $\angle TZS$

Ⓑ $\angle SZY$

Ⓒ $\angle XZT$

Ⓓ $\angle TZY$

13. Which names an acute angle in the figure to the right?

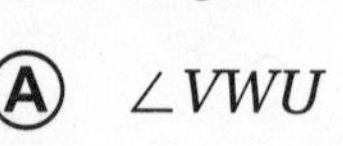

Ⓐ $\angle VWU$

Ⓑ $\angle VTU$

Ⓒ $\angle TUW$

Ⓓ $\angle WUT$

T U V W

Figure *M*

14. Which of the following terms best describes the figure below?

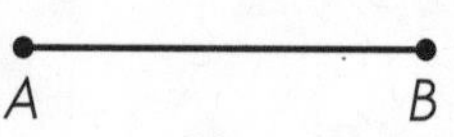

Ⓐ angle

Ⓑ line segment

Ⓒ ray

Ⓓ line

15. **Multi-Step** What is the total number of rays in the figures to the right?

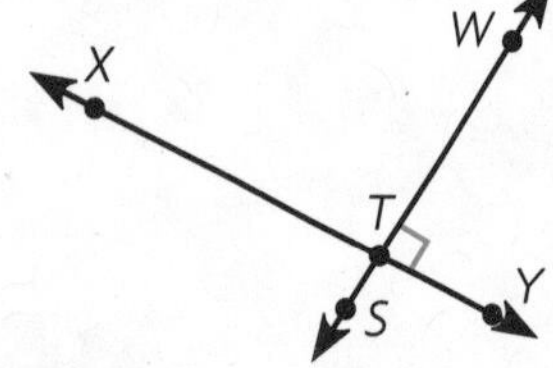

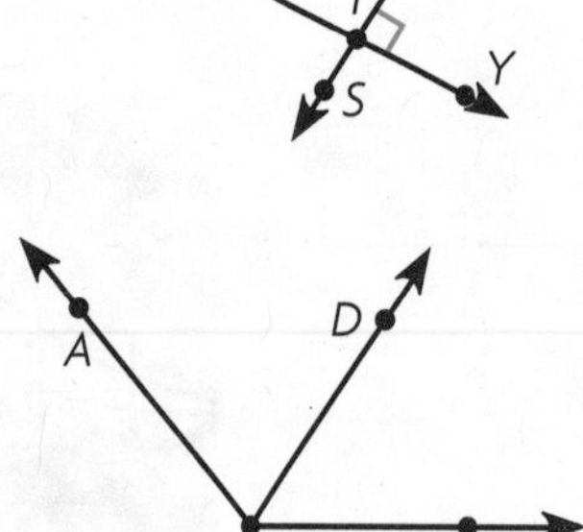

Ⓐ 6

Ⓑ 2

Ⓒ 5

Ⓓ 7

16.  **Multi-Step** How many right angles are in Figure *X*?

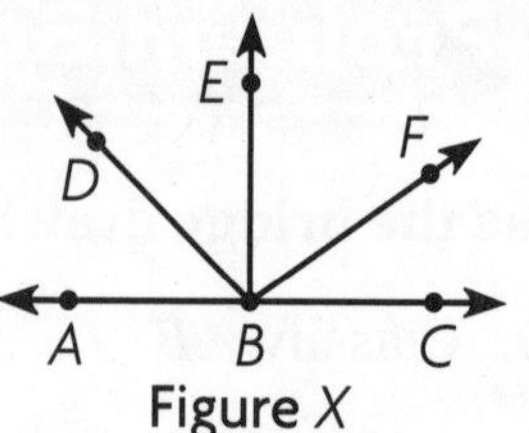

Figure *X*

Ⓐ 4

Ⓑ 2

Ⓒ 3

Ⓓ 1

Name ________________________________

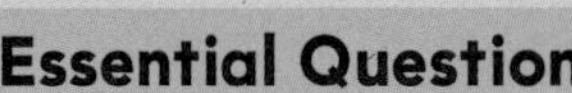

13.2 Classify Triangles

Essential Question How can you classify triangles by the size of their angles?

Unlock the Problem

A triangle is a polygon with three sides and three angles. You can name a triangle by the vertices of its angles.

Triangle	Possible Names	
(triangle with vertices A, B, C)	△ABC	△ACB
	△BCA	△BAC
	△CAB	△CBA

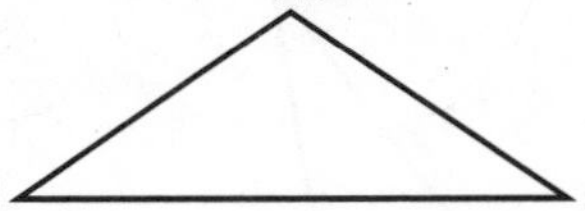

Read Math

When you see "△ABC," say "triangle ABC."

An angle of a triangle can be right, acute, or obtuse.

Activity 1 Identify right, acute, and obtuse angles in triangles.

Materials ■ color pencils

Use the Triangle Color Guide to color the triangles below.

Triangle Color Guide	
RED	one right angle
BLUE	one obtuse angle
ORANGE	three acute angles

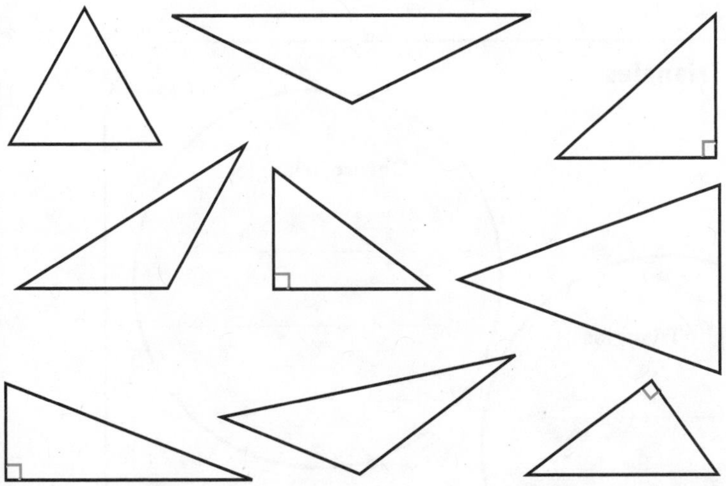

Math Talk Mathematical Processes

Can a triangle have more than one obtuse angle? Explain.

Try This!

a. Name the triangle with one right angle. ______

b. Name the triangle with one obtuse angle. ______

c. Name the triangle with three acute angles. ______

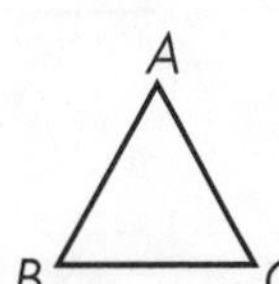

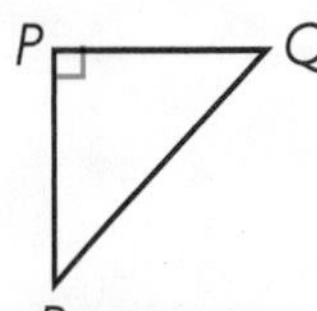

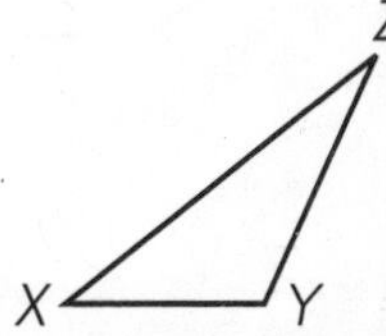

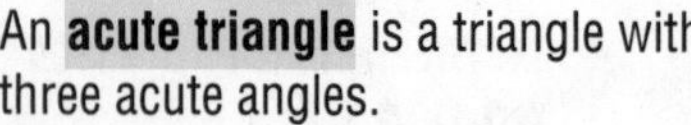

An **acute triangle** is a triangle with three acute angles.	An **obtuse triangle** is a triangle with one obtuse angle.	A **right triangle** is a triangle with one right angle.
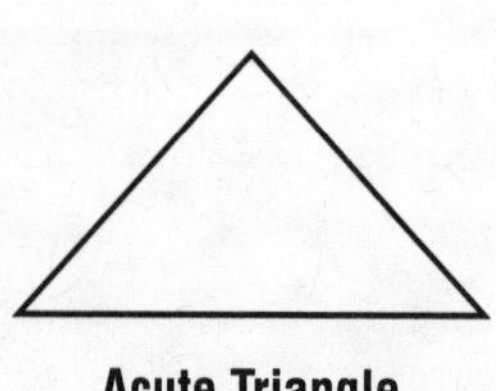	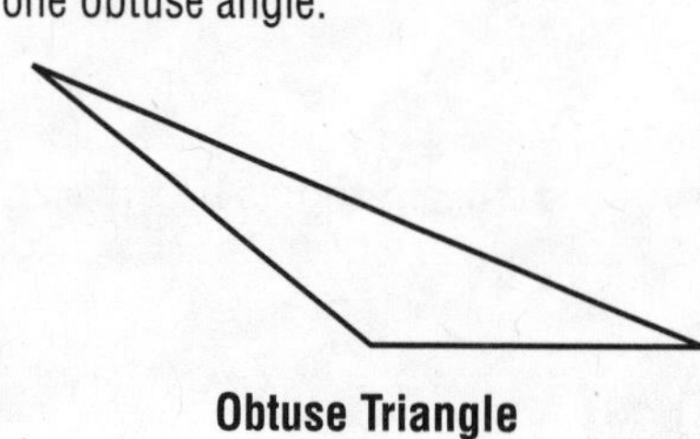	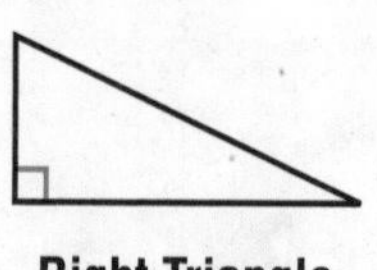
Acute Triangle	**Obtuse Triangle**	**Right Triangle**

Activity 2 Use a Venn diagram to classify triangles.

Write the names of the triangles in the Venn diagram.

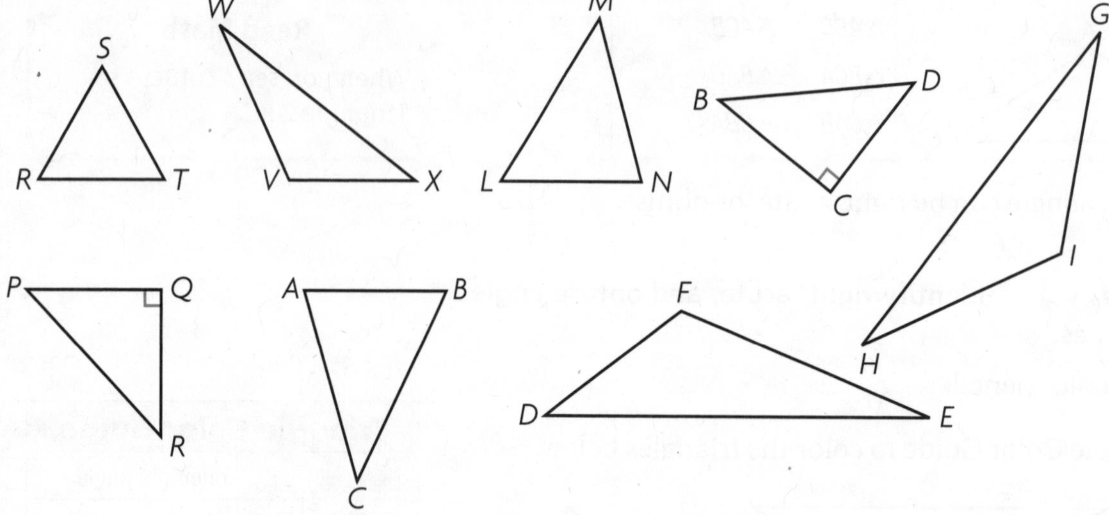

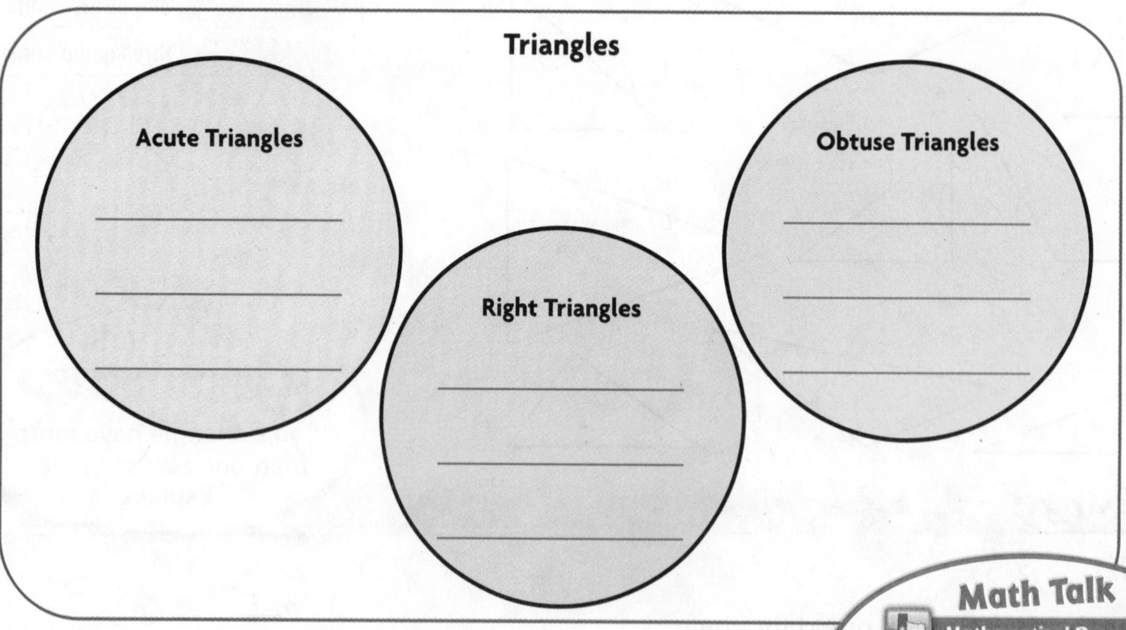

Math Talk
Mathematical Processes
Explain why the three circles in this Venn diagram do not overlap.

Name ________________________________

Share and Show

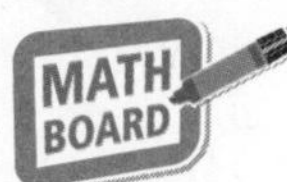

1. Name the triangle. Tell whether each angle is *acute, right,* or *obtuse.*

   A name for the triangle is ____________.

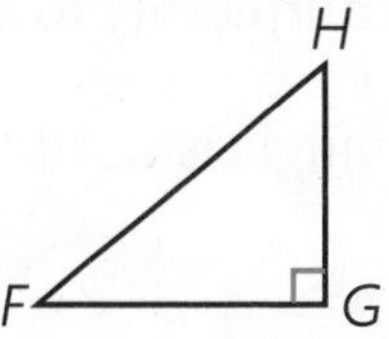

$\angle F$ is ____________. | $\angle G$ is ____________. | $\angle H$ is ____________.

Classify each triangle. Write *acute, right,* or *obtuse.*

2.

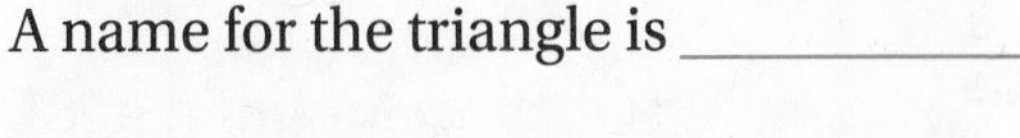

____

3.

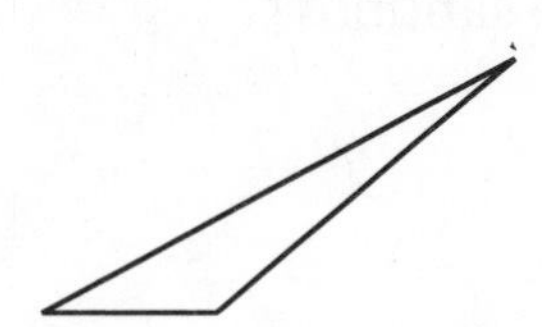

____

4.

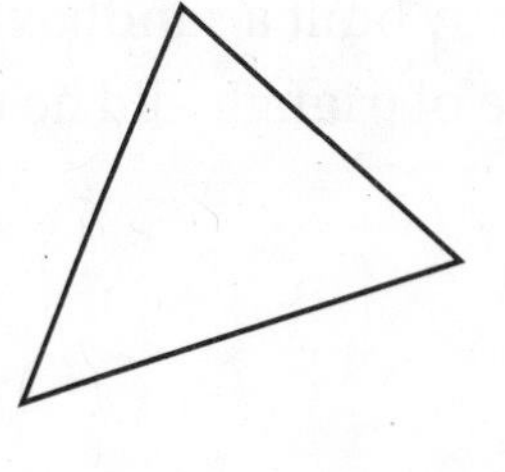

____

Problem Solving

Use the Venn diagram for 5–6.

5. **H.O.T.** **Multi-Step** Which triangles do NOT have an obtuse angle? **Explain.**

____

____

____

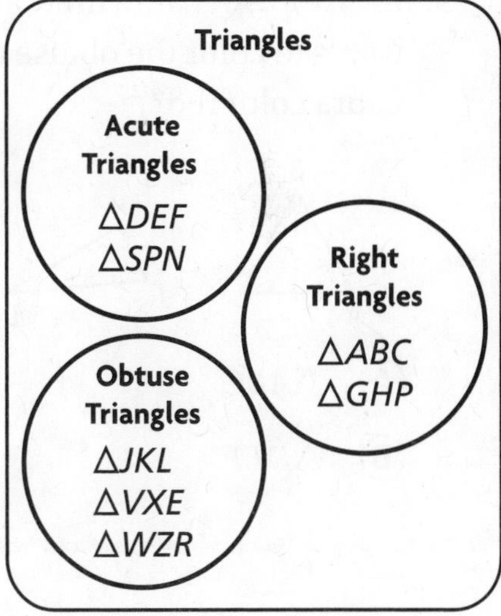

6. **H.O.T.** **Communicate** How many triangles have *at least* two acute angles? **Explain.**

____

____

____

____

Daily Assessment Task

Fill in the bubble completely to show your answer.

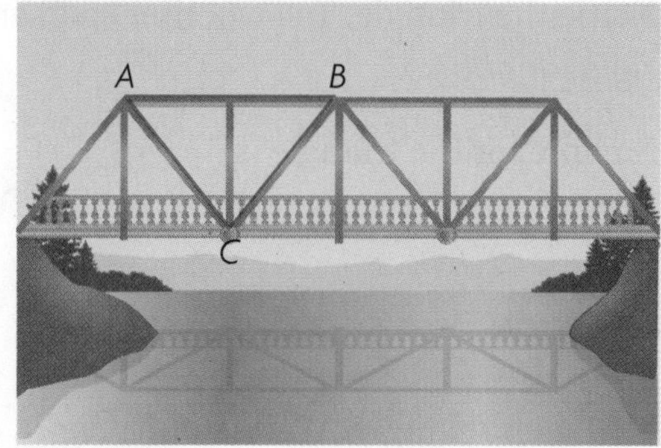

7. What type of triangle is $\triangle ABC$?

Ⓐ right

Ⓑ acute

Ⓒ obtuse

Ⓓ straight

8. Bobby built a sandbox in the shape of the triangle below. Which type of triangle did he use to build the sandbox?

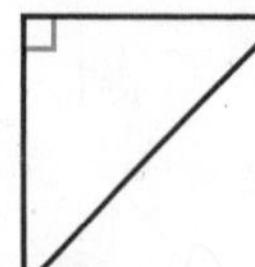

Ⓐ obtuse

Ⓑ right

Ⓒ equilateral

Ⓓ acute

9. **Multi-Step** Laura drew and labeled the triangles below. She wants to color the obtuse triangle red. Which triangle should Laura color red?

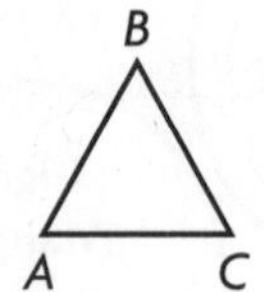

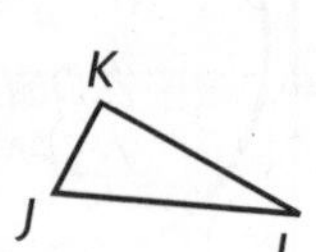

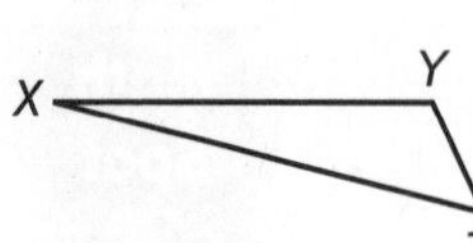

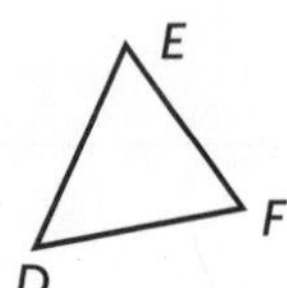

Ⓐ $\triangle ABC$

Ⓑ $\triangle DEF$

Ⓒ $\triangle XYZ$

Ⓓ $\triangle JKL$

TEXAS Test Prep

10. How many acute angles are in an obtuse triangle?

Ⓐ 0

Ⓑ 1

Ⓒ 2

Ⓓ 3

Homework and Practice

TEKS Geometry and Measurement—4.6.C, 4.6.D
MATHEMATICAL PROCESSES 4.1.D, 4.1.E

Name ______________________

13.2 Classify Triangles

Classify each triangle. Write *acute, right,* or *obtuse.*

1.

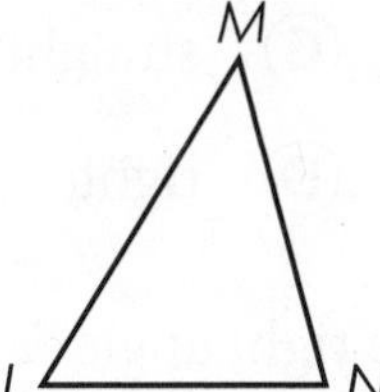

____

2.

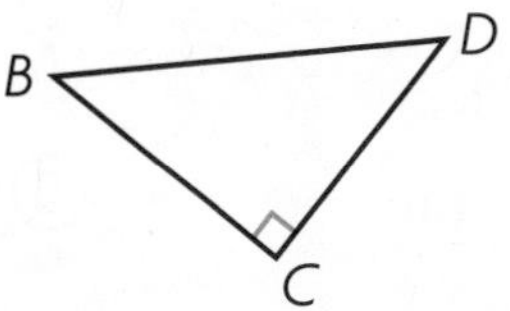

____

3.

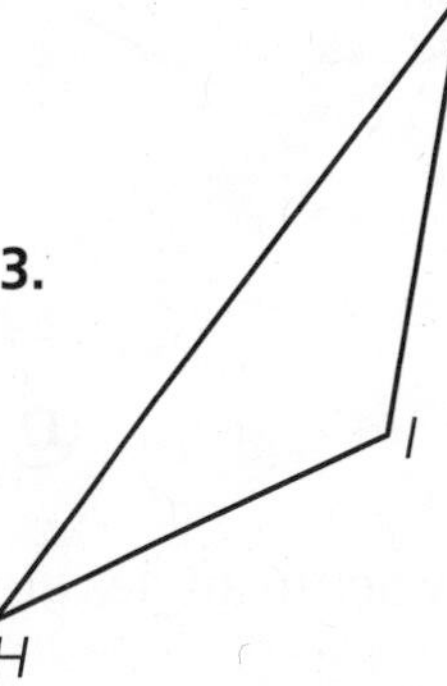

____

4.

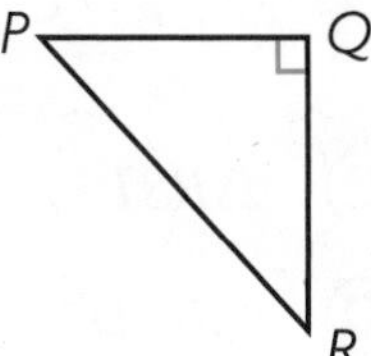

____

5.

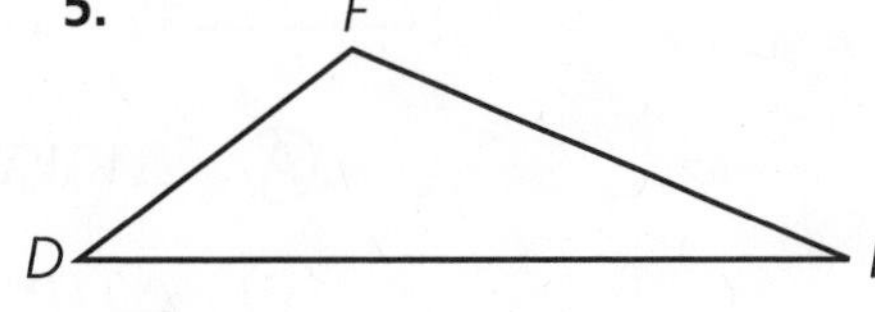

____

6.

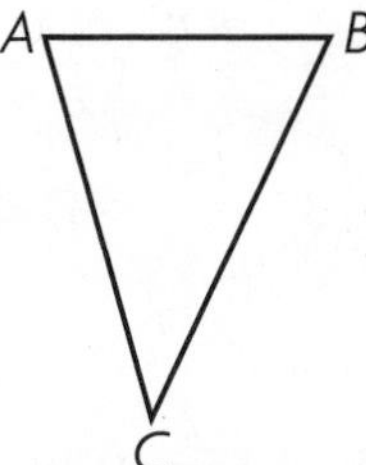

____

7. Name the triangle. Tell whether each angle is *acute, right* or *obtuse.*

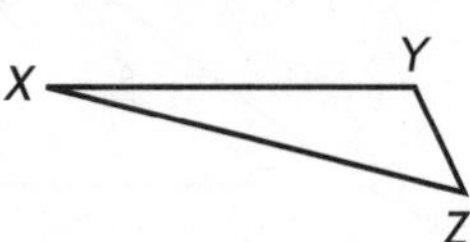

A name for the triangle is ______________________.

$\angle X$ is __________. $\angle Y$ is __________. $\angle Z$ is __________.

Problem Solving

8. Mark folded a flag into a triangle and built a frame for it in the shape of the triangle below. Which type of triangle did he use to build the frame?

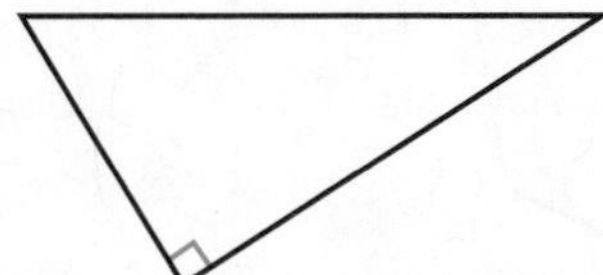

____

9. Cassie added a flower garden to the corner of her yard in the shape of the triangle below. Which type of triangle did she use to add to the garden?

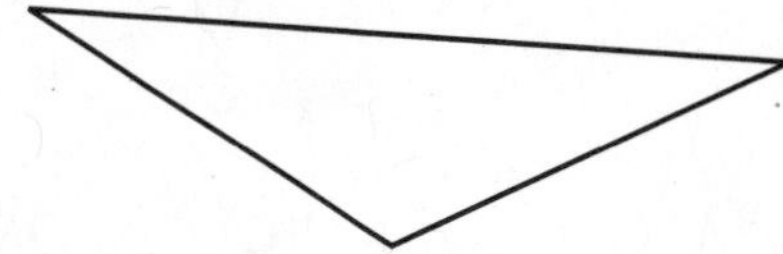

____

Lesson Check

Fill in the bubble completely to show your answer.

10. What type of triangle is $\triangle DEF$?

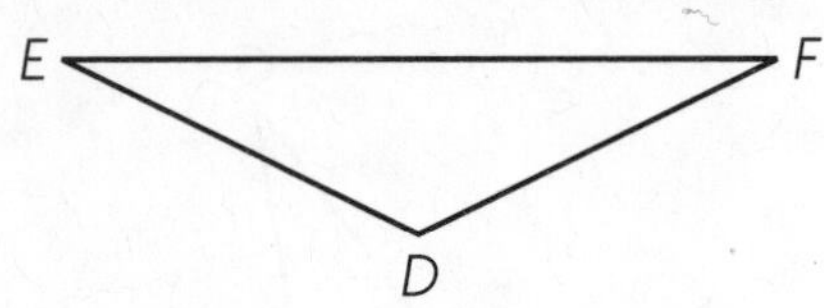

Ⓐ acute
Ⓑ right
Ⓒ obtuse
Ⓓ equilateral

11. What type of triangle is $\triangle JKL$?

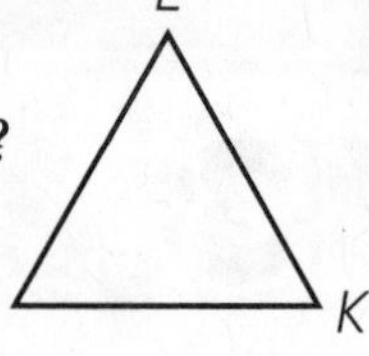

Ⓐ acute
Ⓑ obtuse
Ⓒ straight
Ⓓ right

12. How many acute angles are in a right triangle?

Ⓐ 0
Ⓑ 1
Ⓒ 2
Ⓓ 3

13. Which triangle has one right angle?

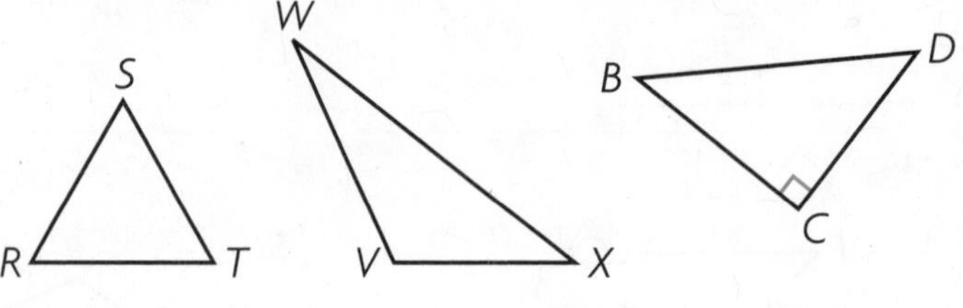

Ⓐ $\triangle VWX$
Ⓑ $\triangle TUV$
Ⓒ $\triangle RST$
Ⓓ $\triangle BCD$

14. Multi-Step Which triangle has both acute and obtuse angles?

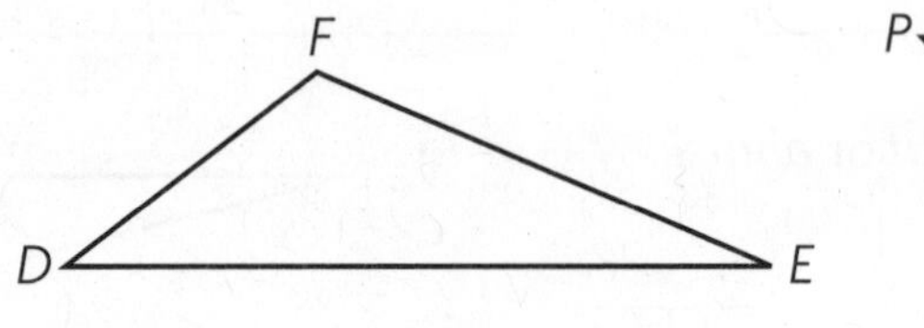

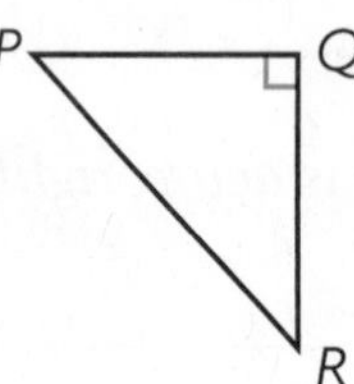

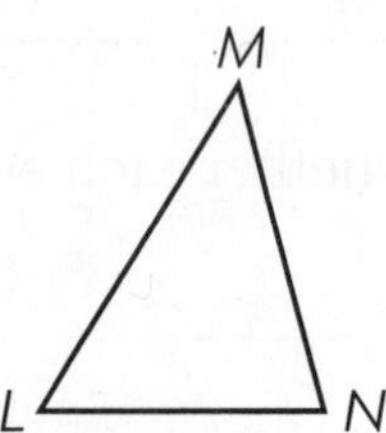

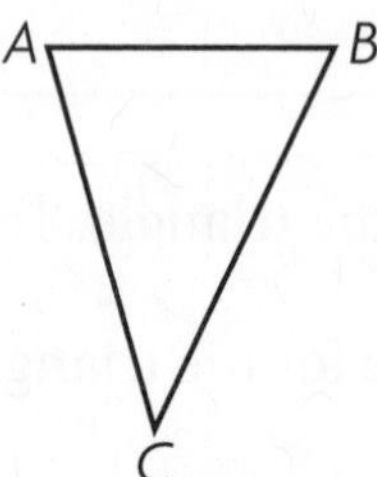

Ⓐ $\triangle DEF$
Ⓑ $\triangle ABC$
Ⓒ $\triangle PQR$
Ⓓ $\triangle LMN$

15. Multi-Step Which triangle has one right angle and no obtuse angles?

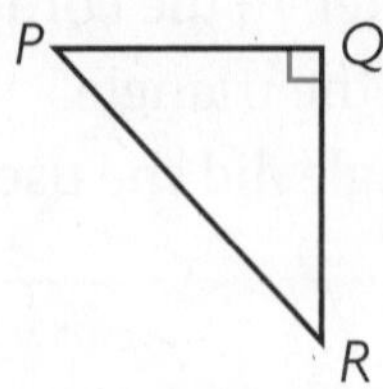

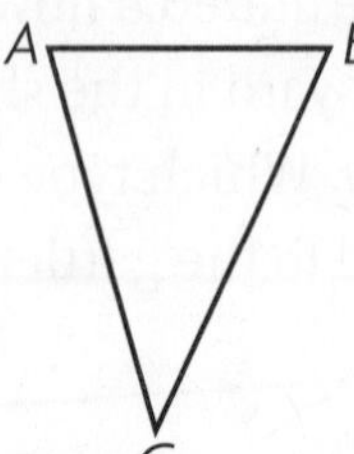

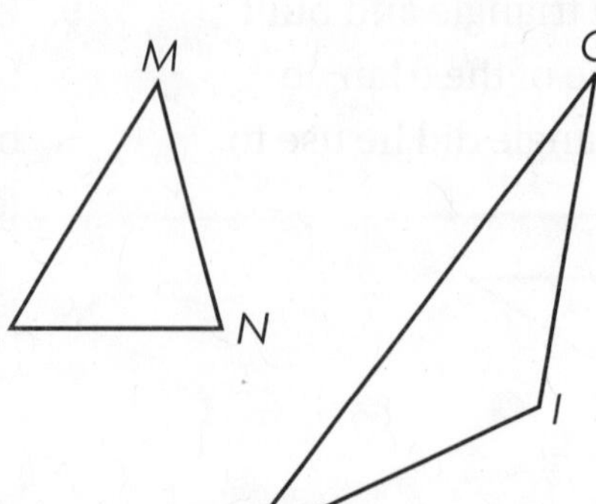

Ⓐ $\triangle ABC$
Ⓑ $\triangle GHI$
Ⓒ $\triangle PQR$
Ⓓ $\triangle LMN$

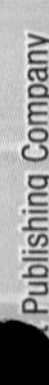

Name ______________________________

13.3 Parallel Lines and Perpendicular Lines

Essential Question

How can you identify and draw parallel lines and perpendicular lines?

Unlock the Problem

Real World

You can find models of lines in the world around you. For example, two streets that cross each other model intersecting lines. Metal rails on a train track that never cross model parallel lines.

Term and Definition	Draw It	Read It	Write It
Intersecting lines are lines in a plane that cross at exactly one point. Intersecting lines form four angles.	H, K, X, J, I	Line *HI* intersects line *JK* at point *X*.	$\overleftrightarrow{HI}$ and $\overleftrightarrow{JK}$ intersect at point *X*
Parallel lines are lines in a plane that are always the same distance apart. Parallel lines never intersect.	D, E, F, G	Line *DE* is parallel to line *FG*.	$\overleftrightarrow{DE} \parallel \overleftrightarrow{FG}$ The symbol $\parallel$ means "is parallel to."
Perpendicular lines are lines in a plane that intersect to form four right angles.	N, L, M, O	Line *LM* is perpendicular to line *NO*.	$\overleftrightarrow{LM} \perp \overleftrightarrow{NO}$ The symbol $\perp$ means "is perpendicular to."

Math Talk Mathematical Processes

Can two rays be parallel? Explain.

Try This! Tell how the streets appear to be related. Write *perpendicular, parallel,* or *intersecting.*

- W 36th St and Broadway ______________________
- W 35th St and 7th Ave ______________________
- W 37th St and W 36th St ______________________

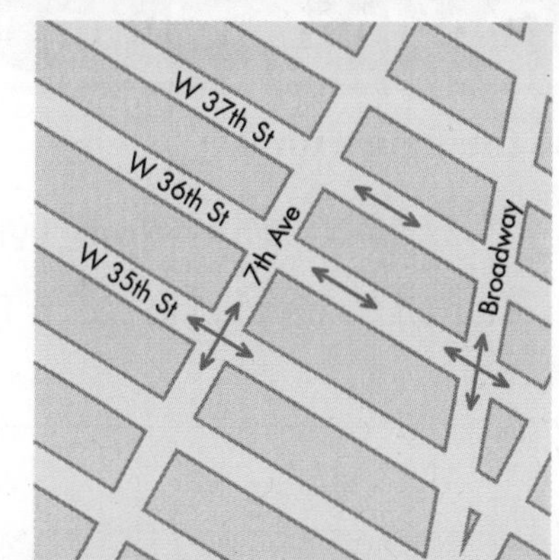

Activity Draw and label $\overrightarrow{YX} \perp \overrightarrow{YZ}$ intersecting at point Y.

Materials ■ straightedge

STEP 1: Draw and label $\overrightarrow{YX}$.

STEP 2: Then draw and label $\overrightarrow{YZ}$.

• How can you check if two rays are perpendicular?

STEP 3: Make sure $\overrightarrow{YX}$ and $\overrightarrow{YZ}$ intersect at point Y.

STEP 4: Make sure the rays are perpendicular.

Share and Show

Math Talk

Explain how the symbols ⊥ and ∥ help you remember which relationships they describe.

1. Draw and label $\overline{QR} \parallel \overline{ST}$.

   Think: Parallel lines never intersect. Parallel line segments are parts of parallel lines.

Use the figure for 2 and 3.

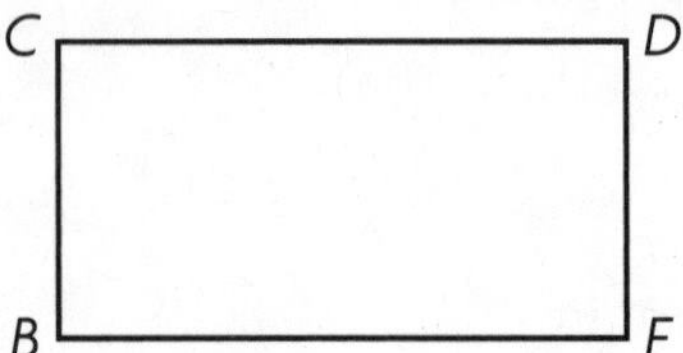

2. Name two sides that appear to be parallel.

3. Name two sides that appear to be perpendicular.

Problem Solving Real World

Use the figure for 4.

4. **H.O.T.** **Multi-Step What's the Error?** Dan says that $\overleftrightarrow{HL}$ is parallel to $\overleftrightarrow{IM}$. Is Dan correct? **Explain.**

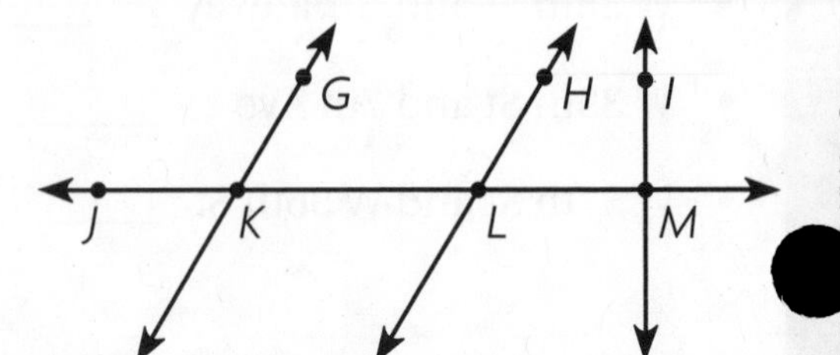

Name ________________________

Problem Solving Real World

Use the house plan at the right for 5–7.

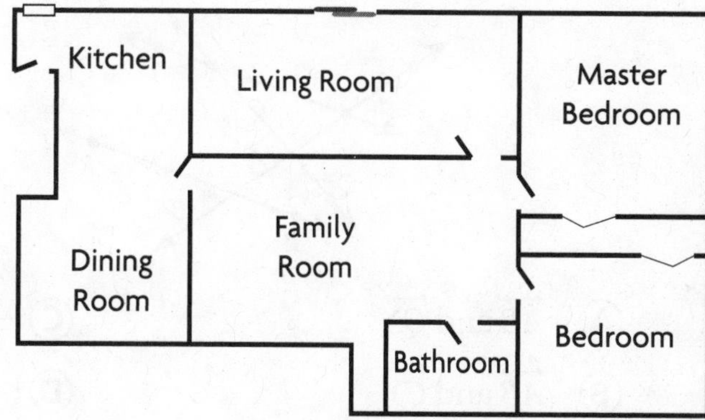

5. What geometric term describes a corner of the living room?

6. **Use Diagrams** Name three parts of the plan that show line segments.

7. H.O.T. Name a pair of line segments that appear to be parallel.

Write Math ▶ Show Your Work

Use the map at the right for 8–10.

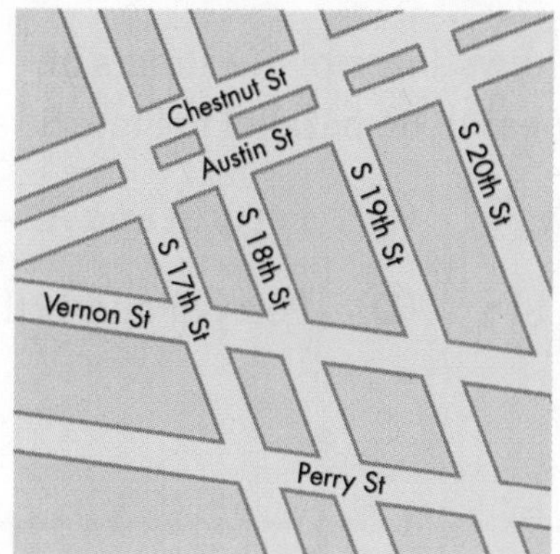

8. Name a street that appears to be parallel to S 17th Street.

9. Name a street that appears to be parallel to Vernon Street.

10. Name a street that appears to be perpendicular to S 19th Street.

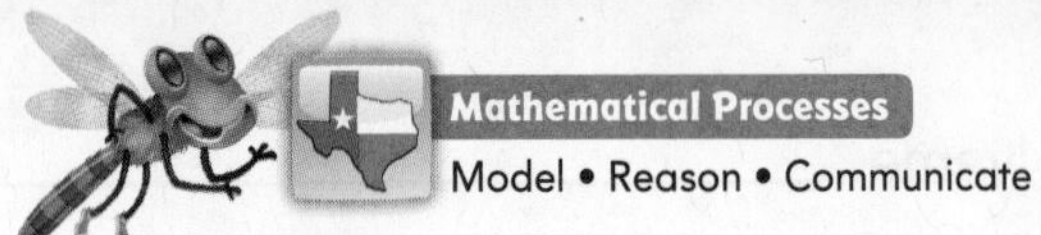

Daily Assessment Task

Fill in the bubble completely to show your answer.

11. Which pair of lines appear to be parallel?

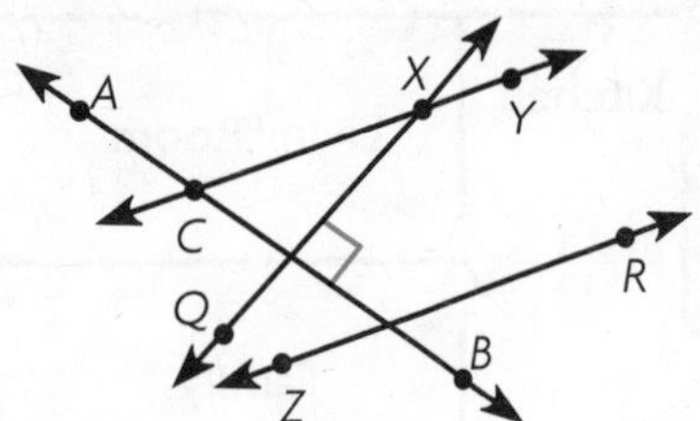

Ⓐ $\overleftrightarrow{AB}$ and $\overleftrightarrow{QX}$

Ⓑ $\overleftrightarrow{AB}$ and $\overleftrightarrow{CY}$

Ⓒ $\overleftrightarrow{CY}$ and $\overleftrightarrow{ZR}$

Ⓓ $\overleftrightarrow{ZR}$ and $\overleftrightarrow{QX}$

12. Which figure appears to show $\overline{QR} \perp \overline{XY}$?

Ⓐ 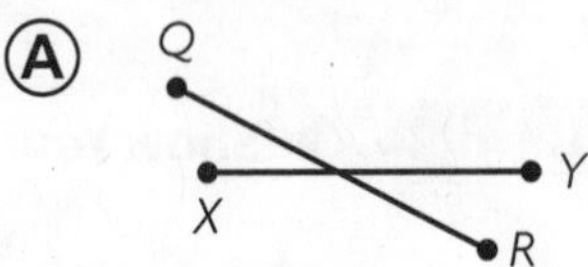

 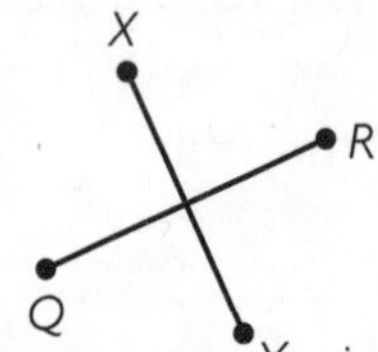

Ⓑ 

 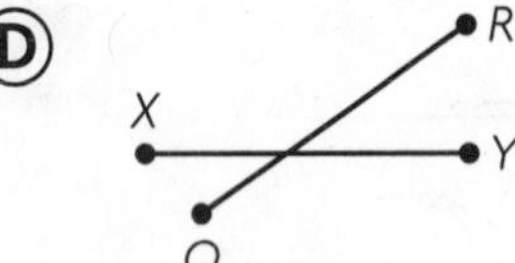

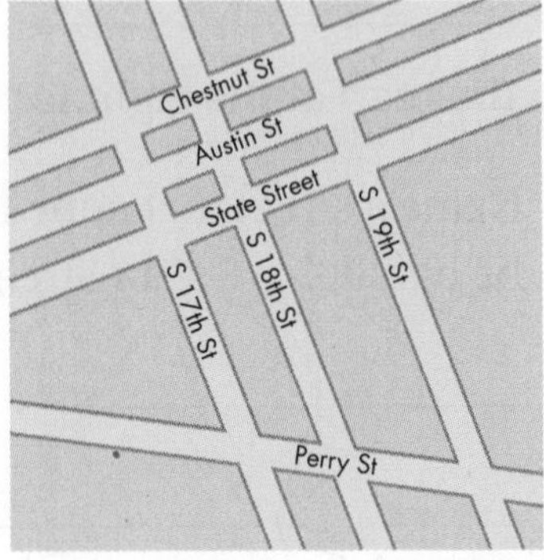

13. Multi-Step The map below shows some of the streets in Matt's town. Which streets appear to be parallel to State Street?

Ⓐ Chestnut St and Austin St

Ⓑ 17th St, 18th St, and 19th St

Ⓒ Perry St and Austin St

Ⓓ Perry St and 17th St

TEXAS Test Prep

14. Which best describes perpendicular lines?

Ⓐ They never meet.

Ⓑ They form four right angles.

Ⓒ They form one acute angle.

Ⓓ They form one obtuse angle.

Homework and Practice

TEKS Geometry and Measurement—4.6.A
MATHEMATICAL PROCESSES 4.1.D, 4.1.E

Name ________________

13.3 Parallel Lines and Perpendicular Lines

Use the figure for 1–3.

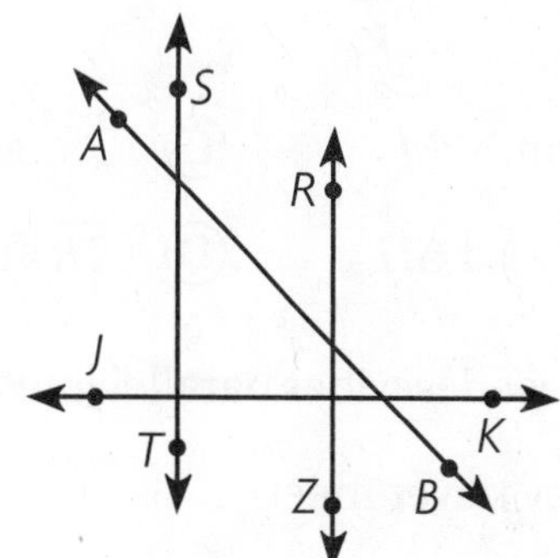

1. Name two lines that appear to be parallel.

____

2. Name two lines that appear to be perpendicular.

____

3. Name two lines that intersect but do not appear to be perpendicular.

____

____

Problem Solving Real World

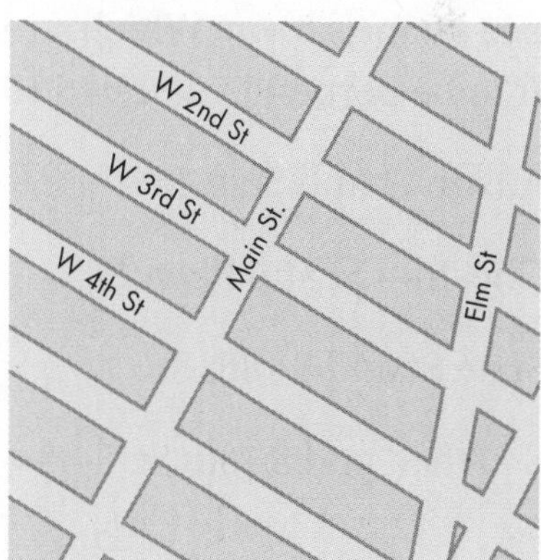

4. Connie says that Main St. appears to be parallel to Elm St. Is Connie correct? **Explain.**

____

____

____

5. Daniel says that Main St. and 3rd Street appear to be perpendicular. Is Daniel correct? **Explain.**

____

____

____

Lesson Check

TEXAS Test Prep

Fill in the bubble completely to show your answer.

6. Which pair of lines appear to be perpendicular?

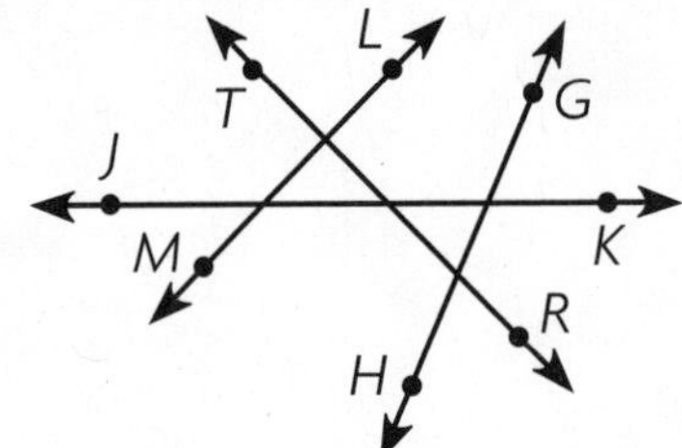

Ⓐ $\overleftrightarrow{JK}$ and $\overleftrightarrow{LM}$
Ⓑ $\overleftrightarrow{LM}$ and $\overleftrightarrow{GH}$
Ⓒ $\overleftrightarrow{LM}$ and $\overleftrightarrow{TR}$
Ⓓ $\overleftrightarrow{TR}$ and $\overleftrightarrow{GH}$

7. Which figure appears to show parallel lines?

Ⓐ 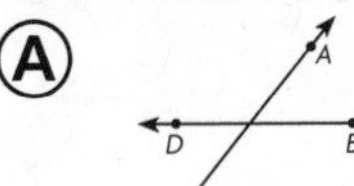

Ⓑ 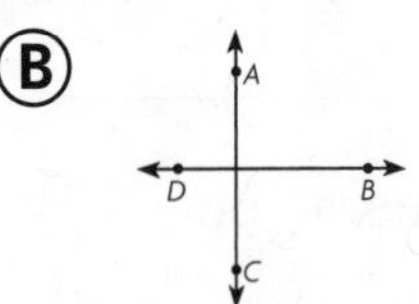

Ⓒ 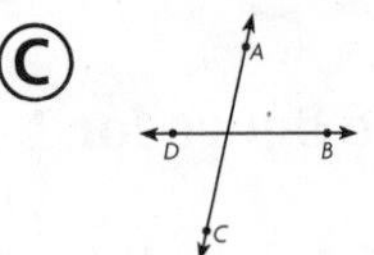

Ⓓ 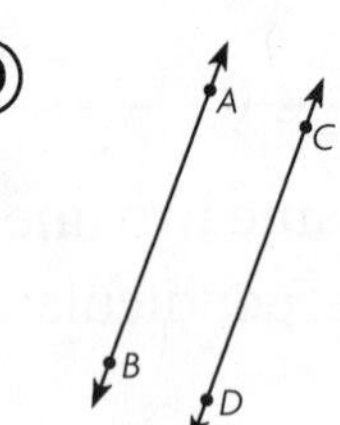

8. Which best describes parallel lines?

Ⓐ They never meet.
Ⓑ They intersect at one point.
Ⓒ They form one acute angle.
Ⓓ They form one obtuse angle.

9. Which does NOT describe intersecting lines?

Ⓐ They cross at exactly one point.
Ⓑ They form four angles.
Ⓒ They are the same distance apart.
Ⓓ They may form a right angle.

10. **Multi-Step** The map shows some of the streets in Diana's town. Which streets appear to be perpendicular to S 19th St?

Ⓐ Austin St and State St
Ⓑ Chestnut St and Perry St
Ⓒ State St and S 18th St
Ⓓ S 17th St and S 18th St

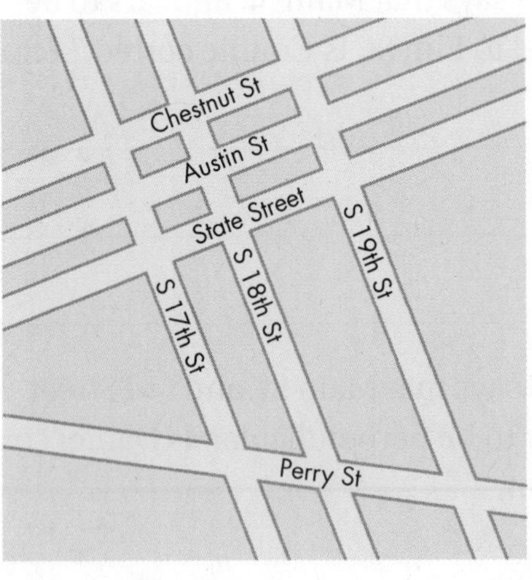

11. **Multi-Step** Which streets appear to be parallel to S 17th St?

Ⓐ State St and Chestnut St
Ⓑ S 18th St and S 19 St
Ⓒ Perry St and Austin St
Ⓓ S 19 St and Perry St

Name ___________________________

13.4 Classify Quadrilaterals

TEKS Geometry and Measurement—4.6.D
MATHEMATICAL PROCESSES 4.1.D, 4.1.E

Essential Question How can you sort and classify quadrilaterals?

Unlock the Problem

A quadrilateral is a polygon with four sides and four angles. You can name a quadrilateral by the vertices of its angles.

Quadrilateral *ABCD* is a possible name for the figure shown at the right. Quadrilateral *ACBD* is not a possible name, since points *A* and *C* are not endpoints of the same side.

Assume that line segments that appear to be parallel are parallel.

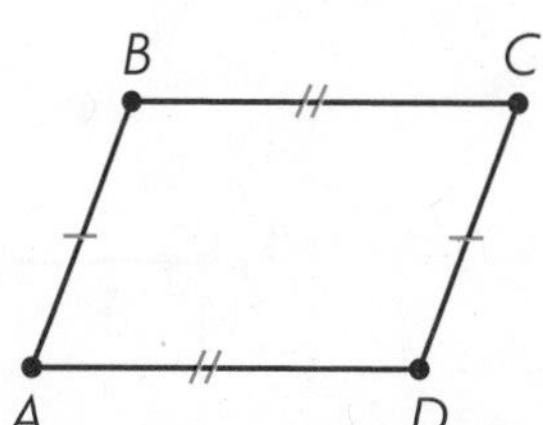

The tick marks on the line segments show that they have the same length. Sides *AD* and *BC* have the same length. Sides *AB* and *CD* have the same length.

Common Quadrilaterals

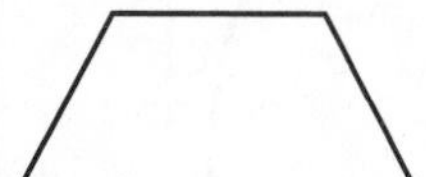

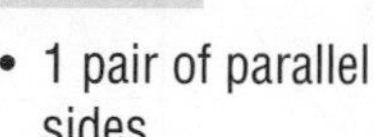

Trapezoid
- 1 pair of parallel sides

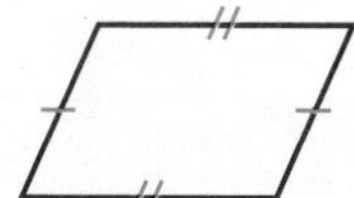

Parallelogram
- 2 pairs of parallel sides
- 2 pairs of sides of equal length

Rhombus
- 2 pairs of parallel sides
- 4 sides of equal length

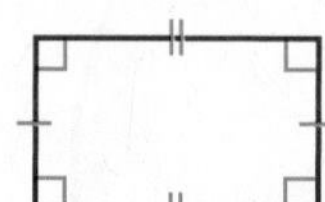

Rectangle
- 2 pairs of parallel sides
- 2 pairs of sides of equal length
- 4 right angles

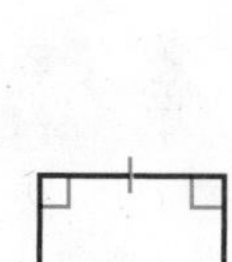

Square
- 2 pairs of parallel sides
- 4 sides of equal length
- 4 right angles

Activity 1 Identify right angles in quadrilaterals.

Materials ■ color pencils

Use the Quadrilateral Color Guide to color the quadrilaterals.

Quadrilateral Color Guide	
RED	exactly 4 right angles
BLUE	exactly 2 right angles
ORANGE	exactly 1 right angle

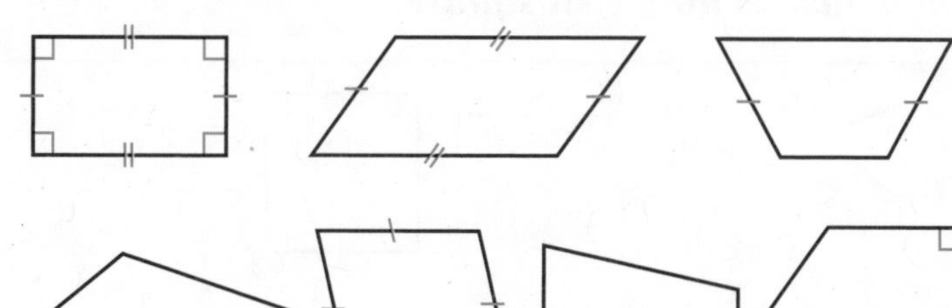

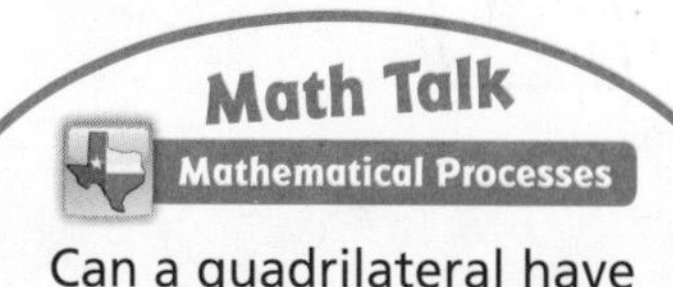

Math Talk Mathematical Processes

Can a quadrilateral have exactly 3 right angles? Explain.

Activity 2 Use a Venn diagram to sort quadrilaterals.

Write the names of the quadrilaterals in the Venn diagram.

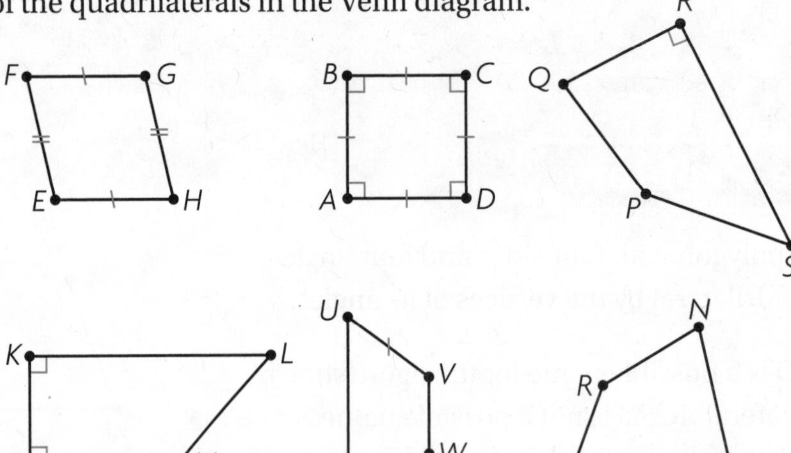

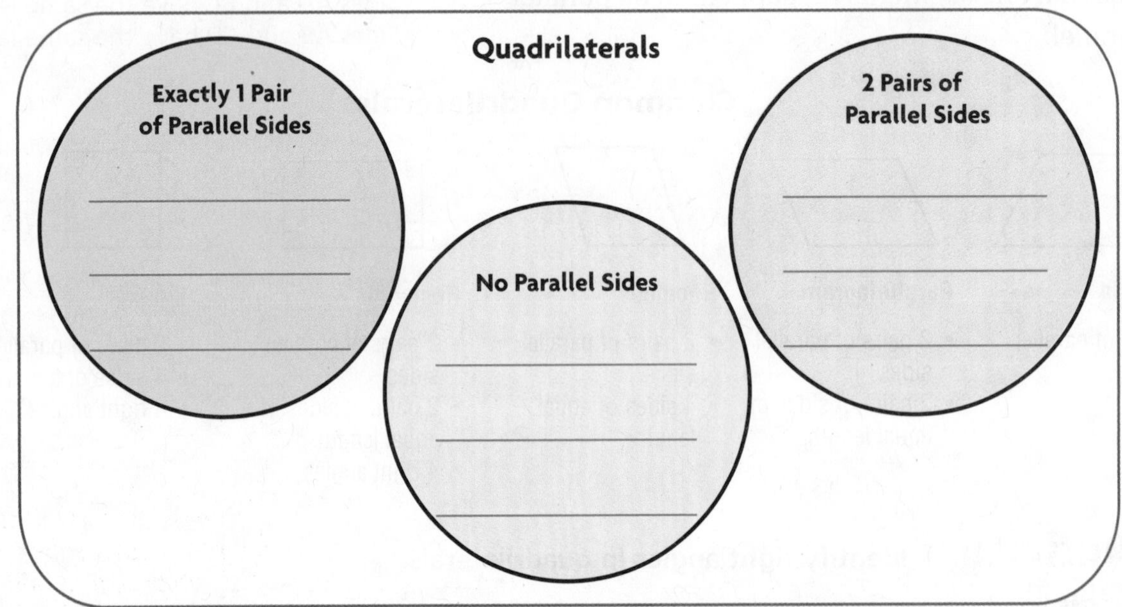

Try This! **Classify each figure as many ways as possible. Write *quadrilateral, trapezoid, parallelogram, rhombus, rectangle,* or *square.***

a. ____________________

b. ____________________

c. ____________________

Name ______________________________

Share and Show

1. Tell whether the quadrilateral is also a trapezoid, parallelogram, rhombus, rectangle, or square.

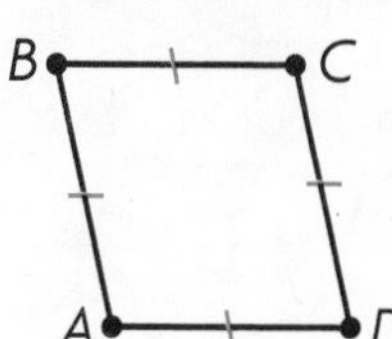

Think: ______ pairs of parallel sides

______ sides of equal length

______ right angles

Quadrilateral *ABCD* is also a ____________________.

Classify each figure as many ways as possible. Write *quadrilateral, trapezoid, parallelogram, rhombus, rectangle,* or *square.*

2. 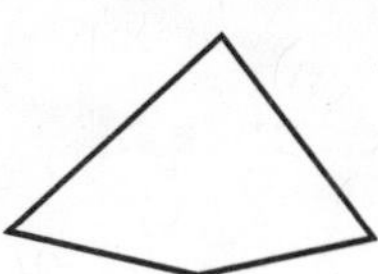

____

____

____

3. 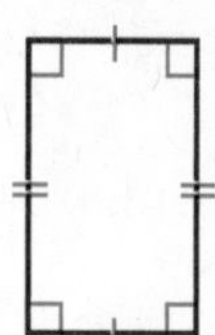

____

____

____

4. 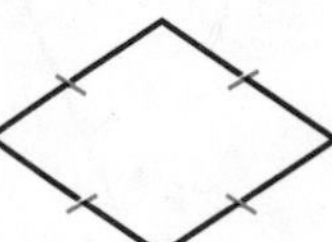

____

____

____

Math Talk
Mathematical Processes

How would you classify a figure with 4 sides, none of which are parallel? Explain.

Problem Solving

5. **H.O.T.** Multi-Step **Explain** how a rhombus and square are alike, and how they are different.

____

____

____

____

6. **H.O.T.** Communicate **Describe** the quadrilaterals you see in the diagram.

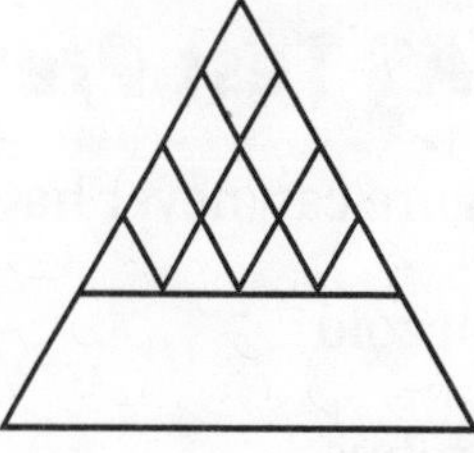

____

____

____

Daily Assessment Task

Fill in the bubble completely to show your answer.

7. What is the name of the figure shown below?

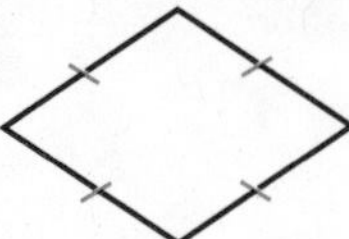

Ⓐ rectangle
Ⓑ trapezoid
Ⓒ rhombus
Ⓓ square

8. Jason wants to classify the figure below in as many ways as possible.

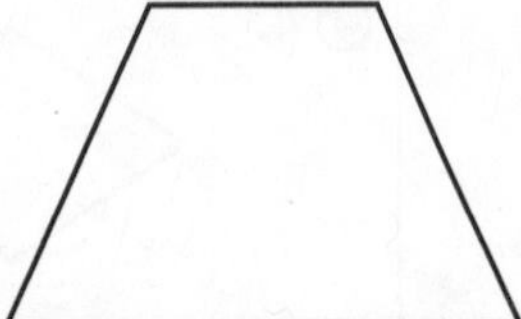

Which shows how Jason classifies the figure?

Ⓐ square, trapezoid
Ⓑ quadrilateral, rectangle
Ⓒ rhombus, square, trapezoid
Ⓓ quadrilateral, trapezoid

9. **Multi-Step** Jane draws two quadrilaterals on construction paper, and then cuts them out. One quadrilateral has one more pair of parallel sides than the other quadrilateral. Which two quadrilaterals could Jane have drawn?

Ⓐ rhombus and square
Ⓑ rectangle and trapezoid
Ⓒ rhombus and rectangle
Ⓓ rectangle and square

TEXAS Test Prep

10. Which figure can never have 2 pairs of parallel sides?

Ⓐ trapezoid
Ⓑ rhombus
Ⓒ rectangle
Ⓓ quadrilateral

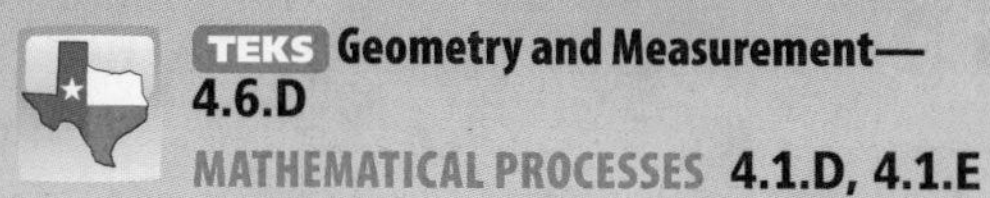

Name ______________________

13.4 Classify Quadrilaterals

Classify each figure as many ways as possible. Write *quadrilateral, trapezoid, parallelogram, rhombus, rectangle,* or *square.*

1. 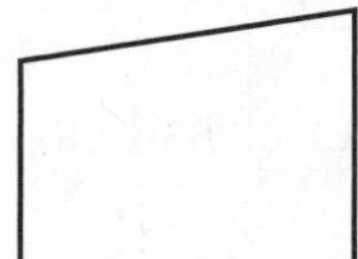

____

____

2. 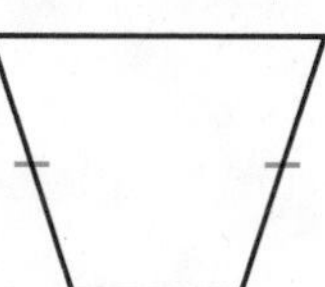

____

____

3. 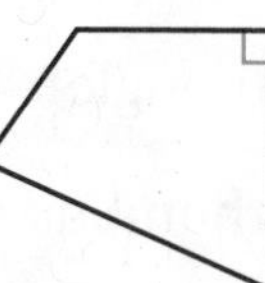

____

____

4. 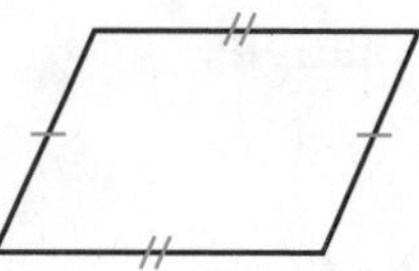

____

____

____

____

5. 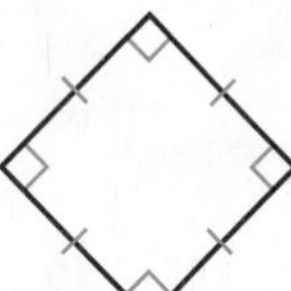

____

____

____

____

6. 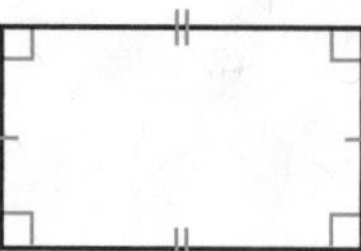

____

____

____

____

Problem Solving

7. **Explain** how a trapezoid and a parallelogram are alike, and how they are different.

____

____

____

____

____

8. Jake thinks that a rhombus is not always a parallelogram. Is Jake correct? **Explain.**

____

____

____

____

____

Lesson Check

TEXAS Test Prep

Fill in the bubble completely to show your answer.

9. What is the name of the figure shown below?

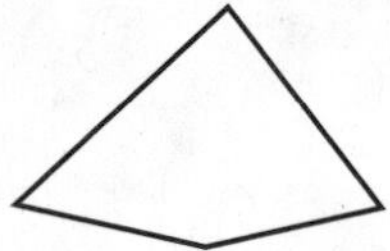

Ⓐ triangle
Ⓑ rhombus
Ⓒ quadrilateral
Ⓓ parallelogram

10. Peter wants to classify the figure below as many ways as possible.

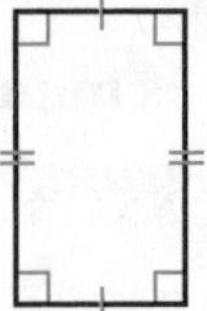

Which shows how Peter classifies the figure?

Ⓐ rhombus, rectangle, quadrilateral
Ⓑ square, parallelogram, rectangle
Ⓒ trapezoid, rectangle, quadrilateral
Ⓓ quadrilateral, rectangle, parallelogram

11. What is the name of a quadrilateral that always has 4 right angles?

Ⓐ trapezoid
Ⓑ rectangle
Ⓒ rhombus
Ⓓ parallelogram

12. What is the name of the figure shown below?

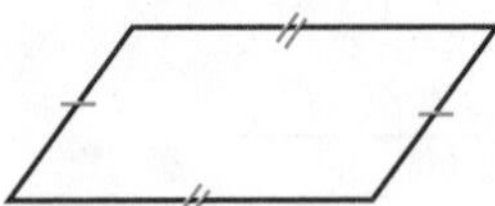

Ⓐ parallelogram
Ⓑ rhombus
Ⓒ trapezoid
Ⓓ square

13. **Multi-Step** Chris has 2 short craft sticks of equal length and 2 longer craft sticks of equal length. What are two quadrilaterals he can make with the sticks?

Ⓐ trapezoid and square
Ⓑ rhombus and square
Ⓒ parallelogram and rectangle
Ⓓ trapezoid and rectangle

14. **Multi-Step** Miranda has four craft sticks of equal length. What are two quadrilaterals she can make with the sticks?

Ⓐ rhombus and square
Ⓑ parallelogram and trapezoid
Ⓒ trapezoid and rectangle
Ⓓ 2 rectangles that are not squares

Name ____________________________

13.5 Line Symmetry

TEKS Geometry and Measurement—4.6.B

MATHEMATICAL PROCESSES 4.1.B, 4.1.C, 4.1.E, 4.1.F

Essential Question

How can you check if a figure has line symmetry?

Unlock the Problem (Real World)

One type of symmetry found in geometric figures is line symmetry. This sign is in the hills above Hollywood, California. Do the letters in the Hollywood sign show line symmetry?

A figure has **line symmetry** if it can be folded about a line so that its two parts match exactly. A fold line, or a **line of symmetry**, divides a figure into two parts that are the same size and shape.

Activity Explore line symmetry.

Materials ■ pattern blocks ■ scissors ■ tracing paper

A Does the letter W have line symmetry?

STEP 1 Use pattern blocks to make the letter W.

STEP 2 Trace the letter.

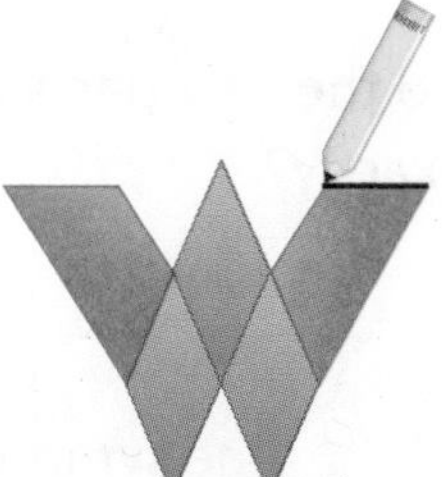

STEP 3 Cut out the tracing.

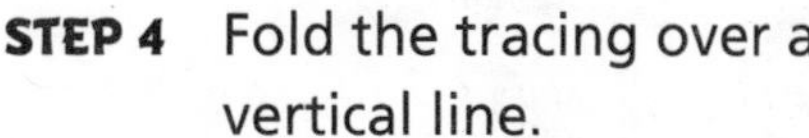

STEP 4 Fold the tracing over a vertical line.

Think: The two parts of the folded W match exactly. The fold line is a line of symmetry.

So, the letter W __________ line symmetry.

Math Idea

A vertical line goes up and down. ↕

A horizontal line goes left and right. ↔

A diagonal line goes through vertices of a polygon that are not next to each other. It can go up and down and left and right.

Math Talk Mathematical Processes

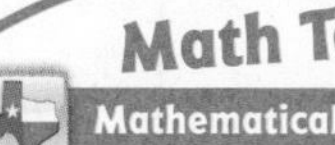

Why is it important to use a fold line to check if a figure has line symmetry?

B **Does the letter L have line symmetry?**

STEP 1

Use pattern blocks or grid paper to make the letter L.

STEP 2

Trace the letter.

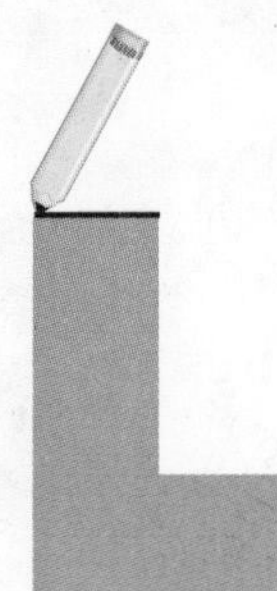

STEP 3

Cut out the tracing.

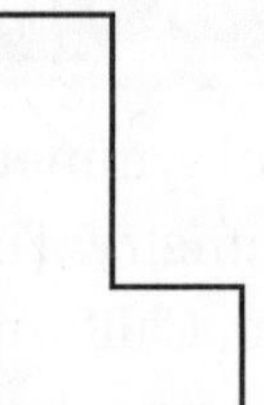

STEP 4

Fold the tracing over a vertical line.

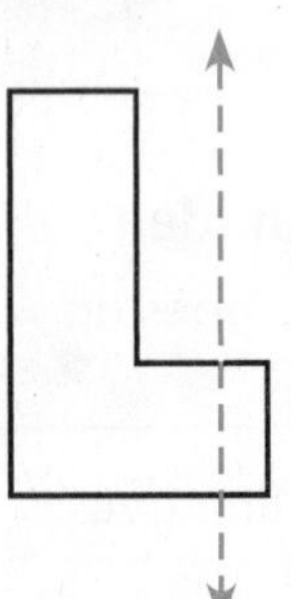

Do the two parts match exactly?

____

STEP 5

Then open it and fold it horizontally.

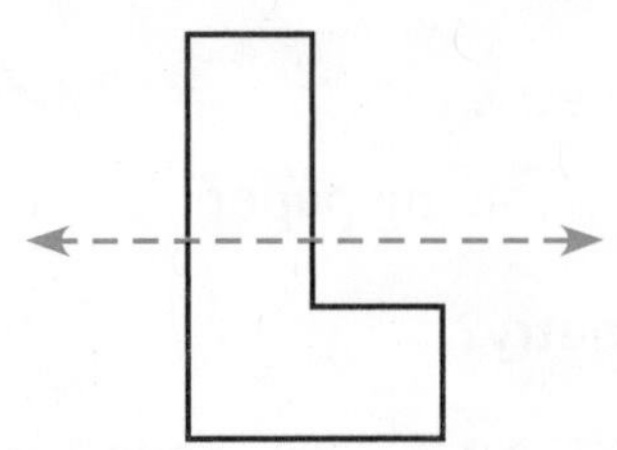

Do the two parts match exactly?

____

STEP 6

Then open it and fold it diagonally.

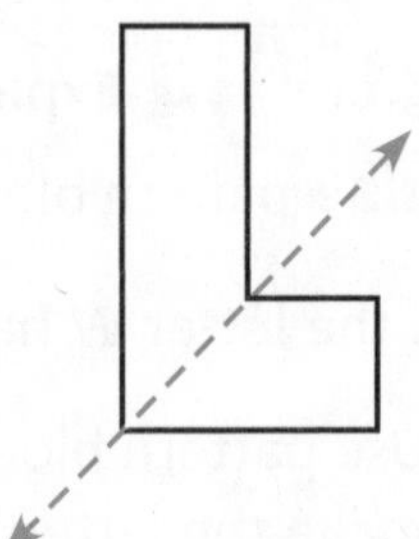

Do the two parts match exactly?

____

So, the letter L _______________ line symmetry.

Math Talk

Mathematical Processes

Explain how you can use paper folding to check if a figure has line symmetry.

Share and Show

Tell whether the parts on each side of the line match. Is the line a line of symmetry? Write *yes* or *no*.

1. 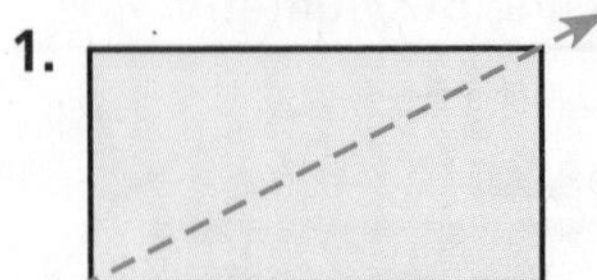

____

2. 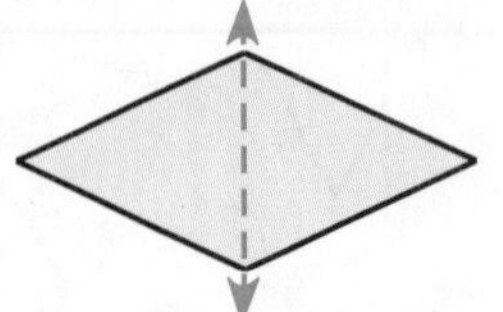

____

3. 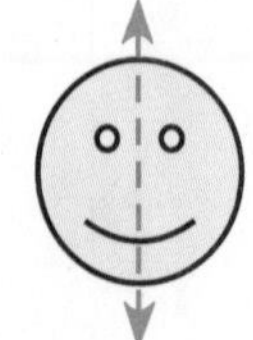

____

4. 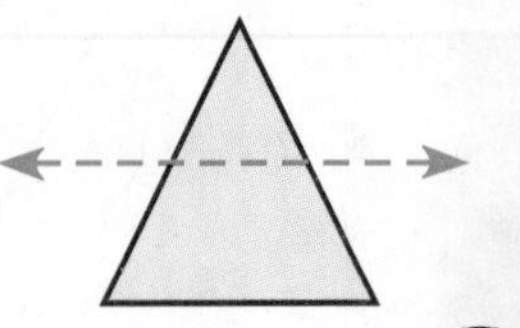

____

Name ____________________

Problem Solving

H.O.T. **Complete the design by reflecting over the line of symmetry.**

5.
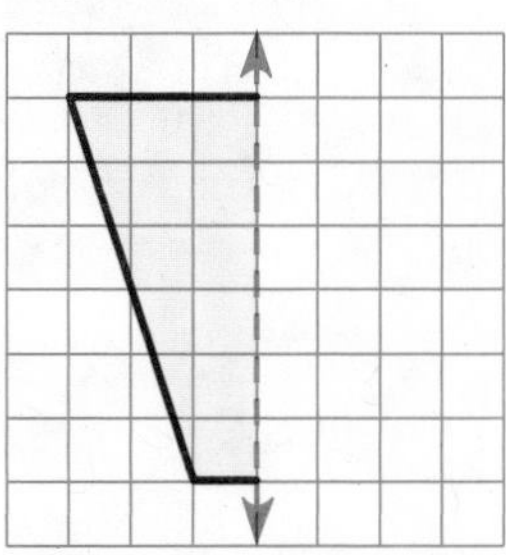

6.
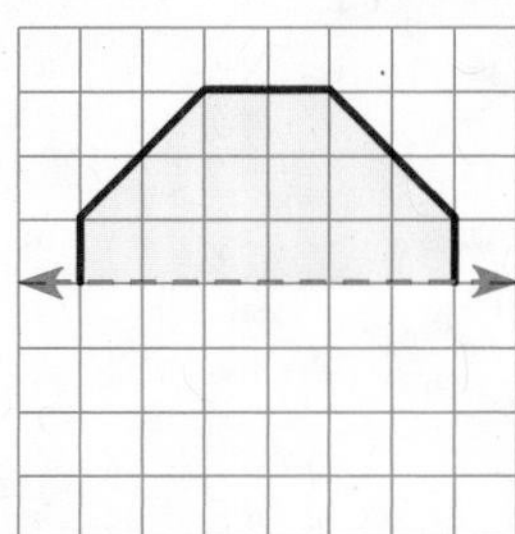

7.
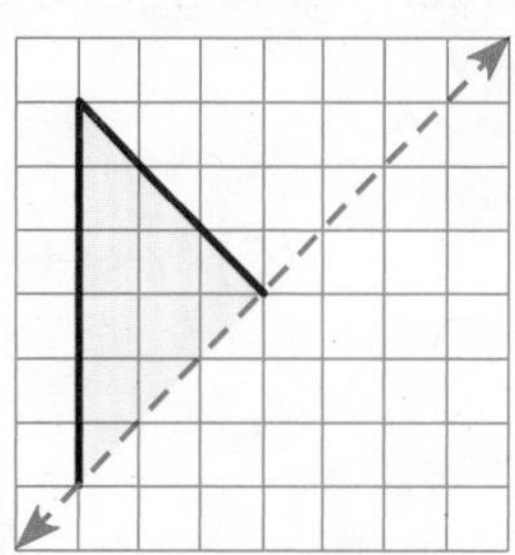

8.
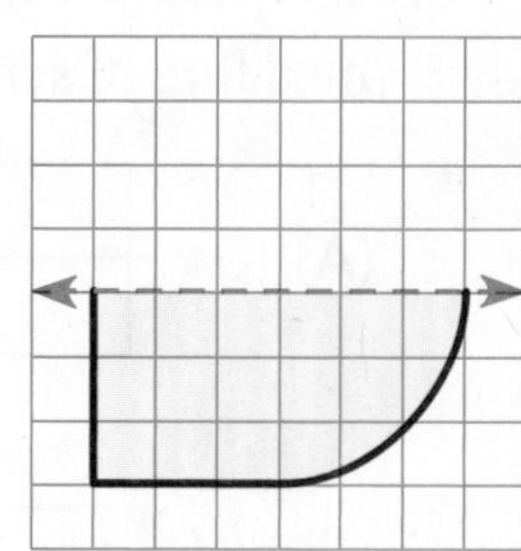

Unlock the Problem

9. **H.O.T.** **Multi-Step** Which figure has a correctly drawn line of symmetry?

Ⓐ

Ⓒ
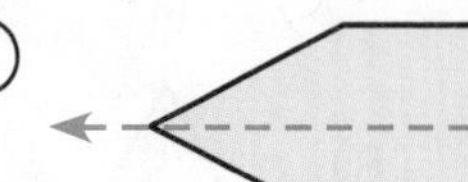

Ⓑ
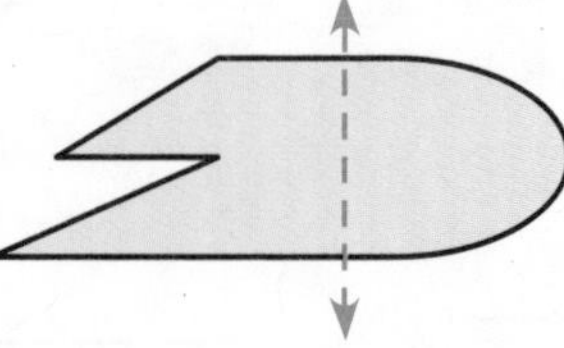

Ⓓ
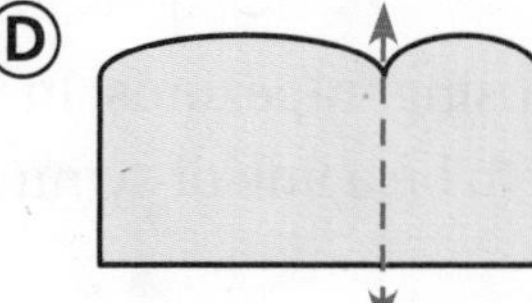

a. What do you need to find? ____________________

____

b. How can you tell if the line of symmetry is correct?

____

____

c. Tell how you solved the problem.

____

____

d. Fill in the bubble for the correct answer choice above.

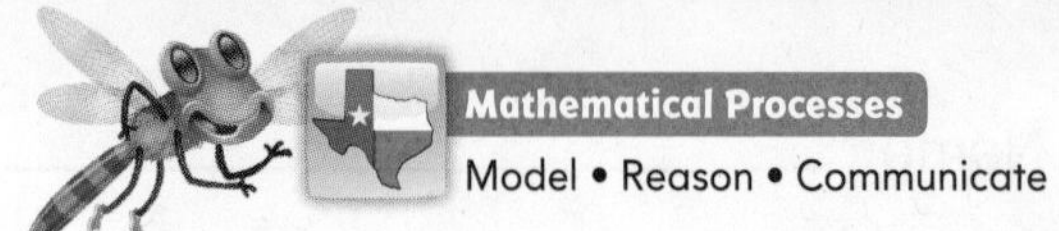

Daily Assessment Task

Fill in the bubble completely to show your answer.

10. **Use Diagrams** In which figure does the blue line appear not to be a line of symmetry?

Ⓐ 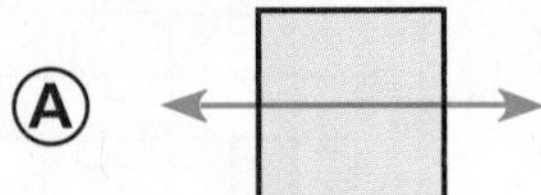

Ⓒ 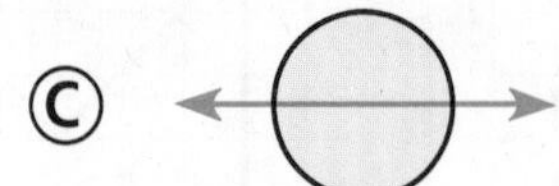

Ⓑ 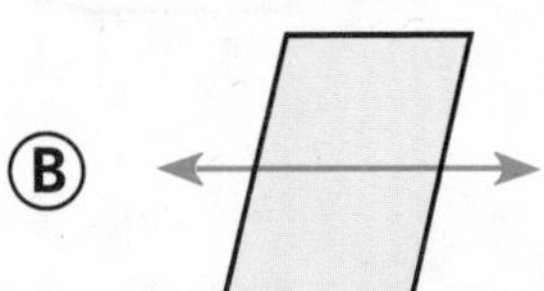

Ⓓ 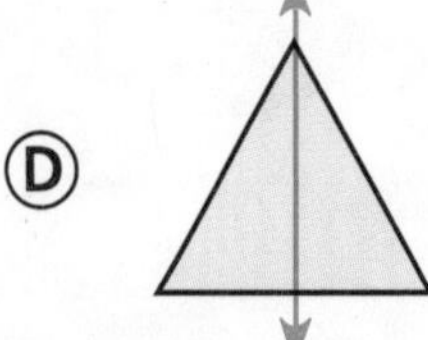

11. Casey is using foam stickers in different shapes to make a design. In which figure does the blue line appear to be a line of symmetry?

Ⓐ 

Ⓑ 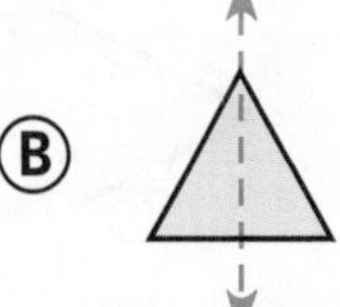

Ⓒ 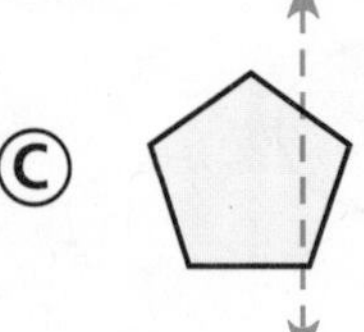

Ⓓ 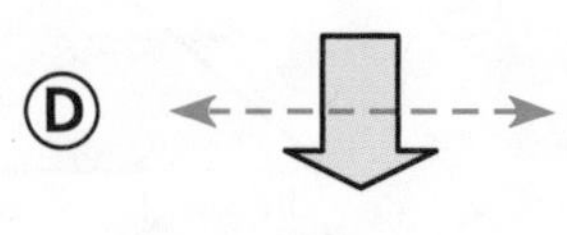

12. Riley is making a pattern using trapezoids. In which trapezoid does the blue line appear to be a line of symmetry?

Ⓐ 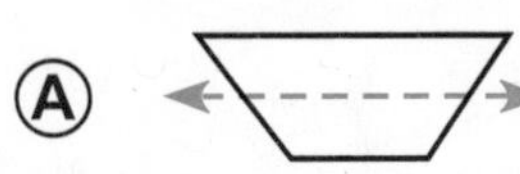

Ⓑ 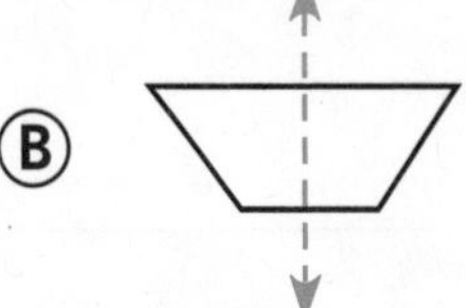

Ⓒ 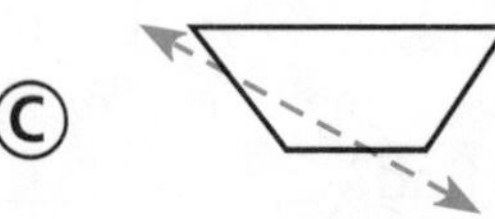

Ⓓ 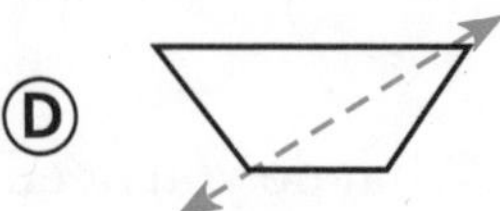

TEXAS Test Prep

13. Which best describes the line of symmetry in the letter M?

M

Ⓐ horizontal

Ⓑ diagonal

Ⓒ vertical

Ⓓ rotational

Homework and Practice

TEKS Geometry and Measurement—4.6.B
MATHEMATICAL PROCESSES 4.1.B, 4.1.C, 4.1.E, 4.1.F

Name ____________________

13.5 Line Symmetry

Tell whether the parts on each side of the line match. Is the line a line of symmetry? Write *yes* or *no*.

1.

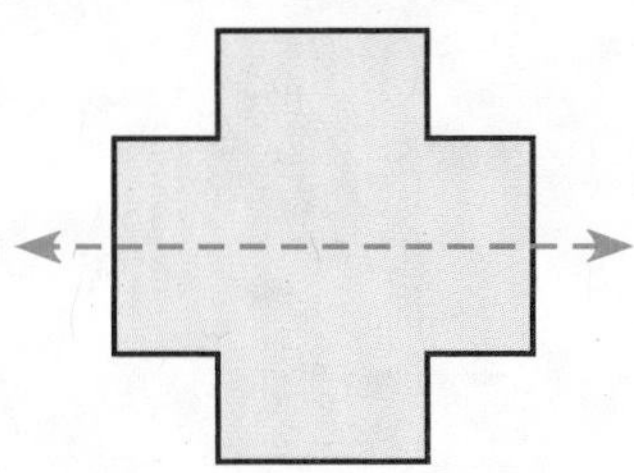

____

2.

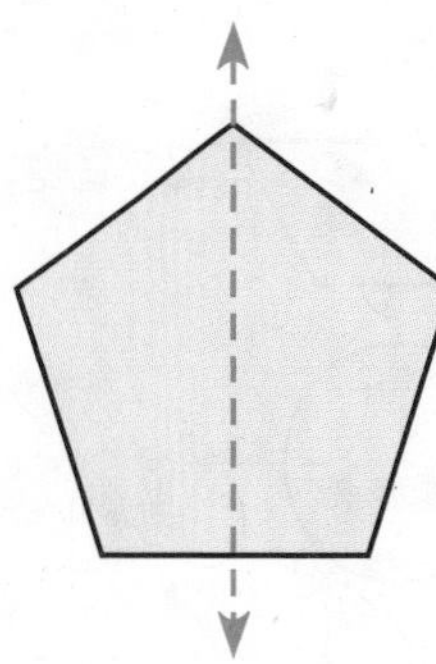

____

3.

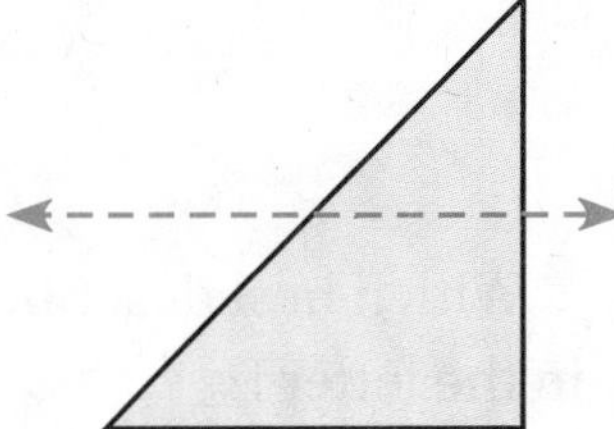

____

4.

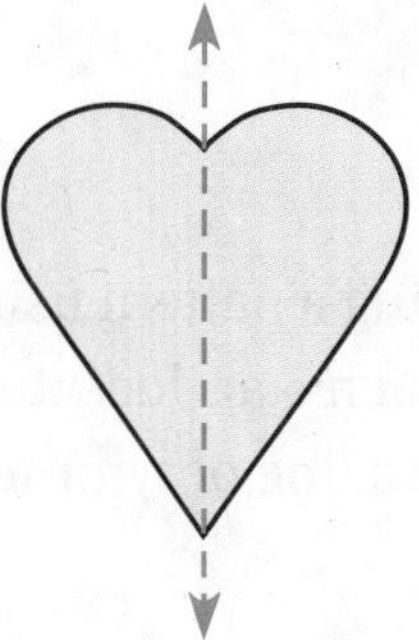

____

Problem Solving

Complete the design by reflecting over the line of symmetry.

5.

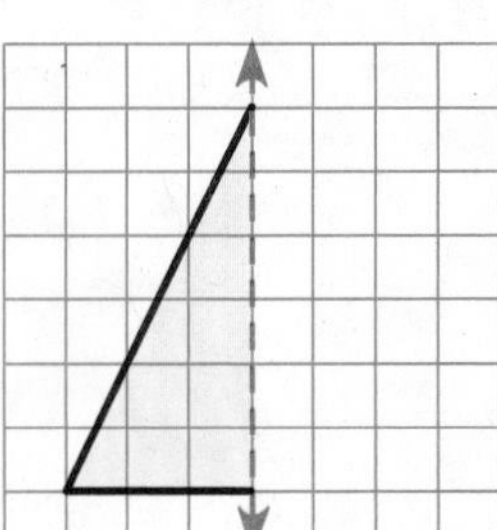

6.

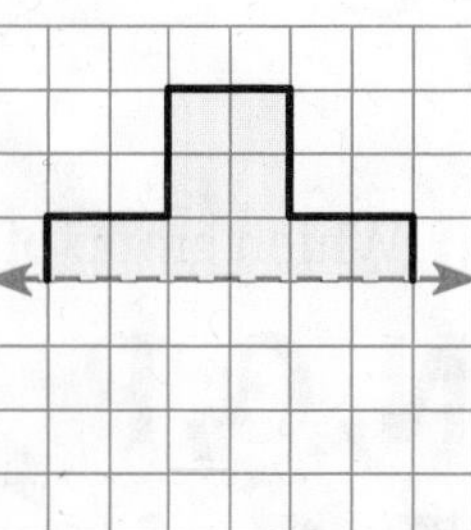

Lesson Check

TEXAS Test Prep

Fill in the bubble completely to show your answer.

7. In which figure does the blue line appear to be a line of symmetry?

Ⓐ 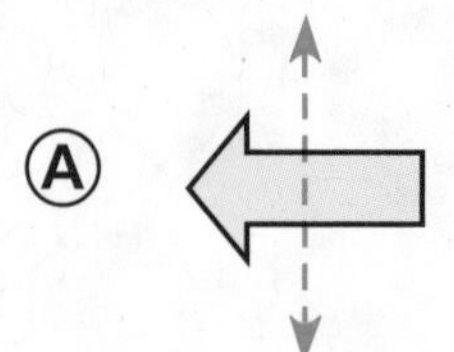

Ⓑ 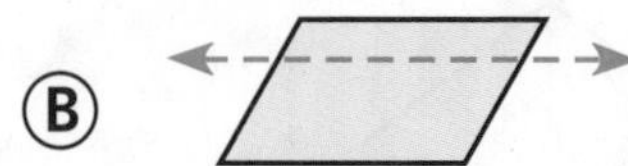

Ⓒ 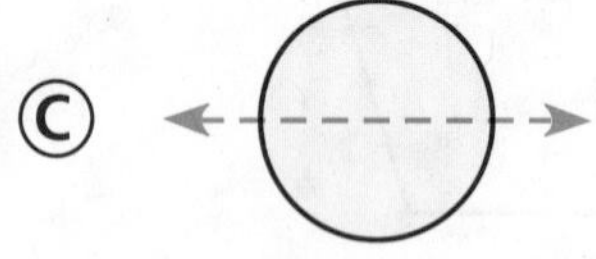

Ⓓ 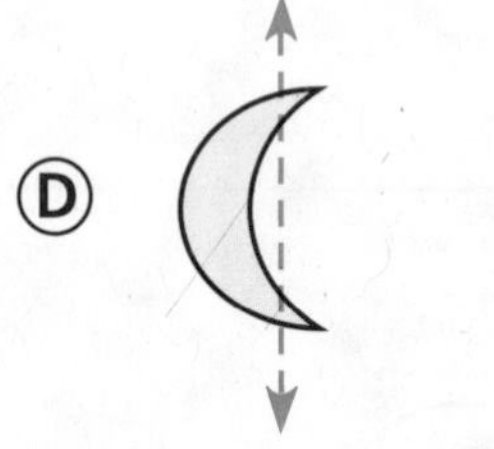

8. Which of the letters has line symmetry?

Ⓐ C

Ⓑ F

Ⓒ J

Ⓓ P

9. Nora is making a pattern using a star shape. In which star does the blue line appear to be a line of symmetry?

Ⓐ 

Ⓒ 

Ⓑ 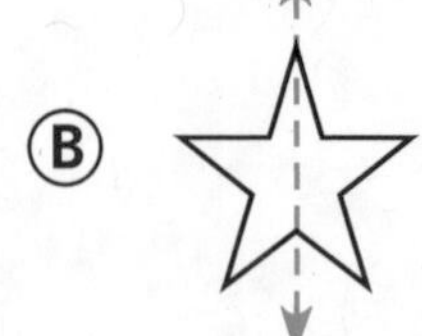

Ⓓ 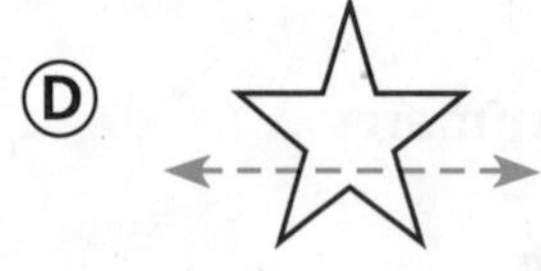

10. **Multi-Step** Which best describes the symmetry in the letter I?

I

Ⓐ vertical only

Ⓑ horizontal only

Ⓒ vertical and horizontal

Ⓓ diagonal and vertical

11. **Multi-Step** Which group of letters has no line of symmetry?

Ⓐ L, N, O, P

Ⓒ Q, S, T, M

Ⓑ Z, F, G, J

Ⓓ C, D, S, V

Name ____________________

13.6 Find and Draw Lines of Symmetry

Essential Question How do you find lines of symmetry?

Unlock the Problem

How many lines of symmetry does each polygon have?

Activity 1 Find lines of symmetry.

Materials ■ isometric and square dot paper ■ straightedge

STEP 1

Draw a triangle like the one shown, so all sides have equal length.

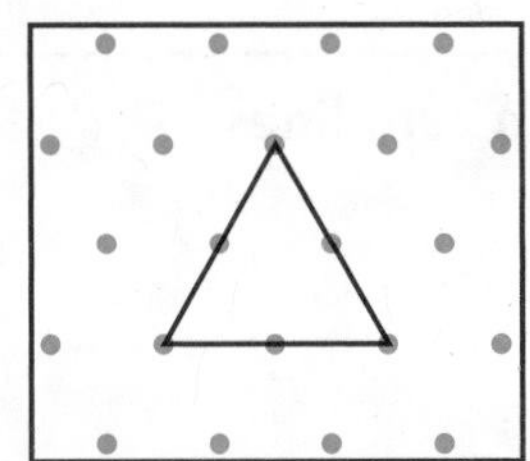

STEP 2

Fold the triangle in different ways to test for line symmetry. Draw along the fold lines that are lines of symmetry.

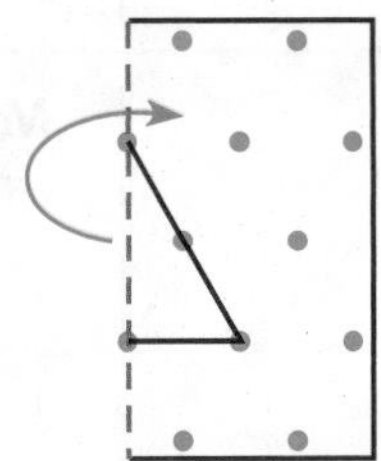

- Is there a line of symmetry if you fold the paper horizontally?

____

STEP 3

Repeat the steps for each polygon shown. Complete the table.

Polygon	Triangle	Square	Parallelogram	Rhombus	Trapezoid	Hexagon
Number of Sides	3					
Number of Lines of Symmetry	3					

- In a regular polygon, all sides are of equal length and all angles are equal. What do you notice about the number of lines of symmetry in regular polygons?

____

____

Math Talk

How many lines of symmetry does a circle have? **Explain.**

Activity 2 Make designs that have line symmetry.

Materials ■ pattern blocks

ERROR Alert

To avoid errors, you may use a mirror to check for line symmetry.

Make a design by using more than one pattern block. Record your design. Draw the line or lines of symmetry.

Make a design with 2 lines of symmetry.

Make a design with 1 line of symmetry.

Make a design with more than 2 lines of symmetry.

Make a design with zero lines of symmetry.

Share and Show

MATH BOARD

1. The figure at the right has line symmetry. Draw the 2 lines of symmetry.

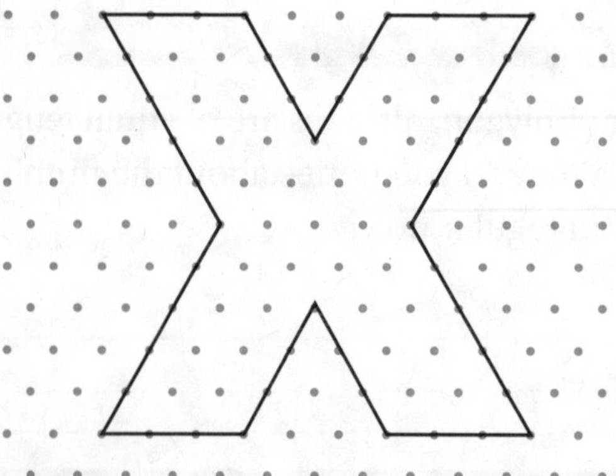

Name ______________________

Tell whether the figure appears to have zero lines, 1 line, or more than 1 line of symmetry. Write *zero, 1,* or *more than 1*.

2.  ______

3.  ______

4.  ______

5.  ______

Math Talk
Mathematical Processes
Explain how you can find lines of symmetry for a figure.

Problem Solving Real World

Use the chart for 6–8.

A	H	S
B	I	T
C	J	U
D	K	V
E	L	W

6. Which letters appear to have only 1 line of symmetry?

____

7. Which letters appear to have zero lines of symmetry?

____

8. H.O.T. The letter C has horizontal symmetry. The letter A has vertical symmetry. Which letters appear to have both horizontal and vertical symmetry?

____

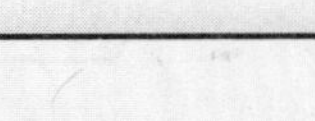

9. H.O.T. **Justify** Sense or Nonsense? Jeff says that the figure has only 2 lines of symmetry.

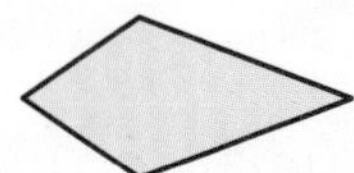

Does his statement make sense? **Explain.**

____

____

____

10. H.O.T. **Communicate** Multi-Step Draw a figure that has at least 2 lines of symmetry. Then write instructions that explain how to find the lines of symmetry.

____

____

Daily Assessment Task

Fill in the bubble completely to show your answer.

11. How many lines of symmetry does the shell have?

Ⓐ 0 Ⓒ 2

Ⓑ 3 Ⓓ 1

12. Which shows all the lines of symmetry for the figure below?

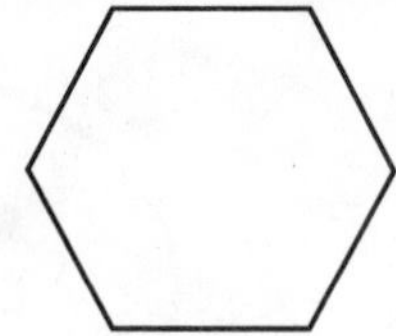

Ⓐ 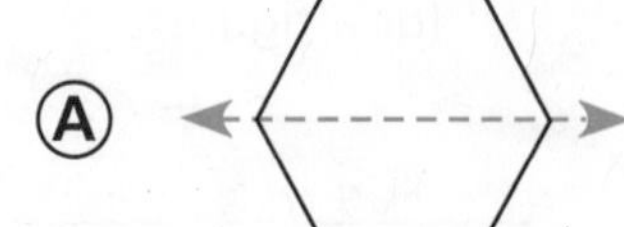

Ⓒ 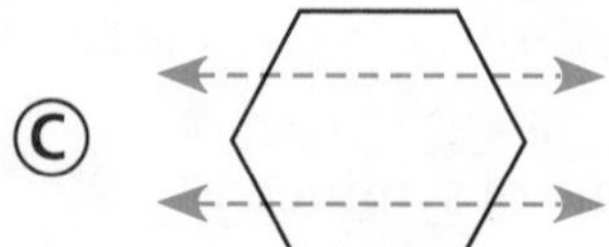

Ⓑ 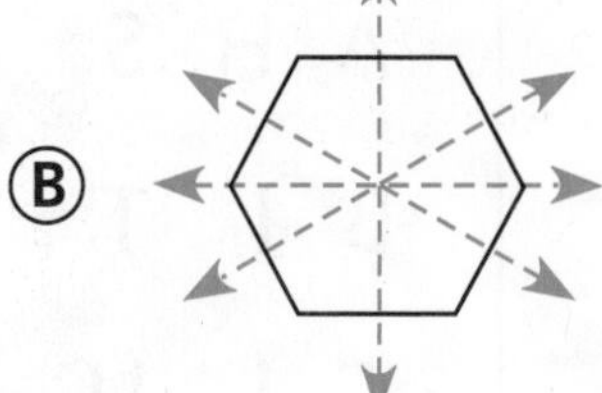

Ⓓ 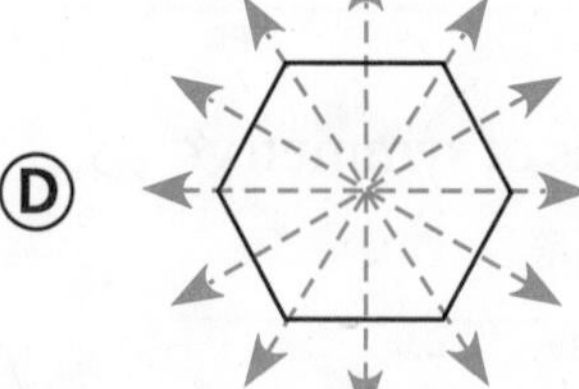

13. Which describes the figure?

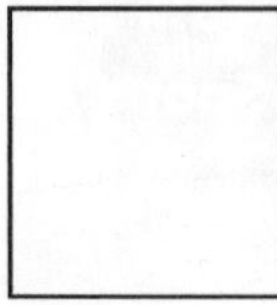

Ⓐ zero lines of symmetry Ⓒ more than 2 lines of symmetry

Ⓑ 2 lines of symmetry Ⓓ 1 line of symmetry

TEXAS Test Prep

14. How many lines of symmetry does the figure to the right have?

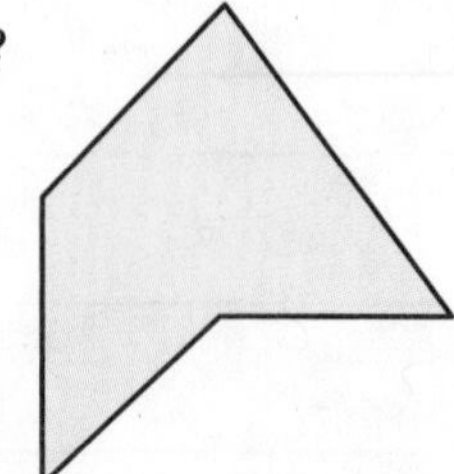

Ⓐ 10 Ⓒ 5

Ⓑ 3 Ⓓ 0

Name ______________________________

13.6 Find and Draw Lines of Symmetry

Tell whether the shape appears to have zero lines, 1 line, or more than 1 line of symmetry. Write *zero, 1,* or *more than 1.*

1. 

____

2. 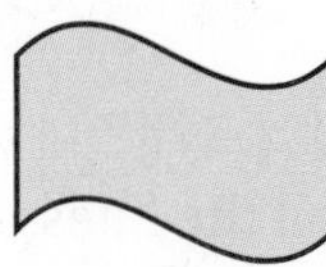

____

3. 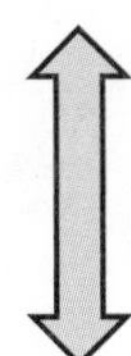

____

4. 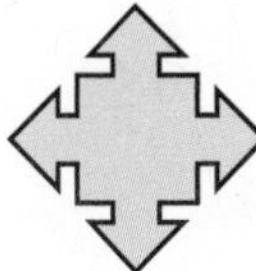

____

Problem Solving

Use the poster for 5–6.

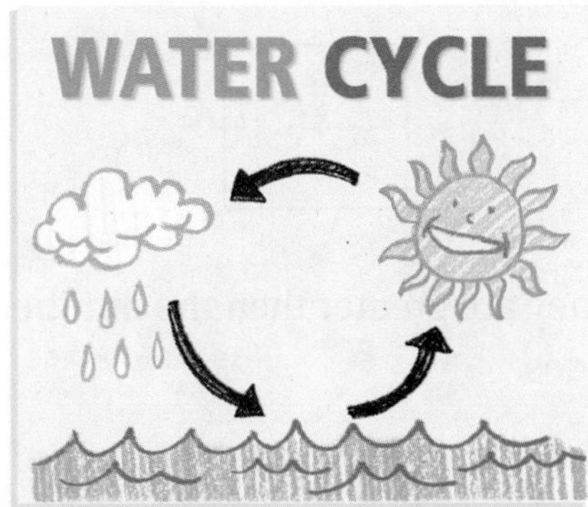

5. Erica is cutting out letters for a science poster. Which letters on Erica's poster appear to have only 1 line of symmetry?

____

6. Which letters on Erica's poster appear to have zero lines of symmetry?

____

7. Write your own poster words. Include letters that have zero, one, and two lines of symmetry. Then draw the lines of symmetry.

____

Lesson Check

Fill in the bubble completely to show your answer.

8. How many lines of symmetry does the jar have?

Ⓐ 0
Ⓑ 1
Ⓒ 2
Ⓓ 3

9. Which describes this figure?

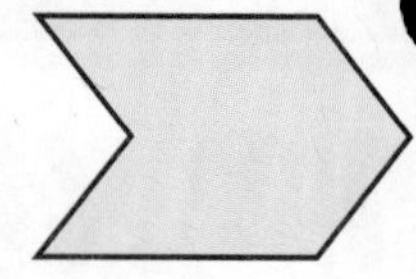

Ⓐ zero lines of symmetry
Ⓑ 1 line of symmetry
Ⓒ 2 lines of symmetry
Ⓓ more than 2 lines of symmetry

10. Which shows all the lines of symmetry for the figure?

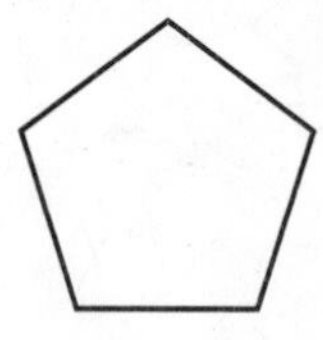

Ⓐ
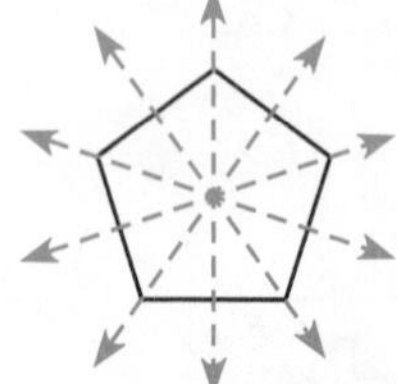

Ⓑ
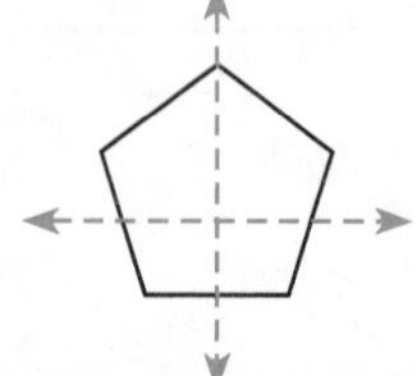

Ⓒ Ⓓ
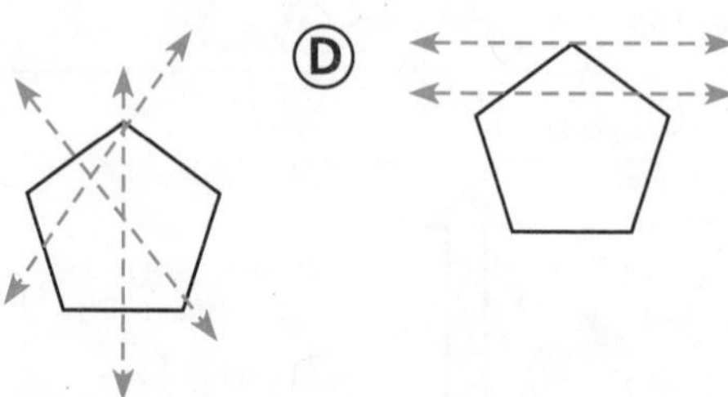

11. How many lines of symmetry does the figure have?

Ⓐ 3 Ⓑ 2 Ⓒ 1 Ⓓ 0

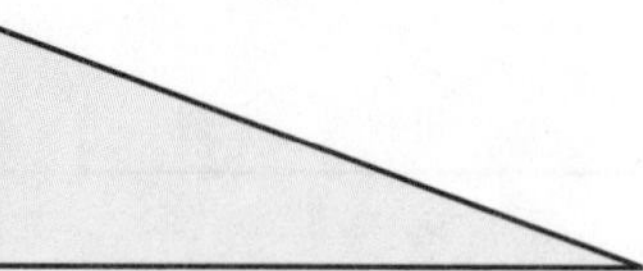

12. Multi-Step Which statement about the number of lines of symmetry is true?

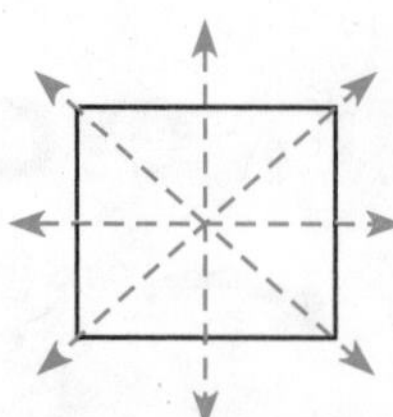

Ⓐ They are greater than the number of sides.
Ⓑ They are less than the number of angles.
Ⓒ They are the same as the number of sides.
Ⓓ They are greater than the number of angles.

13. Multi-Step Lance drew this figure with two lines of symmetry. Which statement is true about the number of lines of symmetry?

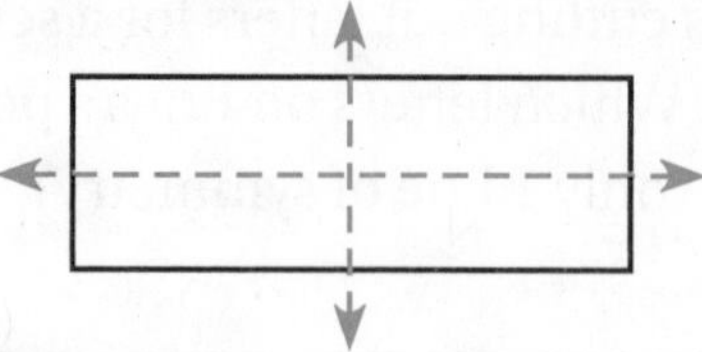

Ⓐ They are the same as the number of sides.
Ⓑ They are greater than the number of sides.
Ⓒ They are less than the number of pairs of sides of equal length.
Ⓓ They are the same as the number of pairs of sides of equal length.

Name ______________________________

Module 13 Assessment

Vocabulary

Vocabulary
acute angle
line segment
obtuse angle
ray
right angle
straight angle

Choose the best term from the box to complete the sentence.

1. A ______________ is part of a line between two endpoints. (p. 449)
2. A ______________ forms a square corner. (p. 450)
3. An ______________ is greater than a right angle and less than a straight angle. (p. 450)
4. The two-dimensional figure that has one endpoint is a ______________. (p. 449)
5. An angle that forms a line is called a ______________. (p. 450)

Concepts and Skills

Use Figure *A* for 6–11. TEKS 4.6.A

6. Name a ray.

____

7. Name an acute angle.

____

8. Name a point.

____

9. Name a line segment.

____

10. Name a pair of perpendicular lines.

____

11. Name an obtuse angle.

____

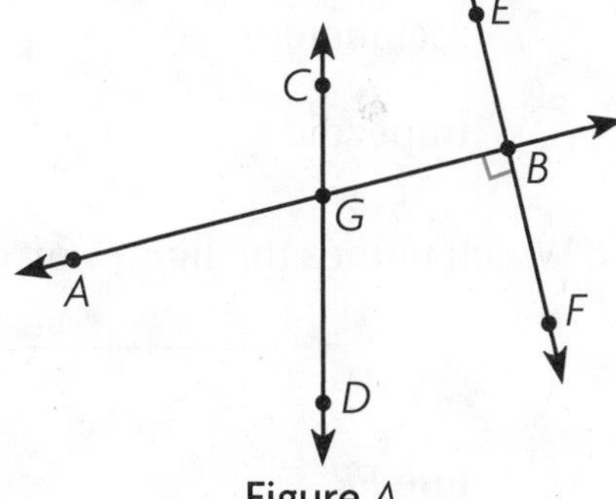

Figure *A*

Classify each triangle. Write *acute, right* or *obtuse*. TEKS 4.6.C

12. 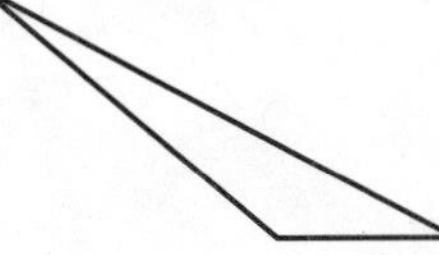

____

13. 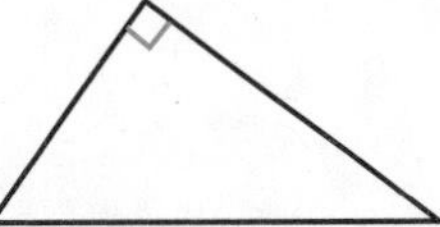

____

14. 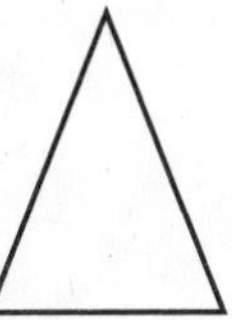

____

Fill in the bubble completely to show your answer.

15. Which describes the figure? TEKS 4.6.B

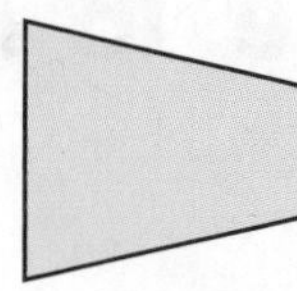

Ⓐ zero lines of symmetry

Ⓑ 1 line of symmetry

Ⓒ 2 lines of symmetry

Ⓓ more than 2 lines of symmetry

16. Which figure has 2 pairs of sides that appear to be parallel? TEKS 4.6.D

Ⓐ 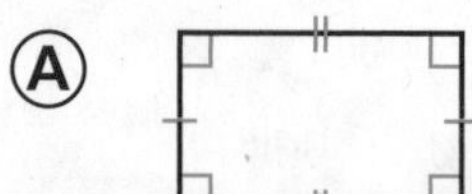

Ⓒ 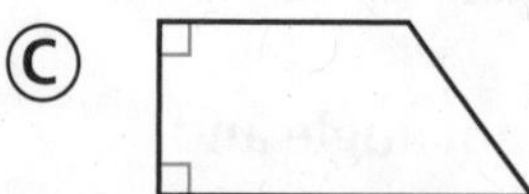

Ⓑ 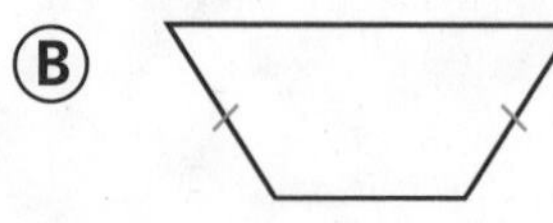

Ⓓ 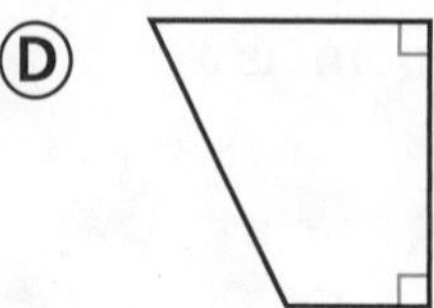

17. Which quadrilateral can have 2 pairs of parallel sides, all sides with equal length, and no right angles? TEKS 4.6.D

Ⓐ square

Ⓑ rhombus

Ⓒ rectangle

Ⓓ trapezoid

18. Which names the figure correctly? TEKS 4.6.A

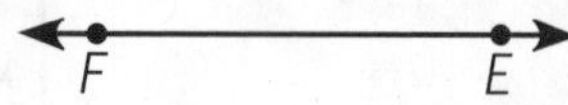

Ⓐ line *FE*

Ⓑ ray *FE*

Ⓒ angle *FE*

Ⓓ ray *EF*

Name ____________________

14.1 Angles and Fractional Parts of a Circle

Essential Question How can you relate angles and fractional parts of a circle?

Investigate

Materials ■ fraction circles

A. Place a $\frac{1}{12}$ piece on the circle. Place the tip of the fraction piece on the center of the circle. Trace the fraction piece.

What figure is formed by the fraction piece? ____________

What parts of the fraction piece represent the rays of the angle? ____________

On what part of the circle is the vertex of the angle?

____

B. Shade the angle cut out by the $\frac{1}{12}$ piece. Label it $\frac{1}{12}$.

C. Place the $\frac{1}{12}$ piece back on the shaded angle. Turn it counterclockwise. **Counterclockwise** is the direction opposite from the way the hands move on a clock.

Trace the fraction piece in its new position. How many twelfths have you traced in all? ______ Label $\frac{2}{12}$.

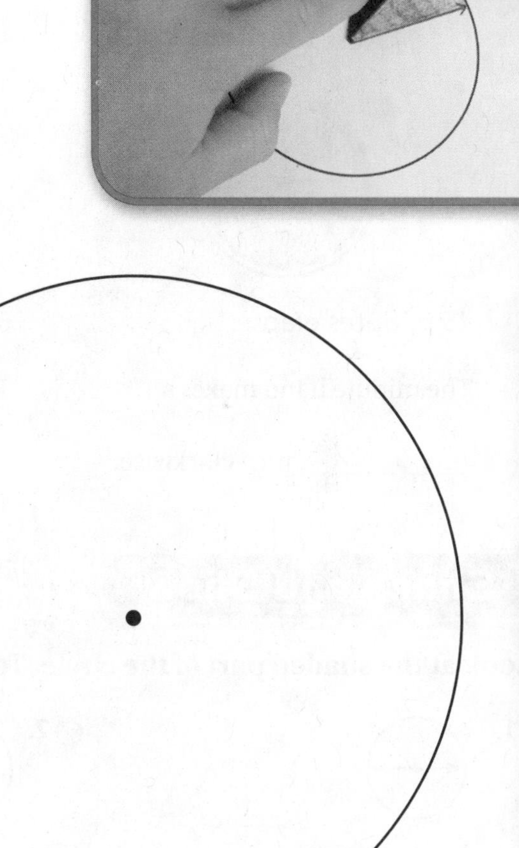

D. Turn the fraction piece counterclockwise again and trace it. Label the total number of twelfths. Continue until you reach the shaded angle. What figure is formed by turning and tracing the fraction piece? ____________

How many times did you need to turn the $\frac{1}{12}$ piece to make a circle? ____________

How many angles came together in the center of the circle? ____________

Make Connections

You can relate fractions and angles to the hands of a clock.

Let the hands of the clock represent the rays of an angle that cuts out a fraction of the clock face. Each 5-minute mark represents a $\frac{1}{12}$ turn **clockwise**.

15 minutes elapse.

The minute hand makes a

__________ turn clockwise.

30 minutes elapse.

The minute hand makes a

__________ turn clockwise.

45 minutes elapse.

The minute hand makes a

__________ turn clockwise.

60 minutes elapse.

The minute hand makes a

__________ turn clockwise.

Math Talk

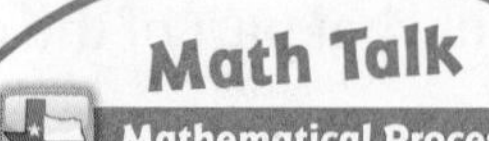

Explain how an angle formed in a circle using a $\frac{1}{4}$-fraction piece is like a $\frac{1}{4}$ turn and 15 minutes elapsing on a clock.

Share and Show

Look at the shaded part of the circle. Tell what fraction of the circle the angle cuts out.

1. 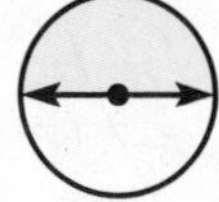 ______

2. 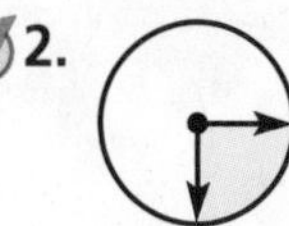 ______

3. 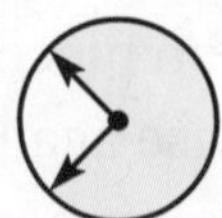 ______

Tell whether the angle on the circle shows a $\frac{1}{4}$, $\frac{1}{2}$, $\frac{3}{4}$, or 1 full turn clockwise or counterclockwise.

4. 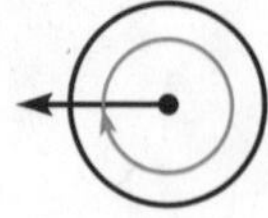 __________

____

5. 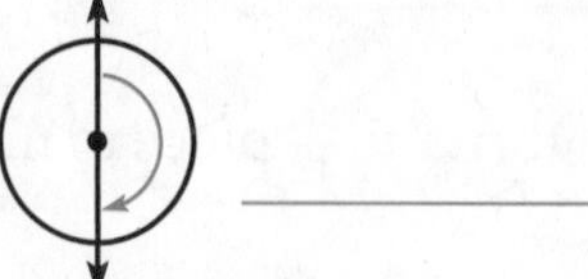 __________

____

6. 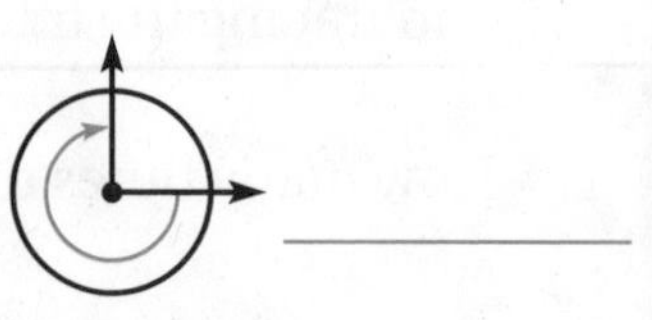 __________

____

Name ____________________

Problem Solving

H.O.T. **Sense or Nonsense?**

7. **Analyze** Whose statement makes sense? Whose statement is nonsense? **Explain** your reasoning.

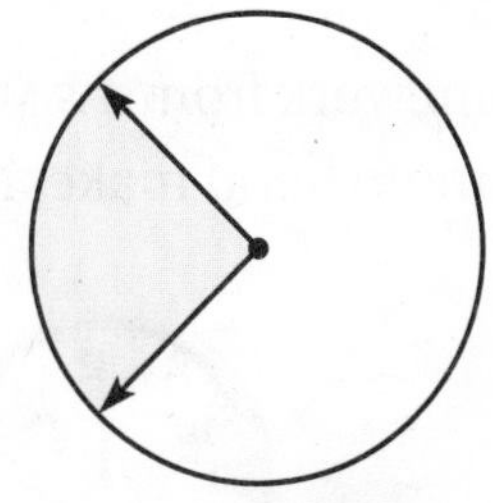

The shaded angle cuts out $\frac{1}{4}$ of the circle.

The shaded angle cuts out $\frac{3}{8}$ of the circle.

Carla's Statement

____

____

____

____

Adam's Statement

____

____

____

____

8. **H.O.T.** Susan watched the game from 1 P.M. to 1:30 P.M. **Describe** the turn the minute hand made.

____

9. **Write Math** Compare the angles in the two circles. Does the position of the angle affect the size of the angle? **Explain**.

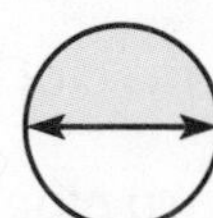

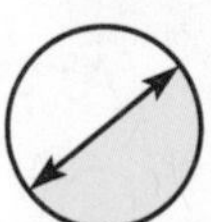

____

____

Mathematical Processes
Model • Reason • Communicate

Daily Assessment Task

Fill in the bubble completely to show your answer.

10. **Multi-Step** Carrie does her homework from 4 P.M. to 4:45 P.M. Which describes the turn the minute hand makes?

Ⓐ $\frac{1}{4}$ turn clockwise

Ⓑ $\frac{3}{4}$ turn clockwise

Ⓒ $\frac{1}{2}$ turn counterclockwise

Ⓓ $\frac{1}{4}$ turn counterclockwise

11. Which angle shows $\frac{1}{2}$ turn counterclockwise?

Ⓐ

Ⓒ 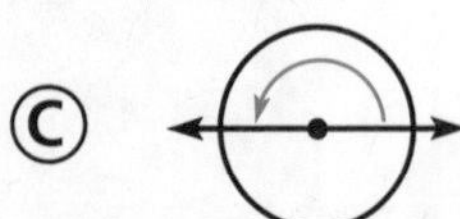

Ⓑ

Ⓓ 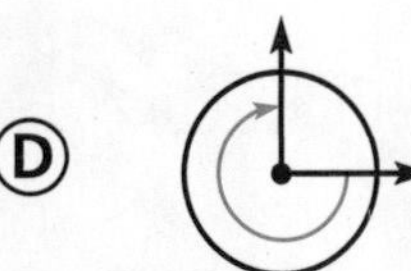

12. Look at the shaded part of the circle. What fraction of the circle does the angle cut out?

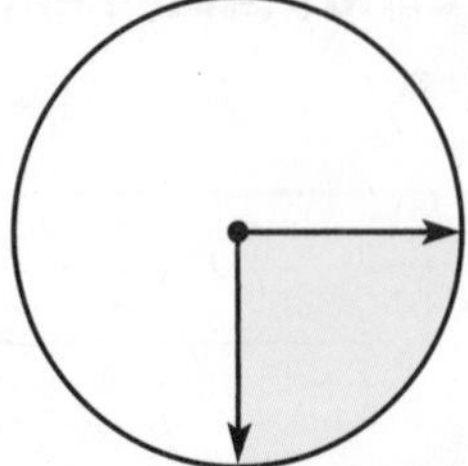

Ⓐ $\frac{1}{4}$

Ⓑ $\frac{1}{12}$

Ⓒ $\frac{3}{4}$

Ⓓ $\frac{1}{2}$

TEXAS Test Prep

13. Phillip watched a beach volleyball game from 1:45 P.M. to 2:00 P.M. What fraction of a turn did the minute hand make?

Ⓐ $\frac{1}{4}$ turn clockwise

Ⓑ $\frac{1}{2}$ turn clockwise

Ⓒ $\frac{3}{4}$ turn clockwise

Ⓓ 1 full turn clockwise

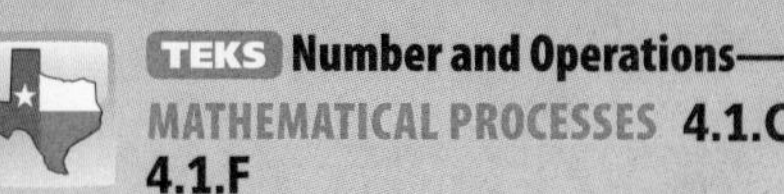

Name ______________________

14.1 Angles and Fractional Parts of a Circle

Look at the shaded part of the circle. Tell what fraction of the circle the angle cuts out.

1.  ________

2. 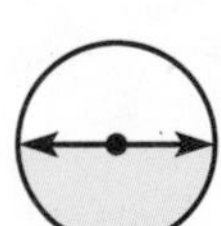 ________

3.  ________

Tell whether the angle on the circle shows a $\frac{1}{4}$, $\frac{1}{2}$, $\frac{3}{4}$, or 1 full turn clockwise or counterclockwise.

4. 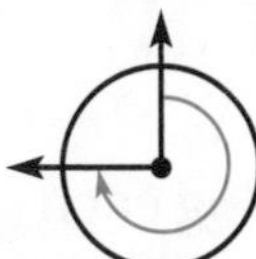 ________

5. 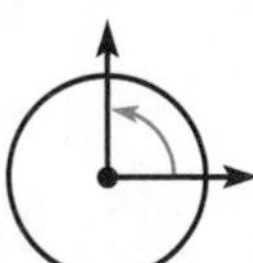 ________

6.  ________

7. 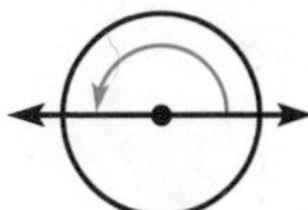 ________

8. 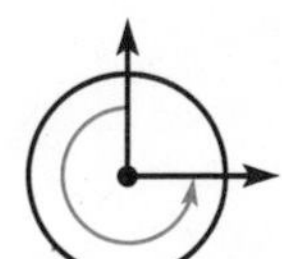 ________

9. 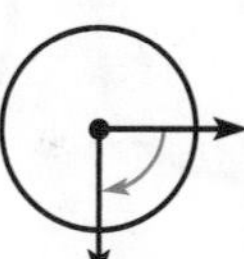 ________

Problem Solving

10. Evan practiced the piano from 3 P.M. to 3:45 P.M. Describe the turn the minute hand made.

____

11. As soon as Evan finished practicing, he ate a snack. When he finished his snack, it was 4:00. Describe the turn the minute hand made.

____

Lesson Check

Fill in the bubble completely to show your answer.

12. Which angle shows a $\frac{3}{4}$ turn counterclockwise?

Ⓐ 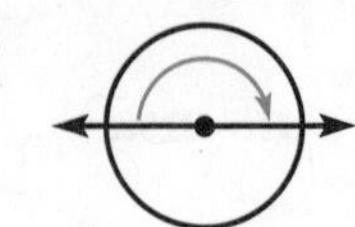

Ⓒ 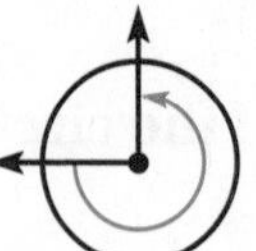

Ⓑ 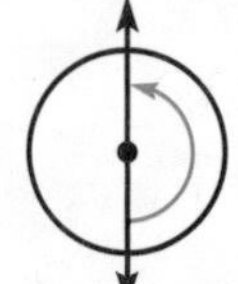

Ⓓ 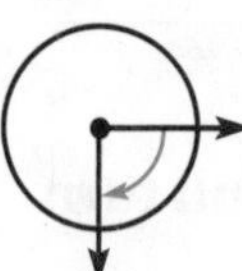

13. Look at the shaded part of the circle. What fraction of the circle does the angle cut out?

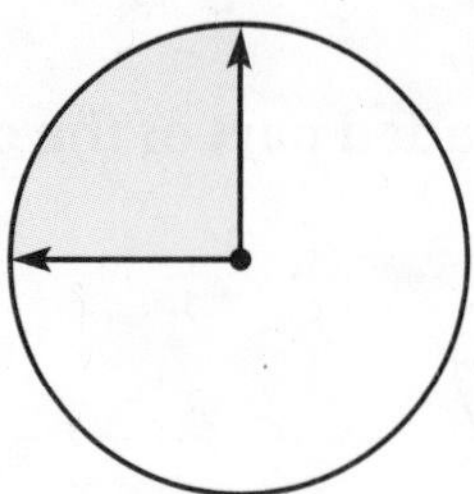

Ⓐ $\frac{1}{2}$ Ⓒ $\frac{1}{3}$

Ⓑ $\frac{3}{4}$ Ⓓ $\frac{1}{4}$

14. **Multi-Step** Hannah takes a break from 10 A.M. to 10:15 A.M. Which describes the turn the minute hand makes?

Ⓐ $\frac{1}{4}$ turn counterclockwise

Ⓑ $\frac{1}{4}$ turn clockwise

Ⓒ $\frac{3}{4}$ turn counterclockwise

Ⓓ $\frac{3}{4}$ turn clockwise

15. **Multi-Step** Inez walks her dog each morning from 7:45 A.M. to 8:15 A.M. Which describes the turn the minute hand makes?

Ⓐ $\frac{1}{2}$ turn clockwise

Ⓑ 1 full turn clockwise

Ⓒ $\frac{1}{2}$ turn counterclockwise

Ⓓ $\frac{1}{4}$ turn clockwise

16. **Multi-Step** Ben babysits his little sister for 15 minutes each day. Which fraction describes the turn of the minute hand on the clock face during the time Ben babysits?

Ⓐ $\frac{1}{2}$ Ⓒ $\frac{12}{12}$

Ⓑ $\frac{3}{4}$ Ⓓ $\frac{1}{4}$

17. **Multi-Step** Standard time begins in the fall. On a certain day each year, many people turn their clocks back one hour. Which fraction describes the turn of the minute hand on the clock face?

Ⓐ $\frac{12}{12}$ Ⓒ $\frac{3}{12}$

Ⓑ $\frac{9}{12}$ Ⓓ $\frac{6}{12}$

Name ______________________________

Degrees

TEKS Geometry and Measurement—4.7.B
Also 4.7.A

MATHEMATICAL PROCESSES
4.1.A, 4.1.F, 4.1.G

Essential Question

How are degrees related to fractional parts of a circle?

Connect You can use what you know about angles and fractional parts of a circle to understand angle measurement. Angles are measured in units called **degrees**. Think of a circle divided into 360 equal parts. An angle that cuts $\frac{1}{360}$ out of the circle measures 1 degree(°).

Math Idea

An angle that cuts $\frac{n}{360}$ out of a circle measures *n* degrees.

Unlock the Problem Real World

The angle between two spokes on the bicycle wheel cuts out or turns through $\frac{10}{360}$ of a circle. What is the measure of the angle between the spokes?

- What part of an angle does a spoke represent?

____

____

Example 1 Use fractional parts to find the angle measure.

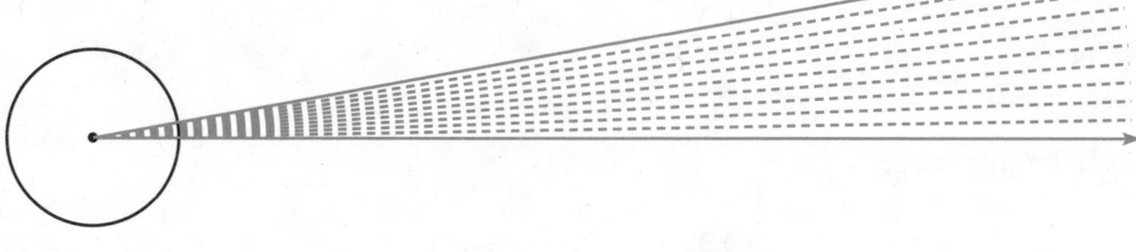

Each $\frac{1}{360}$ turn measures ______ degree.

Ten $\frac{1}{360}$ turns measure ______ degrees.

So, the measure of the angle between the spokes is ______.

Math Talk
Mathematical Processes

How many degrees is the measure of an angle that turns through 1 whole circle? **Explain.**

Example 2 Find the measure of a right angle.

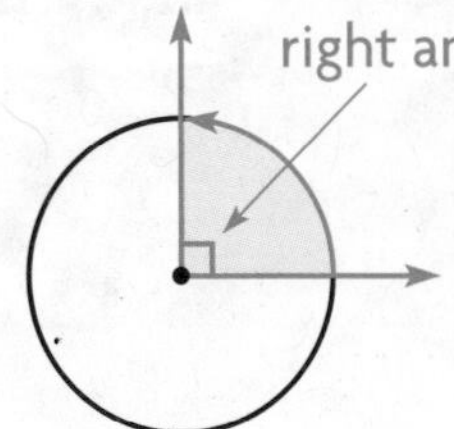

Think: What fraction of a circle does a right angle cut out? ______

STEP 1 Write $\frac{1}{4}$ as an equivalent fraction with 360 in the denominator.

$\frac{1}{4} = \frac{\square}{360}$ **Think:** 4 × 9 = 36, so 4 × ______ = 360.

Remember

To write an equivalent fraction, multiply the numerator and denominator by the same factor.

STEP 2 Write $\frac{90}{360}$ in degrees.

An angle that cuts $\frac{1}{360}$ out of a circle measures ______.

An angle that cuts $\frac{90}{360}$ out of a circle measures ______.

So, a right angle measures ______.

Share and Show

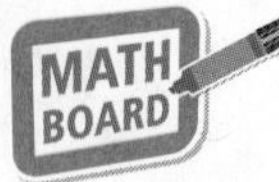

1. Find the measure of the angle.

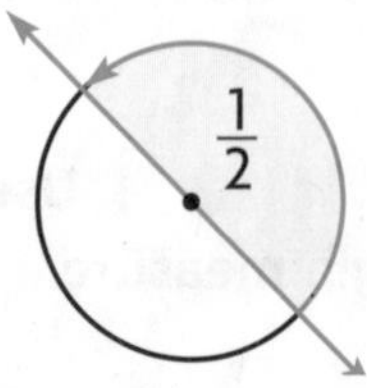

What fraction of the circle does the angle cut out? ______

$\frac{1}{2} = \frac{\square}{360}$ **Think:** 2 × 18 = 36, so 2 × ______ = 360.

So, the measure of the angle is ______.

Tell the measure of the angle in degrees.

2.

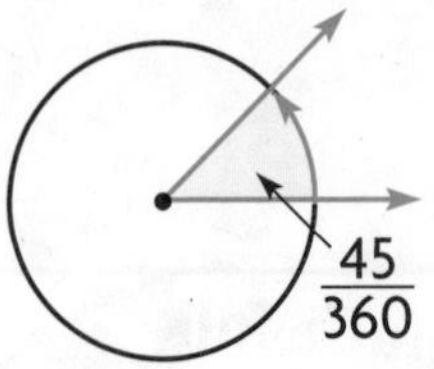

______

3.

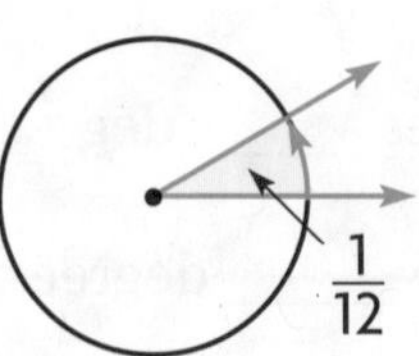

______

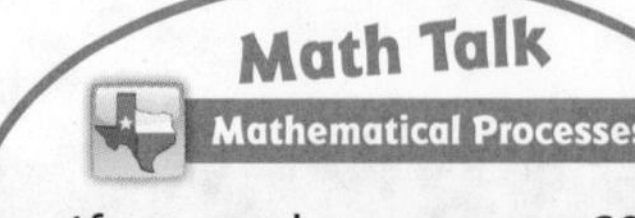

If an angle measures 60°, what fraction of a circle does it cut out? Explain.

Name ________________________________

Unlock the Problem

4. H.O.T. **Multi-Step** Ava started reading at 3:30 P.M. She stopped for a snack at 3:50 P.M. During this time, through what fraction of a circle did the minute hand turn? How many degrees did the minute hand turn?

a. What are you asked to find? ________________________________

____

b. What information can you use to find the fraction of a circle through which the minute hand turned?

____

c. How can you use the fraction of a circle through which the minute hand turned to find how many degrees it turned?

____

____

d. Show how to solve the problem.

$$\frac{1 \times \square}{3 \times \square} = \frac{\square}{360}$$

e. Complete the sentences.

From 3:30 P.M. to 3:50 P.M., the minute hand made a ______ turn clockwise.

The minute hand turned ______ degrees.

5. H.O.T. Write Math
Is this angle measure obtuse? **Explain.**

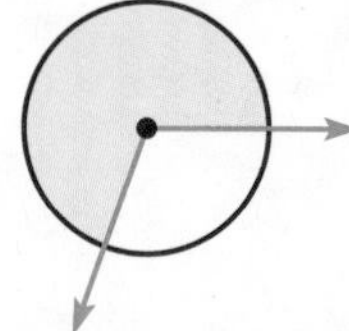

____

____

____

6. **Analyze** What fraction of a circle does a straight angle cut out? What is the measure of a straight angle? **Explain.**

____

____

____

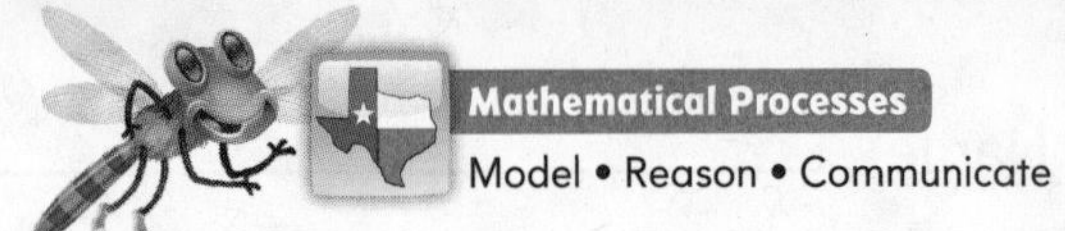

Daily Assessment Task

Fill in the bubble completely to show your answer.

7. What is the measure of the angle in degrees?

Ⓐ 108°

Ⓑ 95°

Ⓒ 3°

Ⓓ 90°

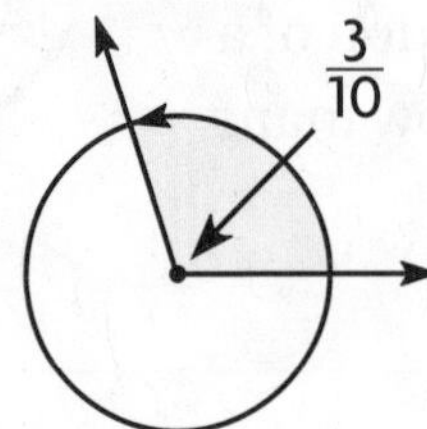

8. **Use Mathematical Language** What type of angle is shown?

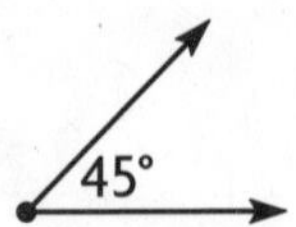

Ⓐ right

Ⓑ obtuse

Ⓒ acute

Ⓓ straight

9. **Multi-Step** A circle is divided into 8 equal sections. An angle measures the same as the total measure of 3 of the sections. What is the measure of the angle?

Ⓐ 270°

Ⓑ 90°

Ⓒ 45°

Ⓓ 135°

TEXAS Test Prep

10. How many degrees are in an angle that cuts $\frac{2}{4}$ of a circle?

Ⓐ 90°

Ⓑ 180°

Ⓒ 270°

Ⓓ 360°

Homework and Practice

TEKS Geometry and Measurement—4.7.B
MATHEMATICAL PROCESSES 4.1.A, 4.1.F, 4.1.G

Name ____________________

14.2 Degrees

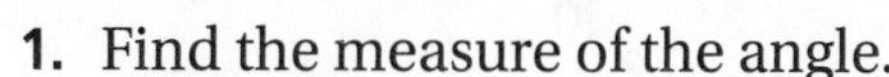

1. Find the measure of the angle.

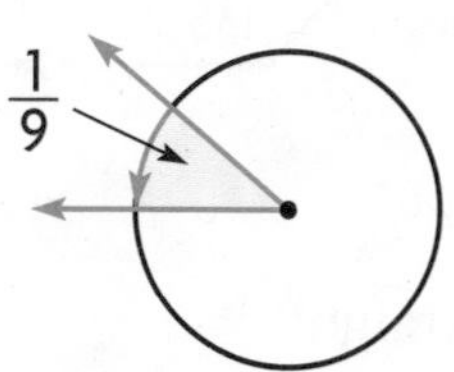

What fraction of the circle does the angle cut out? ______

$\frac{1}{9} = \frac{\square}{360}$

So, the measure of the angle is ______.

Tell the measure of the angle in degrees.

2.

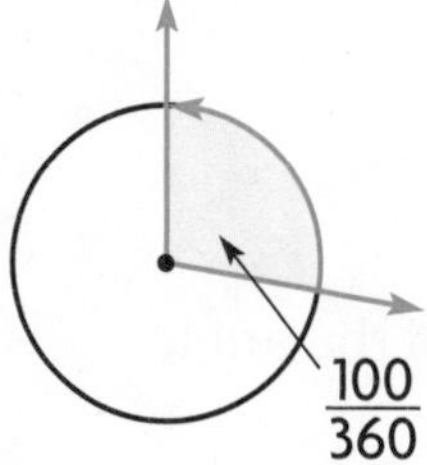

____

3.

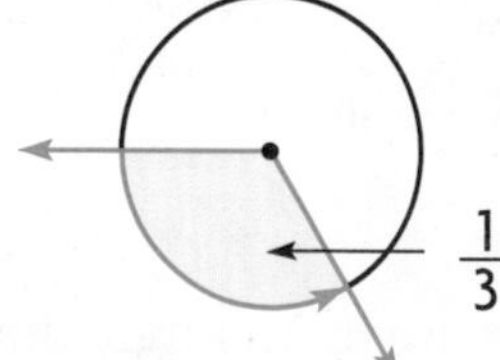

____

Problem Solving

4. At 6:10 P.M., Elena left her house to walk to Claire's house. She arrived at 6:25 P.M. During this time, through what fraction of a circle did the minute hand turn?

____

5. How many degrees did the minute hand turn as it moved from 2 to 5?

____

6. Suppose Elena takes a route that is 15 minutes longer. How would this change your answers to exercises 4 and 5? **Explain.**

____

____

____

Lesson Check

TEXAS Test Prep

Fill in the bubble completely to show your answer.

7. Which type of angle is shown?

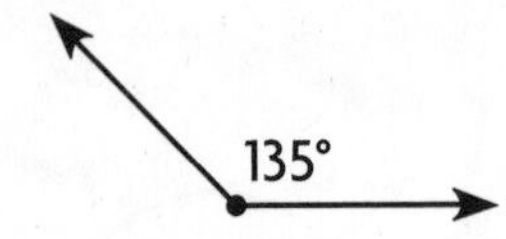

Ⓐ acute

Ⓑ straight

Ⓒ obtuse

Ⓓ right

8. What is the measure of the angle in degrees?

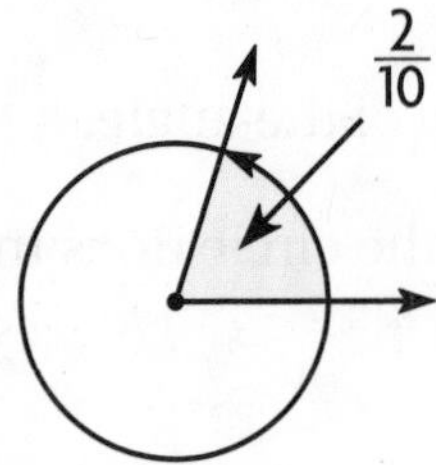

Ⓐ 45°

Ⓑ 72°

Ⓒ 2°

Ⓓ 90°

9. How many degrees are in an angle that cuts $\frac{2}{5}$ of a circle?

Ⓐ 144°

Ⓑ 30°

Ⓒ 180°

Ⓓ 50°

10. What is the measure of the angle in degrees?

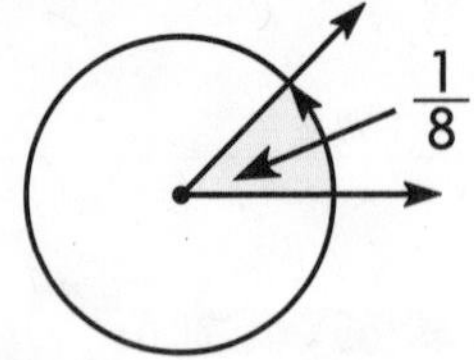

Ⓐ 80°

Ⓑ 90°

Ⓒ 35°

Ⓓ 45°

11. **Multi-Step** Alex cut a pizza into 8 equal slices. He removed 2 of the slices of pizza. What is the measure of the angle made by the missing slices of pizza?

Ⓐ 45°

Ⓑ 20°

Ⓒ 90°

Ⓓ 80°

12. **Multi-Step** Julia woke up at 7:05 A.M. She left for school at 7:25 A.M. How many degrees did the minute hand on the clock turn from the time Julia woke up to the time she left for school?

Ⓐ 120°

Ⓑ 60°

Ⓒ 180°

Ⓓ 90°

Name ______________________

14.3 Measure and Draw Angles

TEKS Geometry and Measurement—4.7.C, 4.7.D
Also 4.7.A

MATHEMATICAL PROCESSES
4.1.A, 4.1.C

Essential Question

How can you use a protractor to measure and draw angles?

Unlock the Problem (Real World)

Emma wants to make a clay sculpture of her daughter as she appears in the photo from her dance recital. How can she measure ∠*DCE*, or the angle formed by her daughter's arms?

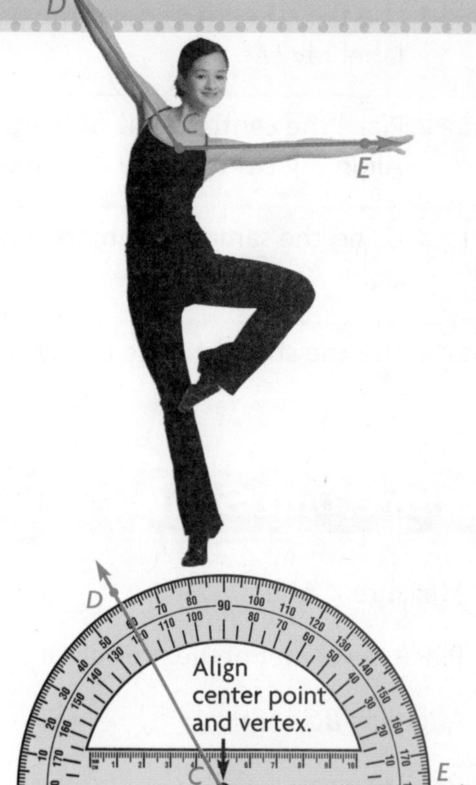

A **protractor** is a tool for measuring the size of an angle.

Activity Measure ∠*DCE* using a protractor.

Materials ■ protractor

STEP 1 Place the center point of the protractor on vertex *C* of the angle.

STEP 2 Align the 0° mark on the scale of the protractor with ray *CE*.

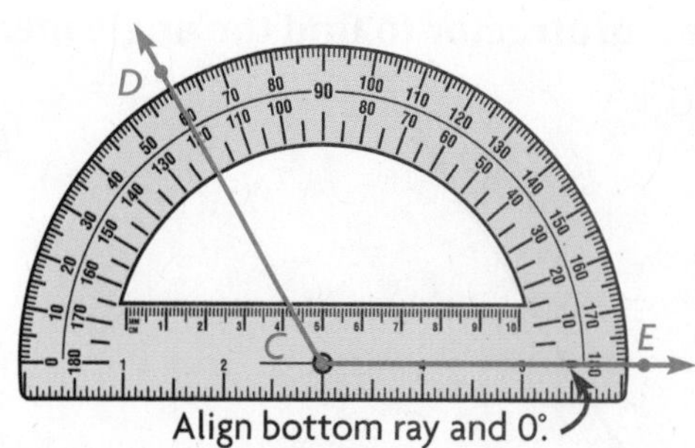

STEP 3 Find where ray *CD* intersects the same scale. Read the angle measure on that scale. Extend the ray if you need to.

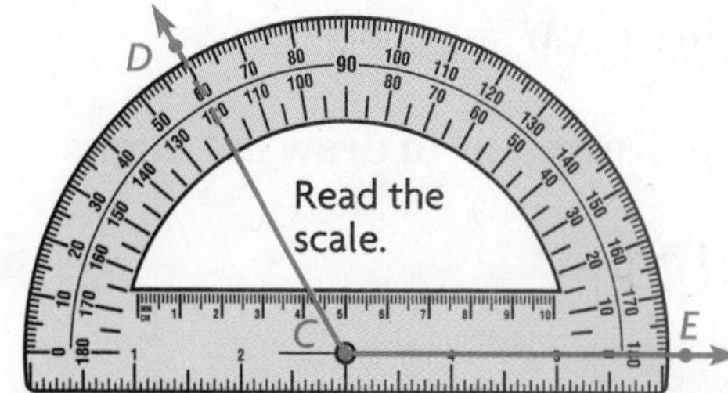

The m∠*DCE* = ______.

Read the m∠*DCE* as the "measure of angle *DCE*".

So, the angle formed by Emma's daughter's arms is ______.

Draw Angles You can also use a protractor to draw an angle of a given measure.

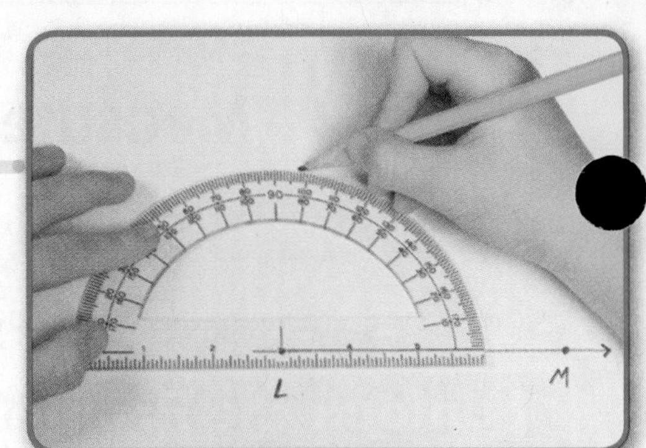

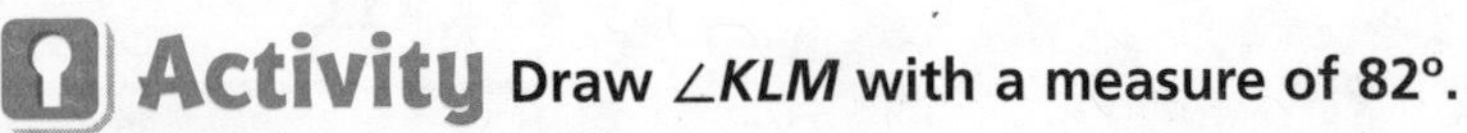

Activity Draw ∠*KLM* with a measure of 82°.

Materials ▪ protractor

STEP 1 Use the straight edge of the protractor to draw and label ray *LM*.

STEP 2 Place the center point of the protractor on point *L*. Align ray *LM* with the 0° mark on the protractor.

STEP 3 Using the same scale, mark a point at 82°. Label the point *K*.

STEP 4 Use the straight edge of the protractor to draw ray *LK*.

Share and Show

1. Measure ∠*ABC*.

   Place the center of the protractor on point ______.

   Align ray *BC* with ______.

   Read where ____________ intersects the same scale.

   So, the m∠*ABC* is ______.

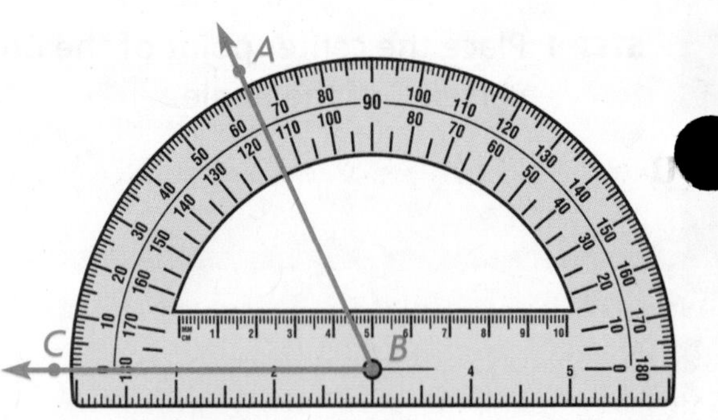

Use a protractor to find the angle measure.

2.

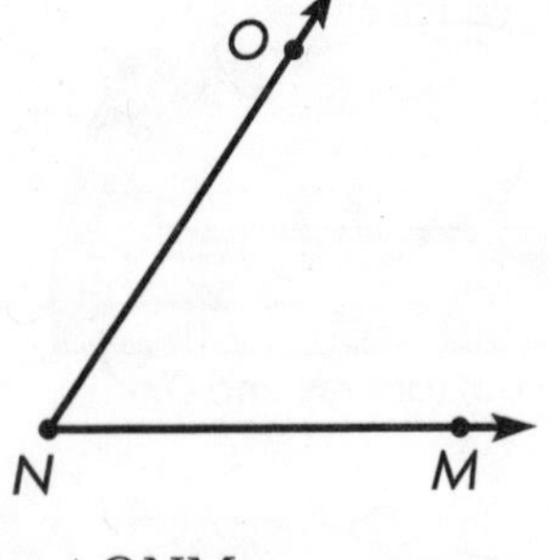

m∠*ONM* = ______

3.

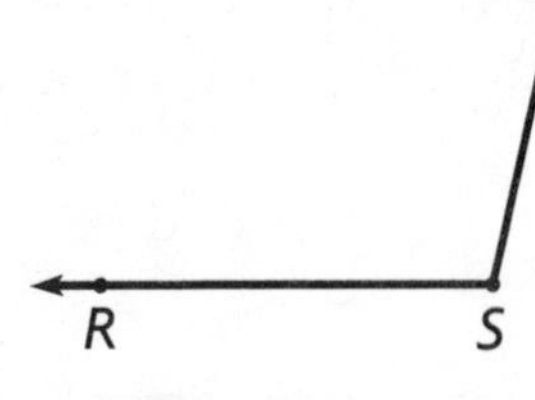

m∠*TSR* = ______

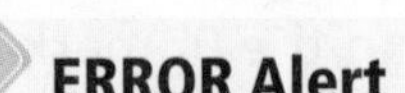

ERROR Alert

Be sure to use the correct scale on the protractor. Ask yourself: Is the measure reasonable?

Use a protractor to draw the angle.

4. 170°

5. 78°

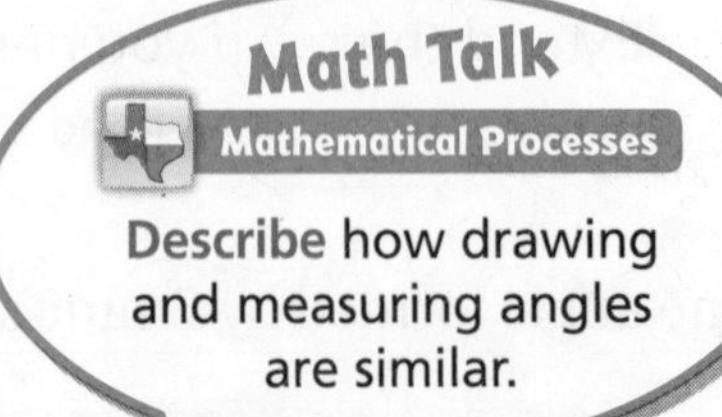

Name ______________________________

Problem Solving Real World

6. **Representations** Mrs. Murphy is building a wheelchair ramp outside her business. The angle of the ramp should be 5°. Draw a picture in the space to the right to show a model of the ramp.

7. H.O.T. Write Math ▶ Draw an angle with a measure of 0°. **Describe** your drawing.

____

____

____

8. H.O.T. **What's the Error?** Tracy measured an angle as 50° that was actually 130°. **Explain** her error.

____

____

Use the diagrams and a protractor for 9–11.

9. **Use Tools** In the Northern Hemisphere, Earth's axis is tilted away from the sun on the first day of winter, which is often on December 21. What is the measure of the marked angle on the first day of winter, the shortest day of the year?

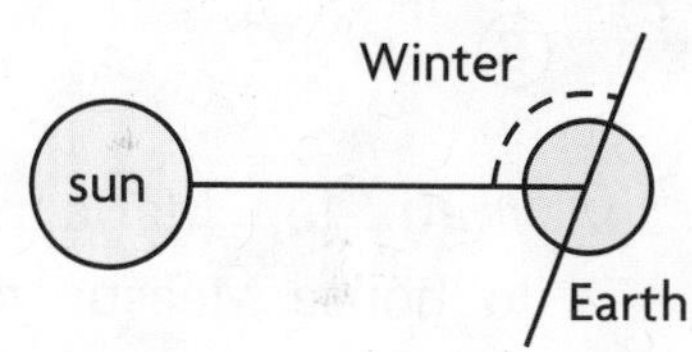

____

10. **Use Diagrams** Earth's axis is not tilted away from or toward the sun on the first days of spring and fall, which are often on March 20 and September 22. What is the measure of the marked angle on the first day of spring or fall?

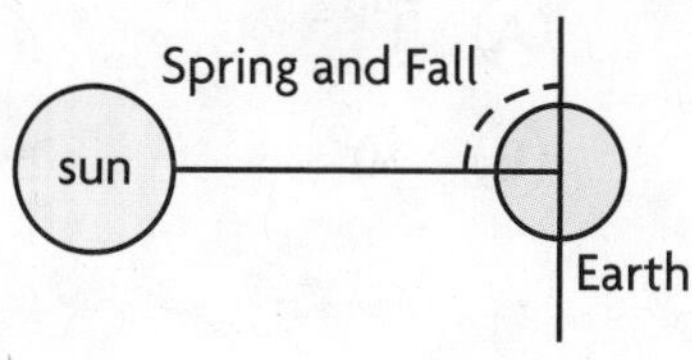

____

11. In the Northern Hemisphere, Earth's axis is tilted toward the sun on the first day of summer, which is often on June 21. What is the measure of the marked angle on the first day of summer, the longest day of the year?

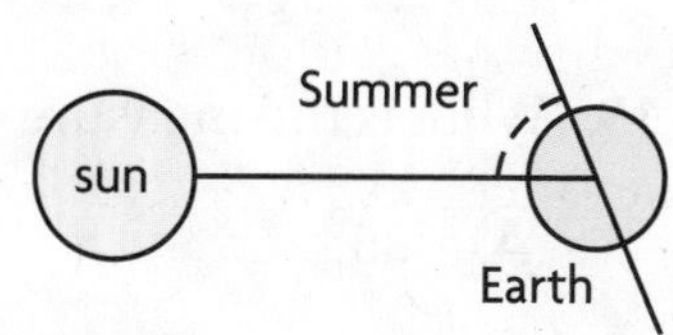

____

Mathematical Processes
Model • Reason • Communicate

Daily Assessment Task

Fill in the bubble completely to show your answer.

12. Kate tosses a stone in the water at a stone-skipping tournament. It forms a 20° angle with the water and skips many times. Which angle measures 20°?

Ⓐ
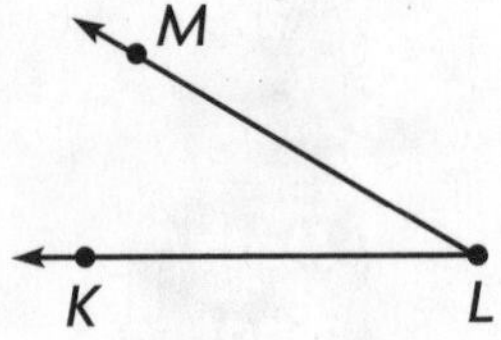

Ⓒ
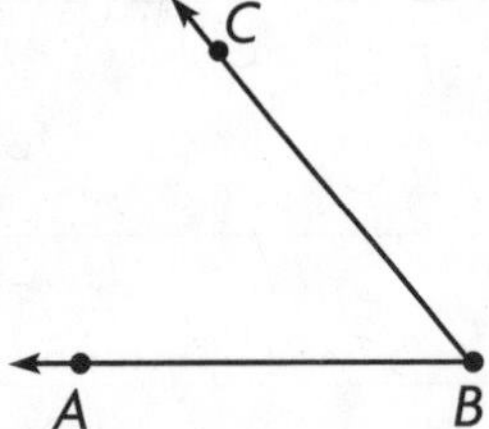

Ⓑ
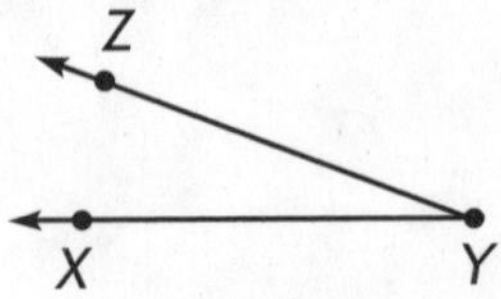

Ⓓ
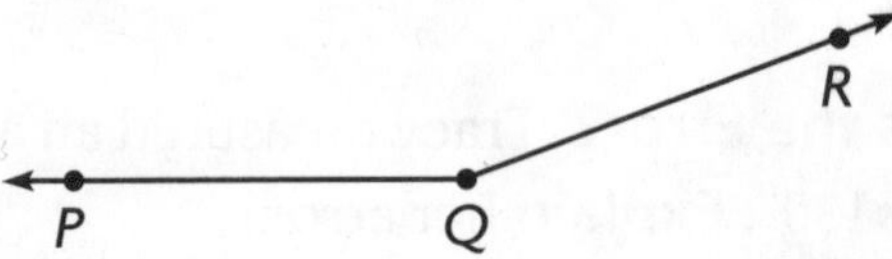

13. Kyle moves furniture up a ramp to get it on a truck. What is the measure of the angle formed by the ramp?

Ⓐ 150° Ⓒ 30°

Ⓑ 80° Ⓓ 60°

K J L

14. Multi-Step Maria builds two sets of stairs in her dollhouse. Measure the angles in the picture at the right. What is the difference between the measures of the angles formed by the stairs?

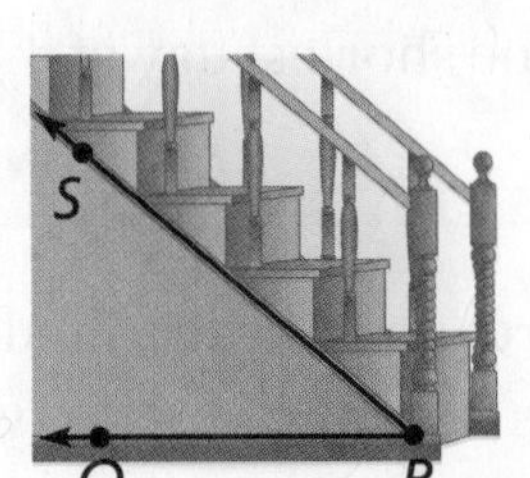

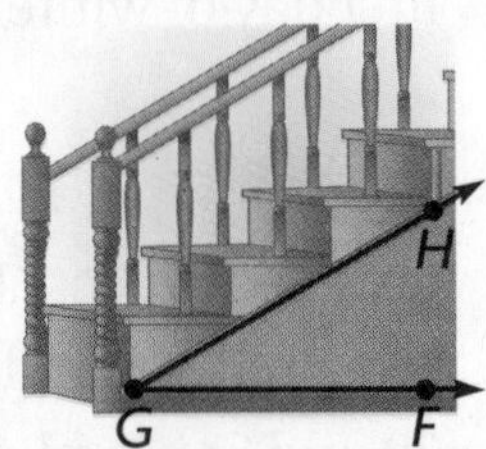

Ⓐ 1°  Ⓒ 40°

Ⓑ 30° Ⓓ 10°

TEXAS Test Prep

15. What is the measure of $\angle QRS$?

Ⓐ 35° Ⓒ 135°

Ⓑ 45° Ⓓ 155°

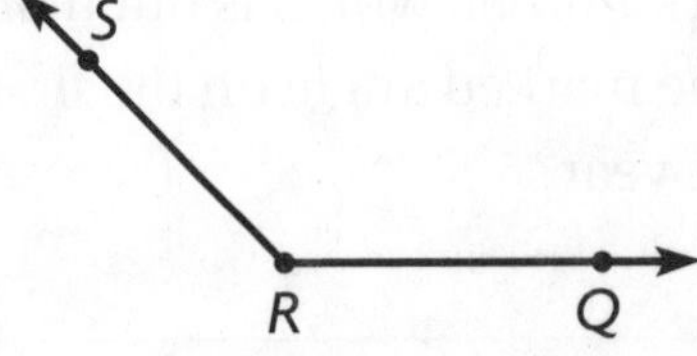

Name ______________________

14.3 Measure and Draw Angles

Use a protractor to find the angle measure.

1.

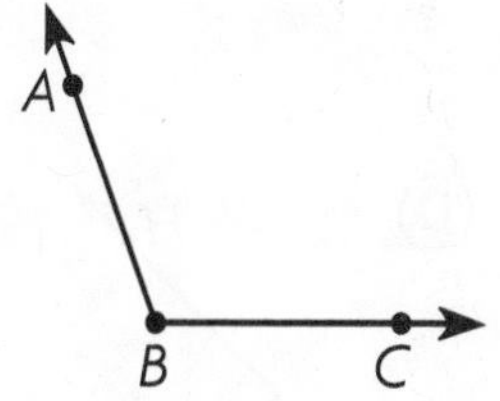

m ∠*ABC* = ______

2.

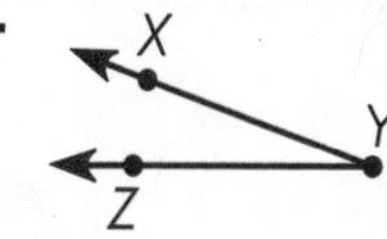

m ∠*XYZ* = ______

Use a protractor to draw the angle.

3. 125°

4. 86°

5. 35°

6. 180°

Problem Solving

7. George leaned a ladder against his house. The angle of the ladder to the ground measured 65°. Draw a picture to show a model of the angle.

8. Grayson built a skateboard ramp. The angle of the ramp is 14°. Draw a picture to show a model of the ramp.

Lesson Check

TEXAS Test Prep

Fill in the bubble completely to show your answer.

9. What is the measure of $\angle LMN$?

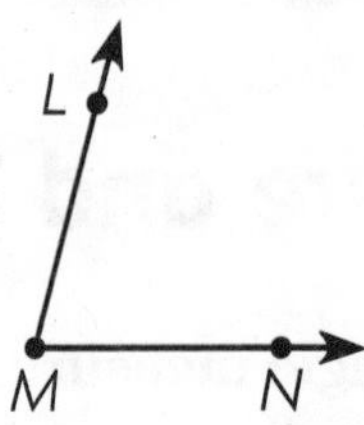

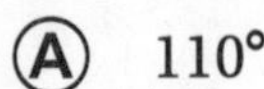
Ⓐ 110° Ⓒ 105°

Ⓑ 70° Ⓓ 75°

10. Whitney drew these angles. Which of the angles has a measure of 130°?

Ⓐ
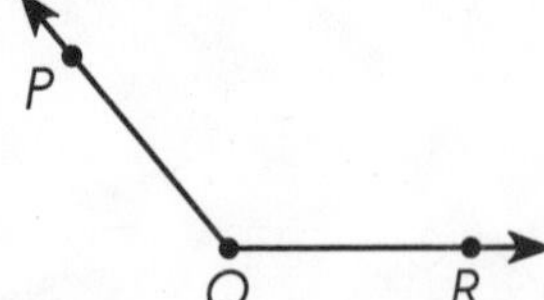

Ⓑ
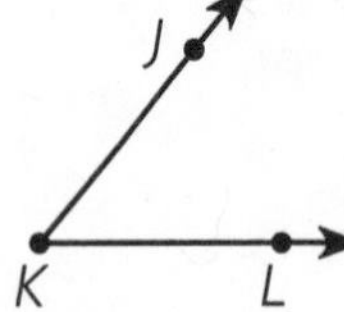

Ⓒ
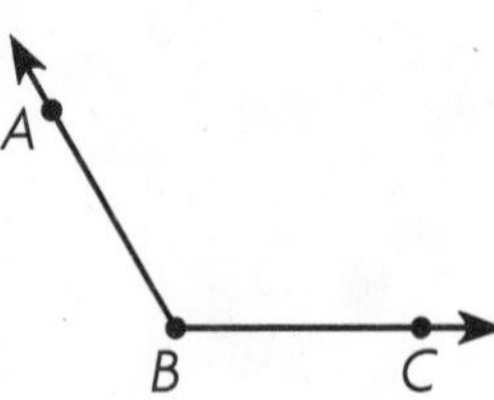

Ⓓ
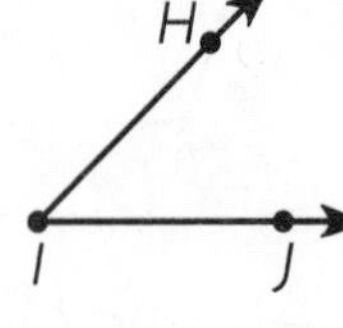

11. An artist is cutting glass triangles to make a star-shaped stained glass window. What is the measure of each of the angles formed at the tips of the star?

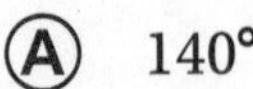
Ⓐ 140°

Ⓒ 40°

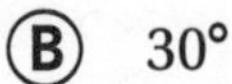
Ⓑ 30° Ⓓ 110°

12. Multi-Step Elizabeth is making a quilt with scraps of fabric. Measure the angles in the picture. What is the difference between the measures of the angles of each scrap of fabric?

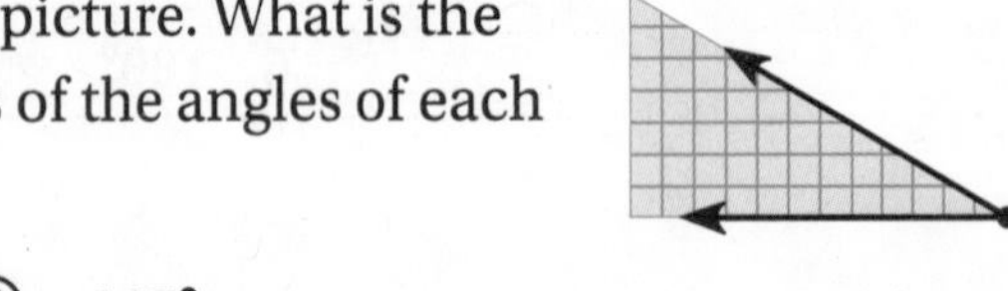

Ⓐ 25°
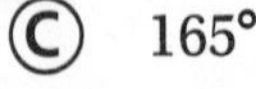
Ⓒ 165°

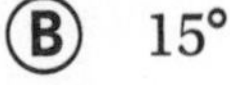
Ⓑ 15° Ⓓ 75°

13. Hector drew a map of his street corner. Use a protractor to find *x*, the measure of an angle formed where Jefferson Street intersects Washington Street.

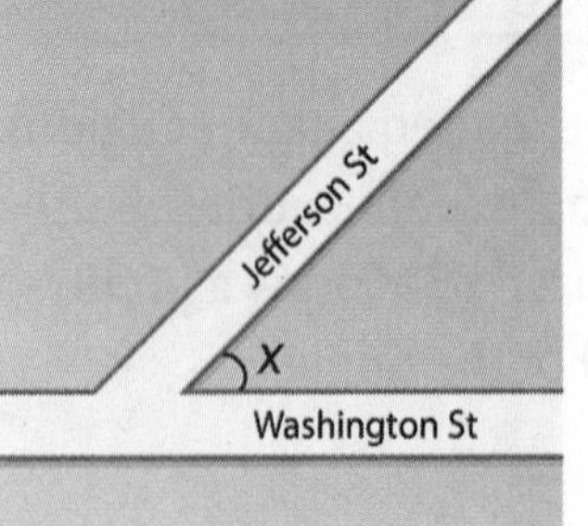

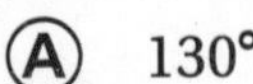
Ⓐ 130° Ⓒ 45°

Ⓑ 135° Ⓓ 62°

14. Multi-Step After eating at a restaurant, Faith had one quarter of her pizza left to take home. She took the pizza home and cut it into three equal slices. What is the angle measure of each of the slices of pizza?

Ⓐ 60° Ⓒ 90°

Ⓑ 40° Ⓓ 30°

Name ____________________

14.4 Join and Separate Angles

TEKS Geometry and Measurement—4.7.C, 4.7.E
MATHEMATICAL PROCESSES 4.1.B, 4.1.C, 4.1.F, 4.1.G

Essential Question

How can you determine the measure of an angle separated into parts?

Investigate

Materials ■ construction paper ■ scissors ■ protractor

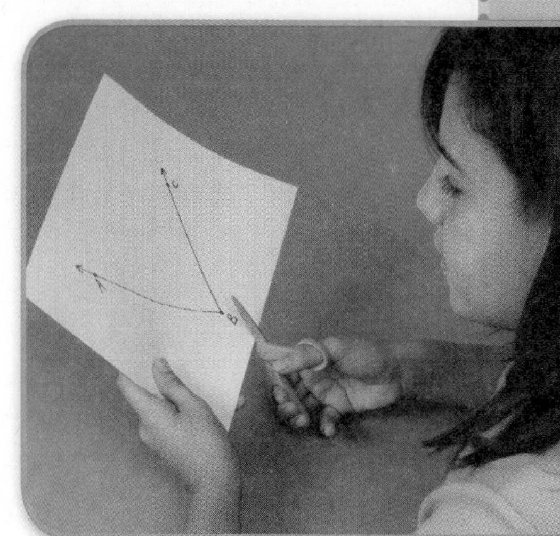

A. Use construction paper. Draw an angle that measures exactly 70°. Label it $\angle ABC$.

B. Cut out $\angle ABC$.

C. Form two new angles from $\angle ABC$ by cutting it into two parts. Begin cutting at the vertex and cut between the rays.

What figures did you form? ____________

D. Use a protractor to measure the two angles you formed.

Record the measures. ____________

E. Find the sum of the angles you formed.

______ + ______ = ______

part + part = whole

F. Join the two angles. Compare the $m\angle ABC$ to the sum of the measures of its parts. **Explain** how they compare.

Math Idea

You can think of $\angle ABC$ as the whole and the two angles you formed as the parts of the whole.

____

____

____

____

Make Connections

Materials ■ protractor

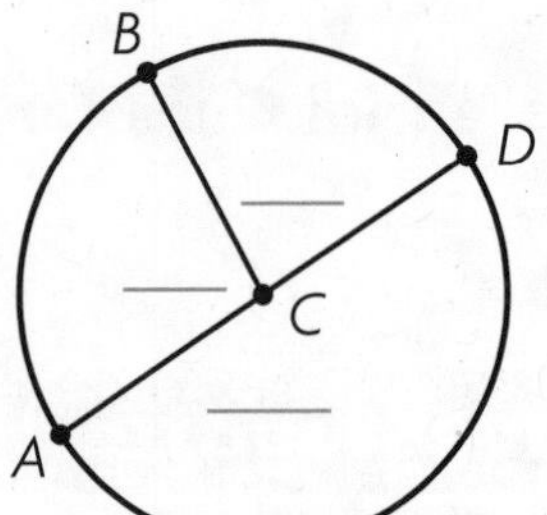

You can write the measure of the angles shown in a circle as a sum.

STEP 1 Use a protractor to find the measure of each angle.

STEP 2 Label each angle with its measure.

STEP 3 Write the sum of the angle measures as an equation.

_____ + _____ + _____ = _____

part + part + part = whole

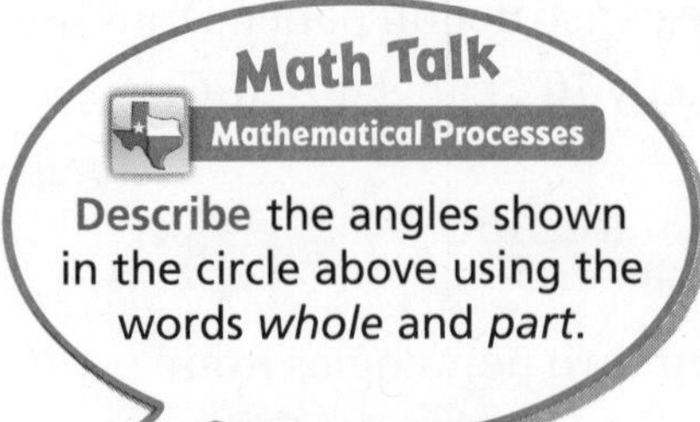

Share and Show

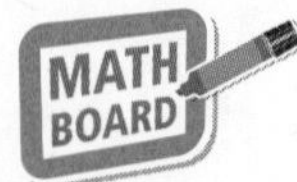

Add to find the measure of the angle. Write an equation to record your work.

1.

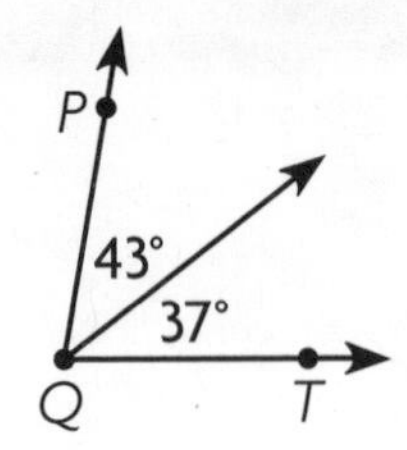

____

$m\angle PQT =$ _____

2.

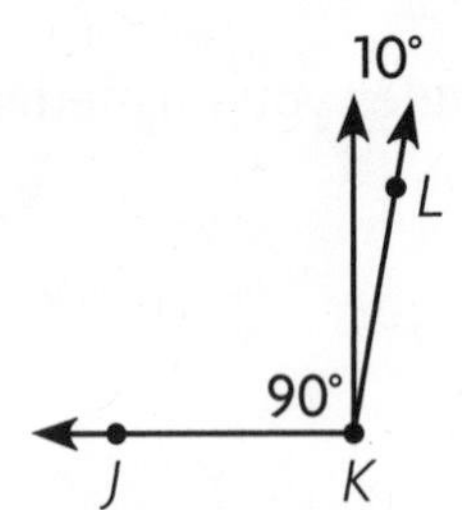

____

$m\angle JKL =$ _____

3.

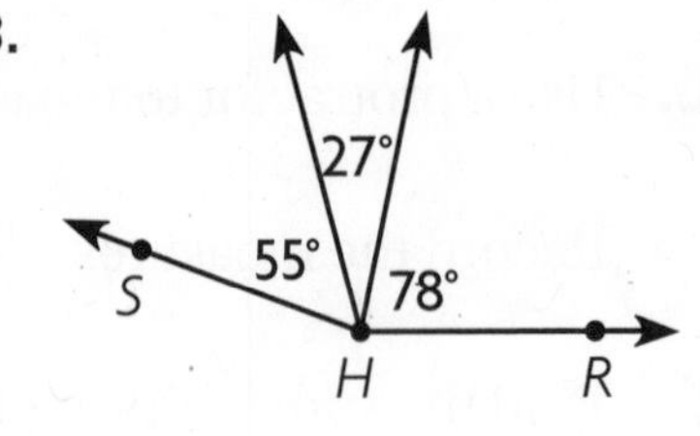

____

$m\angle RHS =$ _____

Use a protractor to find the measure of each angle. Label each angle with its measure. Write the sum of the angle measures as an equation.

4.

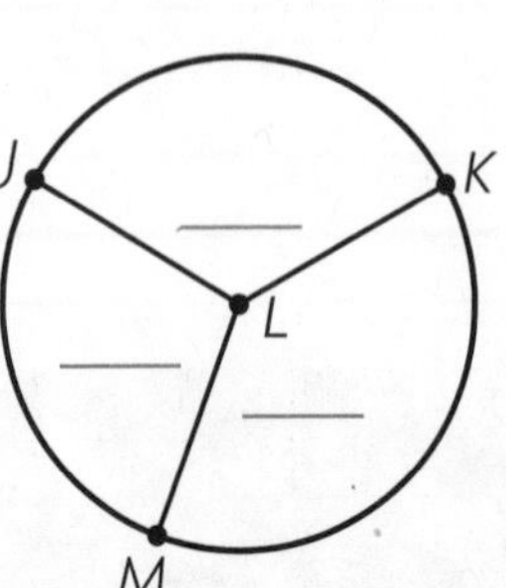

____

5.

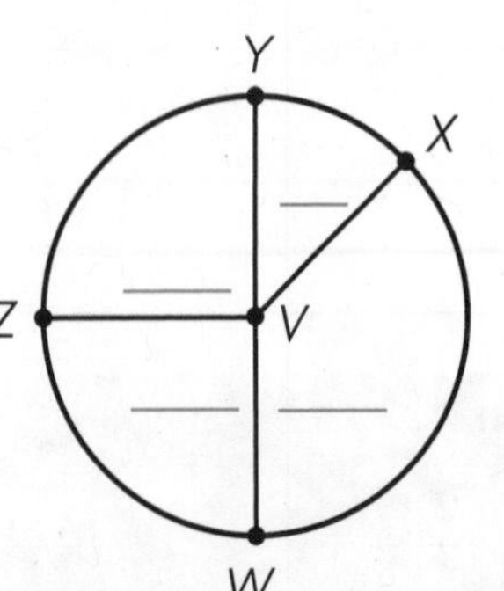

____

Name ____________________________

Unlock the Problem

6. H.O.T. **Multi-Step** Stephanie, Kay, and Shane each ate an equal-sized piece of a pizza. The measure of the angle of each piece was 45°. When the pieces were together, what is the measure of the angle they formed?

Ⓐ 90° Ⓑ 135° Ⓒ 180° Ⓓ 225°

a. What are you asked to find? ____________________________

____

b. What information do you need to use? ____________________________

____

____

c. **Justify** Tell how you can use addition to solve the problem. ____________________________

____

____

____

d. Fill in the bubble for the correct answer choice above.

7. H.O.T. **Multi-Step Reasoning** $\angle DRQ$ is a straight angle. The m$\angle DRB$ is twice the m$\angle QRT$. What is the m$\angle DRB$?

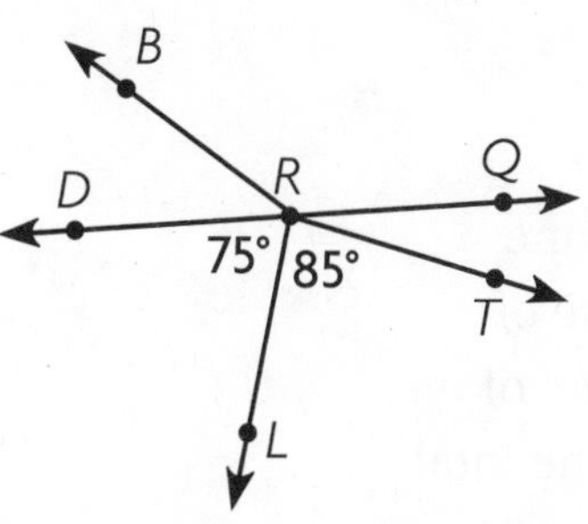

Ⓐ 40° Ⓒ 160°

Ⓑ 150° Ⓓ 220°

8. Which equation can you use to find the m$\angle XZW$?

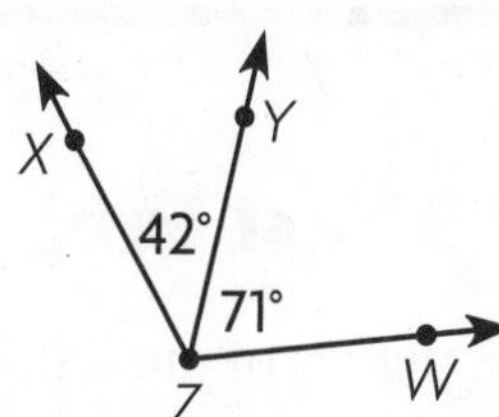

Ⓐ $71° - 42° = ■$

Ⓑ $71° + 42° = ■$

Ⓒ $71° \times 42° = ■$

Ⓓ $180° - 113° = ■$

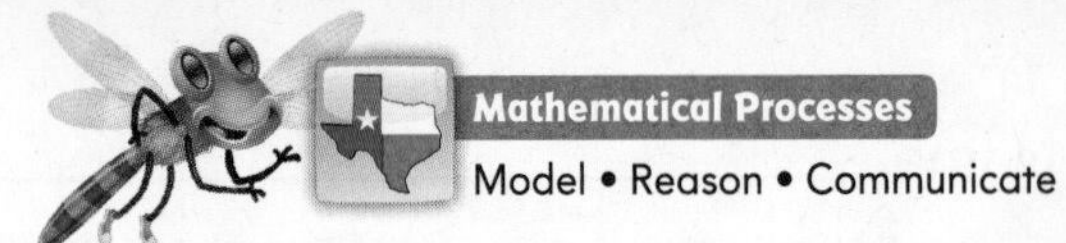

Daily Assessment Task

Fill in the bubble completely to show your answer.

9. **Use Diagrams** A sea turtle walks along a path that forms $\angle ABC$. What is the measure of the angle formed by the path the turtle walked?

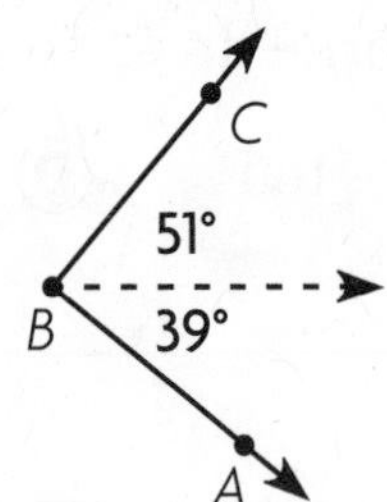

Ⓐ 51°

Ⓑ 12°

Ⓒ 90°

Ⓓ 89°

10. **Use Diagrams** What is the $m\angle DEF$?

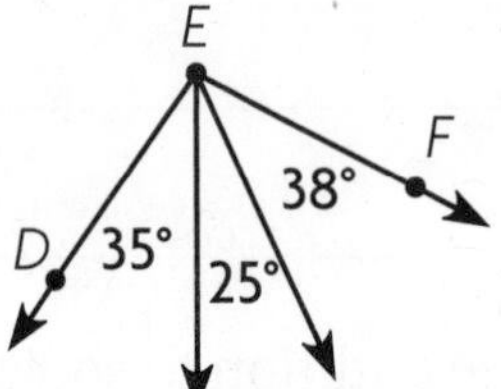

Ⓐ 90°

Ⓑ 73°

Ⓒ 105°

Ⓓ 98°

11. **Multi-Step** Mike used a protractor to find the measure of each angle in the circle below. What is the $m\angle JLK$?

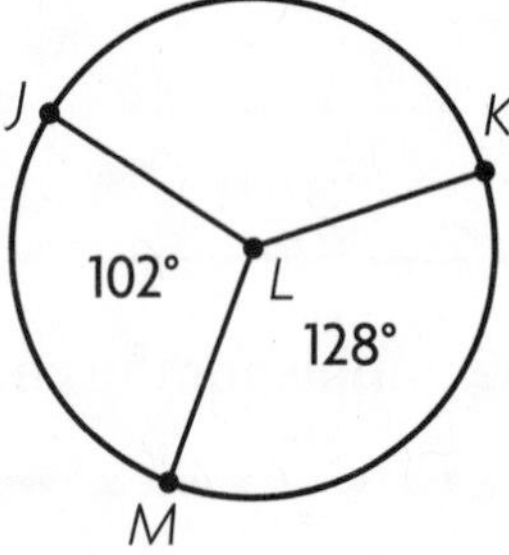

Ⓐ 360°

Ⓑ 130°

Ⓒ 230°

Ⓓ 120°

TEXAS Test Prep

12. Larry has 3 pieces of pie left. The measure of the angle of one piece is 35°. The second piece has an angle with a measure of 25°. The third piece has an angle with a measure that is half of the combined measures of the other two pieces. What is the total measure of the angle formed by all three pieces?

Ⓐ 60°

Ⓑ 90°

Ⓒ 120°

Ⓓ 180°

Name ____________________

14.4 Join and Separate Angles

Add to find the measure of the angle. Write an equation to record your work.

1. 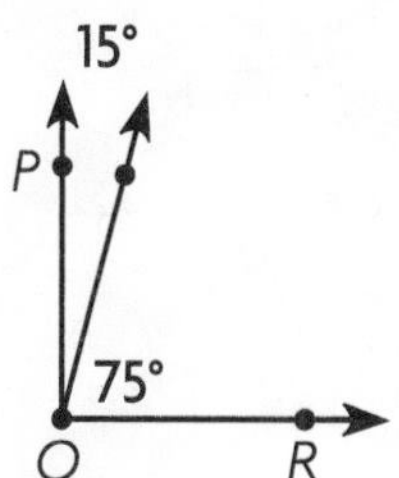

____

m ∠PQR = ____________

2. 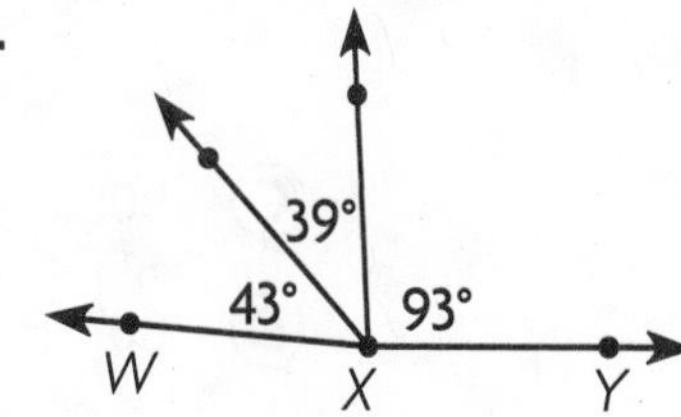

____

m ∠WXY = ____________

Use a protractor to find the measure of each angle. Label each angle with its measure. Write the sum of the angle measures as an equation.

3. 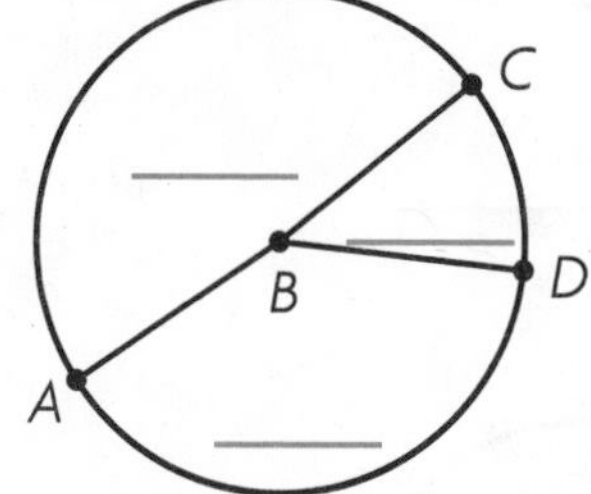

____

4. 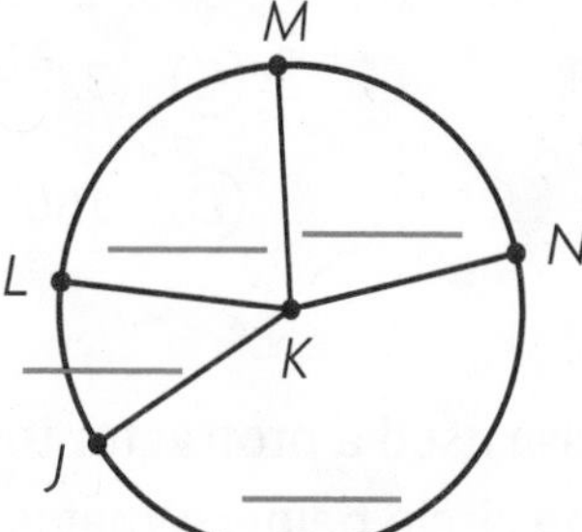

____

Problem Solving

5. Kenny drew and cut out an angle that measured 85°. Beginning at the vertex, he cut the angle into two angles. One of new angles measures 20°. What is the measure of the other new angle?

____

6. Liam and Marcy each have slices of pizza. The measure of the angle of Liam's slice is 40°. The measure of the angle of Marcy's slice is 35°. When the pieces are together, what is the measure of the angle they form?

____

Lesson Check

TEXAS Test Prep

Fill in the bubble completely to show your answer.

7. Which equation can you use to find the m $\angle DEG$?

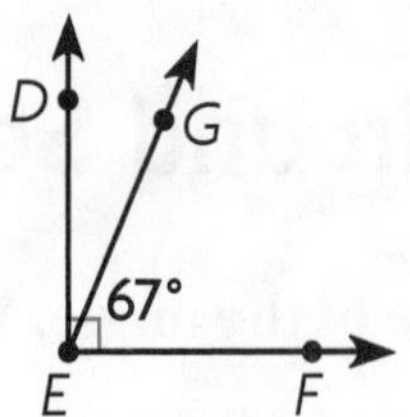

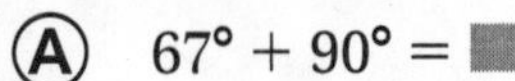

Ⓐ $67° + 90° = ■$ Ⓒ $180° - 90° = ■$

Ⓑ $67° \times 2 = ■$ Ⓓ $90° - 67° = ■$

8. What is the m $\angle KJN$?

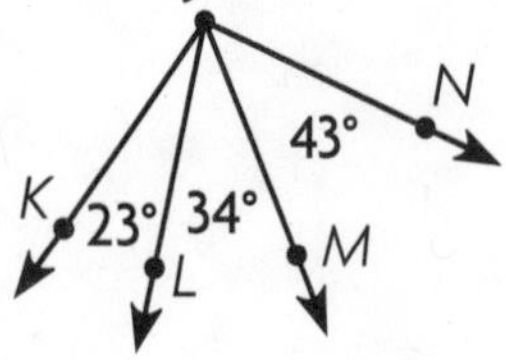

Ⓐ 100° Ⓒ 90°

Ⓑ 77° Ⓓ 80°

9. Hannah cut a pie into three equal parts. What is the measure of the angle of each of the parts of the pie?

Ⓐ 30°

Ⓑ 90°

Ⓒ 100°

Ⓓ 120°

10. Which equation can you use to find the m $\angle PQR$?

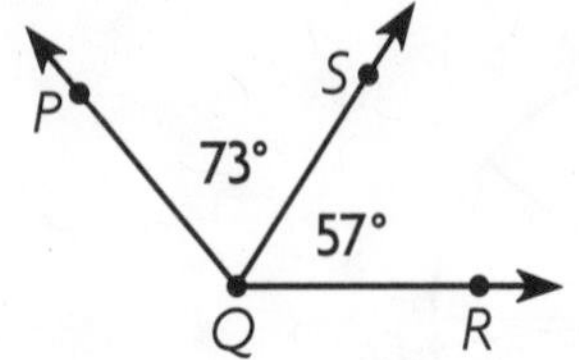

Ⓐ $73° - 57° = ■$ Ⓒ $73° + 57° = ■$

Ⓑ $130° + 90° = ■$ Ⓓ $180° - 130° = ■$

11. Multi-Step Melissa used a protractor to find the measure of each angle in the circle below. What is the m $\angle WZY$?

Ⓐ 218°

Ⓑ 142°

Ⓒ 120°

Ⓓ 238°

12. Multi-Step Angle BAE is a straight angle. The m $\angle FAE$ is half the m $\angle BAC$. What is the m $\angle FAE$?

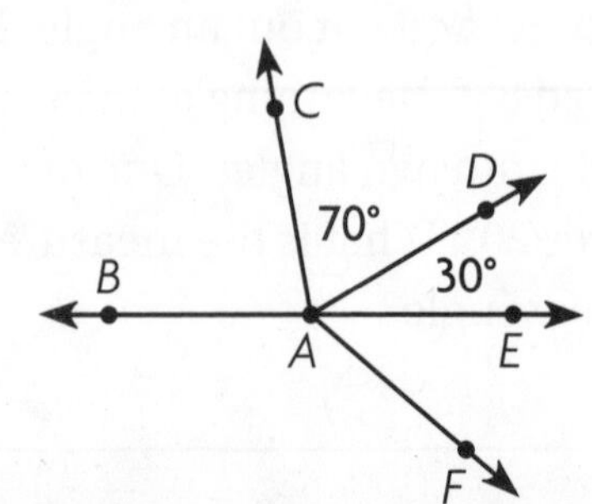

Ⓐ 40° Ⓒ 100°

Ⓑ 80° Ⓓ 30°

Name ____________________

PROBLEM SOLVING • Unknown Angle Measures

TEKS Geometry and Measurement—4.7.E

MATHEMATICAL PROCESSES 4.1.A, 4.1.B, 4.1.E

Essential Question

How can you use the strategy *draw a diagram* to solve angle measurement problems?

Unlock the Problem

Mr. Tran is cutting a piece of kitchen tile as shown at the right. He needs tiles with 45° angles to make a design. After the cut, what is the angle measure of the part left over? Can Mr. Tran use both pieces in the design?

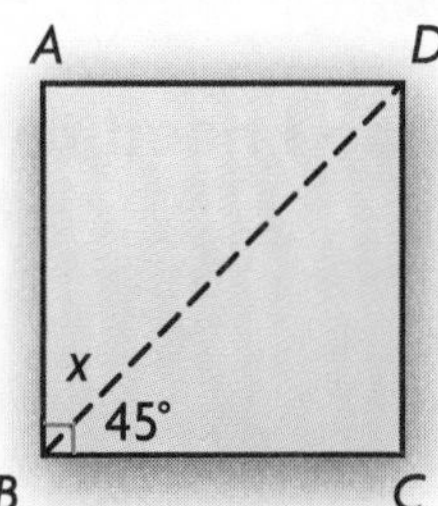

Use the graphic organizer below to solve the problem.

Read

What do I need to find?

I need to find

____

____

What information am I given?

I can use the measures of the angles I know.

____

____

Plan

What is my plan or strategy?

I can draw a strip diagram and use the information to

____

____

Solve

I can draw a strip diagram to represent the problem. Then I can write an equation to solve the problem.

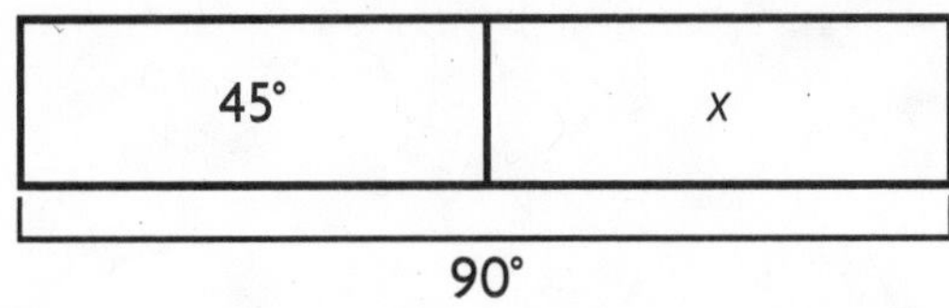

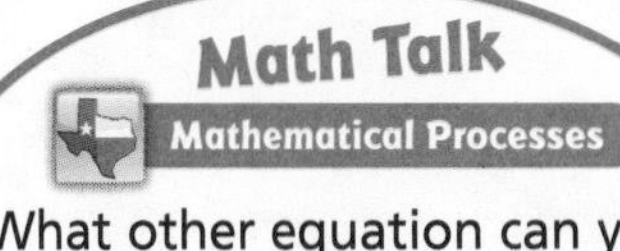

What other equation can you write to solve the problem? Explain.

$m\angle ABD + m\angle CBD = m\angle ABC$

$x +$ ______ $=$ ______

$x =$ ______

The $m\angle ABD =$ ______.

Since both tiles measure ______, Mr. Tran can use both pieces in the design.

Try Another Problem

Marisol is building a frame for a sandbox, but the boards she has are too short. She must join two boards together to build a side as shown. At what angle did she cut the first board?

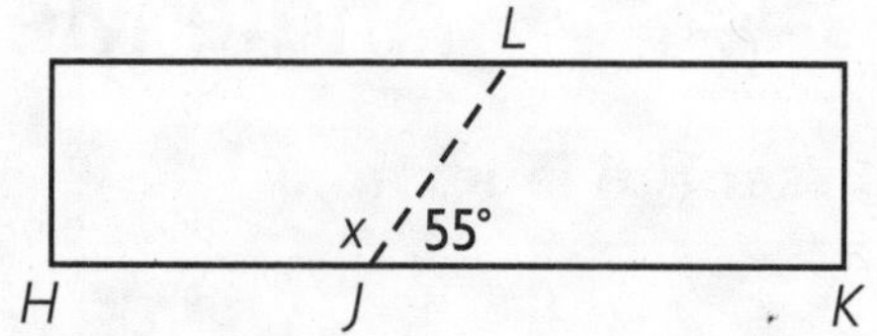

Read		Plan
What do I need to find?	**What information am I given?**	**What is my plan or strategy?**

Solve

- **Explain** how you can check the answer to the problem.

Name ________________________________

Share and Show

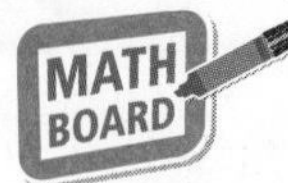

1. Laura cuts a square out of scrap paper as shown. What is the angle measure of the piece left over?

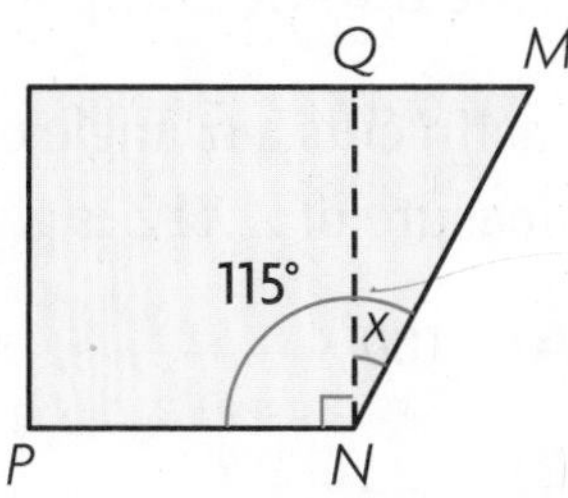

First, draw a strip diagram to represent the problem.

Next, write the equation you need to solve.

____

____

Last, find the angle measure of the piece left over.

The m$\angle MNQ$ = ______.

So, the angle measure of the piece left over is ______.

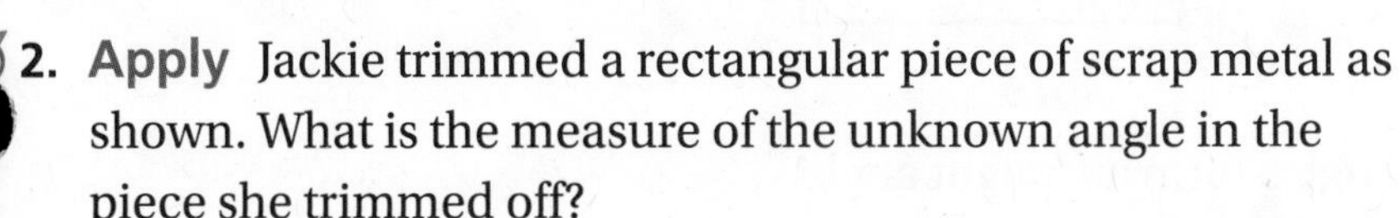

2. **Apply** Jackie trimmed a rectangular piece of scrap metal as shown. What is the measure of the unknown angle in the piece she trimmed off?

____

Problem Solving Real World

3. H.O.T. **What if** in Exercise 1, Laura cut a smaller square as shown? Would the m$\angle MNQ$ be different? **Explain.**

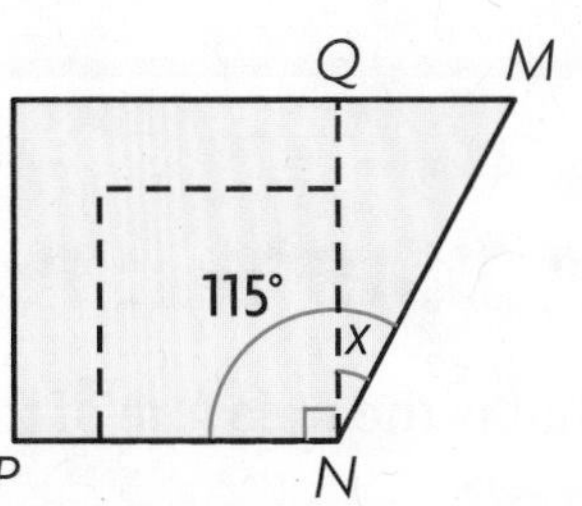

____

____

____

4. H.O.T. **Multi-Step** The map shows Marco's paper route. Marco turns right onto Center Street from Main Street. What is x, the measure of the angle formed by Main Street and Center Street?

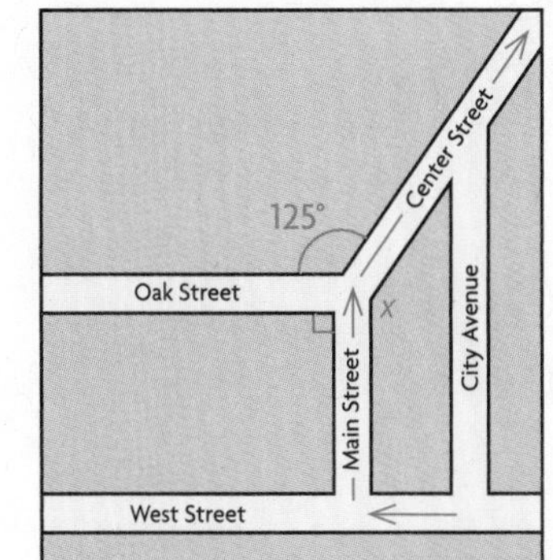

____

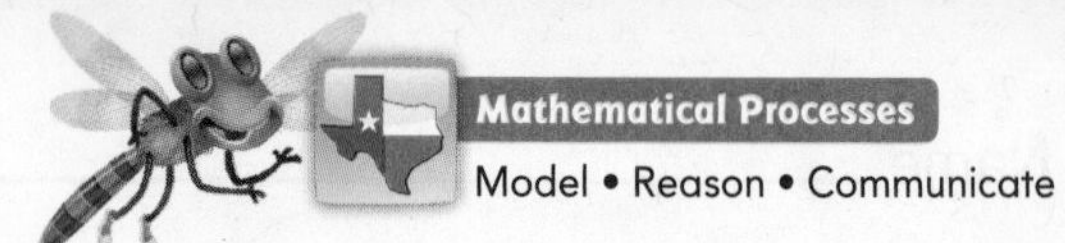

Daily Assessment Task

Fill in the bubble completely to show your answer.

5. Austin cuts a triangle out of some scrap wood as shown. The angle measure of $\angle XYZ$ is given. What is the angle measure of $\angle XYW$?

Ⓐ 180°

Ⓑ 125°

Ⓒ 45°

Ⓓ 135°

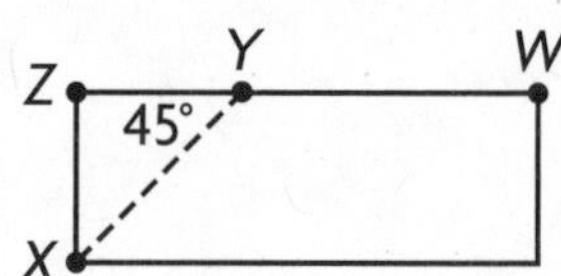

6. Shamika wants to cut a rectangle out of the piece of fabric shown. What is x, the angle measure of the piece of fabric that is left over?

Ⓐ 90°

Ⓑ 22°

Ⓒ 112°

Ⓓ 68°

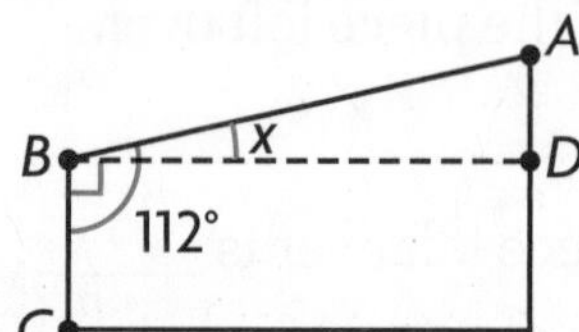

7. **Multi-Step Evaluate** Three angles form a straight angle. One angle measures 90°. Another angle measures 26°. What is the measure of the third angle?

Ⓐ 90°

Ⓑ 26°

Ⓒ 64°

Ⓓ 154°

TEXAS Test Prep

8. What is the measure of the unknown angle in the figure?

Ⓐ 22°

Ⓑ 68°

Ⓒ 90°

Ⓓ 158°

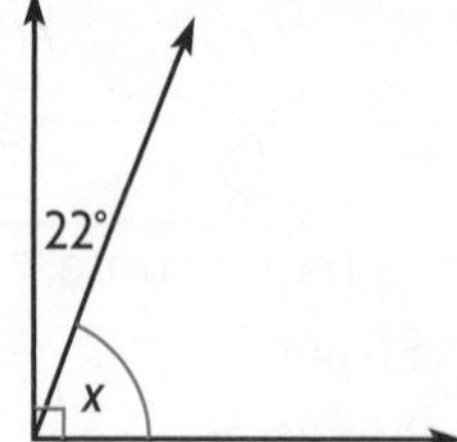

Homework and Practice

TEKS Geometry and Measurement—4.7.E
MATHEMATICAL PROCESSES 4.1.A, 4.1.B, 4.1.E

Name ______________________

14.5 PROBLEM SOLVING • Unknown Angle Measures

Choose a method. Then find the product.

1. Anna cut a square from a scrap to make a patch. What is the angle measure of the piece left over?

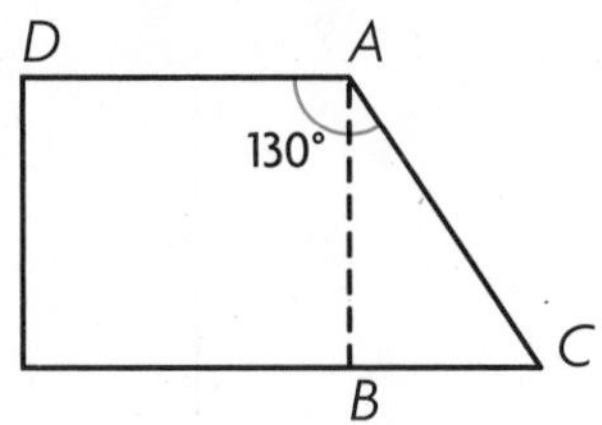

m ∠BAC = ______________

2. Pablo cut a tile at the angle shown. At what angle is the first piece cut?

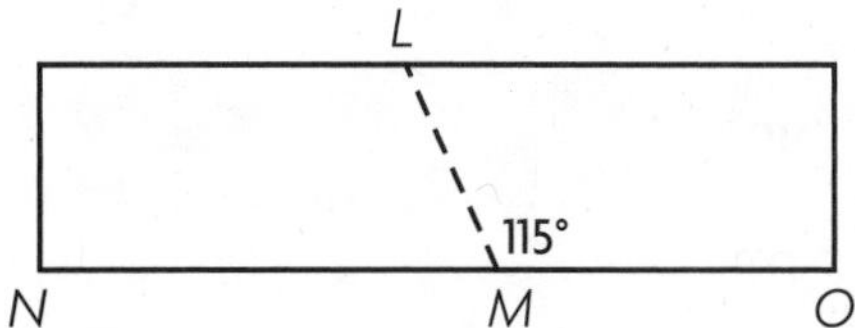

m ∠LMN = ______________

3. Cassie is cutting letters from rectangular sheets of paper. What is x, the measure of the angle of the piece she trimmed off?

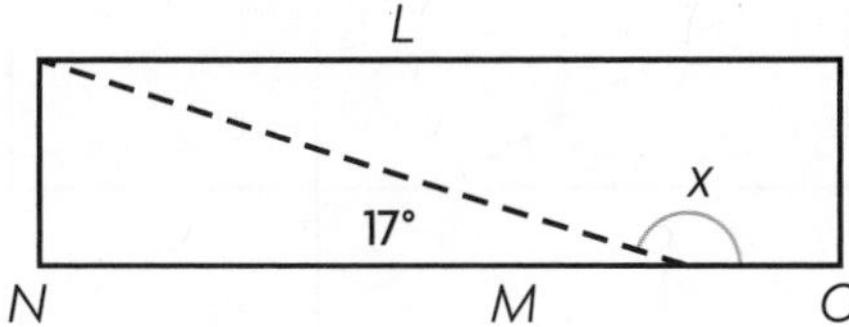

____

4. Walt combined two pieces of tile to fit a corner in his room. What is the measure of ∠ECD?

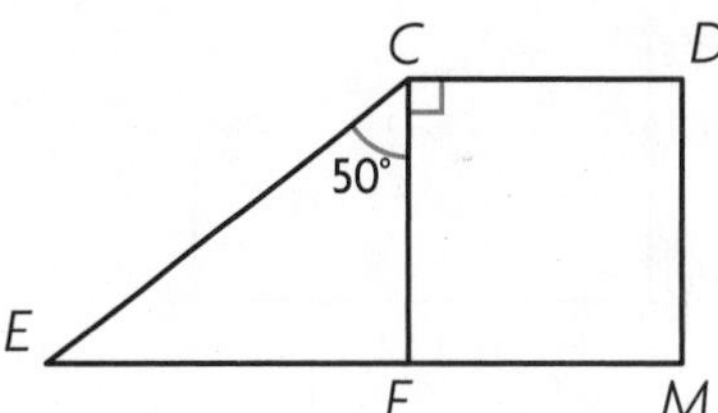

m ∠ECD = ______________

Problem Solving Real World

5. Jaycee cut a square of fabric from a scrap. What is the angle measure of ∠MKJ?

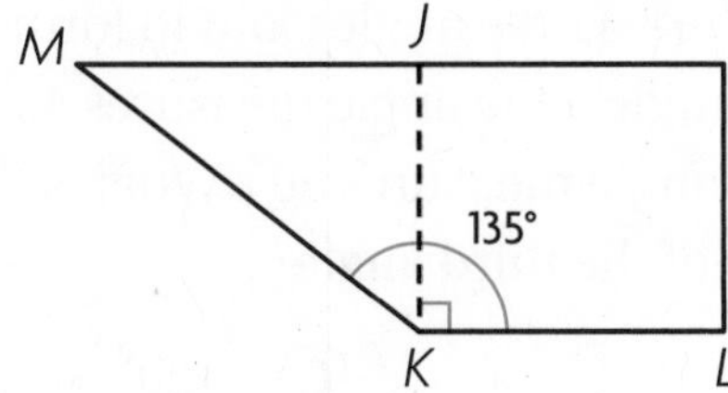

____

6. Mark cut a rectangular piece of wood at the angle shown. What is the measure of ∠SQP in the first piece cut?

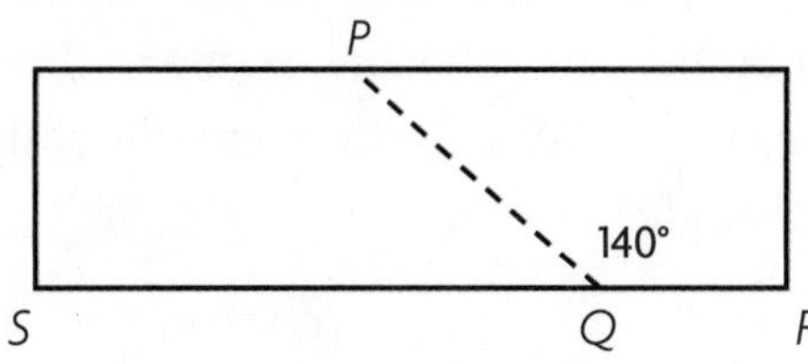

____

Lesson Check

TEXAS Test Prep

Fill in the bubble completely to show your answer.

7. What is the measure of the unknown angle *ABD*? Angle *ABC* is a right angle.

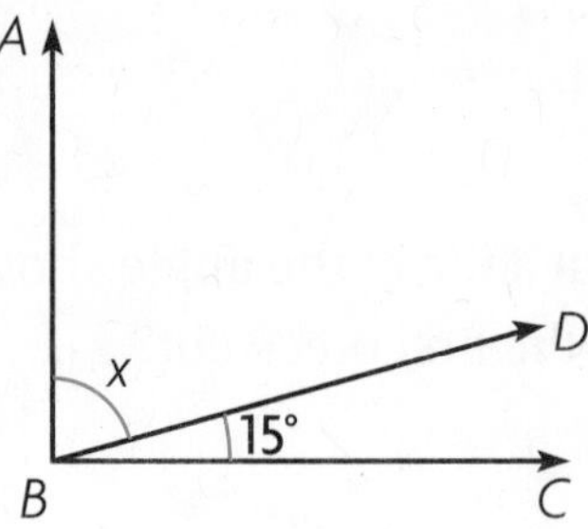

Ⓐ 80°

Ⓑ 105°

Ⓒ 165°

Ⓓ 75°

8. Carol cut a triangle out of a rectangular tile to make a mosaic.

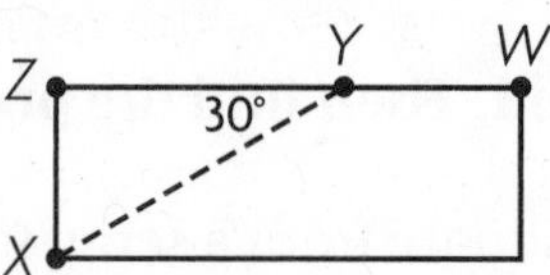

What is the measure of angle *XYW* in the piece leftover?

Ⓐ 180°

Ⓑ 45°

Ⓒ 150°

Ⓓ 60°

9. Jason wants to add a fence to his yard to make it the shape of a rectangle.

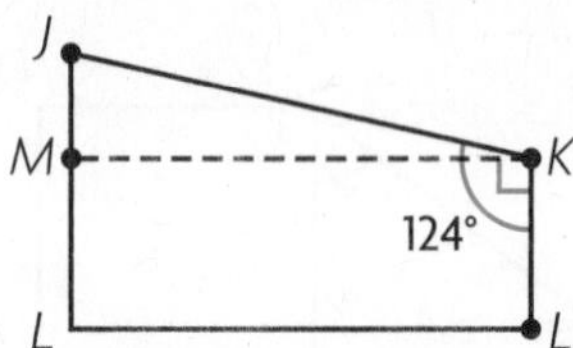

What is the measure of angle *MKJ* in the portion of the yard not inside the fence?

Ⓐ 34°

Ⓑ 146°

Ⓒ 56°

Ⓓ 90°

10. What is the measure of the unknown angle in the figure?

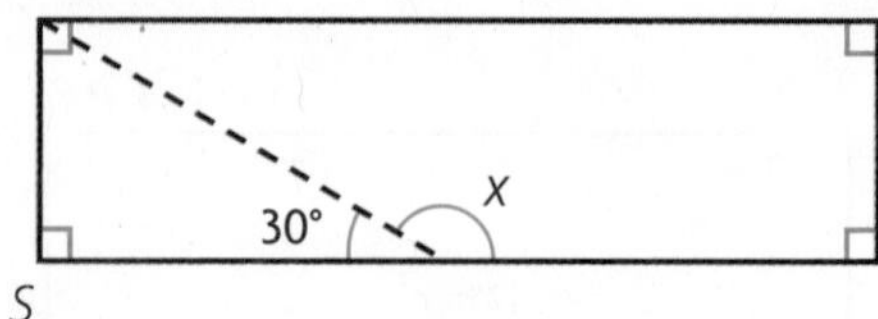

Ⓐ 90°

Ⓑ 150°

Ⓒ 60°

Ⓓ 180°

11. **Multi-Step** Two angles join to form a right angle. The measure of one of the angles is 64°. What is the measure of the other angle?

Ⓐ 116° Ⓒ 90°

Ⓑ 26° Ⓓ 36°

12. **Multi-Step** Three angles join to form a straight angle. One angle measures 45°. Another angle measures 50°. What is the measure of the third angle?

Ⓐ 85° Ⓒ 130°

Ⓑ 95° Ⓓ 100°

Name ________________________________

Module 14 Assessment

Vocabulary

Choose the best term from the box.

Vocabulary
clockwise
counterclockwise
degree (°)
protractor

1. The unit used to measure an angle is called

   a ______________. (p. 493)

2. ______________________ is the opposite of the direction in which the hands of a clock move. (p. 487)

3. A __________________ is a tool for measuring the size of an angle. (p. 499)

Concepts and Skills

Look at the shaded part of the circle. Tell what fraction of the circle the angle cuts out. TEKS 4.7.A

4. 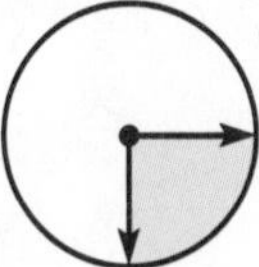

   ____

5. 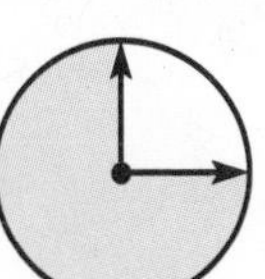

   ____

6. 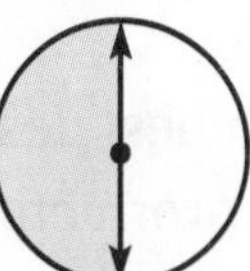

   ____

Tell the measure of the angle in degrees. TEKS 4.7.A, 4.7.B

7. 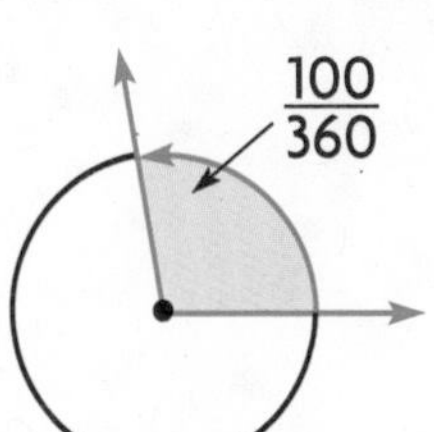

   ____

8. 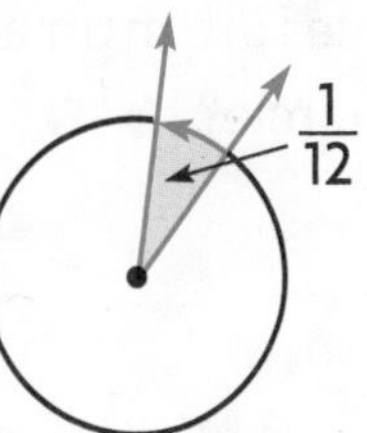

   ____

Use a protractor to draw the angle. TEKS 4.7.D

9. 75°

10. 127°

Fill in the bubble completely to show your answer.

11. What is the measure of the unknown angle in the figure? TEKS 4.7.E

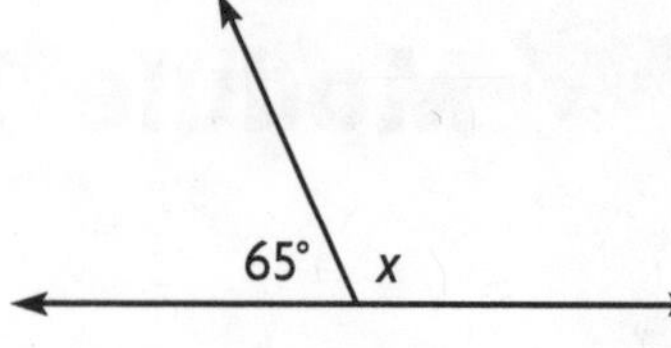

Ⓐ 25°

Ⓑ 115°

Ⓒ 125°

Ⓓ 180°

12. Which equation can you use to find the m∠*WRT*? TEKS 4.7.E

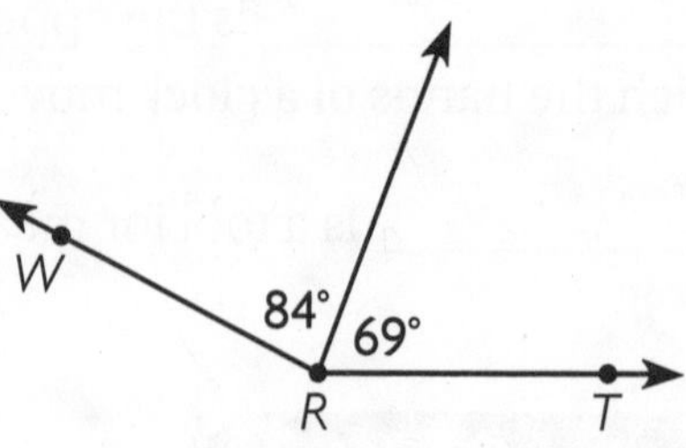

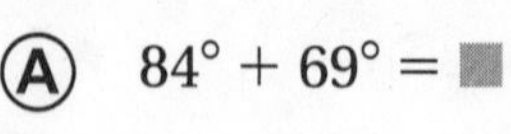
Ⓐ 84° + 69° = ■

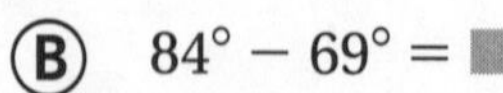
Ⓑ 84° − 69° = ■

Ⓒ 84° × 69° = ■

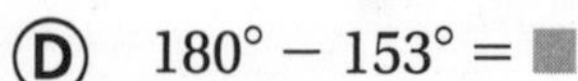
Ⓓ 180° − 153° = ■

13. Which best describes the m∠*CBT*? Use a protractor to help you. TEKS 4.7.C

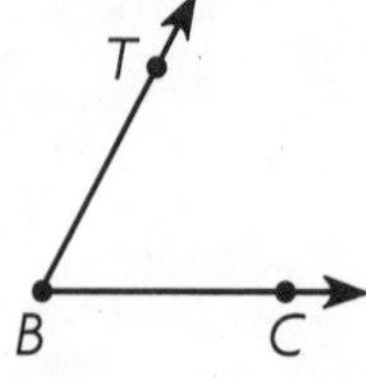

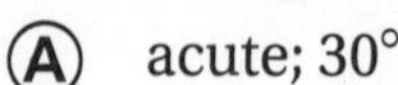
Ⓐ acute; 30°

Ⓑ acute; 60°

Ⓒ obtuse; 118°

Ⓓ obtuse; 80°

14. How many degrees are in an angle that cuts $\frac{1}{360}$ out of a circle? TEKS 4.7.A, 4.7.B

Ⓐ 0°

Ⓑ 90°

Ⓒ 1°

Ⓓ 45°

Name ______________________________

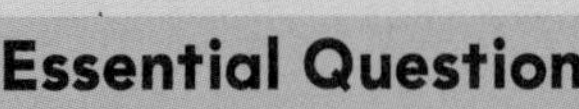

15.1 Measurement Benchmarks

Essential Question How can you use benchmarks to understand the relative sizes of measurement units?

Unlock the Problem

Jake says the length of his bike is about four yards. Use the benchmark units below to determine if Jake's statement is reasonable.

Customary Units of Length			
1 in. about 1 inch	 1 ft about 1 foot	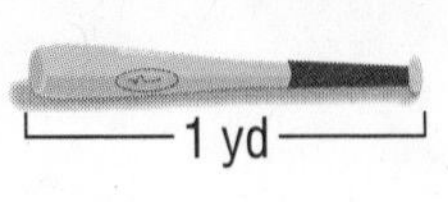 1 yd about 1 yard	 1 mile in about 20 minutes

A **mile** is a customary unit for measuring length or distance. The benchmark shows the distance you can walk in about 20 minutes.

A baseball bat is about one yard long. Since Jake's bike is shorter than four times the length of a baseball bat, his bike is shorter than four yards long.

So, Jake's statement ______ reasonable.

Jake's bike is about ______ baseball bats long.

Example 1 Use the benchmark customary units.

Customary Units of Liquid Volume				
 1 cup = 8 fluid ounces	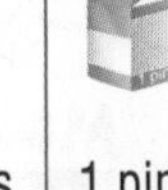 1 pint	 1 quart	 1 half gallon	 1 gallon

- About how much liquid is in a mug of hot chocolate? ____________________

Customary Units of Weight		
 about 1 ounce	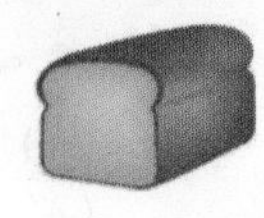 about 1 pound	 about 1 ton

- About how much does a grapefruit weigh? ____________________

Order the units of weight from heaviest to lightest. Use benchmarks to **explain** your answer.

Benchmarks for Metric Units The metric system is based on place value. Each unit is 10 times as large as the next smaller unit. Below are some common metric benchmarks.

Example 2 Use the benchmark metric units.

Metric Units of Length				
about 1 millimeter	about 1 centimeter	about 1 decimeter	about 1 meter	1 kilometer in about 10 minutes

A **kilometer** is a metric unit for measuring length or distance. The benchmark shows the distance you can walk in about 10 minutes.

- Is the length of your classroom greater than or less than one kilometer?

  ____

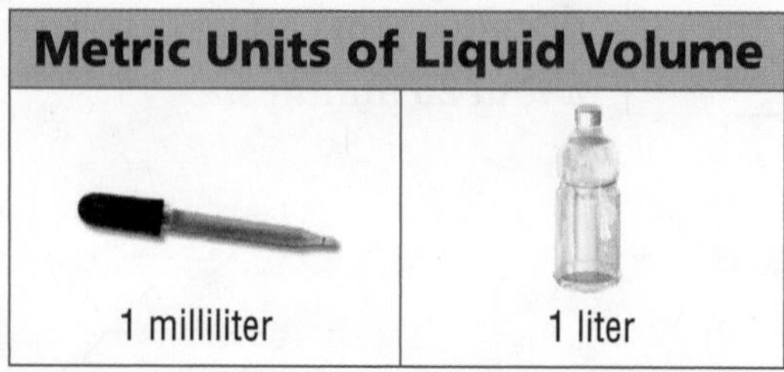

Metric Units of Liquid Volume	
1 milliliter	1 liter

- About how much medicine is usually in a medicine bottle?

  about 120 ______________________

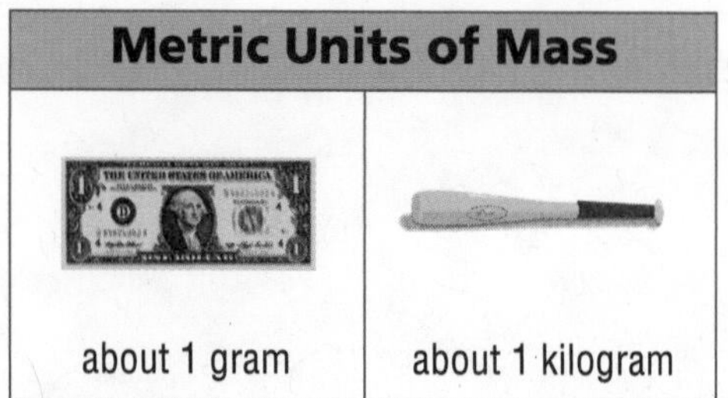

Metric Units of Mass	
about 1 gram	about 1 kilogram

- About how much is the mass of a paper clip?

  ____

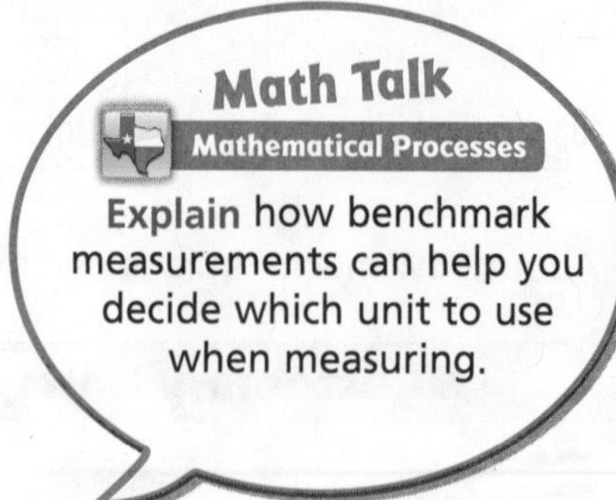

Name ______________________________

Share and Show

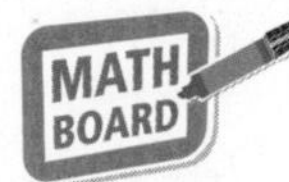

Use benchmarks to choose the customary or the metric unit you would use to measure each.

Metric Units	Customary Units
centimeter	inch
meter	foot
kilometer	yard
gram	ounce
kilogram	pound
milliliter	cup
liter	gallon

1. length of a football field ______________

2. length of a cell phone ______________

Circle the better estimate.

3. width of a teacher's desk

   10 meters or 1 meter

4. the amount of liquid a fish tank holds

   10 cups or 10 gallons

5. distance between Seattle and San Francisco

   6 miles or 680 miles

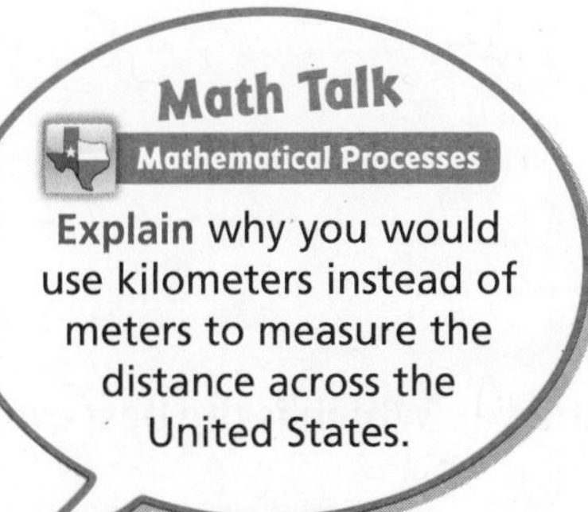

Problem Solving

Solve. For 6–7, use benchmarks to explain your answer.

6. H.O.T. **Apply** Cristina is making macaroni and cheese for her family. Would Cristina use 1 pound of macaroni or 1 ounce of macaroni?

____

____

____

7. H.O.T. **Write Math** Dalton used benchmarks to estimate that there are more cups than quarts in one gallon. Is Dalton's estimate reasonable? **Explain.**

____

____

____

Daily Assessment Task

Fill in the bubble completely to show your answer.

8. A mini-chameleon is about 1 inch long. It spends much of its time on the ground hiding under leaves. Which is the best estimate for the length of a leaf the mini-chameleon might hide under?

Ⓐ 4 inches

Ⓑ 4 ounces

Ⓒ 4 miles

Ⓓ 4 pounds

9. Mrs. Parker paints the school library. Which is the best estimate for the amount of paint she uses?

Ⓐ 18 meters

Ⓑ 18 millimeters

Ⓒ 18 liters

Ⓓ 18 milliliters

10. Roger took his pet canary to the vet. Which is the best estimate of the weight of the canary?

Ⓐ 20 pounds

Ⓑ 20 ounces

Ⓒ 20 feet

Ⓓ 20 inches

TEXAS Test Prep

11. Which is the best estimate for a dose of medicine?

Ⓐ 2 milliliters

Ⓑ 2 liters

Ⓒ 2 millimeters

Ⓓ 2 meters

Homework and Practice

TEKS Geometry and Measurement—4.8.A
MATHEMATICAL PROCESSES 4.1.F, 4.1.G

Name ____________________

15.1 Measurement Benchmarks

Circle the better estimate.

1. width of a computer mouse
2 inches or 2 feet

2. weight of a bag of grapes
3 ounces or 3 pounds

3. height of a stop sign
3 meters or 3 kilometers

4. mass of a mouse
30 grams or 30 kilograms

Problem Solving Real World

Solve. For 5–8, use benchmarks to explain your answer.

5. Which is the better estimate of the height of a basketball hoop, 10 feet or 10 yards?

6. Which is the better estimate of the mass of a wrist watch, 50 grams or 50 kilograms?

7. Which is the better estimate of the amount of water a balloon holds, 1 liter or 1 milliliter?

8. Which is the better estimate of the weight of a football helmet, 3 pounds or 3 ounces?

9. Sandy used benchmarks to estimate that there are more inches than feet in one yard. Is Sandy's estimate reasonable? **Explain.**

10. Jonathan thinks that he rides his bicycle about 4 meters from his house to school each day. Is Jonathan's estimate reasonable? **Explain.**

Lesson Check

TEXAS Test Prep

Fill in the bubble completely to show your answer.

11. Victoria is building a box for her CDs. Which is the best estimate of the width of a CD?

Ⓐ 5 miles
Ⓑ 5 feet
Ⓒ 5 yards
Ⓓ 5 inches

12. Darius is filling a jug with water to take on his trip. Which is the best estimate of the amount of water his jug holds?

Ⓐ 4 gallons
Ⓑ 4 cups
Ⓒ 4 pounds
Ⓓ 4 ounces

13. York School has a new jungle gym and a new swing set on its playground. Which is the best estimate of the height of the jungle gym?

Ⓐ 3 kilograms
Ⓑ 3 meters
Ⓒ 3 kilometers
Ⓓ 3 grams

14. Anna is driving from Dallas to Austin. Which is the best estimate of the distance she will drive?

Ⓐ 320 kilograms
Ⓑ 320 meters
Ⓒ 320 liters
Ⓓ 320 kilometers

15. **Multi-Step** Stan wants to know the weight of his hammer and its length. Which two units should he use?

Ⓐ ounces and inches
Ⓑ pounds and feet
Ⓒ pounds and miles
Ⓓ ounces and feet

16. **Multi-Step** Jodi wants to weigh her dog and measure its height. Which two units should she use?

Ⓐ pounds and inches
Ⓑ ounces and yards
Ⓒ kilograms and kilometers
Ⓓ grams and millimeters

Name ______________________________

TEKS Geometry and Measurement—4.8.A, 4.8.B
Also 4.8.C
MATHEMATICAL PROCESSES
4.1.F, 4.1.G

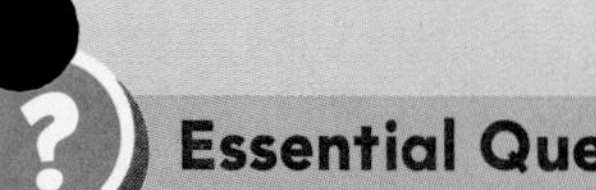

15.2 Customary Units of Length

Essential Question

How can you convert customary units of length?

Unlock the Problem

You can use a ruler to measure length. A ruler that is 1 foot long shows 12 inches in 1 foot. A ruler that is 3 feet long is called a yardstick. There are 3 feet in 1 yard.

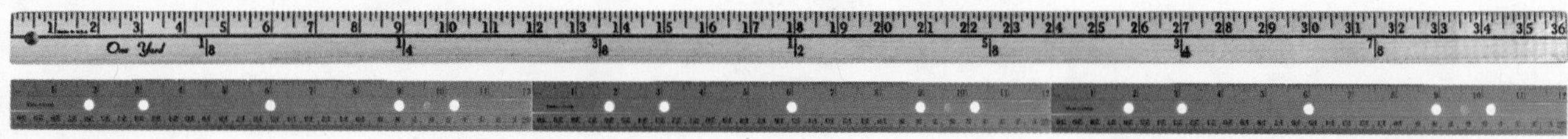

How does the size of a foot compare to the size of an inch?

Activity

Materials ■ 1-inch grid paper ■ scissors ■ tape

STEP 1 Cut out the paper inch tiles. Label each tile 1 inch.

1 inch	1 inch	1 inch	1 inch
1 inch	1 inch	1 inch	1 inch

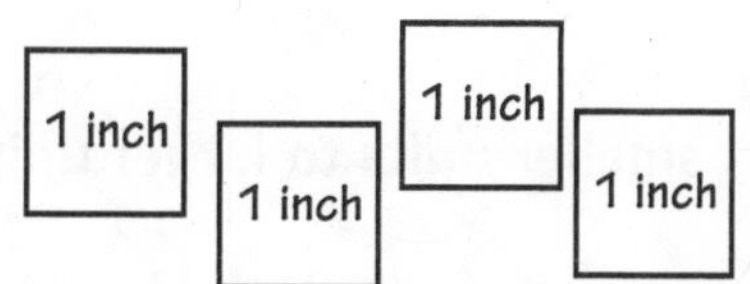

STEP 2 Place 12 tiles end-to-end to build 1 foot. Tape the tiles together.

1 foot

1 inch	1 inch	1 inch	1 inch	1 inch	1 inch	1 inch	1 inch	1 inch	1 inch	1 inch	1 inch

STEP 3 Compare the size of 1 foot to the size of 1 inch.

1 foot

1 inch	1 inch	1 inch	1 inch	1 inch	1 inch	1 inch	1 inch	1 inch	1 inch	1 inch	1 inch

Think: You need 12 inches to make 1 foot.

1 inch

1 inch

So, 1 foot is __12__ times as long as 1 inch.

Math Talk
Mathematical Processes
How many inches would you need to make a yard? Explain.

Example 1 Convert larger units to smaller units.

Emma has 4 feet of thread to make some bracelets. How many inches of thread does Emma have?

Since 1 foot is 12 times as long as 1 inch, you can write feet as inches by multiplying the number of feet by 12.

Make a table that relates feet and inches.

Feet	Inches
1	12
2	24
3	36
4	48
5	60

Think:

1 foot × 12 = 12 inches

2 feet × 12 = 24

3 feet × 12 = 36

4 feet × 12 = 48

5 feet × 12 = 60

So, Emma has 60 inches of thread.

Example 2 Convert smaller units to larger units.

Jason ran 300 feet during recess. How many yards did Jason run?

Make a table that relates feet and yards.

Feet	Yards
120	
150	
210	
240	
300	

120 feet ÷ 3 =

150 feet ÷ 3 =

210 feet ÷ ______ = ______

240 feet ÷ ______ = ______

300 feet ÷ ______ = ______

So, Jason ran a lot yards during recess.

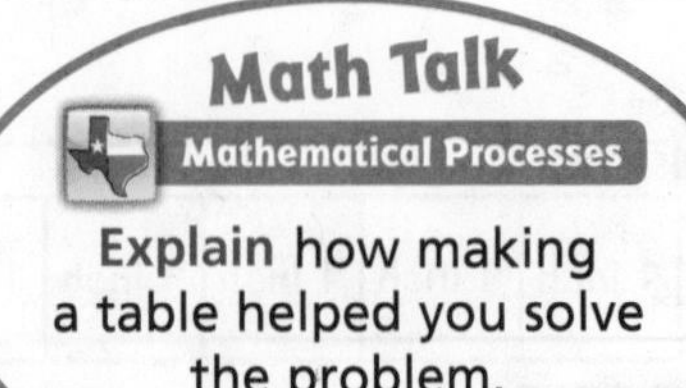

- **What if** Emma had 5 feet of thread? Would she have enough thread to make the bracelets? **Explain.**

yes

Name ___________________________

Share and Show

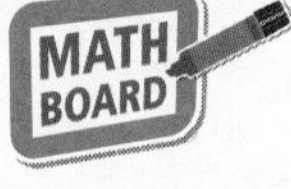

1. Compare the size of a yard to the size of a foot. Use a model to help.

Customary Units of Length
1 foot (ft) = 12 inches (in.) 1 yard (yd) = 3 feet 1 yard (yd) = 36 inches

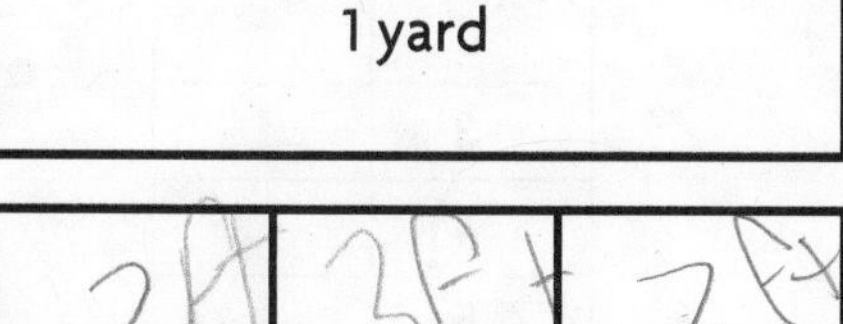

1 yard is ______ times as long as ______ foot.

Complete.

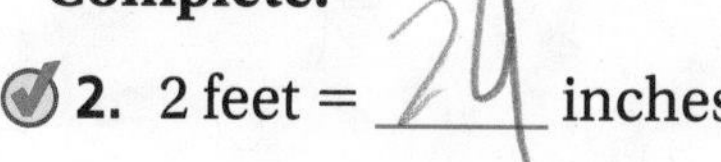

2. 2 feet = ______ inches
3. 3 yards = ______ feet
4. 12 feet = ______ yards
5. 7 yards = ______ feet
6. 144 inches = ______ feet
7. 72 feet = ______ yards

Math Talk
Mathematical Processes

If you measured the length of your classroom in yards and then in feet, which unit would have a greater number of units? **Explain.**

Problem Solving

8. **H.O.T.** **Multi-Step** Joanna has 3 yards of fabric. She needs 100 inches of fabric to make curtains. Does she have enough fabric to make curtains? **Explain.** Make a table to help.

Yards	Inches
1	
2	
3	

9. **H.O.T.** **Justify** Hannah's room is 14 feet wide. She says that her room is 160 inches wide. Is Hannah correct? Explain your answer.

Write Math ▶ **Show Your Work**

Daily Assessment Task

Fill in the bubble completely to show your answer.

10. A spool of thread contains 6 yards of thread. How many feet of thread are on the spool?

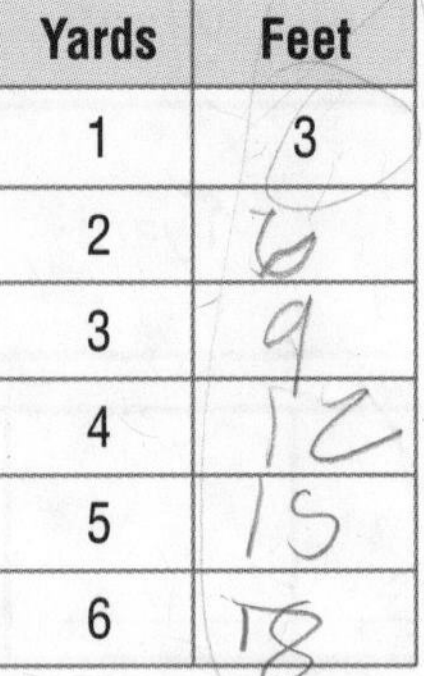

Yards	Feet
1	3
2	
3	
4	
5	
6	

Ⓐ 6 feet

Ⓑ 9 feet

Ⓒ 18 feet

Ⓓ 2 feet

11. Which statement about 8 yards and 25 feet is true?

Ⓐ 25 feet = 8 yards

Ⓑ 25 feet < 8 yards

Ⓒ 8 yards > 25 feet

Ⓓ 8 yards < 25 feet

12. **Multi-Step** Carla has 3 feet of ribbon. She needs 38 inches of ribbon to wrap a present. How many more inches of ribbon does Carla need?

Ⓐ 2 inches

Ⓑ 35 inches

Ⓒ 29 inches

Ⓓ 3 inches

TEXAS Test Prep

13. Jim is putting carpet in his basement. The length of his basement is 12 yards. How many feet is the length of his basement?

Ⓐ 4 feet

Ⓑ 15 feet

Ⓒ 36 feet

Ⓓ 432 feet

Homework and Practice

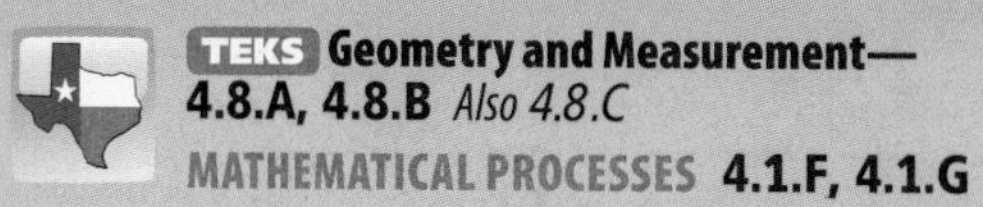

Name ______________________

15.2 Customary Units of Length

Complete.

Customary Units of Length
1 foot (ft) = 12 inches (in.) 1 yard (yd) = 3 feet 1 yard (yd) = 36 inches

1. 3 feet = ______ inches
2. 5 yards = ______ inches
3. 4 yards = ______ feet
4. 72 inches = ______ yards
5. 9 feet = ______ yards
6. 60 inches = ______ feet

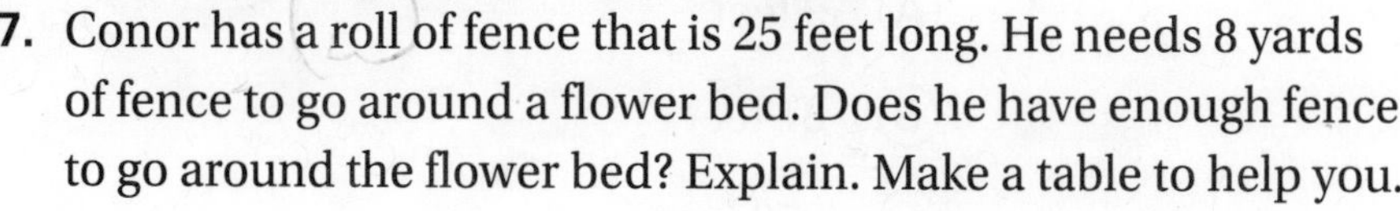

7. Conor has a roll of fence that is 25 feet long. He needs 8 yards of fence to go around a flower bed. Does he have enough fence to go around the flower bed? Explain. Make a table to help you.

____

____

Yards	Feet
1	
2	
3	
4	

8. If you measured the width of a window in inches and then in feet, which measurement would have the greater number of units? **Explain** your answer.

____

____

9. Ginny's house is 20 yards long. She says that the house is 720 feet long. Is Ginny correct? **Explain** your answer.

____

____

____

Lesson Check

TEXAS Test Prep

Fill in the bubble completely to show your answer.

10. Which statement is true?

Ⓐ 15 feet = 3 yards

Ⓑ 15 yards = 3 feet

Ⓒ 15 feet = 5 yards

Ⓓ 15 yards = 5 feet

11. The statement Evan wrote comparing 60 inches and 6 feet is true. Which statement did he write?

Ⓐ 60 inches = 6 feet

Ⓑ 60 inches > 6 feet

Ⓒ 6 feet < 60 inches

Ⓓ 6 feet > 60 inches

12. Hailey has a 5-foot long extension cord. She wants to know its length in inches. How many inches long is the cord?

Ⓐ 60 inches

Ⓑ 180 inches

Ⓒ 15 inches

Ⓓ 48 inches

13. Alex's driveway is 27 yards long and 10 yards wide. How many feet long is the driveway?

Ⓐ 9 feet

Ⓑ 81 feet

Ⓒ 972 feet

Ⓓ 324 feet

14. **Multi-Step** A roll of tape is 50 yards long. How many pieces of tape 2 inches long can be cut from the tape?

Ⓐ 150

Ⓑ 9,000

Ⓒ 900

Ⓓ 300

15. **Multi-Step** Vicky has a 50 inch roll of ribbon. She uses 3 feet of the ribbon to wrap a gift. How many inches of ribbon does she have left?

Ⓐ 4 inches

Ⓑ 41 inches

Ⓒ 14 inches

Ⓓ 24 inches

Name ______________________

15.3 Customary Units of Weight

TEKS Geometry and Measurement—4.8.A, 4.8.B
Also 4.8.C
MATHEMATICAL PROCESSES
4.1.D, 4.1.F, 4.1.G

Essential Question

How can you convert customary units of weight?

Unlock the Problem Real World

Ounces and **pounds** are customary units of weight. How does the size of a pound compare to the size of an ounce?

Activity

Materials ■ color pencils

The number line below shows the relationship between pounds and ounces.

Pounds	0																1
Ounces	0	1	2	3	4	5	6	7	8	9	10	11	12	13	14	15	16

STEP 1 Use a color pencil to shade 1 pound on the number line.

STEP 2 Use a different color pencil to shade 1 ounce on the number line.

STEP 3 Compare the size of 1 pound to the size of 1 ounce.

You need ______ ounces to make ______ pound.

So, 1 pound is ______ times as heavy as 1 ounce.

▲ You can use a spring scale to measure weight.

- **Explain** how the number line helped you to compare the sizes of the units.

____

____

____

____

Math Talk

Which is greater, 9 pounds or 9 ounces? **Explain**.

Example 1 Convert larger units to smaller units.

Nancy needs 5 pounds of flour to bake pies for a festival.
How many ounces of flour does Nancy need to bake the pies?

STEP 1 Make a table that relates pounds and ounces.

Pounds	Ounces
1	16
2	
3	
4	
5	

Think:

1 pound × 16 = 16 ounces

2 pounds × 16 = ______

3 pounds × ______ = ______

4 pounds × ______ = ______

5 pounds × ______ = ______

So, Nancy needs ______ ounces of flour.

Example 2 Convert smaller units to larger units.

Marcel buys 144 ounces of sugar at the grocery store. How many pounds of sugar did Marcel buy?

Ounces	Pounds
80	5
96	
112	
128	
144	

80 ounces ÷ 16 = 5 pounds

96 ounces ÷ 16 = ______

112 ounces ÷ 16 = ______

128 ounces ÷ ______ = ______

144 ounces ÷ ______ = ______

So, Marcel bought ______ pounds of sugar.

Try This! There are 2,000 pounds in 1 **ton**.
Make a table that relates tons and pounds.

Tons	Pounds
1	2,000
2	
3	

1 ton is ______ times as heavy as 1 pound.

Name ______________________

Share and Show

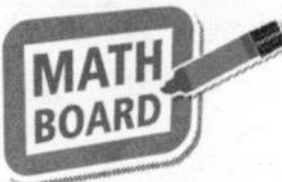

Customary Units of Weight
1 pound (lb) = 16 ounces (oz) 1 ton (T) = 2,000 pounds

1. 4 tons = __________ pounds

   Think: 4 tons × __________ = __________

Complete.

2. 5 tons = __________ pounds
3. 6 pounds = __________ ounces
4. 48 ounces = __________ pounds
5. 128 ounces = __________ pounds

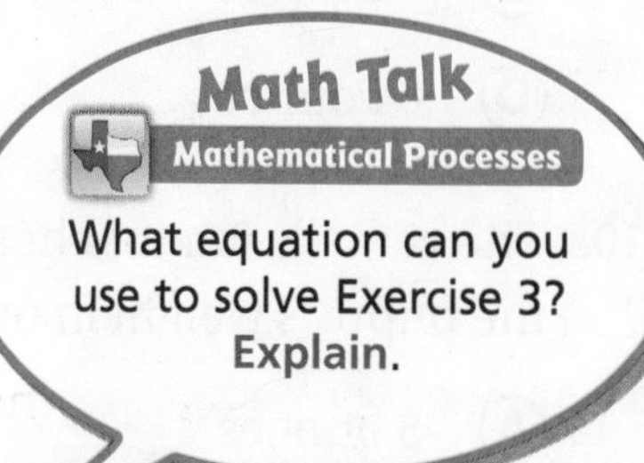

Problem Solving Real World

6. A landscaping company ordered 8 tons of gravel. They sell the gravel in 50 pound bags. How many pounds of gravel did the company order?

____

7. H.O.T. **Communicate** If you could draw a number line that shows the relationship between tons and pounds, what would it look like? **Explain.**

____

____

____

____

Write Math
Show Your Work

8. H.O.T. **Multi-Step** Keith bought 4 steaks from the store. One steak was 14 ounces, one steak was 12 ounces, one steak was 8 ounces and the last steak was 14 ounces. How many pounds of steak did Keith buy from the grocery store? **Explain.**

____

____

____

Daily Assessment Task

Fill in the bubble completely to show your answer.

9. Jill needs 4 pounds of peanut butter to make peanut butter and jelly sandwiches for a party. She buys peanut butter in jars. The weight of peanut butter in jars is given in ounces. How many ounces of peanut butter does Jill need to make the sandwiches?

   Ⓐ 4 ounces

   Ⓑ 16 ounces

   Ⓒ 8 ounces

   Ⓓ 64 ounces

10. The vet tells Jan that her puppy weighs 5 pounds. The scale shows the puppy's weight in ounces. What weight does the scale show?

   Ⓐ 5 ounces

   Ⓑ 80 ounces

   Ⓒ 16 ounces

   Ⓓ 60 ounces

11. **Multi-Step** A truck is transporting 4 new cars to a car dealership. Each car weighs 2 tons. The weight limit for trucks going over bridges is given in pounds. What is the weight of the cars in pounds?

   Ⓐ 16 pounds

   Ⓑ 8,000 pounds

   Ⓒ 16,000 pounds

   Ⓓ 24,000 pounds

TEXAS Test Prep

12. Mike is recording his baby sister's weight in pounds and ounces each week. This week she weighs 10 pounds. How many ounces does she weigh?

   Ⓐ 160 ounces

   Ⓑ 10 ounces

   Ⓒ 20 ounces

   Ⓓ 16 ounces

Homework and Practice

TEKS Geometry and Measurement—4.8.A, 4.8.B *Also 4.8.C*
MATHEMATICAL PROCESSES 4.1.D, 4.1.F, 4.1.G

Name ______________________

15.3 Customary Units of Weight

Complete.

Customary Units of Weight
1 pound (lb) = 16 ounces (oz) 1 ton (T) = 2,000 pounds

1. 48 ounces = ___3___ pounds

2. 3 tons = ___6000___ pounds

3. 7 pounds = ___112___ ounces

4. 10,000 pounds = ___10___ tons

5. 7 tons = ___14000___ pounds

6. 96 ounces = ___90___ pounds

7. 64 ounces = ___4___ pounds

8. 8 pounds = ___70___ ounces

Problem Solving Real World

9. Nathan has a truck that can carry 2 tons. How many pounds can the truck carry?

____

10. Julia bought 40 bags of compost. Each bag weighed 50 pounds. How many tons of compost did she buy?

____

11. Paul bought 3 packages of cheese. The packages weighed 11 ounces, 13 ounces, and 8 ounces. How many pounds of cheese did Paul buy? **Explain.**

____

____

12. Carole needs 4 pounds of nuts for her granola. She has 26 ounces of walnuts and 28 ounces of cashews. How many ounces of peanuts should she buy so she has 4 pounds of nuts? **Explain.**

____

____

____

____

Lesson Check

TEXAS Test Prep

Fill in the bubble completely to show your answer.

13. How many ounces of potatoes are in a 20 pound bag of potatoes?

Ⓐ 40,000 ounces

Ⓑ 3,200 ounces

Ⓒ 320 ounces

Ⓓ 2,000 ounces

14. A construction company orders 12 tons of pea gravel. How many pounds of pea gravel do they order?

Ⓐ 6,000 pounds

Ⓑ 24,000 pounds

Ⓒ 192 pounds

Ⓓ 32,000 pounds

15. At the farmer's market, a bunch of bananas weighs 96 ounces. The price for the bananas is based on the weight in pounds. How many pounds does the bunch of bananas weigh?

Ⓐ 6 pounds

Ⓑ 12 pounds

Ⓒ 1,536 pounds

Ⓓ 96 pounds

16. Which statement about 36 ounces and 2 pounds is true?

Ⓐ 36 ounces $>$ 2 pounds

Ⓑ 2 pounds $=$ 36 ounces

Ⓒ 36 ounces $<$ 2 pounds

Ⓓ 2 pounds $>$ 36 ounces

17. Multi-Step Elizabeth has 4 jars of olives. Each jar contains 12 ounces of olives. How many pounds of olives does Elizabeth have?

Ⓐ 48 pounds

Ⓑ 4 pounds

Ⓒ 3 pounds

Ⓓ 12 pounds

18. Multi-Step Kevin picked 10 pounds of strawberries. He wants to freeze them in 8-ounce packages. How many 8-ounce packages of strawberries can Kevin make?

Ⓐ 16

Ⓑ 32

Ⓒ 80

Ⓓ 20

Name ________________________________

15.4 Customary Units of Liquid Volume

TEKS Geometry and Measurement—4.8.A, 4.8.B
Also 4.8.C
MATHEMATICAL PROCESSES
4.1.D, 4.1.F, 4.1.G

Essential Question How can you convert customary units of liquid volume?

Unlock the Problem

Liquid volume is the measure of the space a liquid occupies. Some basic units for measuring liquid volume are **gallons**, **half gallons**, **quarts**, **pints**, and **cups**.

1 cup = 8 fluid ounces
1 pint = 2 cups
1 quart = 4 cups

The bars below model the relationships among some units of liquid volume. The largest units are gallons. The smallest units are **fluid ounces**.

1 gallon

1 gallon															
1 half gallon								1 half gallon							
1 quart				1 quart				1 quart				1 quart			
1 pint		1 pint		1 pint		1 pint		1 pint		1 pint		1 pint		1 pint	
1 cup	1 cup	1 cup	1 cup	1 cup	1 cup	1 cup	1 cup	1 cup	1 cup	1 cup	1 cup	1 cup	1 cup	1 cup	1 cup
8 fluid ounces	8 fluid ounces	8 fluid ounces	8 fluid ounces	8 fluid ounces	8 fluid ounces	8 fluid ounces	8 fluid ounces	8 fluid ounces	8 fluid ounces	8 fluid ounces	8 fluid ounces	8 fluid ounces	8 fluid ounces	8 fluid ounces	8 fluid ounces

Example How does the size of a gallon compare to the size of a quart?

Math Talk Mathematical Processes
Describe the pattern in the units of liquid volume.

STEP 1 Draw two bars that represent this relationship. One bar should show gallons and the other bar should show quarts.

STEP 2 Shade 1 gallon on one bar and shade 1 quart on the other bar.

STEP 3 Compare the size of 1 gallon to the size of 1 quart.

So, 1 gallon is ______ times as much as 1 quart.

Example 1 Convert larger units to smaller units.

Serena is making 3 gallons of lemonade to sell with her friend. Her friend wants to know how many fluid ounces of lemonade Serena made. How many fluid ounces of lemonade did Serena make?

STEP 1 Use the model on page 537. Find the relationship between gallons and fluid ounces.

1 gallon = ______ cups

1 cup = ______ fluid ounces

1 gallon = ______ cups × ______ fluid ounces

1 gallon = ______ fluid ounces

STEP 2 Make a table that relates gallons and fluid ounces.

Gallons	Fluid Ounces
1	128
2	
3	

Think:

1 gallon = 128 fluid ounces

2 gallons × 128 = ______ fluid ounces

3 gallons × 128 = ______ fluid ounces

So, Serena made ______ fluid ounces of lemonade.

Example 2 Convert smaller units to larger units.

Allison needs to make 36 cups of fruit punch for a party. The recipe she has uses quarts instead of cups. How many quarts of fruit punch does Allison need to make for the party?

Cups	Quarts
16	4
24	
32	
36	

Think:

16 cups ÷ 4 = 4 quarts

24 cups ÷ 4 = ______________

32 cups ÷ ______ = ______________

36 cups ÷ ______ = ______________

So, Allison made ______ quarts of fruit punch.

Name ___________________________

Share and Show 

1. Compare the size of a quart to the size of a pint.
Use a model to help.

1 quart	
______	______

Customary Units of Liquid Volume
1 cup (c) = 8 fluid ounces (fl oz)
1 pint (pt) = 2 cups
1 quart (qt) = 2 pints
1 quart (qt) = 4 cups
1 gallon (gal) = 4 quarts
1 gallon (gal) = 8 pints
1 gallon (gal) = 16 cups

1 quart is ______ times as much as ______ pint.

Complete.

2. 4 cups = ______ pints
3. 12 quarts = ______ gallons
4. 6 quarts = ______ cups
5. 20 cups = ______ quarts
6. 3 gallons = ______ pints
7. 16 pints = ______ cups

Math Talk
Mathematical Processes
Explain how the conversion chart above relates to the model in Exercise 1.

Problem Solving 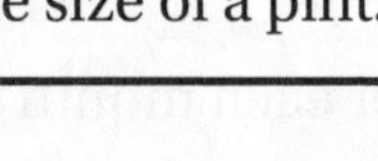

8. H.O.T. **Use Representations Multi-Step** A soccer team has 25 players. The team's thermos holds 4 gallons of water. If the thermos is full, is there enough water for each player to have 2 cups? **Explain.** Make a table to help.

____

____

____

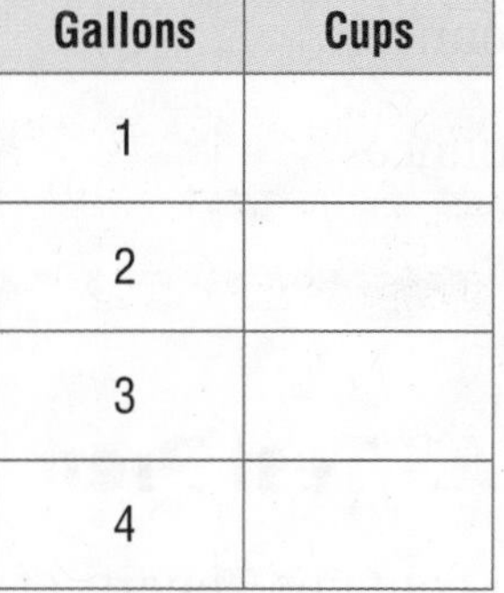

Gallons	Cups
1	
2	
3	
4	

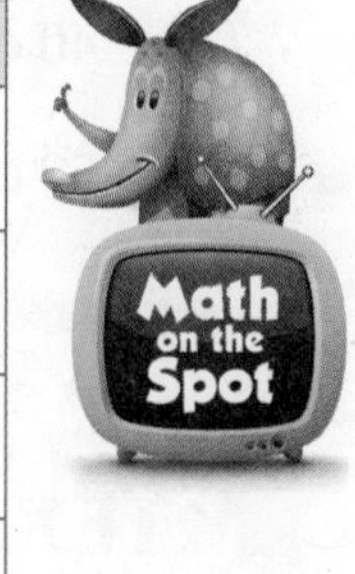

9. H.O.T. Penelope drank 64 fluid ounces of water each day for 7 days.
How many cups of water did Penelope drink during those 7 days? **Explain.**

____

____

____

Daily Assessment Task

Fill in the bubble completely to show your answer.

10. A corn plant gives off about 9 gallons of water each month during the growing season. How many pints of water does the corn plant give off each month?

Ⓐ 144 pints

Ⓑ 36 pints

Ⓒ 72 pints

Ⓓ 18 pints

11. Ken makes 6 quarts of fruit juice. He serves the juice in glasses that hold 1 cup. How many glasses of fruit juice does Ken serve?

Ⓐ 12 glasses

Ⓑ 24 glasses

Ⓒ 96 glasses

Ⓓ 48 glasses

12. **Multi-Step** Marty's pitcher holds 64 ounces of water. She drinks 4 cups of water in the morning and 2 cups in the afternoon. How much water is left in the pitcher?

Ⓐ 40 ounces

Ⓑ 52 ounces

Ⓒ 32 ounces

Ⓓ 16 ounces

TEXAS Test Prep

13. A pitcher contains 5 quarts of water. How many cups of water does the pitcher contain?

Ⓐ 4 cups

Ⓑ 10 cups

Ⓒ 20 cups

Ⓓ 40 cups

Homework and Practice

TEKS Geometry and Measurement—4.8.A, 4.8.B *Also 4.8.C*
MATHEMATICAL PROCESSES 4.1.D, 4.1.F, 4.1.G

Name ______________________

15.4 Customary Units of Liquid Volume

Complete.

Customary Units of Liquid Volume
1 cup (c) = 8 fluid ounces (fl oz)
1 pint (pt) = 2 cups
1 quart (qt) = 2 pints
1 quart (qt) = 4 cups
1 gallon (gal) = 4 quarts
1 gallon (gal) = 8 pints
1 gallon (gal) = 16 cups

1. 5 gallons = __40__ pints

2. 20 cups = __5__ quarts

3. 3 cups = __24__ fluid ounces

4. 6 pints = __3__ quarts

5. 16 quarts = __3__ gallons

6. 40 fluid ounces = __5__ cups

Problem Solving Real World

7. Marina's mug holds 12 fluid ounces of liquid. She drinks 6 mugs of liquid a day. How many cups of liquid does she drink? **Explain.** Make a table to help you.

Cups	Fluid Ounces
1	
2	
3	
4	

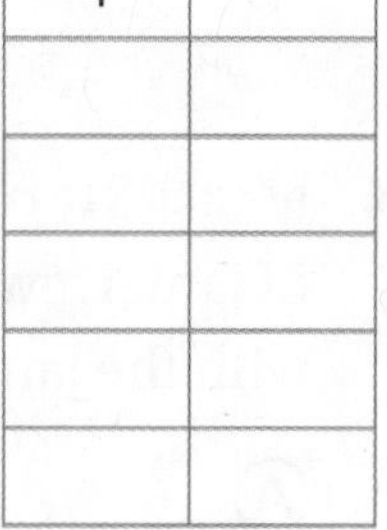

____

____

____

8. Joshua made 5 gallons of maple syrup. How many pint jars does he need to hold the syrup? **Explain.**

____

____

9. The label on a bottle of apple juice says it contains 128 fluid ounces. How many quarts of juice are in the bottle? **Explain.**

____

____

Lesson Check

TEXAS Test Prep

Fill in the bubble completely to show your answer.

10. Michael has a pail that holds 5 gallons of water. How many quarts of water does the pail hold?

Ⓐ 40 quarts
Ⓑ 20 quarts
Ⓒ 10 quarts
Ⓓ 15 quarts

11. Emily needs 12 cups of fruit juice for a punch recipe. The juice comes in quart bottles. How many bottles of juice should Emily buy?

Ⓐ 6
Ⓑ 4
Ⓒ 2
Ⓓ 3

12. **Multi-Step** Marsha's thermos holds 3 pints of tea. She drinks 2 cups of tea on her break and 1 cup of tea for lunch. How many cups of tea are left in the thermos?

Ⓐ 3 cups
Ⓑ 2 cups
Ⓒ 6 cups
Ⓓ 4 cups

13. **Multi-Step** Each batch of pancakes Arlo makes needs 2 cups of milk. How many batches of pancakes can Arlo make with 2 quarts of milk?

Ⓐ 8
Ⓑ 4
Ⓒ 2
Ⓓ 16

14. **Multi-Step** Antonia made 64 fluid ounces of jam. How many pint jars can Antonia fill with the jam?

Ⓐ 6
Ⓑ 2
Ⓒ 4
Ⓓ 8

15. **Multi-Step** Peter's glasses each hold 8 fluid ounces. How many glasses of juice can Peter pour from a bottle that holds 2 quarts?

Ⓐ 8
Ⓑ 4
Ⓒ 16
Ⓓ 12

Name ______________________________

15.5 Mixed Measures

TEKS Geometry and Measurement—4.8.C
Also 4.8.B

MATHEMATICAL PROCESSES
4.1.A, 4.1.C, 4.1.G

Essential Question How can you solve problems involving mixed measures?

Unlock the Problem (Real World)

Herman is building a picnic table for a new campground. The picnic table is 5 feet 10 inches long. How long is the picnic table in inches?

- Is the mixed measure greater than or less than 6 feet?
  ____
- How many inches are in 1 foot?
  ____

Change a mixed measure.

Think of 5 feet 10 inches as 5 feet + 10 inches.

Write feet as inches.

5 feet
+ 10 inches

Think: 5 feet × 12 = 60 inches →

___ inches
+ ___ inches
___ inches

So, the picnic table is ______ inches long.

Example 1 Add mixed measures.

Herman built a deck behind his house in 2 days. The first day he worked he made the deck 12 feet 6 inches wide. The second day he worked he made the deck 8 feet 4 inches wider. How wide is the deck that Herman built?

STEP 1 Add the inches.

12 ft 6 in.
+ 8 ft 4 in.
___ in.

STEP 2 Add the feet.

12 ft 6 in.
+ 8 ft 4 in.
___ 10 in.

So, the deck Herman built was ________________ wide.

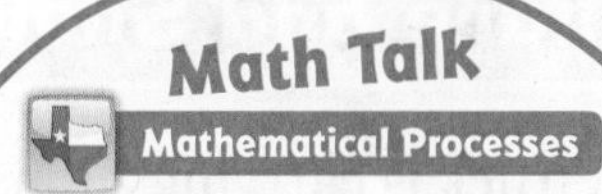

Math Talk Mathematical Processes
How is adding mixed measures similar to adding tens and ones? How is it different? **Explain.**

- **What if** Herman added an extra 2 inches on the deck width? How wide would the deck be then? **Explain.**

____

____

Example 2 Subtract mixed measures.

Alicia is building a fence around the picnic area. She has a pole that is 6 feet 6 inches long. She cuts off 1 foot 7 inches from one end. How long is the pole now?

STEP 1 Subtract the inches.

Think: 7 inches is greater than 6 inches. You need to regroup to subtract.

6 ft 6 in. = 5 ft 6 in. + 12 in.

= 5 ft ______ in.

```
  5    18
  6 ft  6 in.
– 1 ft  7 in.
       ___ in.
```

ERROR Alert

Be sure to check that you are regrouping correctly. There are 12 inches in 1 foot.

STEP 2 Subtract the feet.

```
  5    18
  6 ft  6 in.
– 1 ft  7 in.
___ ft 11 in.
```

So, the pole is now ____________________ long.

Try This! Subtract.

3 pounds 5 ounces − 1 pound 2 ounces

4 gallons 7 cups − 1 gallon 12 cups

Share and Show

1. A truck is carrying 2 tons 500 pounds of steel. How many pounds of steel is the truck carrying?

Think of 2 tons 500 pounds as 2 tons + 500 pounds. Write tons as pounds.

```
  2 tons          Think: 2 tons × 2,000 =  →      pounds
+ 500 pounds      _________ pounds             +  pounds
                                                  pounds
```

So, the truck is carrying __________ pounds of steel.

Name ___________________________

Rewrite each measure in the given unit.

2. 1 yard 2 feet _____ feet	**3.** 3 pints 1 cup _____ cups	**4.** 3 weeks 1 day _____ days

Add or subtract.

5. 2 lb 4 oz + 1 lb 6 oz	**6.** 3 gal 4 qt − 1 gal 5 qt	**7.** 4 ft 6 in − 2 ft 8 in

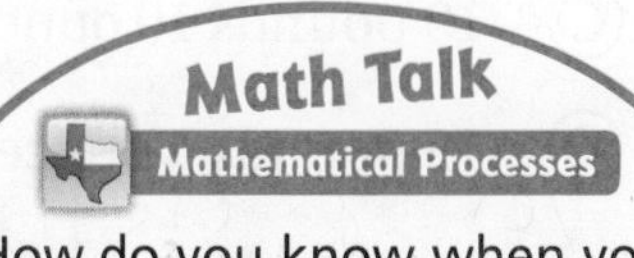

How do you know when you need to regroup to subtract? **Explain.**

Problem Solving Real World

8. H.O.T. **Justify** Jackson has a rope 1 foot 8 inches long. He cuts it into 4 equal pieces. How many inches long is each piece?

9. H.O.T. **Sense or Nonsense?** Sam and Dave each solve the problem at the right. Sam says the sum is 4 feet 18 inches. Dave says the sum is 5 feet 6 inches. Whose answer makes sense? Whose answer is nonsense? **Explain.**

  2 ft 10 in.
+ 2 ft 8 in.

10. H.O.T. **Multi-Step** Don has 5 pieces of pipe. Each piece is 3 feet 6 inches long. If Don joins the pieces end to end to make one long pipe, how long will the new pipe be? **Explain.**

Daily Assessment Task

Fill in the bubble completely to show your answer.

11. Mark had a dog that weighed 21 pounds 8 ounces. The dog lost 1 pound 14 ounces. How much does the dog weigh now?

Ⓐ 20 pounds 4 ounces

Ⓑ 20 pounds 10 ounces

Ⓒ 19 pounds 10 ounces

Ⓓ 19 pounds 4 ounces

12. Linda is making a costume. She needs 3 feet 9 inches of purple fabric and 4 feet 7 inches of orange fabric. How much fabric does Linda need to make the costume?

Ⓐ 8 feet 16 inches

Ⓑ 7 feet 4 inches

Ⓒ 8 feet 4 inches

Ⓓ 1 foot 4 inches

13. **Multi-Step** Tara makes orange smoothies for a party. She combines 2 gallons 3 quarts of milk with 1 gallon 2 quarts of orange juice. Party guests drink 2 gallons 3 quarts of the smoothies. How much is left of the orange smoothie?

Ⓐ 4 gallons 1 quart

Ⓑ 1 gallon 2 quarts

Ⓒ 2 gallons 2 quarts

Ⓓ 1 gallon 1 quart

TEXAS Test Prep

14. Maya's cat weighed 7 pounds 2 ounces last year. The cat gained 1 pound 8 ounces this year. What is the weight of Maya's cat now?

Ⓐ 5 pounds 10 ounces

Ⓑ 8 pounds 2 ounces

Ⓒ 8 pounds 10 ounces

Ⓓ 9 pounds

Homework and Practice

TEKS Geometry and Measurement—4.8.C
Also 4.8.B
MATHEMATICAL PROCESSES 4.1.A, 4.1.C, 4.1.G

Name ______________________

15.5 Mixed Measures

Rewrite each measurement in the given unit.

1. 1 pound 8 ounces

32 ounces

2. 3 feet 1 inch

 inches

3. 2 gallons 3 quarts

7 quarts

Rewrite each measurement in the given unit.

4. 4 yd 2 ft
+ 1 yd 3 ft

55

5. 5 gal 1 qt
− 2 gal 3 qt

6. 2 lb 10 oz
+ 3 lb 12 oz

5 22

Problem Solving Real World

7. Clayton filled 5 containers with water. Each container holds 2 gallons and 2 quarts. How many quarts of water does Clayton have? **Explain.**

____

____

____

8. Michael bought 2 pounds 12 ounces of cashews and 3 pounds 6 ounces of almonds. How many more ounces of almonds did Michael buy? **Explain.**

____

____

____

____

Lesson Check

TEXAS Test Prep

Fill in the bubble completely to show your answer.

9. **Multi-Step** A snake is 2 feet 4 inches long. How many inches long is the snake?

Ⓐ 28 inches

Ⓑ 76 inches

Ⓒ 24 inches

Ⓓ 42 inches

10. Mike has a board that is 38 inches long. How many feet and inches is the board?

Ⓐ 1 foot 11 inches

Ⓑ 2 feet 8 inches

Ⓒ 3 feet 1 inch

Ⓓ 3 feet 2 inches

11. **Multi-Step** Debbie shipped 2 packages. One weighed 2 pounds 10 ounces. The other weighed 4 pounds 12 ounces. What is the total weight of the two packages?

Ⓐ 88 ounces

Ⓑ 130 ounces

Ⓒ 94 ounces

Ⓓ 118 ounces

12. **Multi-Step** Ted is 6 feet 4 inches tall. Lisa is 5 feet 7 inches tall. How much taller is Ted?

Ⓐ 7 inches

Ⓑ 11 inches

Ⓒ 9 inches

Ⓓ 8 inches

13. **Multi-Step** Charlie combined 4 quarts of sparkling water with 2 gallons 1 quart of apple juice. Which tells the amount of drink he made?

Ⓐ 9 quarts

Ⓑ 7 quarts

Ⓒ 13 quarts

Ⓓ 21 quarts

14. **Multi-Step** Cindy had 7 feet of yarn. She needed 4 inches to make a bracelet. How many bracelets can she make with the amount of yarn she has?

Ⓐ 18

Ⓑ 21

Ⓒ 27

Ⓓ 29

Name ___________________________

Also 4.8.C

MATHEMATICAL PROCESSES
4.1.C, 4.1.D, 4.1.F

15.6 Metric Units of Length

Essential Question

How can you convert metric units of length?

Investigate

Materials ■ ruler (meter) ■ scissors ■ tape

Meters (m), **decimeters** (dm), centimeters (cm), and **millimeters** (mm) are all metric units of length.

Build a meterstick to show how these units are related.

A. Cut out the meterstick strips.

B. Place the strips end-to-end to build 1 meter. Tape the strips together.

C. Look at your meter strip. What patterns do you notice about the sizes of the units?

1 meter is ______ times as long as 1 decimeter.

1 decimeter is ______ times as long as 1 centimeter.

1 centimeter is ______ times as long as 1 millimeter.

Describe the pattern you see.

____

____

Math Idea

If you lined up 1,000 metersticks end-to-end, the length of the metersticks would be 1 kilometer.

H.O.T. **Apply** What operation could you use to find how many centimeters are in 3 meters? **Explain**.

____

____

____

Make Connections

You can use different metric units to describe the same metric length. For example, you can measure the length of a book as 3 decimeters or as 30 centimeters. Since the metric system is based on the number 10, decimals or fractions can be used to describe metric lengths as equivalent units.

Think of 1 meter as one whole. Use your meterstick to write equivalent units as fractions and decimals.

1 meter = 10 decimeters	1 meter = 100 centimeters
Each decimeter is	Each centimeter is
_____ or _____ of a meter.	_____ or _____ of a meter.

Complete the sentence.

- A length of 51 centimeters is _____ or _____ of a meter.
- A length of 8 decimeters is _____ or _____ of a meter.
- A length of 82 centimeters is _____ or _____ of a meter.

Math Talk

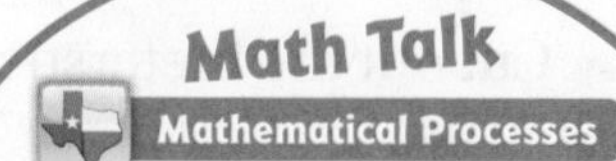

Explain how you are able to locate and write decimeters and centimeters as parts of a meter on the meterstick.

Share and Show

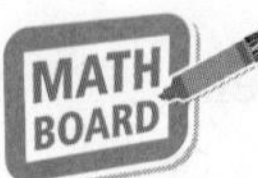

Metric Units of Length
1 centimeter (cm) = 10 millimeters (mm)
1 decimeter (dm) = 10 centimeters
1 meter (m) = 10 decimeters
1 meter (m) = 100 centimeters
1 meter (m) = 1,000 millimeters

Complete.

1. 2 meters = _____ centimeters

2. 3 centimeters = _____ millimeters

3. 5 decimeters = _____ centimeters

Describe the length in meters. Write your answer as a fraction and as a decimal.

4. 65 centimeters = _____ or _____ meter

5. 47 centimeters = _____ or _____ meter

6. 9 decimeters = _____ or _____ meter

7. 2 decimeters = _____ or _____ meter

Name ___

Problem Solving Real World

8. H.O.T. **What's the Error?** Julianne's desk is 75 centimeters long. She says her desk is 7.5 meters long. **Describe** her error.

9. H.O.T. **Communicate Multi-Step** Alexis is knitting a blanket 2 meters long. Every 2 decimeters, she changes the color of the yarn to make stripes. How many stripes will the blanket have? **Explain.**

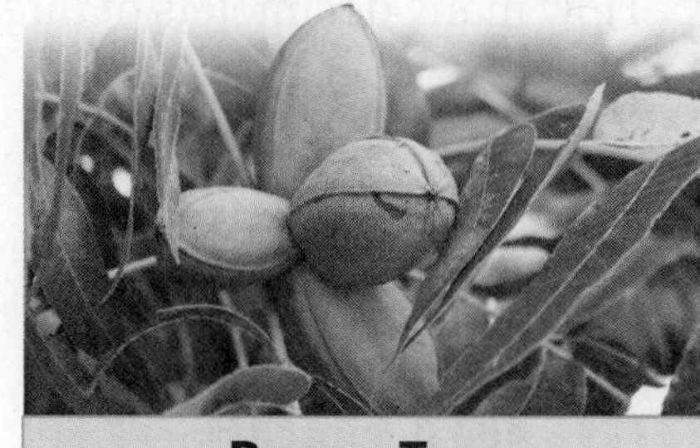

Pecan Tree	
Average Measurements	
Length of nuts	3 cm to 5 cm
Height	21 m to 30 m
Width of trunk	18 dm
Width of leaf	10 cm to 20 cm

H.O.T. Pose a Problem

10. **Multi-Step** Aruna was writing a report on pecan trees. She made the table of information to the right.

Write a problem that can be solved by using the data.

Pose a problem.

Solve your problem.

- **Describe** how you could change the problem by changing a unit in the problem. Then solve the problem.

Mathematical Processes
Model • Reason • Communicate

Daily Assessment Task

Fill in the bubble completely to show your answer.

11. A length of 1 millimeter is what part of a centimeter?

Ⓐ $\frac{1}{10}$

Ⓑ $\frac{1}{1,000}$

Ⓒ $\frac{1}{100}$

Ⓓ $\frac{1}{10,000}$

12. Halle buys a spool of thread containing 40 meters of thread. How many decimeters of thread are on the spool?

Ⓐ 4,000 decimeters

Ⓑ 4 decimeters

Ⓒ 40,000 decimeters

Ⓓ 400 decimeters

13. **Multi-Step** Mia plants flowers in a row along the border of her garden. The border is 4 meters long. She plants a flower at one end of the border and then another flower every 10 centimeters. How many flowers does Mia plant?

Ⓐ 9

Ⓑ 41

Ⓒ 4

Ⓓ 40

TEXAS Test Prep

14. Lucille runs the 50-meter dash in her track meet. How many millimeters long is the race?

Ⓐ 500 millimeters

Ⓑ 50,000 millimeters

Ⓒ 5,000 millimeters

Ⓓ 500,000 millimeters

Name ______________________

15.6 Metric Units of Length

Complete.

Metric Units of Length
1 centimeter (cm) = 10 millimeters (mm)
1 decimeter (dm) = 10 centimeters
1 meter (m) = 10 decimeters
1 meter (m) = 100 centimeters
1 meter (m) = 1,000 millimeters

1. 3 meters = __300__ centimeters
2. 4 centimeters = __40__ millimeters
3. 2 decimeters = __20__ centimeters
4. 5 meters = __50__ decimeters
5. 600 centimeters = __6__ meters

Describe the length in meters. Write your answer as a fraction and as a decimal.

6. 38 centimeters = __________ or __________ meters
7. 91 centimeters = __________ or __________ meters

Problem Solving (Real World)

8. The magazine Barbara is reading is 25 centimeters long. She says it is 0.25 decimeters long. Is she correct? **Explain.**

____

9. Will is building a fence that is 3 meters long. He is using boards that are 2 decimeters wide. How many boards does he need? **Explain.**

____

10. Susan is cutting out squares to make a quilt. Each square is 20 centimeters on a side. How many 20 centimeter squares can she make from a strip 20 centimeters wide and 5 meters long? **Explain.**

____

____

____

Lesson Check

TEXAS Test Prep

Fill in the bubble completely to show your answer.

11. What fraction of a meter is 1 centimeter?

Ⓐ $\frac{1}{1,000}$

Ⓑ $\frac{1}{10}$

Ⓒ $\frac{1}{10,000}$

Ⓓ $\frac{1}{100}$

12. A stamp in Sam's collection is 3 centimeters wide. How many millimeters wide is the stamp?

Ⓐ 0.3

Ⓑ 30

Ⓒ 3,000

Ⓓ 300

13. Pete's dog is 58 centimeters tall. What is the dog's height in meters?

Ⓐ 5.8 meters

Ⓑ 0.58 meters

Ⓒ 50.8 meters

Ⓓ 580 meters

14. A worm is 130 millimeters long. How many centimeters long is the worm?

Ⓐ 13

Ⓑ 13,000

Ⓒ 130

Ⓓ 0.13

15. Multi-Step How many 50 centimeter pieces of ribbon can Casey cut from a roll of ribbon 60 meters long?

Ⓐ 120

Ⓑ 12

Ⓒ 300

Ⓓ 30

16. Multi-Step A sidewalk is 40 meters long. Each section of the sidewalk is 8 decimeters long. How many sections of sidewalk are there?

Ⓐ 5

Ⓑ 500

Ⓒ 50

Ⓓ 0.5

Name ______________________

15.7 Metric Units of Mass and Liquid Volume

TEKS Geometry and Measurement—4.8.B, 4.8.C
Also 4.8.A
MATHEMATICAL PROCESSES
4.1.A, 4.1.D, 4.1.F

Essential Question How can you convert metric units of mass and liquid volume?

Unlock the Problem

Mass is the amount of matter in an object. Metric units of mass include kilograms (kg) and grams (g). Liters (L) and **milliliters** (mL) are metric units of liquid volume.

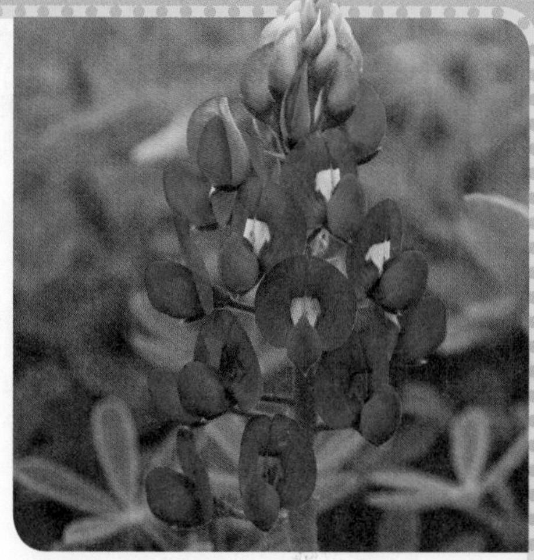

The charts show the relationship between these units.

Metric Units of Mass
1 kilogram (kg) = 1,000 grams (g)

Metric Units of Liquid Volume
1 liter (L) = 1,000 milliliters (mL)

Example 1 Convert larger units to smaller units.

Becky planted a flower garden full of bluebonnets. She used 9 kilograms of soil. How many grams of soil is that?

number of kilograms		grams in 1 kilogram		total grams
9	×	1,000	=	______

So, Becky used ______ grams of soil to plant her bluebonnets.

- Are kilograms larger or smaller than grams?
______
- Will the number of grams be greater than or less than the number of kilograms?
______
- What operation will you use to solve the problem?
______

Example 2 Convert smaller units to larger units.

Becky used 5,000 milliliters of water to water her bluebonnet garden. How many liters of water is that?

number of milliliters		milliliters in 1 liter		total liters
5,000	÷	1,000	=	______

So, Becky used ______ liters of water.

Math Talk

Mathematical Processes

Compare the size of a kilogram to the size of a gram. Then compare the size of a liter to the size of a milliliter.

Share and Show

1. There are 3 liters of water in a pitcher. How many milliliters of water are in the pitcher?

   There are ________ milliliters in 1 liter. Since I am changing

   from a larger unit to a smaller unit, I can ________ 3 by 1,000 to find the number of milliliters in 3 liters.

   So, there are ________ milliliters of water in the pitcher.

Complete.

2. 4 liters = ______ milliliters

3. 6 kilograms = ______ grams

4. 8,000 grams = ______ kilograms

5. 7 liters = ______ milliliters

Math Talk — Mathematical Processes

Explain how you found the number of grams in 6 kilograms in Exercise 3.

Problem Solving Real World

6. Frank wants to fill a fish tank with 8 liters of water. How many milliliters is that?

   ____

7. Kim has 3 water bottles. She fills each bottle with 1,000 milliliters of water. How many liters of water does she have?

   ____

8. H.O.T. **Multi-Step** A 500-gram bag of granola costs $4, and a 2-kilogram bag of granola costs $15. What is the cheapest way to buy 2,000 grams of granola? **Explain.**

   ____

   ____

   ____

   ____

Name ___________________________

9. **Sense or Nonsense?** The world's largest apple had a mass of 1,849 grams. Sue said the mass was greater than 2 kilograms. Does Sue's statement make sense? **Explain.**

____

____

____

____

Unlock the Problem — Real World

10. H.O.T. **Apply** **Multi-Step** Lori bought 600 grams of cayenne pepper and 2 kilograms of black pepper. How many grams of pepper did she buy?

Math on the Spot

a. What are you asked to find?

____

b. What information will you use?

____

c. Tell how you might solve the problem.

____

____

____

d. Show how you solved the problem.

____

____

____

____

e. Complete the sentences.

Lori bought _____ grams of cayenne pepper.

She bought _____ grams of black pepper.

_____ + _____ = _____ grams

So, Lori bought _____ grams of pepper in all.

Daily Assessment Task

Fill in the bubble completely to show your answer.

11. The largest natural pearl in the world has a mass of about 6,000 grams. What is the mass of the pearl in kilograms?

Ⓐ 600 kilograms

Ⓑ 6 kilograms

Ⓒ 60,000 kilograms

Ⓓ 60 kilograms

12. Jen puts 10 liters of water in her aquarium. How many milliliters of water does she put in the aquarium?

Ⓐ 100,000 milliliters

Ⓑ 1,000 milliliters

Ⓒ 100 milliliters

Ⓓ 10,000 milliliters

13. **Multi-Step** Terry buys 3 kilograms of peanuts for a baseball game. He puts the peanuts in bags of 200 grams each. How many bags of peanuts does he have?

Ⓐ 3,000 bags

Ⓑ 150 bags

Ⓒ 15 bags

Ⓓ 50 bags

TEXAS Test Prep

14. Caroline bought a bag of onions that was labeled 5 kilograms. She needs to know how many grams that is for her recipe. How many grams is 5 kilograms?

Ⓐ 5,000 grams

Ⓑ 50 grams

Ⓒ 50,000 grams

Ⓓ 500 grams

Name ____________________

15.7 Metric Units of Mass and Liquid Volume

Complete.

1. 5,000 grams = ________ kilograms

2. 3 liters = ________ milliliters

3. 9 kilograms = ________ grams

4. 6,000 milliliters = ________ liters

Metric Units of Mass
1 kilogram (kg) = 1,000 grams (g)

Metric Units of Liquid Volume
1 liter (L) = 1,000 milliliters (mL)

Problem Solving Real World

5. A bucket holds 10 liters of water. How many milliliters of water does it hold?

6. Jessie's cat has a mass of 5 kilograms. How many grams is Jessie's cat?

7. Austin bought 2,500 grams of red apples and 3,500 grams of green apples. How many kilograms of apples did Austin buy?

8. Kendal has a 5 liter bottle of orange juice and a 3 liter bottle of grapefruit juice. How many more milliliters of orange juice than grapefruit juice does she have?

9. Kent's backpack has a mass of 6 kilograms. Brent's backpack has a mass of 8 kilograms. How many grams greater is the mass of Brent's backpack?

10. A bottle can hold 2 liters of water. The bottle has 500 milliliters of water in it. How many milliliters more can the bottle hold?

11. The maximum amount a picture hook can hold is 5 kilograms. Can Jamie hang a picture that has a mass of 4,600 grams on the hook? **Explain.**

Lesson Check

TEXAS Test Prep

Fill in the bubble completely to show your answer.

12. A punch bowl holds 16 liters. How many milliliters does the punch bowl hold?

Ⓐ 1,600 milliliters

Ⓑ 160 milliliters

Ⓒ 16,000 milliliters

Ⓓ 160,000 milliliters

13. Tim bought a block of cheese that is labeled 4 kilograms. He wants to cut the cheese into blocks that weigh 200 grams. How many blocks of cheese can Tim cut?

Ⓐ 20

Ⓑ 80

Ⓒ 8

Ⓓ 200

14. Allen bought a 3-kilogram squash and a 2-kilogram squash. How many grams of squash did Allen buy in all?

Ⓐ 50,000 grams

Ⓑ 500 grams

Ⓒ 50 grams

Ⓓ 5,000 grams

15. How many 25 milliliter doses of plant food can Tim get from a 1-liter bottle of plant food?

Ⓐ 40

Ⓑ 4

Ⓒ 400

Ⓓ 4,000

16. Multi-Step Maria has a 2-liter bottle of juice. She pours two 300 milliliter glasses of juice. How much juice is left in the bottle?

Ⓐ 1,940 milliliters

Ⓑ 1,400 milliliters

Ⓒ 800 milliliters

Ⓓ 1,700 milliliters

17. Multi-Step Hannah bought a bag of pears that has a mass of 5 kilograms. She used 1,600 grams of pears for a recipe. What is the mass of the pears she has left?

Ⓐ 3,400 grams

Ⓑ 34 kilograms

Ⓒ 3,400 kilograms

Ⓓ 340 grams

Name ____________________

Module 15 Assessment

Vocabulary

Choose the best term from the box to complete the sentence.

Vocabulary
milliliter
millimeter
pint
pound
yard

1. A __________ is a customary unit used to measure weight. (p. 531)
2. The cup and the __________ are both customary units for measuring liquid volume. (p. 537)
3. A __________ is a metric unit for measuring length or distance. (p. 549)
4. A __________ is a metric unit for measuring liquid volume. (p. 555)

Concepts and Skills

Circle the better estimate. TEKS 4.8.A

5. weight of a school bus 11 tons or 1 ton
6. distance between El Paso and Fort Worth 60 miles or 605 miles
7. height of your desk 1 meter or 3 meters
8. the amount of liquid a coffee cup holds 800 fluid ounces or 8 fluid ounces

Complete the sentence. Write *more* or *less*. TEKS 4.8.A

9. A cat weighs __________ than one ounce.
10. Serena's shoe is __________ than one yard long.

Complete. TEKS 4.8.A, 4.8.B, 4.8.C

11. 5 feet = _____ inches
12. 4 tons = _____ pounds
13. 4 cups = _____ pints
14. 4,000 pounds = _____ tons
15. 2 quarts = _____ cups
16. 36 inches = _____ feet
17. 3 meters = _____ decimeters
18. 40 centimeters = _____ decimeters
19. 7 kilograms = _____ grams

Add or subtract. TEKS 4.8.B, 4.8.C

20. 8 ft 4 in.
− 3 ft 11 in.

21. 7 c 4 fl oz
+ 4 c 3 fl oz

22. 9 yd 1 ft
− 5 yd 2 ft

Fill in the bubble completely to show your answer.

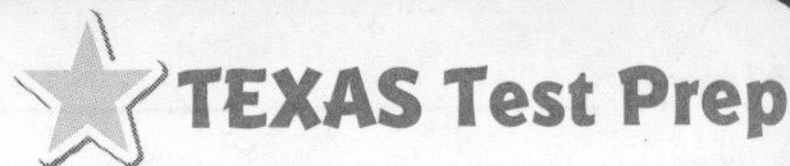

23. A jug contains 8 quarts of water. How many gallons of water does the jug contain? TEKS 4.8.B

Ⓐ 4 gallons

Ⓑ 2 gallons

Ⓒ 3 gallons

Ⓓ 1 gallon

24. Serena bought 4 pounds of dough to make pizzas. The recipe gives the amount of dough needed for a pizza in ounces. How many ounces of dough did she buy? TEKS 4.8.B

Ⓐ 8 ounces

Ⓑ 96 ounces

Ⓒ 64 ounces

Ⓓ 16 ounces

25. Kainoa bought a brick of modeling clay that was labeled 2 kilograms. He needs to separate the clay into balls that are measured in grams. How many grams does he have? TEKS 4.8.B

Ⓐ 20,000 grams

Ⓑ 200 grams

Ⓒ 2,000 grams

Ⓓ 20 grams

26. Lewis fills his thermos with 2 liters of water. Garret fills his thermos with 1 liter of water. How many more milliliters of water does Lewis have than Garret? TEKS 4.8.B, 4.8.C

Ⓐ 1 more milliliter

Ⓑ 2,000 more milliliters

Ⓒ 1,000 more milliliters

Ⓓ 100 more milliliters

Name ________________________________

16.1 Units of Time

TEKS Geometry and Measurement—4.8.C
Also 4.8.B
MATHEMATICAL PROCESSES
4.1.A, 4.1.C

Essential Question

How can you use models to compare units of time?

Unlock the Problem

The analog clock below has an hour hand, a minute hand, and a **second** hand to measure time. The time is 4:30:12.

Read Math

Read 4:30:12 as 4:30 and 12 seconds, or 30 minutes and 12 seconds after 4.

- Are there more minutes or seconds in one hour?

  ____

There are 60 seconds in a minute and 60 minutes in an hour. The clocks below show the length of a second, a minute, and an hour.

Start Time: 3:00:00

1 second elapses.

The time is now 3:00:01.

1 minute, or 60 seconds, elapses. The second hand has made a full turn clockwise.

The time is now 3:01:00.

1 hour, or 60 minutes, elapses. The minute hand has made a full turn clockwise.

The time is now 4:00:00.

Example 1 How does the size of an hour compare to the size of a second?

There are ______ minutes in an hour.

There are ______ seconds in a minute.

60 minutes × ______ = ______ seconds

Think: Multiply the number of minutes in a hour by the number of seconds in a minute.

There are ______ seconds in an hour.

So, 1 hour is ______ times as long as 1 second.

Math Talk
Mathematical Processes

How many full turns clockwise does a minute hand make in 3 hours? Explain.

Example 2 Compare measures.

Materials ■ color pencils

The number line below shows the relationship between days and weeks.

STEP 1 Use a color pencil to shade 1 week on the number line.

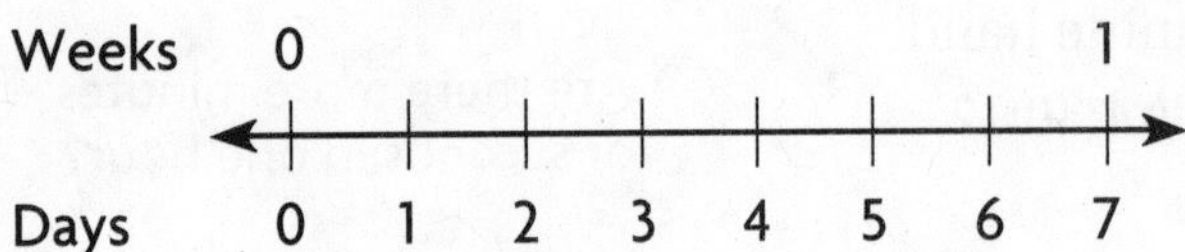

STEP 2 Use a different color pencil to shade 1 day on the number line.

STEP 3 Compare the size of 1 week to the size of 1 day.

There are ______ days in ______ week.

So, 1 week is ______ times as long as 1 day.

Share and Show

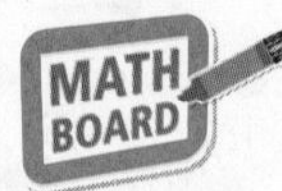

Units of Time
1 minute (min) = 60 seconds (s)
1 hour (hr) = 60 minutes
1 day (d) = 24 hours
1 week (wk) = 7 days
1 year (yr) = 12 months (mo)
1 year (yr) = 52 weeks

1. Compare the length of a year to the length of a month. Use a model to help.

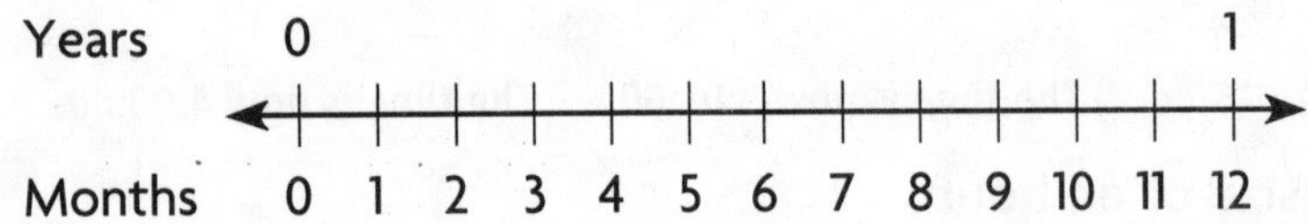

1 year is ______ times as long as ______ month.

Math Talk Mathematical Processes

Explain how the number line helped you compare the length of a year and the length of a month.

Complete.

2. 2 minutes = ______ seconds

3. 4 years = ______ months

Algebra **Compare using <, >, or =.**

4. 3 years ◯ 35 months

5. 2 days ◯ 40 hours

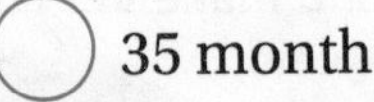

Name ______________________________

Problem Solving Real World

6. Damien has lived in the apartment building for 5 years. Ken has lived there for 250 weeks. Who has lived in the building longer? **Explain**. Make a table to help.

Years	Weeks
1	
2	
3	
4	
5	

7. H.O.T. **Multi-Step** How many hours are in a week? **Explain.**

8. Write Math ▶ **Explain** how you know that 9 minutes is less than 600 seconds.

9. H.O.T. **Apply** Football practice lasts 3 hours. The coach wants to spend an equal number of minutes on each of 4 different plays. How many minutes will the team spend on each play?

10. Martin's brother just turned 2 years old. What is his brother's age in months?

11. **Multi-Step** Mr. Perry drove 2 hours. Mrs. Martin drove 135 minutes. Miss Lawrence drove 25 minutes longer than Mrs. Martin. How much longer did Miss Lawrence drive than Mr. Perry?

12. H.O.T. Shannon's little brother is 7 weeks old. She is exactly 3 years and 3 days older than he is. How old is Shannon in days? Assume that a year is 365 days.

Mathematical Processes
Model • Reason • Communicate

Daily Assessment Task

Fill in the bubble completely to show your answer.

13. Kate's pet cat is 3 years old. How many months old is her cat?

Ⓐ 12 months

Ⓑ 180 months

Ⓒ 13 months

Ⓓ 36 months

14. **Evaluate** Derrick has visited his grandparents for 5 weeks every summer for 6 years. How many days has he visited his grandparents?

Ⓐ 210 days

Ⓑ 42 days

Ⓒ 1,820 days

Ⓓ 420 days

15. **Multi-Step** Damian wants to study for 2 hours. He wants to spend an equal amount of minutes studying each of 3 different subjects. How many minutes will he spend studying each subject?

Ⓐ 120 minutes

Ⓑ 30 minutes

Ⓒ 40 minutes

Ⓓ 180 minutes

TEXAS Test Prep

16. In 7 days, 4 hours and 35 minutes, Michael is flying to Houston. How many minutes is that?

Ⓐ 172 minutes

Ⓑ 10,355 minutes

Ⓒ 207 minutes

Ⓓ 2,760 minutes

Homework and Practice

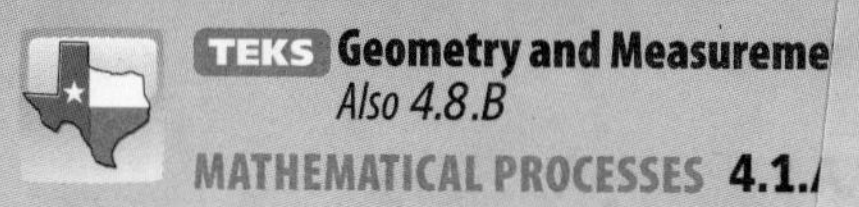

Name ______

16.1 Units of Time

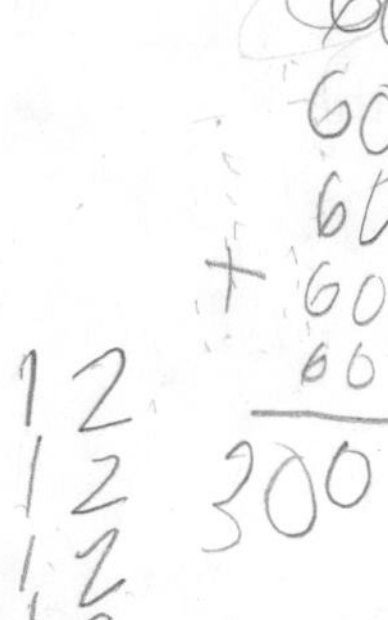

Complete.

1. 9 weeks = __63__ days
2. 4 years = __48__ months
3. 5 minutes = __300__ seconds
4. __72__ hours = 3 days

Units of Time
1 minute (min) = 60 seconds (s)
1 hour (hr) = 60 minutes
1 day (d) = 24 hours
1 week (wk) = 7 days
1 year (yr) = 12 months (mo)
1 year (yr) = 52 weeks

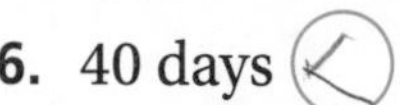

Compare using <, >, or =.

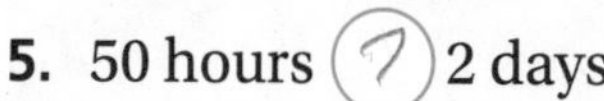

5. 50 hours (>) 2 days
6. 40 days (<) 5 weeks
7. 3 minutes (<) 200 seconds
8. 8 hours (>) 480 minutes

Problem Solving

9. **Multi-Step** It takes Emily 40 minutes to drive to a football game. It takes Mark 1 hour and 15 minutes longer. How many minutes does it take Mark to drive to the football game? **Explain.**

   it takes Mark to drive 1 hour and 55 minutes

10. Brandon was on vacation for 2 weeks and 1 day. He spent the same amount of time with each of his 3 brothers. How many days did he spend with each brother? **Explain.**

   2 weecks and 1 day

Lesson Check

TEXAS Test Prep

Fill in the bubble completely to show your answer.

11. Alison's solar panels have a 10-year guarantee. For how many months is the guarantee good?

Ⓐ 60 months

Ⓑ 120 months

Ⓒ 600 months

Ⓓ 520 months

12. The circus stayed in Bloomington for 3 weeks. How many days was the circus in town?

Ⓐ 21 days

Ⓑ 90 days

Ⓒ 36 days

Ⓓ 72 days

13. Multi-Step Carmen takes 1 breath every 4 seconds. How many breaths will she take in 1 minute?

Ⓐ 40

Ⓑ 28

Ⓒ 15

Ⓓ 20

14. Multi-Step It takes Alden 20 minutes to walk 1 mile. How many miles can Alden walk in 2 hours?

Ⓐ 3 miles

Ⓑ 12 miles

Ⓒ 8 miles

Ⓓ 6 miles

15. Multi-Step Greg spent 3 hours practicing his guitar. He spent the same amount of time practicing each of 4 songs. How many minutes did Greg spend practicing each song?

Ⓐ 45 minutes

Ⓑ 30 minutes

Ⓒ 55 minutes

Ⓓ 10 minutes

16. Multi-Step This summer, Nora spent 8 days visiting her aunt and 2 weeks visiting her grandmother. In all, how many days did she spend visiting?

Ⓐ 10 days

Ⓑ 22 days

Ⓒ 32 days

Ⓓ 14 days

Name ____________________________________

16.2 PROBLEM SOLVING • Elapsed Time

Essential Question How can you use the strategy *draw a diagram* to solve elapsed time problems?

Unlock the Problem

Dora and her brother Kyle spent 1 hour and 35 minutes doing yard work. Then they stopped for lunch at 1:20 P.M. At what time did they start doing yard work?

Use the graphic organizer to help you solve the problem.

Read

What do I need to find?

I need to find the time that Dora and Kyle

____________________.

What information am I given?

I am given the

____

and the time that they

____________________.

Plan

What is my plan or strategy?

I can draw a time line to help me count backward and find the ____________.

Solve

I draw a time line that shows the end time 1:20 P.M. Next, I count backward 1 hour and then 5 minutes at a time until I have 35 minutes.

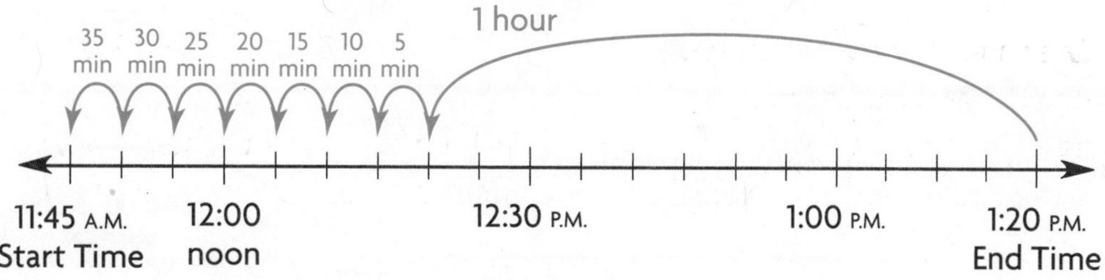

So, Dora and her brother Kyle started doing yard work at ____________.

1. **What if** Dora and Kyle had spent 50 minutes doing yard work and had stopped for lunch at 12:30 P.M.? What time would they have started doing yard work?

____

Try Another Problem

Ben started riding his bike at 10:05 A.M. He stopped 23 minutes later when his friend Robbie asked him to play kickball. At what time did Ben stop riding his bike?

Read		Plan
What do I need to find?	**What information am I given?**	**What is my plan or strategy?**

Solve

10:05 A.M. 10:10 A.M. 10:15 A.M. 10:20 A.M. 10:25 A.M. 10:30 A.M.

2. How did your diagram help you solve the problem?

____

____

Math Talk

Mathematical Processes

Describe another way you could find the time an activity started or ended given the elapsed time and either the start or end time.

Name ______________________________

Share and Show

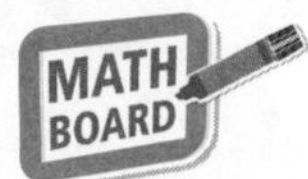

1. Evelyn has dance class every Saturday. It lasts 1 hour and 15 minutes and is over at 12:45 P.M. At what time does Evelyn's dance class begin?

Draw a time line to show the end time and the elapsed time.

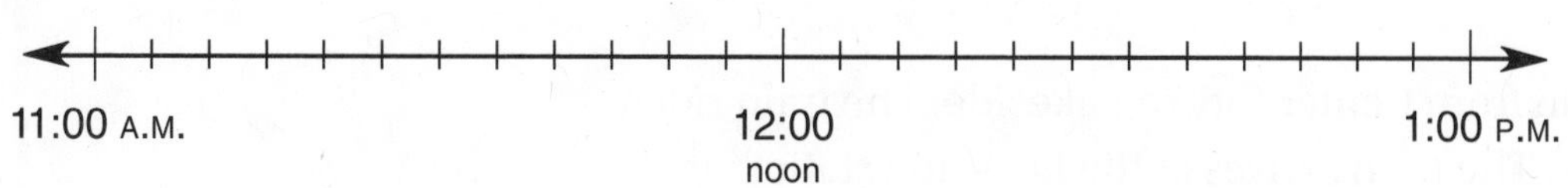

Finally, find the start time.

Evelyn's dance class begins at ___________ .

2. H.O.T. **What if** Evelyn's dance class started at 11:00 A.M. and lasted 1 hour and 25 minutes? At what time would her class end? **Describe** how this problem is different from Problem 1.

____

____

Unlock the Problem

Tips

- Use the Problem Solving MathBoard.
- Choose a strategy you know.
- Underline important facts.

Problem Solving Real World

3. Apply Beth got on the bus at 8:06 A.M. Thirty-five minutes later, she arrived at school. At what time did Beth arrive at school?

____

4. H.O.T. **Multi-Step** Bethany finished her math homework at 4:20 P.M. She did 25 multiplication problems in all. If each problem took her 3 minutes to do, at what time did Bethany start her math homework?

____

Daily Assessment Task

Fill in the bubble completely to show your answer.

5. Leo records his sister's piano recital. The recital starts at 1:15 P.M. and lasts 1 hour and 22 minutes. What time does the recital end?

   Ⓐ 1:37 P.M.
   Ⓑ 2:22 P.M.
   Ⓒ 2:37 P.M.
   Ⓓ 1:22 P.M.

6. James rides the train from Center City to Lakeside. The train ride lasts for 18 minutes. The train arrives at the Lakeside station at 9:12 A.M. What time did the train ride start?

   Ⓐ 9:02 A.M.
   Ⓑ 8:54 A.M.
   Ⓒ 8:30 A.M.
   Ⓓ 8:44 A.M.

7. H.O.T. **Multi-Step** Cleo starts playing softball at 10:18 A.M. She plays for 1 hour and 35 minutes and then stops to eat lunch. Her lunch lasts 25 minutes. What time does Cleo's lunch end?

   Ⓐ 11:53 A.M.
   Ⓑ 12:18 A.M.
   Ⓒ 11:43 A.M.
   Ⓓ 12:18 P.M.

TEXAS Test Prep

8. Vincent began his weekly chores on Saturday morning at 11:20. He worked for 1 hour and 15 minutes with a 10 minute break. At what time did Vincent finish his chores?

   Ⓐ 12:45 A.M.
   Ⓑ 10:15 A.M.
   Ⓒ 12:45 P.M.
   Ⓓ 1:15 P.M.

Homework and Practice

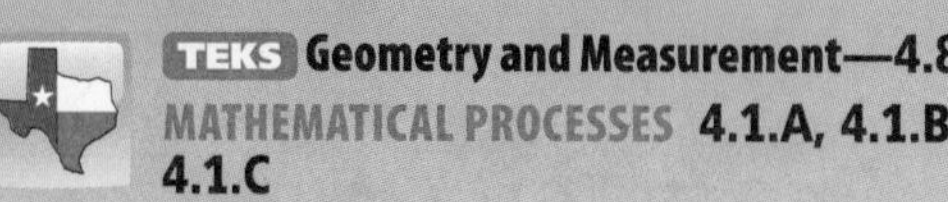

Name ________________

16.2 PROBLEM SOLVING • Elapsed Time

1. Elizabeth goes to chorus practice after school. Practice lasts 1 hour and 20 minutes and is over at 4:40 P.M. At what time does chorus practice begin?

   Draw a time line to show the end time and the elapsed time.

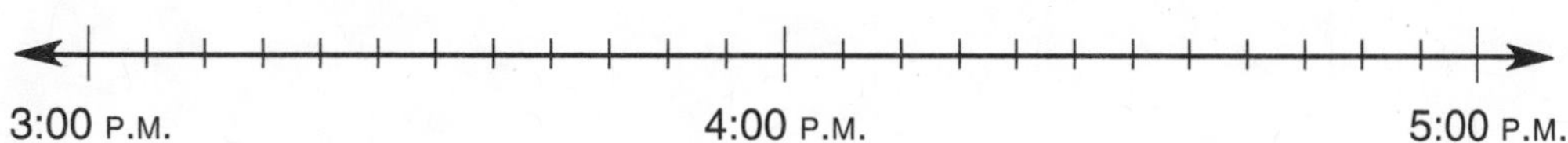

   Chorus practice begins at ________

2. What if chorus practice started at 3:10 P.M. and ended at 4:25 P.M.? How long would chorus practice last? Describe how this problem is different from Problem 1.

____

____

____

Problem Solving

3. Jason left his house at 9:58 A.M. He arrived at the baseball field 16 minutes later. At what time did Jason arrive at the baseball field?

   ____

4. Amanda arranged 5 baskets of flowers. She finished at 4:10 P.M. It took her 20 minutes to arrange each basket of flowers. At what time did Amanda begin?

   ____

5. Play rehearsal started at 8:12 P.M. and ended at 10:05 P.M. How long did play rehearsal last?

   ____

Lesson Check

TEXAS Test Prep

Fill in the bubble completely to show your answer.

6. Karen slept for 8 hours and 10 minutes. She got up at 7:40 A.M. What time did Karen go to bed?

Ⓐ 11:30 P.M.

Ⓑ 3:50 A.M.

Ⓒ 11:30 A.M.

Ⓓ 3:50 P.M.

7. Greg rented a movie that is 2 hours and 18 minutes long. He started the movie at 7:12 P.M. What time will the movie end?

Ⓐ 9:06 P.M.

Ⓑ 10:30 P.M.

Ⓒ 9:30 P.M.

Ⓓ 4:54 P.M.

8. Don is baking cookies. He put a tray of cookies in the oven at 10:50 A.M. The cookies need to bake for 12 minutes. What time will the cookies be done?

Ⓐ 10:02 A.M.

Ⓑ 11:12 A.M.

Ⓒ 10:38 A.M.

Ⓓ 11:02 A.M.

9. Ashley wants to arrive at the airport at 3:30 P.M. It takes her 1 hour and 40 minutes to get there. What time should Ashley leave her house?

Ⓐ 5:50 P.M.

Ⓑ 5:10 P.M.

Ⓒ 1:40 P.M.

Ⓓ 1:50 P.M.

10. **Multi-Step** Cora arrived at school at 7:55 A.M. She left school for 1 hour for a doctor's appointment. She was dismissed from school at 3:15 P.M. How long was Cora at school?

Ⓐ 7 hours and 20 minutes

Ⓑ 6 hours and 20 minutes

Ⓒ 7 hours and 15 minutes

Ⓓ 8 hours and 20 minutes

11. **Multi-Step** Mike starts his run at 11:30 A.M. and runs four 12-minute miles. What time does Mike finish his run?

Ⓐ 12:08 A.M.

Ⓑ 12:18 P.M.

Ⓒ 12:42 P.M.

Ⓓ 12:18 A.M.

Name ______________________________

16.3 Add and Subtract Money

Essential Question How can you use addition and subtraction in problems involving money?

Unlock the Problem Real World

The balance in Marsha's savings account is $423.54. She makes a deposit of $58.95. What is the balance in her savings account now?

The amount of money that is in an account after a deposit or withdrawal is made is called the **balance.** A **deposit** is when money is added to the balance of an account. A **withdrawal** is when money is subtracted from the balance of an account.

Math Idea

You can add and subtract decimals the same way you add and subtract whole numbers if you line up the decimal points first.

Use addition to find the balance after a deposit.

STEP 1

Line up the decimal points. Add the hundredths.

```
  $423.54
+ $ 58.95
```

STEP 2

Add the tenths. Regroup as needed.

```
       1
  $423.54
+ $ 58.95
        9
```

STEP 3

Add the ones, tens, and hundreds. Place the decimal point in the sum.

```
    11
  $ 423.54   starting balance
+ $  58.95   deposit
  $     49   new balance
```

So after the deposit, the balance in Marsha's savings account is __________.

Use subtraction to find the balance after a withdrawal.

Two weeks later, Marsha withdraws $75.34. What is the balance now?

STEP 1

Subtract the hundredths.

```
  $482.49
 −$ 75.34
```

STEP 2

Subtract the tenths.

```
  $482.49
 −$ 75.34
        5
```

STEP 3

Subtract the ones, tens, and hundreds. Place the decimal point in the difference.

```
    712
  $482.49   starting balance
 −$ 75.34   withdrawal
  $    15   new balance
```

So after the withdrawal, the balance in Marsha's savings account is __________.

Share and Show

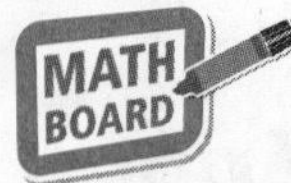

1. Mrs. Freeman has a checking account with a balance of $442.37. She writes a check for $63.92. Then she makes a deposit of $350.00. What is the final balance in her checking account after writing the check and making the deposit?

First use subtraction to find the balance after writing the check.

Starting balance:	**$442.37**
Check amount:	−
Balance after writing the check:	

Then use addition to find the final balance after making the deposit.

Balance after writing the check:	
Deposit amount:	+
Final balance after making the deposit:	

So, Mrs. Freeman's final balance is ________.

2. Jeremy has a school store account with a balance of $16.82. He spends $2.75 to buy a new marker. What is the balance of Jeremy's school store account?

____

3. Sarah has $789.59 in her checking account. She makes a deposit of $65.32. Then she writes a check for $105.00. What is the balance of her checking account after she writes the check?

____

Problem Solving

4. H.O.T. **Analyze** Lana's checking account had a balance of $589.33 at the beginning of the month. She made no deposits that month and the bank charged no fees. At the end of the month, her balance was $472.58. How much had she written in checks that month? **Explain**.

____

____

____

5. **Multi-Step** Ponce went shopping with $20. He bought a shirt for $7.89 at one store and a DVD for $11.79 at another. How much money did he have left after he bought the shirt and the DVD?

____

Name ______________________

Problem Solving Real World

6. **H.O.T.** **Multi-Step** Mitch began the month with $733.12 in his savings account. He deposited his earnings of $24.00 for babysitting and $31.00 for doing chores. That same month, he withdrew $331.76. How much money was in his account at the end of the month?

____

7. **H.O.T.** **Multi-Step** Max has $720.67. He spends $435.22 on an HD television and $102.65 on a DVD player. How much money does Max have now?

____

8. **H.O.T.** **Multi-Step** Paul wants to know what his balance was at the beginning of the month. He knows his balance was $978.45 at the end of the month. During the month, he withdrew $332.70 and deposited $500.00. What was his beginning balance? **Explain** how you got your answer.

____

____

____

____

____

9. **H.O.T.** **Multi-Step** Nick wants to start a lawn mowing business. He will pay his workers $15.25 to mow a lawn. It costs $4.77 for gas to mow one lawn. If Nick charges his customer $32.00 to mow the lawn, how much will he have left after paying his worker and paying for the gas?

____

Write Math ▸ **Show Your Work**

Daily Assessment Task

Fill in the bubble completely to show your answer.

10. **Multi-Step** At the end of March, Vicki had an account balance of $185.78. Since then, she has written two checks, one for $25.50 and another for $18.34. How much is in her account now?

Ⓐ $160.28
Ⓑ $141.94
Ⓒ $178.62
Ⓓ $167.44

11. Mrs. Jackson bought lunch for herself and two friends. The lunches cost $8.25, $6.00, and $10.50. How much do the three lunches cost all together?

Ⓐ $24.00
Ⓑ $11.25
Ⓒ $38.25
Ⓓ $24.75

12. **Multi-Step** Doug bought a pair of sneakers for $47.82 and a shirt for $11.36. If Doug had $100 before his purchase, how much money does he have left now?

Ⓐ $38.18
Ⓑ $59.18
Ⓒ $40.82
Ⓓ $35.82

TEXAS Test Prep

13. Mrs. Proctor worked for a company that gave her $300 for travel. She spent $114.59 for a hotel room, $15.97 for lunch and $25.83 for dinner. How much money did she have left at the end of her trip?

Ⓐ $227.21
Ⓑ $156.39
Ⓒ $143.61
Ⓓ $372.79

Homework and Practice

Name ____________________

16.3 Adding and Subtracting Money

1. Kim had $472.15 in her checking account. She deposited $188.50 and wrote a check for $263.89. How much is in Kim's checking account now?

____

2. Julia sold her bicycle for $88.50. She sold her bicycle helmet for $8.75. She bought a basketball for $35.82. How much money does Julia have now?

____

3. Nick's lunch cost $14.75. Tax was $1.03 and he left a tip of $2.50. How much did Nick pay for his lunch?

____

4. Mario buys a shirt for $28.95 and a pair of socks for $4.29. He gives the clerk at the store two $20 bills. How much change should Mario receive?

____

Problem Solving Real World

5. Susan bought a hat and gave the salesperson at the store $50.00. She got $13.72 back in change. How much did Susan pay for the hat? **Explain** how you got your answer.

____

____

6. At the beginning of the month, Javier had $671.90 in his checking account. At the end of the month, he had $422.15. He knows he wrote 2 checks. One check was for $118.42. How much was the other check for? **Explain** how you got your answer.

____

____

____

____

Lesson Check

Fill in the bubble completely to show your answer.

7. Brad had $515.97 in his savings account at the beginning of the month. At the end of the month he had $648.47 in the account. If Brad withdrew no money that month, how much money did he deposit into his savings account that month?

   Ⓐ $133.50 Ⓒ $1,153.34

   Ⓑ $1,164.44 Ⓓ $132.50

8. Leslie bought a magazine for $5.98. She paid with a $10.00 bill. How much change did Leslie receive?

   Ⓐ $5.02

   Ⓑ $4.12

   Ⓒ $4.02

   Ⓓ $5.12

9. **Multi-Step** Carina had $283.20 in her checking account. She wrote checks for $28.50 and $35.67. How much is left in Carina's checking account?

   Ⓐ $219.03

   Ⓑ $262.13

   Ⓒ $230.03

   Ⓓ $219.13

10. **Multi-Step** Allen wants to buy a television for $789.98. He has $512.16 in savings. He can save another $123.62 this week. How much more money does he need to buy the television?

    Ⓐ $143.20

    Ⓑ $401.44

    Ⓒ $154.20

    Ⓓ $635.78

11. **Multi-Step** Lucy spent $16.08 for a dog collar and $43.57 for a dog bed. She has $25.45 left. How much money did Lucy have before she went shopping?

    Ⓐ $85.10

    Ⓑ $7.06

    Ⓒ $74.90

    Ⓓ $75.12

12. **Multi-Step** Barry had $68.17 in his pocket. His friend Jack returned $20.00 he borrowed from Barry. Then Barry spent $32.91 on groceries. How much money does Barry have now?

    Ⓐ $17.26

    Ⓑ $55.26

    Ⓒ $56.26

    Ⓓ $56.06

Name ____________________

16.4 Multiply and Divide Money

TEKS Geometry and Measurement—4.8.C
MATHEMATICAL PROCESSES
4.1.A, 4.1.C, 4.1.G

Essential Question

How can you use multiplication and division in problems involving money?

Unlock the Problem

Example 1 Mrs. Cleary wants to buy books for her bookstore. The new novel she wants comes in a case containing 48 books. Each book costs her $15. How much would 1 case of the books cost?

Math Idea

Multiplying and dividing money is just like multiplying and dividing whole numbers.

Use place value and regrouping. Multiply. 48 × $15

STEP 1

Think of 48 as 4 tens and 8 ones. Multiply $15 by 8 ones, or 8.

```
   4
 $15
× 48
 ___  ← 8 × 15
```

STEP 2

Multiply 15 by 4 tens, or 40.

```
   2
   4̸
 $15
× 48
 120
 ___  ← 40 × 15
```

STEP 3

Add the partial products. Place a dollar sign in the final product.

```
   2
   4̸
 $15
× 48
 120
+600
 ___
```

So, Mrs. Cleary will pay ____________ for 1 case of the books.

Example 2 Mrs. Cleary paid $584 for 8 cases of a popular magazine. How much did she pay for each case of magazines?

Divide. $584 ÷ 8

STEP 1

Divide the tens.

```
     7
8)$584    Divide: 58 tens ÷ 8
 −___     Multiply: 8 × 7 tens
   ___    Subtract: 58 tens − 56 tens.
```

STEP 2

Divide the ones. Regroup 2 tens as 20 ones.

```
   $ 73
8 )$584    Divide: ______ ones ÷ ______
  −56↓
    24
   −___    Multiply: ______ × ______ ones
    ___    Subtract: ______ ones − ______ ones.
```

Place the dollar sign in the quotient.

So, Mrs. Cleary paid ____________ for each case of magazines.

Share and Show

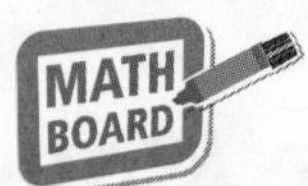

1. Ray bought 18 baseball caps for his baseball team. Each cap costs $29. How much did Ray spend on caps?

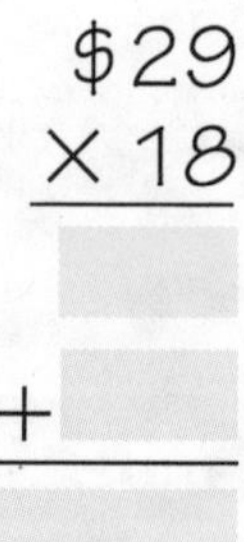

So, Ray spent ___________ on caps.

2. Samantha sold 9 teddy bears that she made. She was paid a total of $126 for all the bears. If the bears were all the same price, what was the price of one bear?

____

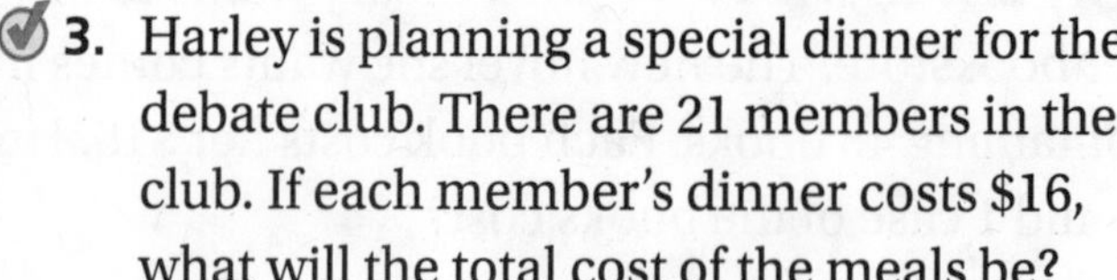

3. Harley is planning a special dinner for the debate club. There are 21 members in the club. If each member's dinner costs $16, what will the total cost of the meals be?

____

Problem Solving

Practice: Copy and Solve

4. $24 \times \$42$

5. $\$453 \div 3$

6. $68 \times \$92$

7. $\$875 \div 7$

8. $\$6{,}295 \div 5$

9. $7 \times \$1{,}372$

10. **H.O.T.** Palo bought a car for $1,284 using money from his savings account. He wants to repay his savings account over the next 6 months. If he saves an equal amount each month, how much will he need to save each month?

____

11. **H.O.T.** **Multi-Step** Lassa bought a car. She paid the dealer $2,220 and then finished paying for her car by making 9 equal payments of $352. How much was the total cost of her car?

____

Name ___________________________

Problem Solving Real World

12. H.O.T. **Multi-Step** Don buys a shirt for $24.85. His friend Daryl spends $3.15 more for his shirt. Sean paid the same price as Daryl for his shirt but bought 2. How much did Sean spend for his 2 shirts?

____

13. H.O.T. **Multi-Step** Stacy buys 3 CDs in a set for $29.75. She saved $6.25 by buying the set instead of buying the CDs separately. If each CD costs the same amount, how much does each of the 3 CDs cost when purchased separately?

____

Write Math ▶ **Show Your Work**

14. H.O.T. **Multi-Step** Julie saved $60. Jeff saved 29 times as much as Julie did. Jeff saved 3 times as much as Marco. How much did Marco save? **Explain** how you found your answer.

____

____

____

____

____

15. H.O.T. **Multi-Step** The grocery store has a sale on soup. One can costs $2.59 but you can buy 8 cans for a total of $16.00. How much do you save per can if you buy 8 at the sale price?

____

16. **Apply** Billy plans to save $55 each month for 5 years. How much will he have at the end of 5 years?

____

Daily Assessment Task

Fill in the bubble completely to show your answer.

17. Jen downloads 7 apps for a total of $24. Two of them cost $2.00 each. If the other apps all cost the same amount, how much does each cost?

Ⓐ $3.43
Ⓑ $3.70
Ⓒ $4
Ⓓ $4.25

18. **Multi-Step** Jeremiah spends $51.25 at the mall. He buys a game for $24.25 and 3 DVDs. If the DVDs are all the same price, how much does 1 DVD cost?

Ⓐ $15
Ⓑ $8
Ⓒ $25
Ⓓ $9

19. **Multi-Step** Delilah buys a loaf of bread, 3 pounds of turkey, and 2 pounds of cheese. The turkey costs $3.00 per pound and the cheese costs $2.00 per pound. A loaf of bread costs $3.49. How much does Delilah spend in all?

Ⓐ $13.75
Ⓑ $16.49
Ⓒ $8.49
Ⓓ $17.49

TEXAS Test Prep

20. While working at the school store, John sold a letter jacket for $40.50 and some notebooks for $2.00 each. If he collected a total of $92.50, how many notebooks did he sell?

Ⓐ 25
Ⓑ 66
Ⓒ 26
Ⓓ 104

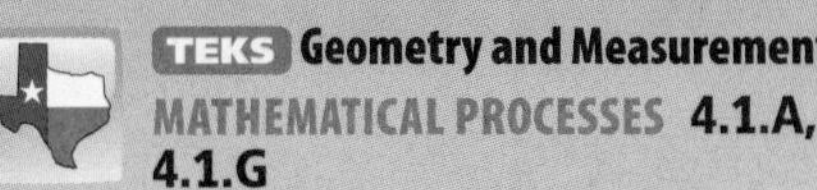

Name ______________________

16.4 Multiplying and Dividing Money

Solve.

1. 26 × $44

2. $318 ÷ 6

3. 35 × $73

4. $572 ÷ 4

5. $7,640 ÷ 5

6. 6 × $1,336

Problem Solving

7. Multi-Step Margie bought 3 identical sweaters for a total of $114. She saved $18 by buying the 3 sweaters on sale rather than at the regular price. What is the regular price of each sweater? **Explain** how you found the answer.

____

____

____

8. Multi-Step Keira rented a car for 3 days. She paid $118 rent each day. Insurance for the 3 days came to a total of $35. How much did Keira pay in all? **Explain** how you found your answer.

____

____

Lesson Check

TEXAS Test Prep

Fill in the bubble completely to show your answer.

9. A box of 5 model race cars costs $115. How much does each model car cost?

   Ⓐ $23
   Ⓑ $25
   Ⓒ $13
   Ⓓ $15

10. Jonathan bought 3 airplane tickets for $478 each. How much did he pay for the three tickets?

   Ⓐ $1,234
   Ⓑ $1,434
   Ⓒ $1,414
   Ⓓ $1,214

11. **Multi-Step** The Wallace family saves the same amount of money each month for vacation. From January 1 to September 30 they saved $1,314. How much does the Wallace family save each month for vacation?

   Ⓐ $156
   Ⓑ $131
   Ⓒ $146
   Ⓓ $152

12. **Multi-Step** A coach bought 3 dozen soccer balls. Each ball cost $28. How much did the coach pay for all of the soccer balls? (Remember, 1 dozen = 12.)

   Ⓐ $84
   Ⓑ $840
   Ⓒ $336
   Ⓓ $1,008

13. **Multi-Step** Tony spent $49 at the fair. Molly spent $14 more than twice as much as Tony spent. How much did the two of them spend in all?

   Ⓐ $112
   Ⓑ $161
   Ⓒ $126
   Ⓓ $140

14. **Multi-Step** Paula bought 8 pairs of socks. She paid $104. Two pairs of socks cost $16 each. The other pairs each cost the same amount. How much did each of the other pairs of socks cost?

   Ⓐ $12
   Ⓑ $17
   Ⓒ $13
   Ⓓ $18

Name ________________________________

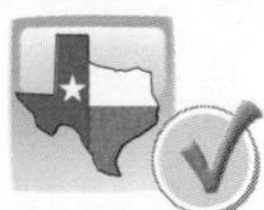

Module 16 Assessment

Vocabulary

Choose the best term from the box to complete the sentence.

Vocabulary
balance
deposit
second
withdrawal

1. A ____________ is a small unit of time. (p. 563)
2. The ____________ is the amount of money that is in an account after a deposit or withdrawal is made. (p. 575)
3. When money is added to the balance of an account it is a ____________. (p. 575)
4. When money is subtracted from the balance of an account it is a ____________. (p. 575)

Concepts and Skills

Complete. TEKS 4.8.B, 4.8.C

Units of Time
1 minute (min) = 60 seconds (s)
1 hour (hr) = 60 minutes
1 day (d) = 24 hours
1 week (wk) = 7 days
1 year (yr) = 12 months (mo)
1 year (yr) = 52 weeks

5. 5 weeks = ______ days
6. 4 minutes = ______ seconds
7. ______ months = 4 years
8. ______ hours = 5 days
9. 8 years = ______ weeks
10. 7 days = ______ hours
11. 14 days = ______ weeks
12. 2 years = ______ weeks

Use a time line to find the start or end time. TEKS 4.8.C.

13. Start time: 11:38 A.M.
Elapsed time: 3 hours 10 minutes
End time: ____________

14. Start time: ____________
Elapsed time: 2 hours 37 minutes
End time: 1:12 P.M.

15. Start time: ____________
Elapsed time: 2 hours 14 minutes
End time: 5:30 P.M.

16. Start time: 7:41 P.M.
Elapsed time: 1 hour 9 minutes
End time: ____________

Fill in the bubble completely to show your answer.

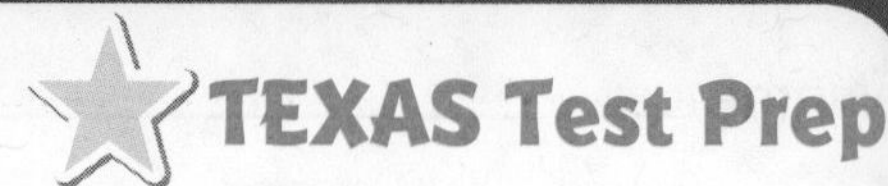

17. Jerome has a balance of $63.45 in his checking account. He withdraws $38.14 to buy a computer game. What is his checking account balance now? TEKS 4.8.C

Ⓐ $35.31

Ⓑ $25.31

Ⓒ $101.59

Ⓓ $5.31

18. Serena buys 3 T-shirts at $12 each and 2 pairs of sandals at $24 each. How much does Serena spend? TEKS 4.8.C

Ⓐ $74

Ⓑ $12

Ⓒ $84

Ⓓ $96

19. Ken had a balance of $1,150.00 in his checking account. He withdrew $85.35 to buy groceries. One week later he deposited $250.00 into his checking account. What is the balance in his checking account now? TEKS 4.8.C

Ⓐ $1,314.65

Ⓑ $900.00

Ⓒ $335.35

Ⓓ $1,335.35

20. Vince bought 8 hardback books to read during the summer. He spent $288 for the books. If each book cost the same amount, how much did one book cost? TEKS 4.8.C

Ⓐ $58

Ⓑ $17

Ⓒ $36

Ⓓ $125

Name ____________________

Unit 4 Assessment

Vocabulary

Vocabulary
acute angle
deposit
milliliter
millimeter
straight angle
withdrawal

1. A ______________ is when money is subtracted from the balance of an account. (p. 575)

2. A ______________ is a metric unit of volume. (p. 555)

3. An angle that is less than 90° is called a(n) ______________. (p. 450)

Concepts and Skills

Tell if the blue line is a line of symmetry. TEKS 4.6.B

4. 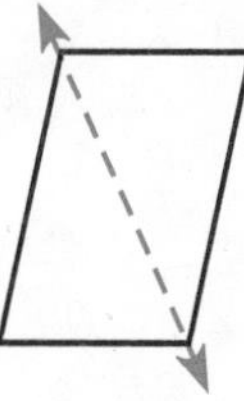

____

5. 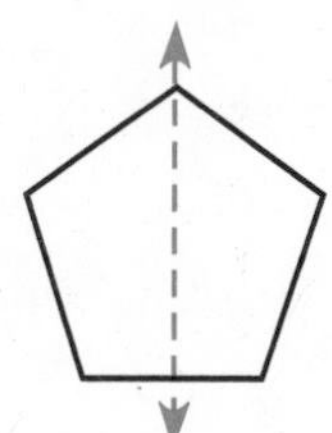

____

6. 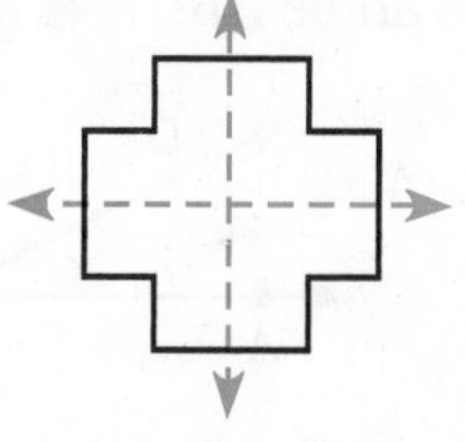

____

Draw all lines of symmetry.

7. 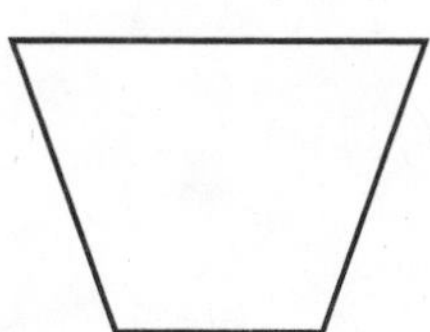

8. 

9. 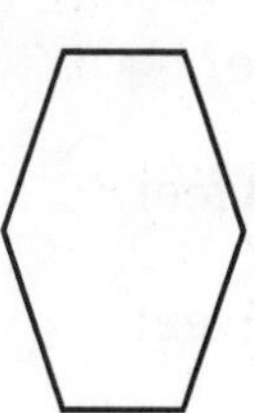

Use the figure for 10–12. TEKS 4.6.A

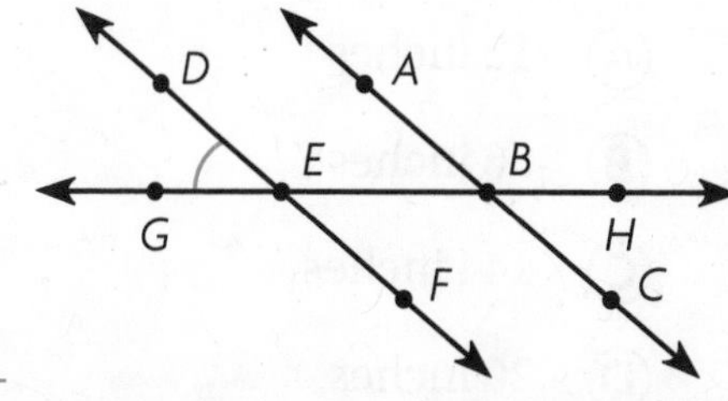

10. Name a pair of parallel lines. ______________

11. Name a ray. ______________

12. Classify angle *DEG*. Write *acute, right, straight,* or *obtuse.*

____

Fill in the bubble completely to show your answer. TEXAS Test Prep

13. Which quadrilateral has only one pair of parallel sides? TEKS 4.6.D

Ⓐ square

Ⓑ rectangle

Ⓒ trapezoid

Ⓓ rhombus

14. Which of the following is true about an acute triangle? TEKS 4.6.C

Ⓐ It has one obtuse angle.

Ⓑ It has one right angle.

Ⓒ It has only one acute angle.

Ⓓ It has three acute angles.

15. Angle *ABC* is a straight angle. What is *x* the measure of the angle *ABD*? TEKS 4.7.E

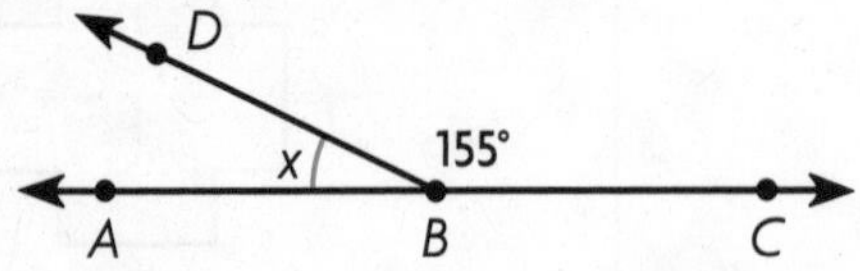

Ⓐ 25°

Ⓑ 65°

Ⓒ 35°

Ⓓ 180°

16. John needs 4 yards of plastic to make his kite. He has 7 feet now. How many more feet of plastic does he need to have enough for his kite? TEKS 4.8.C

Ⓐ 3 feet

Ⓑ 5 feet

Ⓒ 28 feet

Ⓓ 17 feet

17. Paula's dresser is 4 feet tall. Her brother's dresser is 8 inches taller than hers. How many inches tall is her brother's dresser? TEKS 4.8.C

Ⓐ 12 inches

Ⓑ 56 inches

Ⓒ 144 inches

Ⓓ 20 inches

Fill in the bubble completely to show your answer.

18. Maggie's fish tank has 50 gallons of water in it. She takes out 10 quarts. How many quarts of water are now left in the fish tank? TEKS 4.8.B, 4.8.C

Ⓐ 40 quarts

Ⓑ 10 quarts

Ⓒ 190 quarts

Ⓓ 44 quarts

19. Parker's kitten weighed 135 grams when she was born. She now weighs 2 kilograms more than that. How many grams does the kitten weigh? TEKS 4.8.B, 4.8.C

Ⓐ 335 grams

Ⓑ 2,135 grams

Ⓒ 155 grams

Ⓓ 1,370 grams

20. Baxter had 4 kilograms of flour. He made 3 loaves of bread. He used 235 grams to make each loaf. How many grams of flour did he have left? TEKS 4.8.B, 4.8.C

Ⓐ 1,650 grams

Ⓑ 305 grams

Ⓒ 165 grams

Ⓓ 3,295 grams

21. A tour of the island began at 10:25 A.M. It lasted 4 hours and 42 minutes. What time was the tour over? TEKS 4.8.C

Ⓐ 4:17 P.M.

Ⓑ 2:07 P.M.

Ⓒ 3:07 P.M.

Ⓓ 5:17 A.M.

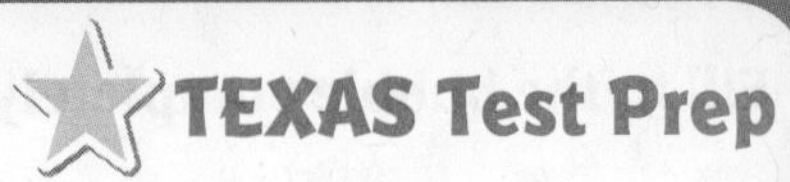

22. Leanne has 6 kilograms of salt. She wants to divide it into portions that are 8 grams each. How many portions will she make?
TEKS 4.8.B, 4.8.C

Ⓐ 750

Ⓑ 14

Ⓒ 48

Ⓓ 75

23. The minute hand of a clock moves clockwise from 3 to 8. What is the measure of the angle that the minute hand cuts? TEKS 4.7.B

Ⓐ 240°

Ⓑ 150°

Ⓒ 75°

Ⓓ 180°

24. Mary has been a member of the debate club for 9 weeks and 5 days. Jack has been a member for 75 days. Who has been a member the longest and by how many days? TEKS 4.8.C

Ⓐ Jack has been a member 12 days longer

Ⓑ Mary has been a member for 20 days longer

Ⓒ Jack has been a member 7 days longer

Ⓓ Not Here

25. Charlotte divided a whole pizza into 4 pieces. One piece formed a straight angle. One piece formed a right angle. Two pieces formed acute angles with the same degree measure. Write an equation that represents the degree measure of the whole pizza as the sum of the measures of its parts. TEKS 4.7.E

____

Unit 5

Data Analysis

Show What You Know

Check your understanding of important skills.

Name ____________________________________

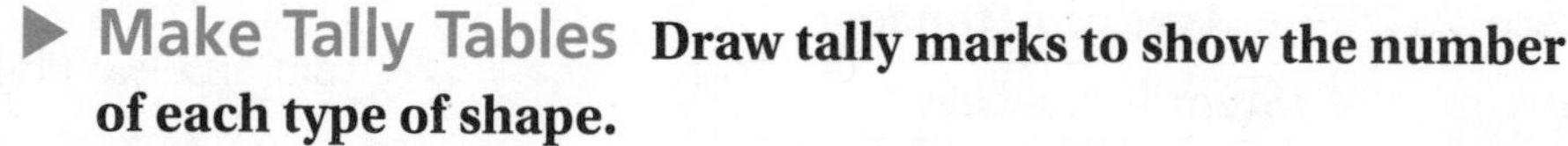

▶ Make Tally Tables Draw tally marks to show the number of each type of shape.

1.

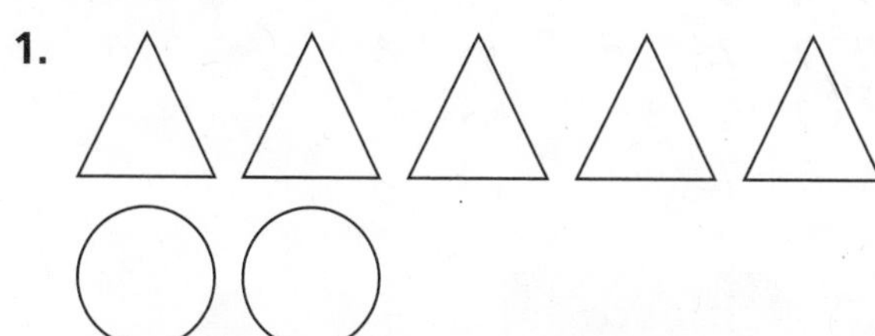

Number of Shapes	
triangle	
circle	

2.

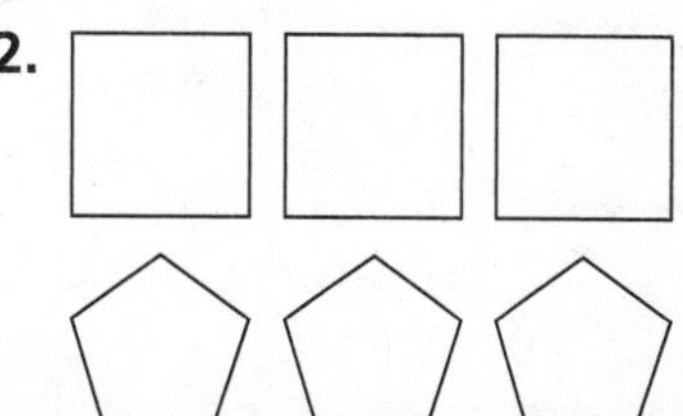

Number of Shapes	
square	
pentagon	

▶ Use Models to Add Fractions with Like Denominators

Shade the fraction strips to show the addition. Write the sum.

3. $\frac{1}{6} + \frac{3}{6}$

1					
$\frac{1}{6}$	$\frac{1}{6}$	$\frac{1}{6}$	$\frac{1}{6}$	$\frac{1}{6}$	$\frac{1}{6}$

4. $\frac{3}{8} + \frac{4}{8}$

1							
$\frac{1}{8}$	$\frac{1}{8}$	$\frac{1}{8}$	$\frac{1}{8}$	$\frac{1}{8}$	$\frac{1}{8}$	$\frac{1}{8}$	$\frac{1}{8}$

▶ Use Models to Subtract Fractions with Like Denominators

Shade the fraction strips to show the subtraction. Write the difference.

5. $\frac{7}{10} - \frac{4}{10}$

1									
$\frac{1}{10}$	$\frac{1}{10}$	$\frac{1}{10}$	$\frac{1}{10}$	$\frac{1}{10}$	$\frac{1}{10}$	$\frac{1}{10}$	$\frac{1}{10}$	$\frac{1}{10}$	$\frac{1}{10}$

6. $\frac{5}{6} - \frac{1}{6}$

1					
$\frac{1}{6}$	$\frac{1}{6}$	$\frac{1}{6}$	$\frac{1}{6}$	$\frac{1}{6}$	$\frac{1}{6}$

GO DIGITAL Assessment Options: Soar to Success Math

Vocabulary Builder

▶ Visualize It

Write the term next to its example.

Review Word
✓ tally table

Preview Words
✓ dot plot
✓ frequency table
✓ stem-and-leaf plot

____

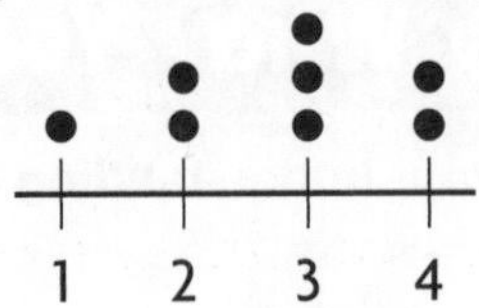

Number of Brothers

____

Ages of Attendees

Stem	Leaves
1	3 4 9
2	0 2 7
3	1 2 2 8
5	3 3 7 9

____

Favorite Subject	
Subject	**Frequency**
English	7
Math	15
History	4
Art	8

▶ Understand Vocabulary

Complete the sentences by using the review and preview words.

1. A ______________ uses tally marks to record data.
2. A graph that records each piece of data on a number line is called a ______________.
3. A ______________ is a graph of data arranged by place value.
4. A table that uses numbers to record data about how often something happens is called a ______________.

GO DIGITAL • Interactive Student Edition • Multimedia eGlossary

Name ______________________________

Vocabulary

In this unit you will make and solve problems using **frequency tables**.

Mr. Jackson surveyed his fourth-grade students. He asked, "How much do you spend for lunch each day?" The tally chart shows his data.

Lunch	
Amount	**Number of Students**
\$1.00	卌 卌 ǀǀ
\$1.25	ǀǀ
\$1.50	卌 ǀǀ
\$1.75	卌 ǀǀǀ
\$2.00	ǀǀǀ
\$2.25	ǀ
\$2.50	ǀǀ

Use the information in the tally chart to answer the questions.

1. How many students spend \$1.75 for lunch? ______

2. How many more students spend \$1.00 for lunch than those that spend \$1.25 and \$2.00 combined? ______

Writing Jessica arrived late to class. She told Mr. Jackson she spent \$2.25 each day for lunch. Does this change the data in the tally table? Explain.

____

Reading Check out this book in your library. *Tiger Math: Learning to Graph from a Baby Tiger* by Ann Whitehead Nagda

Get Ready **Game**

Biking Buddies Dot Plot

Object of the Game Represent and interpret data on a dot plot.

Materials

- 2 number cubes labeled 4–9
- Number lines labeled 8 through 18
- Pencil or marker

Set Up

Each team gets one number line

Number of Players: teams of 2 or 3 players

How to Play

1. Player 1 on each team tosses the two number cubes. The sum of the numbers tossed is the number of miles you ride your bike that day.

Team A

Player 1

2. The player records a dot on the number line for the number of miles.

Player 2

3. Player 2 on each team tosses the two number cubes, finds the sum, and also plots the number of miles on the team's dot plot.

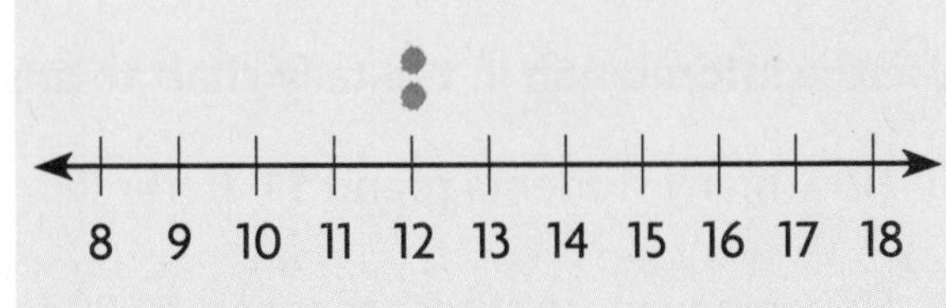

4. Repeat the steps until each player on each team has tossed the cubes 7 times.

5. Teams analyze their dot plots to find the total number of miles the team rode bikes in one week.

6. The team that rode the most number of miles in one week wins the game.

Name ____________________________________

MATHEMATICAL PROCESSES
4.1.C, 4.1.D, 4.1.E

17.1 Frequency Tables

Essential Question How do you make a frequency table from data that is given to you?

Unlock the Problem

A **frequency table** is a table that uses numbers to record data about how often something happens. The **frequency** is the number of times the data occurs.

Example 1

Tony kept a table of the number of minutes he read during a 15 day period. He wants to represent this data in a frequency table. Make a frequency table using the data from the table.

Tony's Reading Times (minutes)				
30	60	30	90	30
120	60	60	30	90
120	120	90	60	30

Make a frequency table.

STEP 1

List the number of minutes from the Tony's Reading Times table in the Minutes column of the frequency table.

STEP 2

Record the frequency of the number of minutes from Tony's Reading Table in the Frequency column.

Complete the frequency table.

Tony's Reading Times	
Minutes	**Frequency**
30	5
60	4
____	____
____	____

- How would the data in Tony's table change if he recorded the number of minutes he read during a 20 day period instead of a 15 day period?

____

- Explain how the frequency table would change to show the new data Tony recorded during 20 day period.

____

____

____

____

Math Talk

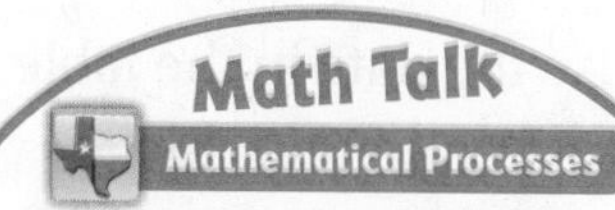

Explain how you used the data in Tony's table to record the numbers in the frequency column.

Example 2

Jasmine went for a walk each day. She recorded the distance she walked in a table. Use the data in the table to make a frequency table.

Make a frequency table to represent the data.

Distance Walked (miles)				
$\frac{1}{2}$	$\frac{1}{4}$	$\frac{3}{4}$	$\frac{3}{4}$	$\frac{1}{2}$
$\frac{3}{4}$	$\frac{1}{2}$	$\frac{3}{4}$	$\frac{1}{2}$	$\frac{1}{4}$

STEP 1

List the distances that Jasmine walked in the Distance column of the frequency table.

STEP 2

Record the frequency of each distance from the Distance Walked table in the Frequency column.

Complete the frequency table.

Distance Walked (miles)	
Distance	**Frequency**
____	____
____	____
____	____

- **Explain** how creating a frequency table whose data is in fractions is similar to creating a frequency table where the data is in whole numbers.

____

____

____

Share and Show

1. Use the data in the table to complete the frequency table.

Time Spent Doing Homework (minutes)				
15	30	30	45	15
45	15	60	45	15
30	60	90	15	30

STEP 1: The title of the frequency table is ____________________

The two column titles are __________ and __________.

STEP 2: List the number of minutes in the Minutes column:

____, ____, ____, ____, ____

STEP 3: List the frequency of the amount of time in the Frequency table:

____, ____, ____, ____, ____

Name ______________________________

2. Make a frequency table using the data in the table.

Time Spent Studying (hour)				
$\frac{1}{2}$	$\frac{1}{4}$	$\frac{1}{2}$	$\frac{3}{4}$	$\frac{1}{2}$
$\frac{1}{4}$	$\frac{1}{4}$	$\frac{3}{4}$	$\frac{1}{2}$	1

3. Make a frequency table using the data in the table.

Distance Traveled on Bike (km)				
4	7	3	9	7
11	3	4	4	9
11	4	7	3	7

Problem Solving

4. H.O.T. **Multi-Step** Gloria likes to hike every Saturday. She records the number of miles she hikes each day. Use the data in the Distance Hiked table to make a frequency table.

Math on the Spot

Distance Hiked (miles)			
7	15	8	12
8	8	7	15
15	15	8	8
12	7	8	12

5. H.O.T. **Explain** how you would use the data in the table to make a frequency table. Then represent the data in a frequency table.

Amount of Pizza Left			
$\frac{1}{8}$	$\frac{1}{8}$	$\frac{1}{2}$	$\frac{1}{4}$
$\frac{1}{4}$	$\frac{3}{8}$	$\frac{1}{4}$	$\frac{1}{2}$
$\frac{1}{2}$	$\frac{1}{4}$	$\frac{3}{8}$	$\frac{1}{8}$

____

____

____

____

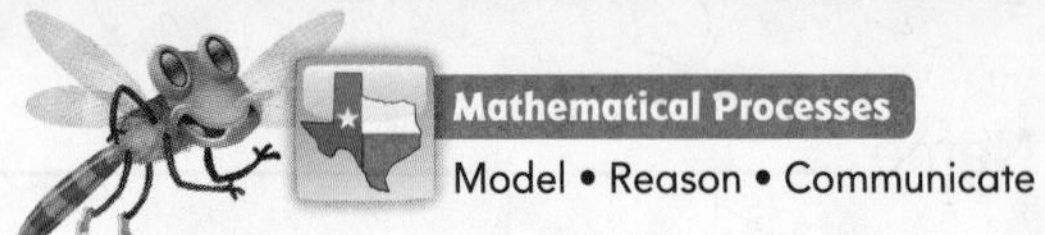

Daily Assessment Task

Fill in the bubble completely to show your answer.

6. Joe made a table to show the length of time he walked.

If Joe were to create a frequency table from this data, what number would he use to show the number of times he walked 45 minutes?

Time Joe Walked (minutes)			
45	30	60	45
90	60	45	90
90	60	30	60
45	60	30	45

Ⓐ 2 Ⓒ 3

Ⓑ 4 Ⓓ 5

Use the table at the right for 7–8.

Jennie has 4 different routes that she goes on when she walks her dog. She made a table to show when she took each of the 4 routes.

Miles Walked With Dog			
$\frac{1}{2}$	$2\frac{1}{8}$	$1\frac{1}{2}$	$1\frac{1}{2}$
$1\frac{3}{4}$	$1\frac{3}{4}$	$\frac{1}{2}$	$1\frac{1}{2}$
$2\frac{1}{8}$	$2\frac{1}{8}$	$1\frac{3}{4}$	$\frac{1}{2}$

7. If Jennie was going to make a frequency table from this data, what number would she put to show the number of times she took the $1\frac{3}{4}$ route?

Ⓐ 3 Ⓒ 2

Ⓑ 5 Ⓓ 4

8. What number would Jennie put for the frequency of $\frac{1}{2}$?

Ⓐ 2 Ⓒ 4

Ⓑ 3 Ⓓ 5

TEXAS Test Prep

9. During a fund-raiser, several students were asked to sell soda during a baseball game. Danny made a table to keep track of the number of sodas students sold.

If Danny were to create a frequency table from this data, what number would he use to show the number of students who sold 10 sodas?

Number of Sodas Sold			
12	10	8	7
7	8	7	10
12	12	10	10
10	10	8	10

Ⓐ 3 Ⓑ 5 Ⓒ 10 Ⓓ 7

TEKS Data Analysis—4.9.A
MATHEMATICAL PROCESSES 4.1.C, 4.1.D, 4.1.E

Name ________________________

17.1 Frequency Tables

1. Make a frequency table using the data in the table.

Number of Laps Run				
3	4	3	5	2
3	5	5	2	1
4	4	3	3	4

2. Make a frequency table using the data in the table.

Books Checked Out				
2	6	3	5	2
3	2	7	3	6
6	3	5	2	3

Problem Solving

3. Paul made a table to show how many hits each baseball player got in 2 games. Use the data from the table to make a frequency table.

Number of Hits					
0	1	1	2	3	3
1	1	1	0	2	3
4	2	2	1	4	0

4. Sahara made a table to show how many cans were left in the recycle bin each day. Use the data from the table to make a frequency table.

Cans Left in Recycling Bin				
10	14	12	10	18
12	18	14	18	14
18	13	10	18	10

Lesson Check

TEXAS Test Prep

Fill in the bubble completely to show your answer.

5. Greg made a table showing the number of baskets he made during 15 basketball practices.

Number of Baskets Made				
12	14	24	18	20
8	17	20	14	14
16	19	20	19	18

If Greg were to make a frequency table from this data, what number would he use to show the number of times he made 14 baskets?

Ⓐ 5
Ⓑ 0
Ⓒ 3
Ⓓ 4

6. Lacy made a table to show the number of miles she walked.

Miles Walked			
1	$\frac{1}{2}$	$\frac{3}{4}$	$\frac{1}{2}$
$1\frac{1}{2}$	1	$\frac{1}{2}$	$\frac{3}{4}$
1	$\frac{3}{4}$	$1\frac{1}{2}$	1

If Lacy were to make a frequency table from this data, what number would she use to show the number of times she walked $\frac{1}{2}$ mile?

Ⓐ 4
Ⓑ 2
Ⓒ 1
Ⓓ 3

Use the table at right for 7–8.

Ellen is training to run a marathon. She made a table to show how many miles she runs each day she trains.

Miles Run Each Day				
10	8	12	10	8
9	13	10	9	13
9	12	8	12	12
12	10	13	9	13

7. **Multi-Step** Ellen made a frequency table from this data. Which mileage will have the greatest frequency?

Ⓐ 12
Ⓑ 13
Ⓒ 9
Ⓓ 10

8. **Multi-Step** Which statement about the frequency table Ellen made is NOT true?

Ⓐ Ellen ran the same number of 9 and 10 mile days.
Ⓑ Ellen ran more 12 mile days than 10 mile days.
Ⓒ Ellen ran four 9, 10, and 13 mile days.
Ⓓ Ellen ran fewer 9 mile days than 8 mile days.

Name ________________________

Problem Solving Real World

Use the frequency table for 4–6.

Number of Miles Hiked	
Miles	Frequency
$2\frac{1}{4}$	15
3	7
$3\frac{1}{2}$	11
$4\frac{3}{4}$	3
$5\frac{1}{8}$	5
$5\frac{3}{4}$	1

4. Jake asked a group of friends he hikes with how many miles they hiked during their vacation. How many of Jake's friends hiked at least $2\frac{1}{4}$ miles during their vacation?

5. H.O.T. Multi-Step How many more friends hiked 3 miles or less than friends that hiked $3\frac{1}{2}$ miles or more? **Explain** your answer.

6. **Use Math Language Explain** how you would find the number of Jake's friends that hiked between $2\frac{1}{4}$ and $4\frac{3}{4}$ miles.

Use the frequency table for 7–8.

7. **Multi-Step** During a fund-raiser, students were asked to sell t-shirts. The school recorded the number of students who sold t-shirts in a frequency table. How many students sold more than 20 t-shirts?

Number of T-Shirts Sold	
T-Shirts	Frequency
15	7
20	8
25	14
30	21
35	3
40	5

8. H.O.T. **Apply** How many t-shirts did the most number of students sell? How many total t-shirts were sold by those students? **Explain**.

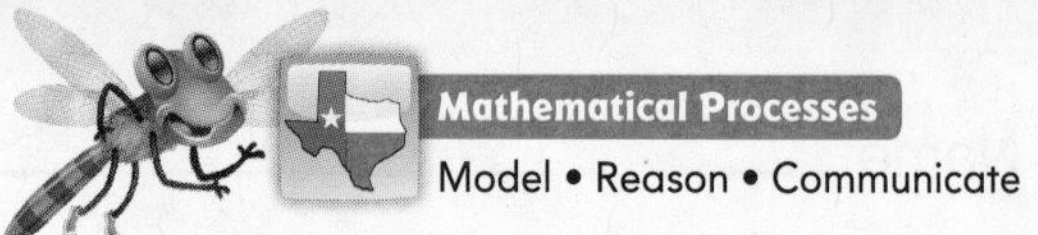

Daily Assessment Task

Fill in the bubble completely to show your answer.

9. **Multi-Step** Monica recorded the frequency of the number of students and the length of time it took them to play a math game. How many more students took $\frac{1}{2}$ hour to play the game than the students that took $\frac{3}{4}$ hour and 1 hour combined?

Time to Complete a Math Game (in hours)	
Time	**Frequency**
$\frac{1}{4}$	11
$\frac{1}{2}$	18
$\frac{3}{4}$	8
1	9

Ⓐ 17

Ⓑ 6

Ⓒ 20

Ⓓ 1

Use the Age of Chorus Members frequency table for 10–11.

Age of Chorus Members	
Age	**Frequency**
10	7
11	4
12	
13	10
14	12
15	1

10. There are half as many 12 year old chorus members than there are 14 year olds. How many 12 year old chorus members are there?

Ⓐ 2 Ⓒ 6

Ⓑ 10 Ⓓ 8

11. **Multi-Step** How many fewer 13 year olds are there in chorus than 10 year olds and 14 year olds combined?

Ⓐ 19 Ⓒ 15

Ⓑ 9 Ⓓ 16

TEXAS Test Prep

12. Dafnie and her friends like to ride bikes. How many of Dafnie's friends rode their bikes either less than 1.1 miles or more than 2.0 miles?

Distance Biked (miles)	
Distance	**Frequency**
0.8	4
1.0	8
1.4	5
1.9	1
2.2	7
2.4	4

Ⓐ 23

Ⓑ 24

Ⓒ 11

Ⓓ 12

TEKS Data Analysis—4.9.B
MATHEMATICAL PROCESSES 4.1.A, 4.1.C, 4.1.D, 4.1.E

Name ______________________

17.2 Use Frequency Tables

Use the frequency table for 1–4.

Number of Boxes of Cookies Sold	
Boxes	**Frequency**
25	4
30	6
35	7
40	5
45	2
50	1

1. Kayla is in charge of cookie sales for her scout troop. How many members sold more than 40 boxes of cookies?

____

2. How many members sold fewer than 40 boxes of cookies?

____

3. How many boxes of cookies did the most number of members sell?

____

4. How many members are represented in Kayla's frequency table?

____

Problem Solving Real World

Use the frequency table for 5–7.

Number of Absences	
Absences	**Frequency**
0	36
1	10
2	15
3	4
4	2

5. The table shows the number of absences in the fourth grade during the school year. How many students were absent either 1 or 2 times during the school year?

____

6. How many students were absent more than 2 times during the school year?

____

7. **Multi-Step** How many more students were absent 2 days or less than students who were absent 3 days or more? **Explain** your answer.

____

____

Lesson Check

Fill in the bubble completely to show your answer.

Use the Grade of Marching Band Members frequency table for 8–9.

Grade of Marching Band Members	
Grade	**Frequency**
9	84
10	51
11	
12	34

8. There are half as many 11th grade students in the band as there are 9th grade students. How many 11th grade students are in the band?

Ⓐ 42 Ⓒ 51

Ⓑ 84 Ⓓ 17

9. How many more 9th grade students are in the band than 10th grade students?

Ⓐ 50 Ⓒ 33

Ⓑ 9 Ⓓ 51

Use the April Rainfall frequency table for 10–11.

April Rainfall (in inches)	
Amount	**Frequency**
$\frac{1}{4}$	5
$\frac{1}{2}$	11
$\frac{3}{4}$	10
1	4

10. **Multi-Step** Olivia recorded the frequency of the amount of rain that fell each day in April. How many more days did it rain less than an inch than it rained 1 inch?

Ⓐ 4 days Ⓒ 26 days

Ⓑ 10 days Ⓓ 22 days

11. **Multi-Step** How many fewer days did it rain $\frac{1}{4}$ inch than $\frac{1}{2}$ inch and $\frac{3}{4}$ inch combined?

Ⓐ 6 days Ⓒ 26 days

Ⓑ 16 days Ⓓ 4 days

Name ___________________________

TEKS Data Analysis—4.9.A

MATHEMATICAL PROCESSES 4.1.C, 4.1.D, 4.1.E

17.3 Dot Plots

Essential Question How do you make a dot plot with whole numbers and fractional data?

Unlock the Problem

A **dot plot** is a graph that shows the frequency of data along a number line.

Example 1

Scott is training to run a half-marathon. He recorded the distances he ran in a table. Use the data in the table to make a dot plot.

Distance Scott Ran (miles)				
4	8	8	7	5
9	9	9	7	9
9	5	7	8	4

STEP 1

Order the data from the least to the greatest distance.

4, 4, ______, ______, ______, ______, ______, ______,

______, ______, ______, ______, ______, ______, ______

Draw a number line. Label it with the distances. Write a title below the number line to describe the data.

Label the distances on the number line from the least value of the data to the greatest. The data points for this dot plot will be

______, ______, ______, ______, ______, and ______.

STEP 2

To represent the data values, place two dots above the 4 on the number line to show how many times Scott ran that distance.

Complete the dot plot by placing the correct number of dots above the distances on the number line.

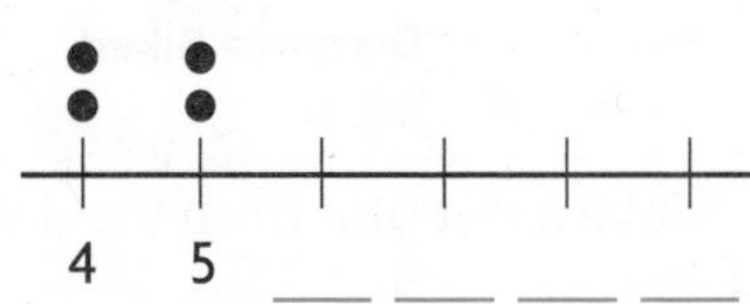

- **Explain** why a dot plot is a useful way to organize and present data.

____

____

Example 2

Kristen practices her tennis serve every day. She records the amount of time she practices, in fractions of an hour. Use the data in the table to make a dot plot to represent the data.

Time Spent Practicing Serving (hour)				
$\frac{1}{4}$	$\frac{3}{4}$	$\frac{3}{4}$	$\frac{3}{4}$	$\frac{1}{2}$
$\frac{3}{4}$	$\frac{1}{2}$	$\frac{1}{4}$	$\frac{1}{2}$	$\frac{1}{2}$
$\frac{1}{4}$	$\frac{1}{2}$	$\frac{1}{2}$	$\frac{1}{4}$	$\frac{1}{2}$

STEP 1

Order the data from the least to greatest fractional part of an hour. Draw a number line. Label it with the fractions. Write a title below it to describe the data.

The data points should start with the least fraction and end with the greatest fraction. The data points for this dot plot will be ____, ____, ____.

STEP 2

Place a dot above each fraction on the number line to show how many times Kristen spent that time practicing her serve.

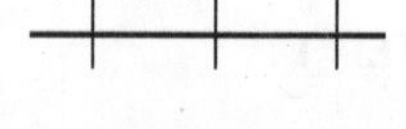

___ ___ ___

Time Spent Practicing Serving

Share and Show

1. Use the data in the Distance Biked table to complete the dot plot.

Distance Biked (km)				
3	5	12	2	1
8	5	8	6	3
11	8	6	4	10
10	9	6	6	6
5	2	1	2	3

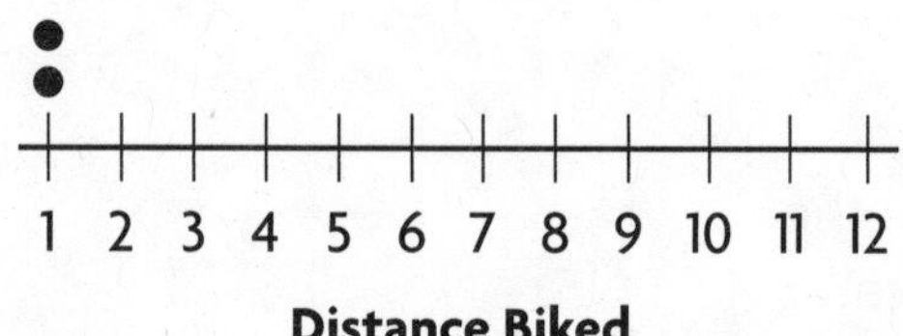

Distance Biked

2. Make a dot plot from the data in the table.

Number of Siblings				
2	2	1	1	3
4	0	1	1	0
2	2	1	3	4
1	0	0	2	0

Name ________________________________

3. Make a dot plot using the data in the table.

Size of Water Samples (gallons)				
$\frac{1}{4}$	$\frac{1}{2}$	$\frac{1}{4}$	$\frac{3}{4}$	$\frac{1}{2}$
$\frac{1}{2}$	$\frac{3}{4}$	$\frac{3}{4}$	$\frac{1}{4}$	$\frac{1}{2}$
$\frac{1}{4}$	$\frac{1}{2}$	$\frac{1}{2}$	$\frac{3}{4}$	$\frac{1}{4}$

4. Make a dot plot using the data in the table.

Number of Cars Sold per Month				
11	14	12	12	11
14	16	11	10	14
10	10	11	13	10

Problem Solving Real World

5. H.O.T. **Multi-Step** Martin wants to build some tool boxes for his friends. He plans to use wood that he already has. He listed the different lengths of the wood he has in a table. Use this data to create a dot plot so Martin can easily visualize what lengths of wood he has.

Length of Wood Pieces (ft)			
$2\frac{5}{8}$	$2\frac{3}{8}$	$2\frac{1}{8}$	$2\frac{4}{8}$
$2\frac{2}{8}$	$2\frac{6}{8}$	$2\frac{3}{8}$	$2\frac{2}{8}$
$2\frac{6}{8}$	$2\frac{1}{8}$	$2\frac{5}{8}$	$2\frac{1}{8}$

6. H.O.T. **Use Graphs Explain** how you would use the data in the table to make a dot plot. Then represent the data in a dot plot.

Number of CDs Owned				
18	23	16	12	15
12	20	14	18	19
14	15	17	12	15

____

____

____

Daily Assessment Task

Fill in the bubble completely to show your answer.

7. Some of the students in Jose's class counted the number of animals each of them saw during recess. Jose wants to make a dot plot to represent the data. How many dots will he place above the number 5?

Number of Animals Seen								
5	3	1	7	2	1	3	5	3

Ⓐ 1 Ⓒ 2

Ⓑ 3 Ⓓ 5

8. Sara went to the beach for a week. She recorded the length of the shells she found each day in the table below. She wants to make a dot plot to represent the lengths she recorded. Which shows the way Sara should label the fraction lengths on the number line?

Length of Seashells Found (in inches)								
$\frac{1}{2}$	$\frac{3}{4}$	$\frac{1}{4}$	$\frac{1}{2}$	$\frac{3}{4}$	1	$\frac{1}{4}$	$\frac{1}{4}$	1

Ⓐ $\frac{1}{4}$ $\frac{1}{2}$ $\frac{3}{4}$ 1

Ⓒ 1 $\frac{3}{4}$ $\frac{1}{4}$ $\frac{1}{2}$

Ⓑ 1 $\frac{1}{2}$ $\frac{1}{4}$ $\frac{3}{4}$

Ⓓ $\frac{1}{4}$ $\frac{3}{4}$ $\frac{1}{2}$ 1

TEXAS Test Prep

9. The data in the table shows the lengths of some pieces of carpet that Justin has. He wants to make a dot plot to show the data. How many dots will Justin place above the $3\frac{1}{2}$?

Ⓐ 0 Ⓒ 3

Ⓑ 1 Ⓓ 4

Length of Carpet Pieces (ft)			
$3\frac{3}{4}$	$2\frac{3}{4}$	$2\frac{1}{2}$	$1\frac{1}{4}$
$2\frac{1}{4}$	$3\frac{1}{2}$	$1\frac{1}{2}$	$2\frac{1}{8}$
$3\frac{1}{4}$	$2\frac{1}{8}$	$1\frac{1}{8}$	$1\frac{1}{8}$

Name ______________________________

17.3 Dot Plots

1. Make a dot plot using the data in the table.

Number of Vowels in First Name			
1	2	2	2
3	4	4	5
1	2	2	2
3	3	1	2
2	2	2	2

2. Make a dot plot using the data in the table.

Time Spent Practicing Piano (in hours)			
$\frac{3}{4}$	1	$\frac{1}{2}$	$\frac{3}{4}$
$1\frac{1}{4}$	$\frac{1}{2}$	$\frac{3}{4}$	1
1	$1\frac{1}{4}$	1	$\frac{1}{2}$
1	$\frac{1}{2}$	1	$\frac{1}{2}$

Problem Solving

3. Jerome took a walk through his neighborhood. He recorded the number of trees he saw in each yard. Use the data in the table to make a dot plot to represent the data.

Number of Trees			
3	0	3	5
4	1	2	0
5	4	4	6
0	5	5	0
1	2	4	2
2	0	1	0

4. Tiffany recorded the amount of time it took her to walk to school each day. Use the data in the table to make a dot plot to represent the data.

Time Spent Walking (in minutes)			
20	18	19	16
18	15	20	18
19	20	15	20
16	19	20	19

Lesson Check

Fill in the bubble completely to show your answer.

5. Mrs. Thompson counted the number of books that students in her class checked out from the library. She wants to make a dot plot to represent the data. How many dots will she place above the number 3?

Number of Books Checked Out								
2	5	4	5	2	3	2	3	2

Ⓐ 6

Ⓑ 3

Ⓒ 9

Ⓓ 2

6. Hector recorded the time he spent watering his yard each day. He wants to make a dot plot to represent the times he recorded. Which shows the way Hector should label the times on the number line?

Time Spent Watering (in minutes)							
16	20	16	18	16	20	19	18

Ⓐ 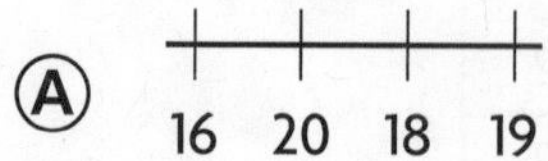

Ⓑ 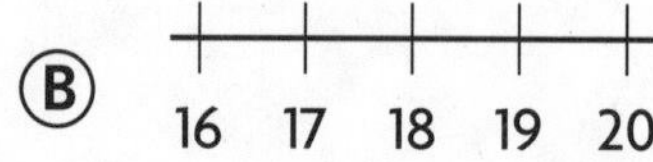

Ⓒ 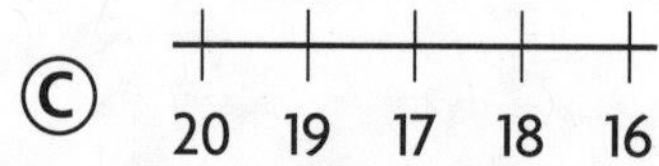

Ⓓ 16 18 19 20

Use the table at right for 7–8.

7. **Multi-Step** Mr. Davis recorded the grades his students scored on a math test. He wants to make a dot plot to represent the data. How many more dots will he place above the 100 than above the 70, 75, and 80 combined?

Ⓐ 2

Ⓑ 6

Ⓒ 3

Ⓓ 4

Grade Scored on Test			
100	85	90	95
85	95	100	80
100	90	70	100
75	95	100	75
90	100	85	95

8. **Multi-Step** Which statement about the dot plot is NOT true?

Ⓐ Fewer students scored 90 than 95.

Ⓑ More students scored 75 than 80.

Ⓒ More students scored 95 than 80 and 85 combined.

Ⓓ The same number of students scored 85 and 90.

Name ____________________

17.4 Use Dot Plots

Essential Question

How do you use dot plots to answer questions involving whole numbers, fractions, and decimals?

Unlock the Problem

You can use a dot plot to organize data to make the data visually easier to read.

Example 1

The dot plot shows the lengths of the buttons in Jen's collection. For an art project, she wants to know how many buttons in her collection are longer than $\frac{1}{4}$. How can she use a dot plot to find the answer?

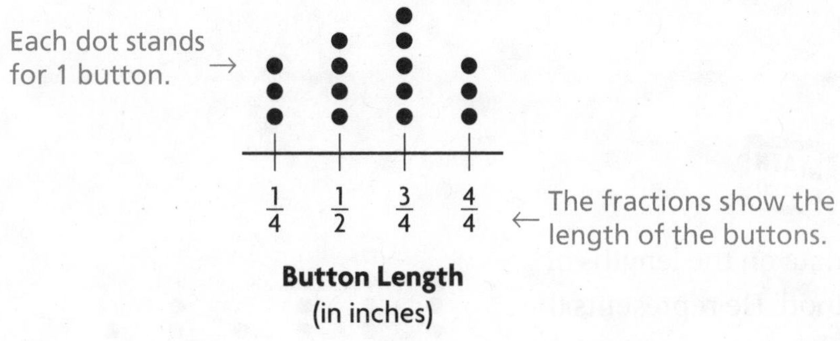

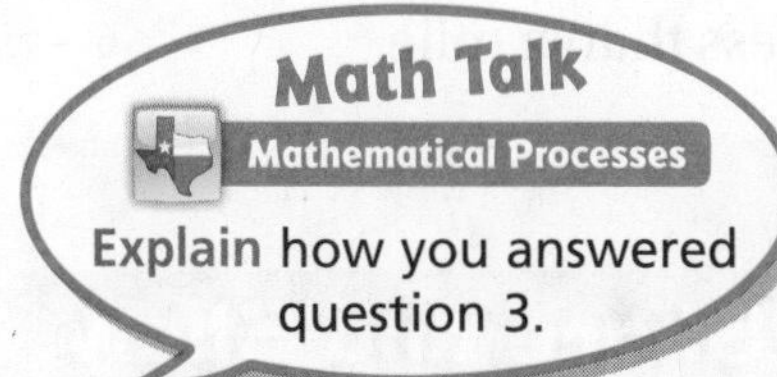

Count the number of dots above each of the button lengths on the dot plot. There are ______ dots above $\frac{1}{4}$, ______ dots above $\frac{1}{2}$, ______ dots above $\frac{3}{4}$, and ______ dots above $\frac{4}{4}$.

Since you are trying to find the number of buttons that have a length greater than ______, count the number of dots above the other fractions to find the answer.

So, ______ buttons in Jen's collection are longer than $\frac{1}{4}$ inch.

1. How many buttons does Jen have in her collection? __________

2. How many buttons are less than $\frac{3}{4}$ inch long? __________

3. What is the difference in length between the longest button and the shortest button in Jen's collection? __________

Example 2 Solve a multi-step problem.

Some of the students in Ms. Lee's class walk around the track during recess.The dot plot shows the distances that the students walked. How many more students walked 1 or more miles than walked less than a mile?

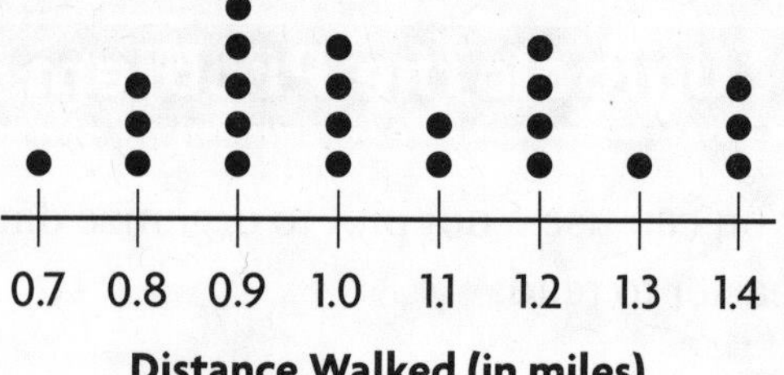

STEP 1 Count the number of dots above 0.7, 0.8, and 0.9.

______ students walked less than ______ mile.

STEP 2 Count the number of dots above 1.0, 1.1, 1.2, 1.3, and 1.4.

______ students walked mile or more.

STEP 3 ______ − ______ = ______

So, ______ more students walked 1 or more miles than walked less than a mile.

Share and Show

1. A restaurant manager collected data on the lengths of time customers waited for their food. He represents the data he collected in a dot plot. How many customers waited for 15 minutes for their food?

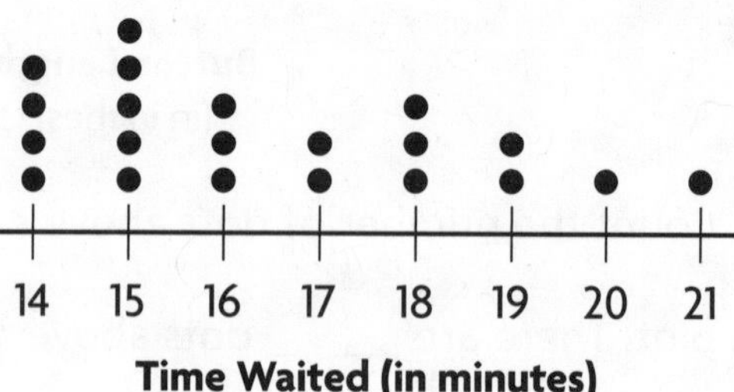

Think: Count the number of • above the 15.

There are ______ dots above the 15 on the dot plot.

So, ______ people waited 15 minutes for their food.

2. How many people did the restaurant manager collect data about?

____

3. How many people waited 17 minutes or less for their food?

____

4. How many more people waited 17 minutes or less than waited 19 minutes or more?

____

Math Talk
Mathematical Processes
Explain how the dot plot helps you answer the question for Exercise 2.

Name ______________________________

Problem Solving Real World

Use the dot plot for 5–6.

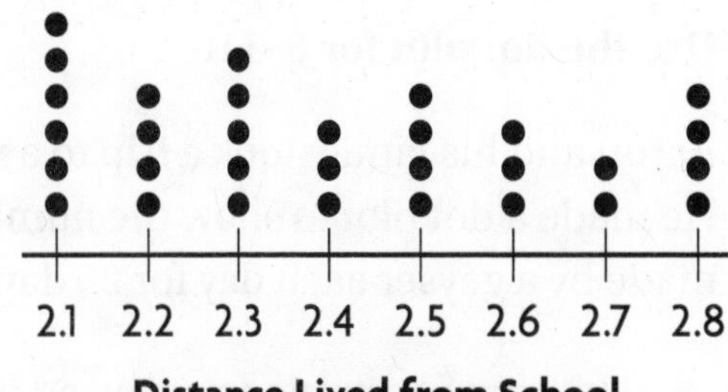

Distance Lived from School (in miles)

5. **Use Graphs** A school collected data from some students about how far they live from the school. How many students live either 2.1 or 2.2 miles from the school?

____

6. **H.O.T.** **Apply** **Multi-Step** Martha wants to know how many more students live more than 2.0 and less than 2.4 miles from school than live more than 2.5 and less than 2.9 miles from school. **Explain** how Martha will determine the answer.

____

____

Unlock the Problem

7. **H.O.T.** **Multi-Step** The dot plot shows the distances some of the track team ran to practice for an upcoming track meet, in miles. Altogether, did the students run more or less than 5 miles?

$\frac{1}{5}$ $\frac{2}{5}$ $\frac{3}{5}$ $\frac{4}{5}$ $\frac{5}{5}$

Distance Track Team Ran (in miles)

a. What are you asked to find? ______________________________

____

b. What information do you need to use? ______________________________

____

c. How will the dot plot help you solve the problem? ______________

____

d. Show the steps to solve the problem. ______________________________

e. Complete the sentences. The team members ran a total of ______ miles.

Since ______ miles ______ 5 miles, the students ran ______ than 5 miles.

Daily Assessment Task

Fill in the bubble completely to show your answer.
Use the dot plot for 8–11.

Aaron and his family took a trip to a national park. He made a dot plot to show the number of eruptions made by a geyser each day for 20 days.

Number of Eruptions Each Day	12	13	14	15	16	17	18	19
Dots	•••	•	•••	•	•••	•••••	••	••

8. How many eruptions occurred the most number of days?

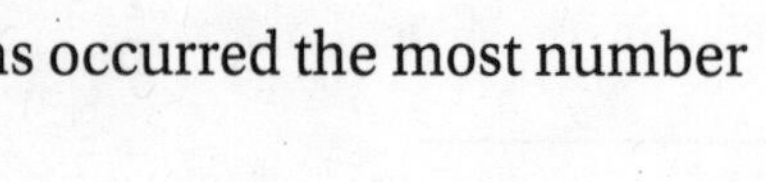

Ⓐ 18

Ⓑ 14

Ⓒ 17

Ⓓ 16

9. What is the least number of eruptions the geyser has in one day?

Ⓐ 18

Ⓑ 15

Ⓒ 13

Ⓓ 12

10. **Multi-Step** How many more times does the geyser have 17 daily eruptions than it has 15 and 16 eruptions combined?

Ⓐ 3

Ⓑ 1

Ⓒ 2

Ⓓ 5

TEXAS Test Prep

11. How many times did Aaron and his family see either 12, 13, 14, or 15 eruptions?

Ⓐ 8

Ⓑ 9

Ⓒ 7

Ⓓ 12

Homework and Practice

TEKS Data Analysis—4.9.B
MATHEMATICAL PROCESSES 4.1.C, 4.1.D, 4.1.E

Name ______________________

17.4 Use Dot Plots

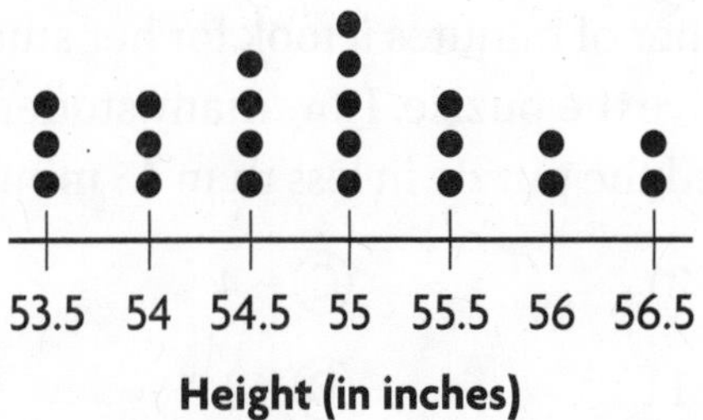

1. Mr. Dominguez collected data on the heights of the students in his class. He represents the data he collected in a dot plot. How many students are 54.5 inches tall?

____

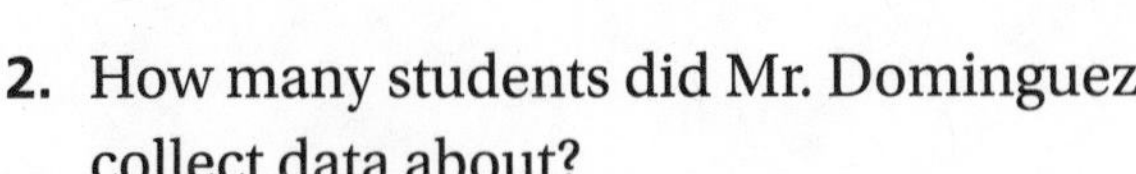

2. How many students did Mr. Dominguez collect data about?

____

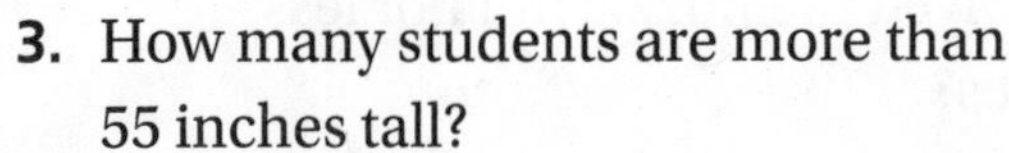

3. How many students are more than 55 inches tall?

____

4. How many students are more than 56 inches tall or less than 54 inches tall?

____

5. What is the height of the most students in the class?

____

6. What is the difference between the number of students who are 55 inches or less tall and students who are more than 55 inches tall?

____

Problem Solving Real World

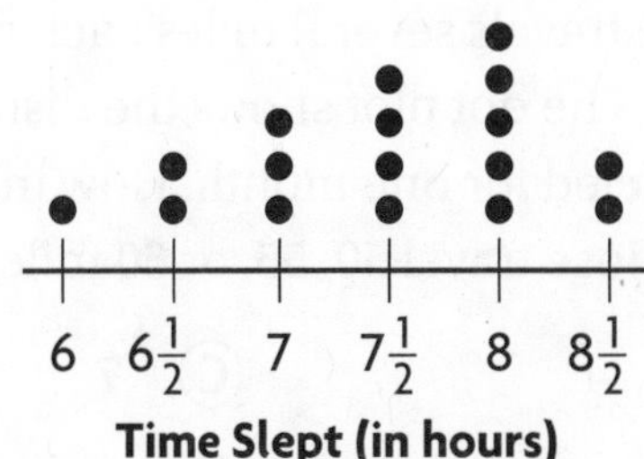

7. Adam asked several people how many hours they slept each night. He represents the data he collected in a dot plot. How many hours of sleep do most of the people sleep?

____

8. How many people sleep less than $7\frac{1}{2}$ hours each night?

____

9. **Multi-Step** How many more people sleep 8 or more hours than people who sleep 7 or less hours? **Explain.**

____

____

____

____

Lesson Check

Fill in the bubble completely to show your answer.
Use the dot plot for 10–12.

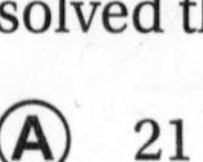

10. Mrs. Sanders gave her students a puzzle to solve. She made a dot plot to show the number of minutes it took for her students to solve the puzzle. How many students solved the puzzle in less than 15 minutes?

Ⓐ 21 Ⓒ 4
Ⓑ 11 Ⓓ 17

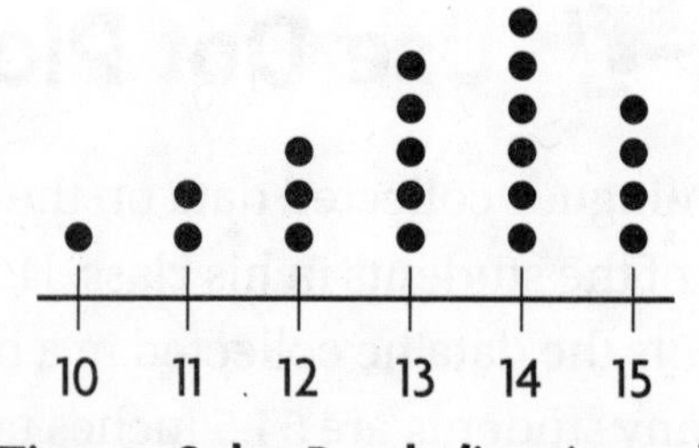

11. What number represents the time that the greatest number of students solved the puzzle?

Ⓐ 12 Ⓒ 14
Ⓑ 13 Ⓓ 15

12. Multi-Step How many more students solved the puzzle in 14 or more minutes than solved the puzzle in 11 or less minutes?

Ⓐ 10 Ⓒ 8
Ⓑ 7 Ⓓ 3

Use the dot plot for 13–15.

13. Jose travels several miles each day for his job. The dot plot shows the distances he traveled for one month. How many days did Jose travel 50, 55, or 60 miles?

Ⓐ 4 Ⓒ 7
Ⓑ 2 Ⓓ 13

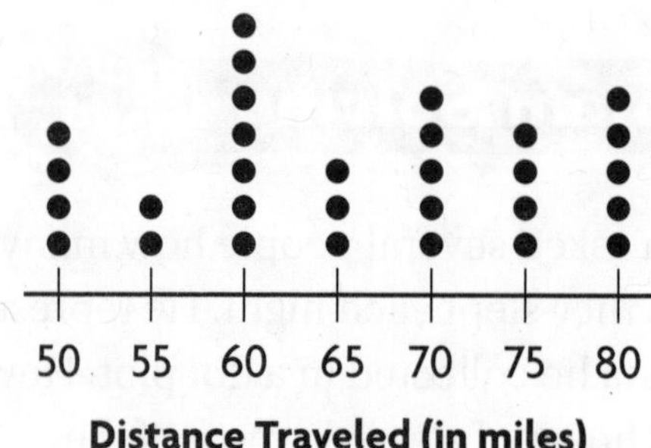

14. How many more days did Jose travel 70 miles than 65 miles?

Ⓐ 5 Ⓒ 1
Ⓑ 2 Ⓓ 3

15. Multi-Step How many more days did Jose travel 60 or less miles than he traveled 75 or more miles?

Ⓐ 4 Ⓒ 3
Ⓑ 7 Ⓓ 9

Name ______________________________

17.5 Stem-and-Leaf Plots

Essential Question How do you make stem-and-leaf plots with whole numbers?

Unlock the Problem

Henry kept track of the points of each of his words when he played a word game with his friend.

Word Game Score							
13	15	19	31	22	33	27	22

Then he used a stem-and-leaf plot to show the data.

A **stem-and-leaf plot** shows groups of data arranged by place value.

Make a stem-and-leaf plot.

STEP 1

Group the data by the tens digits.

10: 13, 15, ______

20: 22, ______, ______

______: 31, ______

STEP 2

Order the tens digits from least to greatest. Draw a line.

1 | Each tens digit is
2 | called a stem.
3 |

STEP 3

Write each ones digit in order from least to greatest to the right of its tens digit.

1 | 3, ______, ______ Each ones
2 | 2, ______, ______ digit is called
3 | 1, ______ a leaf.

STEP 4

Include a title, labels, and a key.

Points Scored in Word Game

Stem	Leaves
1	3 ______
______	______
______	______

Key: 1 | 3 represents 13 points

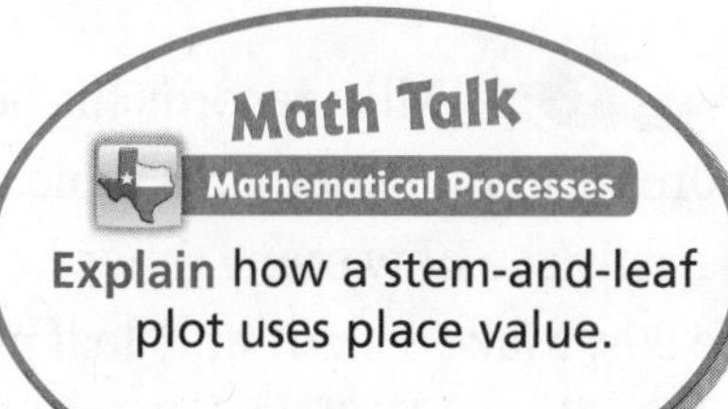

Explain how a stem-and-leaf plot uses place value.

Share and Show

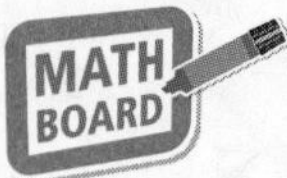

1. Use the data in the table to make a stem-and-leaf plot.

Numbers of Floors of High Rise Buildings							
31	37	48	26	33	34	43	38
38	30	27	32	40	45	38	39
27	29	30	33	28	45	43	43

Order the data in the table from ___________

to ___________.

The numbers _____, _____, _____ are stems.

The leaves for stem 2 are _____, _____, _____,

_____, _____.

Complete the stem-and-leaf plot.

Numbers of Floors of High Rise Buildings

Stem	Leaves

Key: 2 | 6 represents 26 floors

2. Use the data in the Number of Jumps table to make a stem-and-leaf plot.

Number of Jumps							
10	22	12	11	20	25	31	26

3. Use the data in the Number of Different Beads table to make a stem-and-leaf plot.

Number of Different Beads							
12	33	10	14	24	26	31	37

Problem Solving

4. H.O.T. Mike records his bowling scores and puts them in a table. He wants to easily see how many times he bowled in the 90s. Make a stem-and-leaf plot from the data in the table. Explain how Mike used the stem-and-leaf plot to determine how many times he bowled in the 90s.

Mike's Bowling Scores							
76	92	85	73	94	98	61	74
79	73	81	85	92	86	86	75
69	67	82	86	93	89	76	80

____

____

Name ________________________________

5. **Use Graphs Multi-Step** Naomi conducted a science experiment where she recorded the high temperature each day for 24 days. She chose a stem-and-leaf plot to display her data. Make Naomi's stem-and-leaf plot.

High Temperature (°F)		
67	73	62
75	79	76
86	79	72
87	85	72
67	68	65
72	86	83
88	75	89
84	87	86

6. H.O.T. **Use Graphs Multi-Step** Jenny was asked to make teams based on the height of the students in her class. She recorded the student's height, in inches, in a table. To more clearly see the different heights, she made a stem-and-leaf plot. Make Jenny's stem-and-leaf plot.

Student's Height (in.)					
49	52	61	48	55	60
54	50	63	56	62	54
55	57	60	60	58	59

7. H.O.T. **Use Math Language** Explain the steps you would use to make the stem-and-leaf plot from the data in the table. Then make the stem-and-leaf plot.

Time Spent Reading (min)					
32	41	55	24	44	30
26	41	29	35	37	22
55	24	47	36	29	30

____

____

____

Daily Assessment Task

Fill in the bubble completely to show your answer.

Use the table for 8–11.

The data shows the number of jumping jacks completed by 15 students in one minute. Robert is making a stem-and-leaf plot to display the information.

Number of Jumping Jacks Completed in One Minute				
55	51	50	50	45
48	52	51	39	53
42	38	55	44	44

8. What are the stems for the stem-and-leaf plot?

Ⓐ 3, 5, 6
Ⓑ 0, 3, 4, 5, 9
Ⓒ 3, 4, 5
Ⓓ 0, 1, 2, 3, 5, 8, 9

9. How many leaves are in the stem-and-leaf plot?

Ⓐ 12
Ⓑ 10
Ⓒ 15
Ⓓ 3

10. Which could be a key for the stem-and-leaf plot?

Ⓐ 4 | 8 represents 84 jumping jacks.
Ⓑ 3 | 8 represents 38 jumping jacks.
Ⓒ 5 | 0 represents 5 jumping jacks.
Ⓓ 4 | 4 represents 4 jumping jacks.

TEXAS Test Prep

11. In the stem-and-leaf plot that Robert is making, which stem would have the most leaves?

Ⓐ 3
Ⓑ 4
Ⓒ 5
Ⓓ 0

Name ______________________

17.5 Stem-and-Leaf Plots

1. Use the data in the Daily Temperatures table to make a stem-and-leaf plot.

Daily Temperatures (°F)							
88	91	95	95	84	79	92	96

2. Use the data in the Minutes Spent Doing Homework table to make a stem-and-leaf plot.

Minutes Spent Doing Homework						
25	14	30	34	13	39	28

Problem Solving

3. Cade recorded the number of points his team scored in ten basketball games and put them in a table. Make a stem-and-leaf plot from the data.

Points Scored in a Game				
24	34	25	28	28
25	26	30	32	32

4. The school librarian recorded the total number of books checked out from the library each day for two weeks. She put the data in a table. Make a stem-and-leaf plot from the data.

Number of Books Checked Out				
94	72	75	87	90
83	85	94	74	88

Lesson Check

Fill in the bubble completely to show your answer.

Use the table at right for 5–7.

The data show the number of hours 16 students exercise in one month. Jen is making a stem-and-leaf plot to display the information.

Number of Hours Exercised in One Month			
18	28	22	20
34	30	19	25
42	19	27	41
25	38	26	28

5. What are the stems for the stem-and-leaf plot?

Ⓐ 0, 1, 2, 4, 5, 6, 7, 8, 9,
Ⓑ 0, 1, 2, 3, 4
Ⓒ 1, 2, 3, 4
Ⓓ 2, 3, 4

6. Which stem has the most leaves?

Ⓐ 1
Ⓑ 2
Ⓒ 3
Ⓓ 4

7. Multi-Step How many more leaves are there for 2 than there are for 3 and 4 combined?

Ⓐ 5
Ⓑ 2
Ⓒ 3
Ⓓ 1

Use the table at right for 8–10.

The data show the height of plants grown for Javier's science experiment. Javier is making a stem-and-leaf plot to display the information.

Height of Plants (in.)			
15	14	14	12
21	18	21	20
12	14	10	22

8. How many leaves are in the stem-and-leaf plot?

Ⓐ 2
Ⓑ 12
Ⓒ 9
Ⓓ 10

9. Which could be a key for the stem-and-leaf plot?

Ⓐ 2 | 2 represents 22 inches.
Ⓑ 3 | 2 represents 23 inches.
Ⓒ 2 | 1 represents 12 inches.
Ⓓ 2 | 0 represents 2 inches.

10. Multi-Step How many leaves are in the plot for 12 and 14?

Ⓐ 3
Ⓑ 1
Ⓒ 2
Ⓓ 5

Name ___________________________

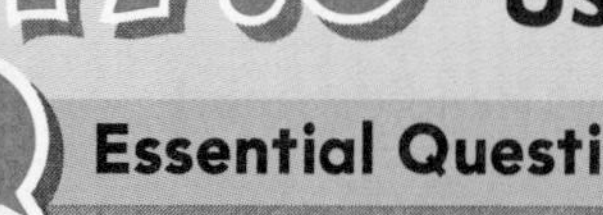

17.6 Use Stem-and-Leaf Plots

TEKS Data Analysis—4.9.B

MATHEMATICAL PROCESSES 4.1.C, 4.1.D, 4.1.E

Essential Question How do you solve problems using a stem-and-leaf plot?

Unlock the Problem

Example 1

While doing research for a project, Lila made a stem-and-leaf plot of the number of floors that different buildings in Chicago have. How many buildings have more than 40 floors?

Number of Floors in Chicago Buildings

Stem	Leaves
1	2 2 5 7 7 7 7 9
2	5 6 7
3	4 6
4	1 4
5	0 1
6	0 4

Key: 1 | 2 represents 12 floors

Think: 41 is represented by 4 | 1 on the stem-and-leaf plot.

The number of floors in the buildings that have more than 40 floors are: ____________

So, ______ buildings have more than 40 floors.

- How many buildings have more than 11 floors but less than 19 floors? ______

Example 2

Each time Glenda practiced her free throws, she recorded the number of made baskets in a stem-and-leaf plot. How many times did Glenda make more than 20 free throws?

Number of Free Throws Made

Stem	Leaves
0	4 6 9 9
1	1 1 2 4 5 9
2	0 0 4 5 6 8 9
3	0 0 2 2 2 2 7

Key: 0 | 4 represents 4 free throws

The number of times Glenda practiced her free throws and made more than 20 of them was: ______

So, Glenda made more than 20 free throws ______ times.

- How many times did Glenda either make less than 10 free throws or more than 26 free throws? **Explain.**

____

____

Share and Show

Use the stem-and-leaf plot for 1–3.

Time Spent Reading (min)

Stem	Leaves
1	3 5 5 5
2	0 0 0 5 8 8
3	0 0 3 3 5 9
4	0 0 2 5 5 5
5	0 2 3 5 5
6	3

Key: 1 | 3 represents 13 min

1. Martin kept track of the time he spent reading in a stem-and-leaf plot. How many times did Martin read for 40 or more minutes?

Think: Count the number of leaves that are after stems 4, 5, 6.

Martin read for 40 or more minutes _____ times.

2. How many times did Martin read for less than 30 minutes?

____

3. How many more times did Martin read for less than 39 minutes than he read for more than 39 minutes?

____

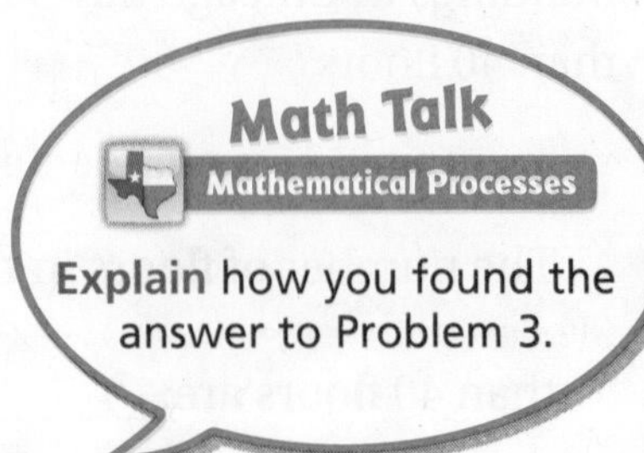

Problem Solving Real World

Use the stem-and-leaf plot for 4–7.

Minutes Spent Doing Chores

Stem	Leaves
2	2 2 4 6
3	0 5 5 8
4	0 6
5	5 8
6	2
7	1 4

Key: 2 | 2 represents 22 min

4. Stephanie asked her 23 classmates how much time they spent doing chores in a week. She recorded the data in a stem-and-leaf plot. How many classmates said that they spend some time doing chores in a week?

____

5. How many of Stephanie's classmates said they did more than an hour of chores a week?

____

6. H.O.T. **Multi-Step** How many classmates said that they spent more than 20 minutes and less than 40 minutes doing chores a week?

____

7. How many classmates said they didn't do any chores? **Explain** your answer.

____

____

____

Use the stem-and-leaf plot for 8–10.

Daily Low Temperature (°F)

Stem	Leaves
3	7 9 9
4	1 4 4 8
5	0 3 4 9 9
6	1 1 2

Key: 3 | 7 represents 37 °F

8. Tina records the daily low temperature for 15 days. She recorded the data in the stem-and-leaf plot. How many days was the low temperature in the 50s?

____

9. **Use Graphs** On how many days was the daily low temperature in the 30s and 40s?

____

10. H.O.T. **Use Math Language** Explain how to find how many more days the low temperature was greater than 53°F than less than 53°F.

____

____

____

Use the stem-and-leaf plot for 11–14.

Score of Basketball Games

Stem	Leaves
4	0 5 8
5	1 4 4 6 7
6	2 2 7 8 9 9
7	4 4 6 6
8	1
9	0

Key: 4 | 5 represents 45 points

11. Nick recorded the number of points his basketball team scored during their season in a stem-and-leaf plot. How many games did Nick's basketball team play?

____

12. During how many games did Nick's team score between 55 and 75 points?

____

13. **Multi-Step** During how many more games did Nick's team score less than 68 points than they scored more than 68 points?

____

14. **Reasoning** Explain how the stem-and-leaf plot would change if Nick's basketball team played 8 more games and they scored more than 65 points each game?

____

____

Daily Assessment Task

Fill in the bubble completely to show your answer.

15. The stem-and-leaf plot at the right shows the number of programs that different vendors sold during a sporting event. How many vendors sold between 20 and 30 programs?

Ⓐ 1
Ⓑ 4
Ⓒ 5
Ⓓ 3

Programs Sold

Stem	Leaves
1	3
2	1 3 6 6 8
3	2 5 4
4	1 7 7

Key: 1 | 3 represents 13 programs sold

Use the stem-and-leaf plot for 16-17.

The stem-and-leaf plot at the right shows the bowling scores for members of a bowling team.

Bowling Scores

Stem	Leaves
6	0 4 5 5 5 9
7	1 2
8	6 6 8 9
9	0 1 4 5 6 9

Key: 6 | 4 represents 64 points

16. What is the highest score that is bowled?

Ⓐ 69
Ⓑ 99
Ⓒ 78
Ⓓ 95

17. Multi-Step How many team members bowled a 64 or a 65?

Ⓐ 0
Ⓑ 4
Ⓒ 2
Ⓓ 3

TEXAS Test Prep

18. The stem-and-leaf plot at the right shows the number of stuffed animals Sara and her friends have. How many of Sara's friends have more than 10 stuffed animals?

Ⓐ 12
Ⓑ 6
Ⓒ 8
Ⓓ 7

Number of Stuffed Animals Owned

Stem	Leaves
0	3 5 5 8 8
1	0 2 2 2 3
2	1 1 4

Key: 0 | 3 represents 3 stuffed animals

TEKS Data Analysis—4.9.B
MATHEMATICAL PROCESSES 4.1.C, 4.1.D, 4.1.E

Name ________________

17.6 Use Stem-and-Leaf Plots

1. Blake used a stem-and-leaf plot to record the number of football cards that he and his friends have collected. How many friends have collected 50 or more cards?

____

Number of Football Cards Collected

Stem	Leaves
1	9
2	3 5
3	6 8 9
4	2 2 4 8
5	1 3 5 6 9
6	1 4 7

Key: 2 | 3 represents 23 cards.

2. How many friends have collected 25 or fewer cards?

____

3. How many friends have collected between 30 and 50 cards?

____

4. **Multi-Step** How many more friends have collected more than 40 cards than less than 40 cards?

____

Problem Solving

5. The girls on Stacy's soccer team sold boxes of cards to raise money for new uniforms. Stacy recorded data about their sales in a stem-and-leaf plot. How many girls sold more than 30 boxes of cards?

____

Boxes of Cards Sold

Stem	Leaves
2	2 2 4
3	1 3 4 5 5 9
4	5 8 9
5	1

Key: 2 | 2 represents 22 boxes.

6. What is the greatest number of boxes sold by one girl?

____

7. How many girls on the team sold cards? **Explain.**

____

____

8. **Explain** how the stem-and-leaf plot would change if another girl on Stacy's soccer team sold 60 boxes of cards.

____

____

Lesson Check

Fill in the bubble completely to show your answer.

Use the table at right for 9–11.

Ages of People Who Attended a Dog Obedience Class

Stem	Leaves
0	9
1	2 5 5 5 8 9
2	1 3 4 4 6
3	3 4
4	2

Key: 0 | 9 represents 9 years of age.

9. The stem-and-leaf plot at the right shows the ages of people who attended a dog obedience class. How many people were between 20 and 40 years old?

Ⓐ 7

Ⓑ 5

Ⓒ 8

Ⓓ 6

10. Which age group was most widely represented at the class?

Ⓐ teens
Ⓒ thirties
Ⓑ twenties
Ⓓ forties

11. Multi-Step How many people were more than 20 years old than were less than 20 years old?

Ⓐ 8
Ⓒ 2
Ⓑ 1
Ⓓ 7

Use the table at right for 12–14.

Number of Laps Swam in 26 Days

Stem	Leaves
1	0 4 5 6 6 7 8 9
2	0 1 1 2 3 3 4 4
	5 5 5 6 7 9
3	1 1 4 4

Key: 3 | 1 represents 31 laps.

12. Kyle kept track of the number of laps he swam each day. He used a stem-and-leaf plot to display his data. What is the greatest number of laps that Kyle swam in one day?

Ⓐ 44
Ⓒ 26
Ⓑ 34
Ⓓ 43

13. Multi-Step How many days did Kyle swim 30 or more laps?

Ⓐ 1 days
Ⓒ 2 days
Ⓑ 3 days
Ⓓ 4 days

14. Multi-Step How many days did Kyle swim 23, 24, or 25 laps?

Ⓐ 3 days
Ⓒ 11 days
Ⓑ 7 days
Ⓓ 9 days

Name ________________________________

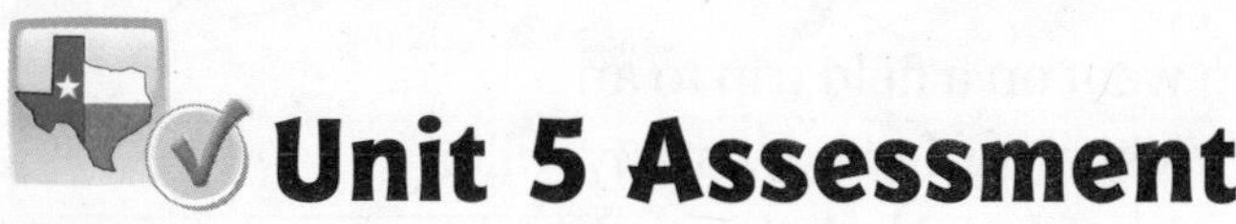

Unit 5 Assessment

Vocabulary

Choose the best term from the box.

Vocabulary
frequency table
frequency
dot plot
stem-and-leaf plot

1. A ______________________ shows groups of data arranged by place value. (p. 621)

2. A ______________________ is a graph that shows the frequency of data along a number line. (p. 609)

3. The ______________________ is the number of times data occurs. (p. 597)

Concepts and Skills

Use the Number of Apples Picked table for 4–6. TEKS 4.9.A

Janet and her classmates went to an apple orchard to pick apples. Janet recorded the number of apples some of her classmates picked.

Number of Apples Picked				
7	12	9	18	24
35	18	20	20	35
25	12	18	20	20

4. If Janet represents this data in a stem-and-leaf plot, how many leaves would there be? ________

5. Janet wants to make a frequency table from this data. Which number of apples picked has the greatest frequency? ________

6. Janet decided that instead of a frequency table, she wants to make a dot plot. How many dots will be above the number 20? ________

Use the Amount of Raisins Used table for 7–8. TEKS 4.9.A

Barry and his classmates made trail mix. They each used different amounts of raisins. Barry recorded the amounts of raisins that the classmates used.

Amount of Raisins Used (cups)				
$\frac{1}{4}$	$\frac{1}{2}$	$\frac{1}{4}$	$\frac{1}{2}$	$\frac{1}{4}$
$\frac{1}{4}$	$\frac{1}{2}$	$\frac{1}{2}$	$\frac{3}{4}$	$\frac{3}{4}$

7. Barry wants to make a dot plot with the data. How many total dots will go above $\frac{1}{4}$ and $\frac{3}{4}$? ________

8. If Barry created a frequency table with this data, what number would be in the frequency column for $\frac{1}{2}$? ________

Use the Roller coasters Ridden dot plot for 9–10.

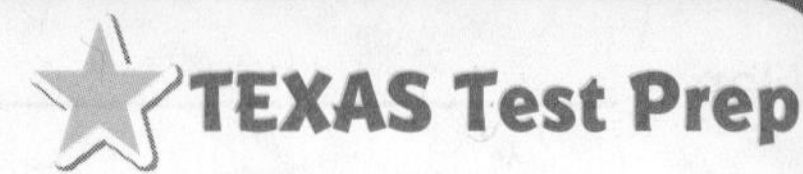

The campers from a summer camp went on a field trip to an amusement park. During the trip, Vicki recorded how many roller coasters each camper went on. She recorded the data in a dot plot.

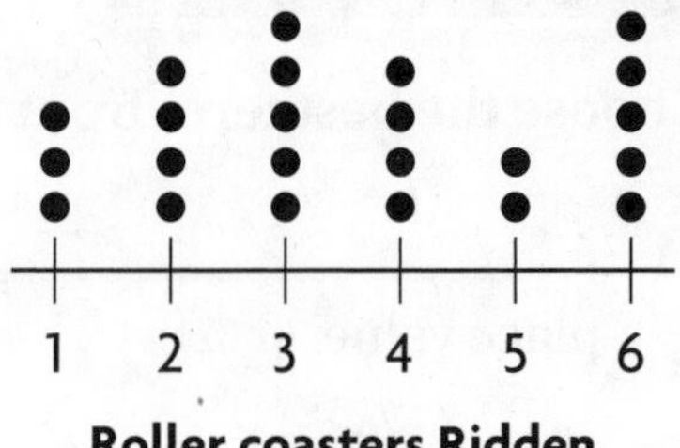

9. How many campers rode either 3 or 5 roller coasters? TEKS 4.9.B

Ⓐ 7 Ⓒ 4

Ⓑ 8 Ⓓ 11

10. How many campers rode 2 or more roller coasters? TEKS 4.9.B

Ⓐ 18 Ⓒ 19

Ⓑ 25 Ⓓ 21

Use the Length of Leaves frequency table for 11–12.

Several scientists went to a field to collect various leaves. When they got back to the lab, they measured each leaf, in feet. They recorded the data in a frequency table.

Length of Leaves (ft)

Length	Frequency
$\frac{1}{8}$	11
$\frac{1}{4}$	19
$\frac{3}{8}$	7
$\frac{1}{2}$	3

11. How many leaves were less than $\frac{3}{8}$ ft in length? TEKS 4.9.B

Ⓐ 19 Ⓒ 7

Ⓑ 30 Ⓓ 9

12. How many more leaves are $\frac{1}{4}$ ft than $\frac{3}{8}$ ft and $\frac{1}{2}$ ft combined? TEKS 4.9.B

Ⓐ 19 Ⓒ 7

Ⓑ 30 Ⓓ 9

13. Sasha asked her friends how many books they read during their two week vacation. She recorded their responses in a frequency table. How many of her friends read 1 or more books during their vacation? TEKS 4.9.B

Ⓐ 8 Ⓒ 13

Ⓑ 15 Ⓓ 12

Number of Books Read

Books	Frequency
0	2
1	3
2	4
3	1
4	2
5	3

Use the Weight of Rocks dot plot for 14–15.

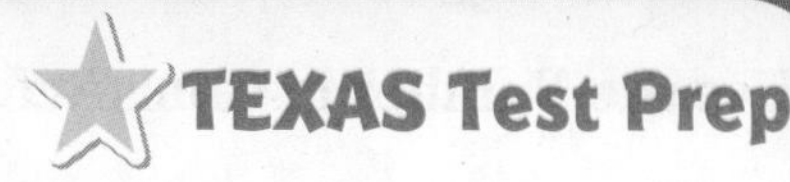

Frank wants to record the weights of the different rocks in his collection. He weighs each rock in pounds and records the data in a dot plot.

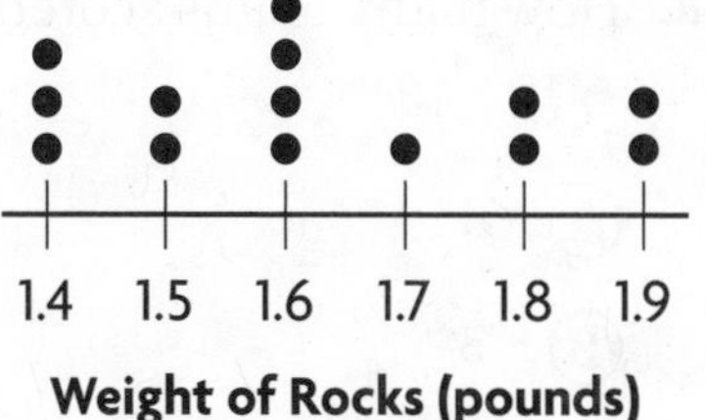

14. How many rocks does Frank have that weigh more than a pound but less than 1.7 pounds? TEKS 4.9.B

Ⓐ 9 Ⓒ 14

Ⓑ 7 Ⓓ 10

15. How many rocks does Frank have in his collection? TEKS 4.9.B

Ⓐ 10 Ⓒ 13

Ⓑ 11 Ⓓ 14

16. Kerry kept track of the time he spent on the computer in a frequency table. How many more times did Kerry spend 4 hours or less than he spent 5 hours or more using the computer? TEKS 4.9.B

Time Spent Using Computer (hours)	
Hours	**Frequency**
2	12
3	10
4	13
5	5
6	9
7	1

Ⓐ 17 Ⓒ 19

Ⓑ 20 Ⓓ 23

17. Jackson asked the 3rd grade students to find the distance that they live from the school, in miles. Jackson recorded the students' answers in a frequency table. How many total students live less than 1 mile or more than 2 miles from the school? TEKS 4.9.B

Distance Lived from School (miles)	
Distance	**Frequency**
0.4	4
0.8	8
1.1	3
1.4	6
1.8	6
2.1	2
2.2	1
2.5	4

Ⓐ 18 Ⓒ 26

Ⓑ 20 Ⓓ Not here

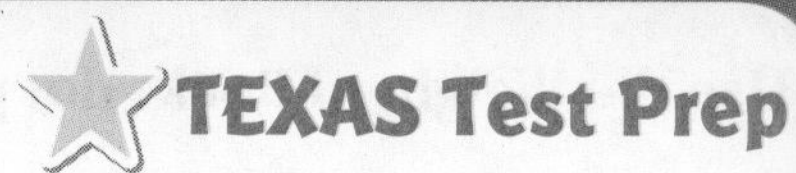

Use the Number of Goals Scored stem-and-leaf plot for 18–19.

During the soccer season, Dylan kept record of the number of goals scored by each team. At the end of the season, Dylan made a stem-and-leaf plot to show the total number of goals scored by each team.

Number of Goals Scored

Stem	Leaf
1	1 4 6
2	0 4 7 8 9
3	1 2 3
4	4

Key: 1 | 1 represents 11 goals

18. How many teams scored less than 20 goals during the season? TEKS 4.9.B

Ⓐ 4　　Ⓒ 8

Ⓑ 3　　Ⓓ 5

19. How many more teams scored less than 30 goals than scored more than 30 goals during the season? TEKS 4.9.B

Ⓐ 3　　Ⓒ 5

Ⓑ 8　　Ⓓ 4

Use the Time Spent Practicing dot plot for 20–21.

20. Chad recorded the number of times he spent practicing his saxophone. How many more times did Chad practice for $\frac{9}{12}$ hour or more than he practiced for $\frac{6}{12}$ hour or less? TEKS 4.9.B

Ⓐ 2　　Ⓒ 3

Ⓑ 4　　Ⓓ 6

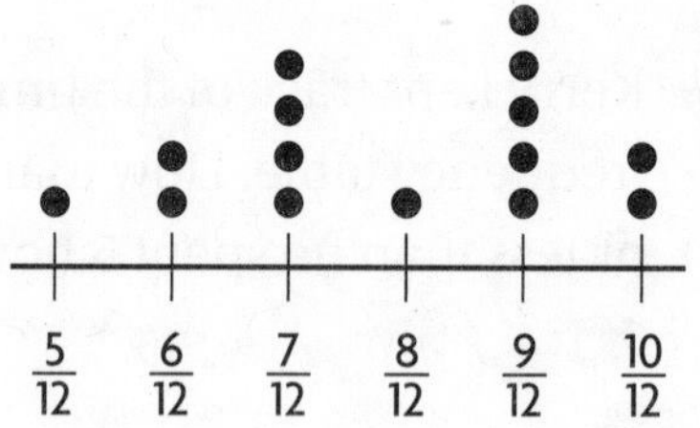

Time Spent Practicing (hour)

21. How many times did Chad practice for $\frac{7}{12}$ hour? TEKS 4.9.B

Ⓐ 2　　Ⓒ 4

Ⓑ 3　　Ⓓ 5

22. Brandon borrowed a book from the library. The data show the lengths of time Brandon read the book each day until he finished it. Explain how you would use the data to label and plot the dots on a dot plot. What is the difference between the longest time and shortest time Brandon spent reading the book? TEKS 4.9.B

Time Reading Book (In hours)
$\frac{1}{4}, \frac{1}{4}, 1, \frac{1}{4}, \frac{1}{2}, \frac{3}{4}, \frac{1}{2}, \frac{1}{4}$

Unit 6

Personal Financial Literacy

Show What You Know 

Check your understanding of important skills.

Name ______________________________

▶ Add Decimals Estimate. Then find the sum.

1. Estimate:

		2	.	1	8
+	+	3	.	3	2

2. Estimate:

		4	.	7	5
+	+	2	.	6	1

▶ Subtract Decimals Estimate. Then find the difference.

3. Estimate:

		7	.	4	4
−	−	3	.	9	3

4. Estimate:

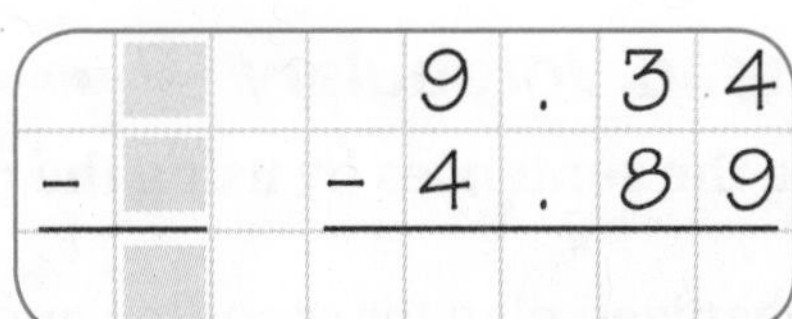

		9	.	3	4
−	−	4	.	8	9

▶ Multiply 3-Digit and 4-Digit Numbers by 1-Digit Numbers

Find the product.

5. 684 × 7

	T	H	T	O
		6	8	4
×				7

6. 1,152 × 4

	T	H	T	O
	1	1	5	2
×				4

GO DIGITAL Assessment Options: Soar to Success Math

Vocabulary Builder

Preview Words

budget	interest	variable expense
financial institution	loan	
fixed expense	profit	

▶ Visualize It

Write an example for each term in the chart.

Term	Example
financial institution	
fixed expense	
variable expense	
loan	
interest	

▶ Understand Vocabulary

Complete the sentences by using the preview words.

1. An organized plan for spending and saving money is called a __________.

2. A _______________ is one in which the amount changes based on need or choice.

3. A _______________ occurs regularly and the amount does not change.

4. Money that is lent by a bank or other financial institution is called a ______.

5. __________ is the amount left after all the expenses are subtracted from the amount of money received from selling an item or service.

6. A ____________________ keeps money safe, lends money, and borrows money.

GO DIGITAL
- Interactive Student Edition
- Multimedia eGlossary

Name ______________________________

Vocabulary

You can use what you know about adding and subtracting whole numbers to add and subtract money amounts.

1. On the way home from school, Janine bought a bunch of bananas for $3.00. She gave the clerk a ten-dollar bill. How much change should she get back?

$$\begin{array}{r} \$10.00 \\ -\ 3.00 \\ \hline \end{array}$$

An input/output table shows how input numbers and output numbers are related. A rule tells what to do to the input to get the output. You can use an input/output table to help you solve problems.

Janine wants to know how much it will cost her to buy 4 bunches of bananas. Complete the input/output table to show how much the bananas will cost.

	Input (Number of bunches)	Output (Total Cost)
	1	$3.00
2.	2	
3.	3	
4.	4	

5. The rule is: ______________________________

6. Four bunches of bananas will cost ____________.

7. How much would 8 bunches of bananas cost? ____________

Writing Make an input/output table that shows the total cost of 5 DVDs if each DVD costs $13.00.

____

Reading Look for this book in your library. *Once Upon a Dime: A Math Adventure*, by Nancy Kelly Allen

Get Ready Game

Make a Profit

Object of the Game Determine expenses and calculate the profit.

Materials

- 3 number cubes each labeled 1–6
- Monthly Worksheet
- Pencil or marker

Set Up

Each player becomes the owner of a made up company that sells items. Each player uses a worksheet to find the company's expenses and profit for one month.

Number of Players: 2 to 4 players

How to Play

1. Player 1 tosses 3 cubes and arranges the digits in any order to determine the company's fixed expenses.

2. Player 1 tosses one cube, and multiplies by 4 to determine the company's monthly variable expenses. Player 1 then finds their total expenses.

3. Player 1 tosses two cubes and arranges the digits in any order to determine the price of each item sold.

4. Player 1 tosses one cube and multiplies by 90 to determine the number of items sold. Player 1 then finds the total amount received for the number of items sold.

5. Each player repeats the four steps and computes his or her profit for the month.

6. The player with the greatest profit for the month wins the game.

Monthly Worksheet

Fixed expenses: $☐☐☐

Variable expenses: $☐ × 4

Total expenses: ___________

Price per item sold: $☐☐

Number of items sold: ☐ × 90

Total amount received: ___________

Profit: ___________

Name ______________________

18.1 Fixed and Variable Expenses

Essential Question What is the difference between fixed and variable expenses?

Money that you need to pay for electricity or phone service are your expenses. Expenses that occur regularly and the amount does not change are **fixed expenses**. Expenses in which the amount does change based on need or choice are **variable expenses**.

Unlock the Problem

Erin has some fixed and variable expenses. She pays $23.75 every 12 weeks for the newspaper to be delivered to her home every day. She and her family like to eat out. Monday night, Erin spent $45.78 to eat a meal at Restaurant A. Tuesday night, she spent $58.12 for a meal at Restaurant B. Wednesday night, she spent $37.64 for a meal at Restaurant C.

Example 1 Complete.

Erin's ____________ is a ____________ expense because she pays the same amount and the cost does not change. The money Erin spends on meals is a ____________ expense because the amount ____________ depending on which restaurant she goes to or the type of meal she buys.

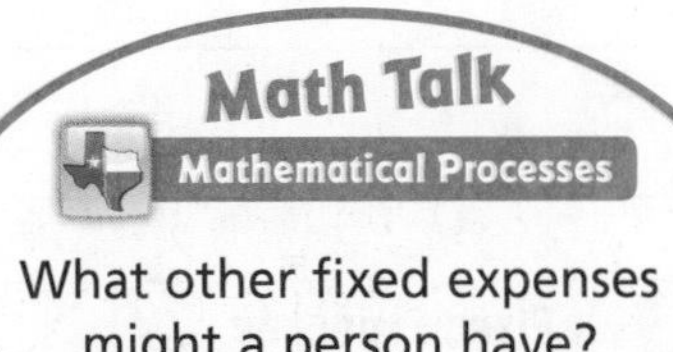

Example 2 Find the amount Erin spends on fixed expenses for 24 weeks.

Erin pays $____________ every 12 weeks for the newspaper.

In 24 weeks, she pays $____________ + $____________ =

$____________.

Erin spends $____________ in fixed expenses for 24 weeks.

Example 3 Solve.

How much does Erin spend on variable expenses?

__________ + __________ + __________ = __________

Monday night   Tuesday night   Wednesday night   Total spent

So Erin spent $__________ on variable expenses.

Share and Show

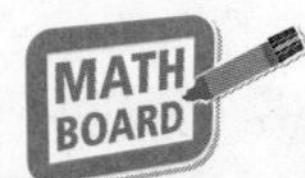

1. Betsy pays a trash service to pick up the household trash once a week. The cost is $23 a month. Trash pick-up is a __________ expense. In 6 months, the family pays

   6 × __________ = __________.

2. Mrs. Beyer goes grocery shopping once a week. In one month she spent $99.65, $122.56, $130.45, and $145. What was the total monthly expense? Grocery bills are a __________ expense. In a month, Mrs. Beyer spent __________ for groceries.

3. **Write Math** ▸ Use the list at the right. Sort the topics into fixed expenses and variable expenses. Choose one and explain why you placed it there.

____

____

____

- clothing
- car payments
- vacation
- groceries
- entertainment
- electric bills
- cell phone
- house payments
- gasoline
- loan payments

Fixed Expenses	Variable Expenses

Math Talk

Mathematical Processes

Explain why some of the topics could be either fixed or variable expenses.

Name ______________________________

Problem Solving Real World

Use the numbers in the picture for 4–5.

4. How much has the price of gas increased from the lowest to the highest price shown?

____

5. **Multi-Step** Maya filled her car with gas once at each price shown. Her gas tank holds 15 gallons. Estimate the amount that she spent to fill her tank these four times. Is this a fixed or variable expense?

____

6. **Apply** Mario paid off his car loan this year. His payments were $259 a month for each of the first 8 months. The last payment, in the ninth month, was $125. What was the total Mario paid in car payments this year? Are the payments Mario paid the first 8 months a fixed or variable expense?

____

Show Your Work

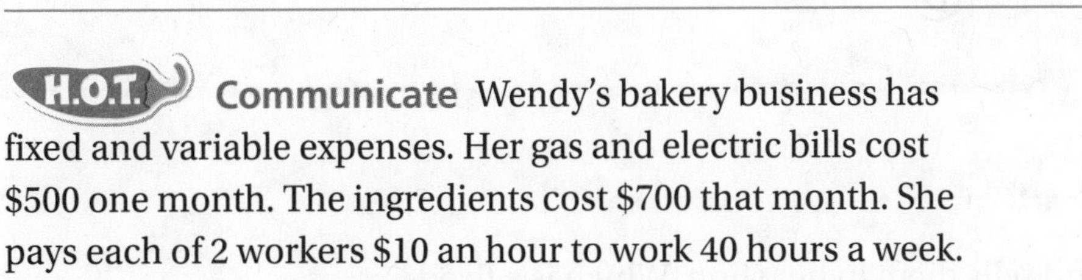

7. **H.O.T. Multi-Step** Mrs. Xavier buys 1 or 2 books a month for $13.99 each. A magazine subscription costs her $19.99 a year. She buys the Sunday paper for $2.05 each week. Estimate the most she could spend for her reading material in a year.

____

8. **H.O.T. Communicate** Wendy's bakery business has fixed and variable expenses. Her gas and electric bills cost $500 one month. The ingredients cost $700 that month. She pays each of 2 workers $10 an hour to work 40 hours a week. **Explain** how you can find her total business expenses for a month.

____

____

____

____

____

Daily Assessment Task

Fill in the bubble completely to show your answer.

9. Lexi is taking 3 courses at Community College. She pays $835 for each college course. She spends about $45 a week for 20 weeks to drive to school. How much does she spend on fixed expenses?

Ⓐ $2,505 Ⓒ $900

Ⓑ $2,400 Ⓓ $2,700

10. Every month, Jack's mother pays the following expenses: the house payment, the club membership, the car payment, and the cost of food. Which is a variable expense?

Ⓐ the club membership

Ⓑ the house payment

Ⓒ the car payment

Ⓓ the cost of food

11. Multi-Step Josh has a new cell phone plan. He gets unlimited voice calls and text messages to other devices in his area for $35 a month. Voice calls outside of his area cost $0.10 a minute and text messages cost $0.99 a message. What is Josh's bill if he uses 10 minutes for calls and makes one text outside his area?

Ⓐ $35.10 Ⓒ $35.00

Ⓑ $36.99 Ⓓ $35.99

TEXAS Test Prep

12. Dara makes bracelets and sells them in her shop. Which is a fixed expense for Dara's business?

Ⓐ the cost of the beads

Ⓑ the cost of the string

Ⓒ the cost of advertising

Ⓓ rent for her shop

Homework and Practice

TEKS Personal Financial Literacy—4.10.A
Also 4.4.A, 4.4.H
MATHEMATICAL PROCESSES 4.1.A, 4.1.D

Name ________________

18.1 Fixed and Variable Expenses

1. Bruce buys 7 cans of dog food a week and a bag of dog food every 4 weeks. Cans of dog food cost $1.29 each.

A bag of dog food costs $67.59. Dog food is a ________ expense. In 4 weeks, Bruce spends

28 × ________ + ________ = ________ for dog food.

2. Use the list of Expenses for Dog Owners. Sort the expenses into fixed expenses and variable expenses. Choose one expense and explain why you put it where you did.

Expenses for Dog Owners
food
treats
toys
bed
collar and leash
veterinary care
daily dog walking
boarding
Training Classes

Fixed Expenses	Variable Expenses	

____

Problem Solving Real World

3. Gretchen has a cat. She buys a bag of litter every month. Litter costs $38.59 a bag. How much will litter for a year cost? Is the expense fixed or variable? ________________

4. In March, Gretchen bought a brush and a toy for her kitten. The brush cost $6.79. The toy cost $3.88. In April, she bought a cat carrier for $87.68. How much did she spend for these items? Are the expenses fixed or variable? **Explain.** ________________

____

____

Lesson Check

TEXAS Test Prep

Fill in the bubble completely to show your answer.

5. Mark pays a gardener $100 each week. He bought a fence for the garden and 2 flats of plants. He also bought a shovel and a hoe. Which expense is fixed?

   Ⓐ gardener

   Ⓑ plants

   Ⓒ fence

   Ⓓ shovel

6. Leslie rides the bus to work and back 5 days a week. The bus costs $1.25 each way. Sometimes she buys a newspaper to read on the bus. The newspaper costs $0.75 a day. How much does she spend for fixed expenses every week?

   Ⓐ $6.25

   Ⓑ $12.50

   Ⓒ $18.75

   Ⓓ $10.00

7. Every month, Wesley writes checks to pay each of the bills listed below. Which is a variable expense?

   Ⓐ rent

   Ⓑ cable television

   Ⓒ electricity

   Ⓓ gym membership

8. Which of Victoria's monthly car expenses is fixed?

   Ⓐ car payment

   Ⓑ gas

   Ⓒ bridge tolls

   Ⓓ parking

9. **Multi-Step** A store owner pays $1,200 each month for rent. She pays the clerk who works in the store $15 an hour. The clerk works 60 hours each month. What is the total of the monthly fixed expenses?

   Ⓐ $2,100

   Ⓑ $1,290

   Ⓒ $1,800

   Ⓓ $3,000

10. **Multi-Step** Jenny spends $2.20 for a school lunch every day. She also buys a muffin at the bakery every day on her way home from school. The muffin costs $1.25. What are Jenny's fixed expenses for a 5-day school week?

    Ⓐ $15.05

    Ⓑ $15.75

    Ⓒ $22.25

    Ⓓ $17.25

Name ________________________________

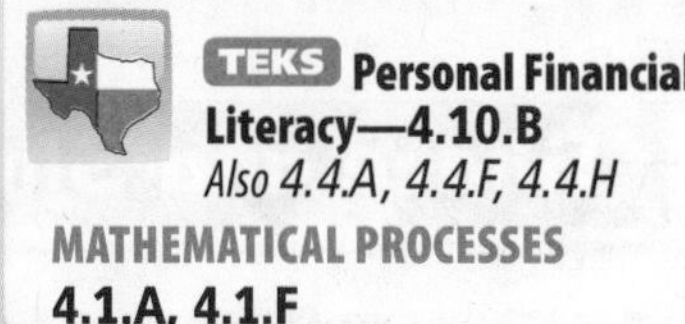

18.2 Find Profit

Essential Question

How can you determine if you make a profit?

Unlock the Problem Real World

Jasmine makes cow sock puppets to earn money to donate to the Future Farmers Club. She buys all of the items shown in the table. Each sock makes one puppet. She will sell the cow puppets for $8 each. Will Jasmine make a profit if she sells all of her puppets?

Puppet Supplies	Cost
3 pieces felt fabric, (one each, red, pink, and black)	$6 each
6-pack white socks (12 total)	$12
assorted buttons	$3.69
Craft glue	$4.99
Craft scissors	$9.99
10-pack of poster board	$5.33

Profit is the amount of money left after all the expenses are subtracted from the amount of money received from selling an item or service.

Example

A Find the total expenses.

Think: Find the cost of the 3 pieces of felt.

Felt: ______ pieces × $______ = $______.

Add the cost of all the puppet supplies she bought.

____ = ______

Jasmine spent a total of $______ on her supplies.

B Amount received from selling puppets.

Jasmine has ______ socks, so she can make ______ puppets.

She sells the puppets for $8 each.

Think: to find the amount of money she receives, you must multiply.

______ puppets × $______ per puppet = $______

Jasmine receives ______ from selling all the puppets.

C Find the profit.

Subtract the total expenses from the amount received.

$______ − $______ = $______

So, Jasmine makes a ___________ of $______.

Math Talk

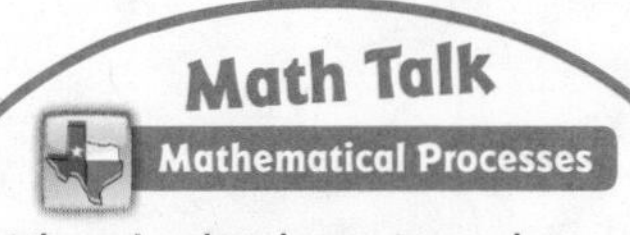

What is the least number of puppets Jasmine has to sell and still make a profit? **Explain.**

Share and Show

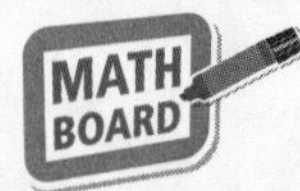

1. Diego runs his own lawn mowing business. His expenses for one week are listed in the chart. He charges his customers $45 to mow a lawn. How much profit did Diego make in the week of June 4th?

Diego's Lawn Mowing-Week of June 4th	
Expenses	**Cost**
Gas for truck and tools	$67.40
Other truck costs	$89
New garden edger	$198.99

A. What were his expenses for the week of June 4th?

_______ + _______ + _______ = _______

B. In the week of June 4th, he had 15 customers. How much money did he take in?

_______ lawns × _______ per lawn = _______

C. What was Diego's profit?

Think: Amount received − expenses = profit

_______ − _______ = _______

2. During the week of August 6th, Diego had to buy a new lawn mower for $378. His gas expenses were $45, and his other truck expenses were $89. How much profit did Diego make if he had 12 customers that week?

Expenses: _______ + _______ + _______ = _______

Profit: _______ − _______ = _______

So, Diego made a profit of _______.

Find the profit.

3. Expenses: $222
Earnings: $791

____

4. Expenses: $96
Earnings: $149.59

____

5. Expenses: $195.75
Earnings: $500

____

6. Expenses: $950.01
Earnings: $1,203.12

____

7. Expenses: $109.90
Earnings: $860

____

8. Expenses: $810.50
Earnings: $2,002.25

____

Name ______________________

Problem Solving Real World

Use the table for 9–11.

9. **Multi-Step** Ava starts a business making oil paintings of people's pets. She buys the items shown in the table. She has her paints and other supplies. She charges $75 for an unframed painting. If she sells 20 paintings, how much profit will she make?

Ava's Animal Portraits	
Expenses	**Cost**
canvas (set of 20)	$44.89
Master brush set	$231.21

____

10. H.O.T. What is the least number of paintings Ava needs to sell in order to make a profit? Explain how you found your answer.

____

____

____

____

____

11. **Apply** Ava buys another 20 canvasses. She needs paint, now, so she buys 3 tubes at $11 each. She does not need brushes. What is her profit if she sells 5 paintings?

____

12. H.O.T. **Reasoning** David and Diane decide to decorate tote bags and sell them. The profit will go to the community garden project. They buy 8 tote bags for $5.93 each and 8 fabric paints for $4.02 each. Estimate the amount they should charge for each tote bag so they make a profit of about $40. **Explain.**

____

____

____

Write Math ▶ **Show Your Work**

Daily Assessment Task

Fill in the bubble completely to show your answer.

13. Jamie builds and sells boxes for worm farms. The materials to build each box cost $13. She sells the boxes for $20 each. How much profit will Jamie make if she sells 5 boxes?

Ⓐ $100

Ⓑ $115

Ⓒ $13

Ⓓ $35

14. Simon makes a profit of $1.35 on each hot dog he sells. If a hot dog costs him $0.85 to make, how much does Simon sell each hot dog for?

Ⓐ $2.20

Ⓑ $1.35

Ⓒ $0.50

Ⓓ $2.55

15. **Multi-Step** Jenny sells her homemade granola bars for $2 each. Each bar costs $1 to make. If she sells 50 granola bars at a street fair, how much profit does Jenny make?

Ⓐ $100

Ⓑ $50

Ⓒ $75

Ⓓ $175

TEXAS Test Prep

16. John has an income tax preparation business. He spent $99 on computer software and $16 on books. He charges each client $25. How much profit can he make if he has 18 clients?

Ⓐ $334

Ⓑ $335

Ⓒ $450

Ⓓ $173

Homework and Practice

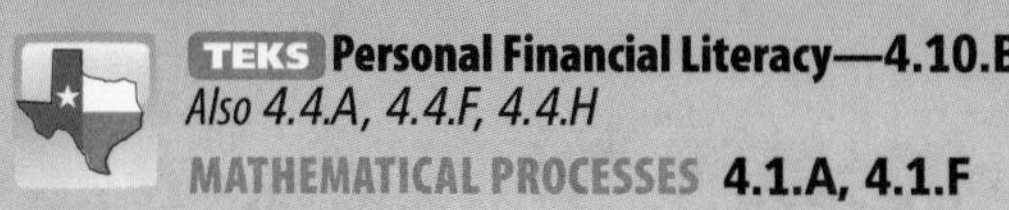

Name ________________________

18.2 Find Profit

Jackie is making jam to sell at the farmers' market. Her expenses are shown in the chart.

Jam-Making Expenses	
Berries	$24.69
Sugar	$4.75
Lemons	$3.29

1. What are Jackie's expenses?

   ________ + ________ + ________ = ________

2. Jackie made 21 jars of jam. She sold all of the jam for $5.50 a jar. How much money did she take in?

   ________ × ________ = ________

3. What was Jackie's profit?

   ________ − ________ = ________

Problem Solving

Use the table for 4–6.

Supplies for Making Loop Potholders	
Loom	**$17.94**
Includes enough loops for 3 potholders	
Bag of Loops	**$19.95**
Enough loops for 8 potholders	

4. Sam and Carla are going to make and sell potholders to earn money for the animal shelter. They need 2 looms, so they will buy 2 loom kits. If they also buy 2 bags of loops and sell the 22 potholders for $4.00 each, how much profit will they make? **Explain.**

   ____

   ____

   ____

5. Sam and Carla decide to buy 2 looms and 10 bags of loops. What is their profit if they sell all 86 potholders for $4.50 each? ________________

6. If Sam and Carla buy just the 2 loom kits and sell only the 6 potholders, how much do they need to charge for each potholder to make a profit? **Explain.**

   ____

   ____

Lesson Check

TEXAS Test Prep

Fill in the bubble completely to show your answer.

7. **Multi-Step** Connor sells pretzels for $1.50 each. The pretzels cost $0.45 each to make. How much profit will Connor make if he sells 40 pretzels?

   Ⓐ $58.00
   Ⓑ $60.00
   Ⓒ $78.00
   Ⓓ $42.00

8. Priscilla makes a profit of $24.50 on every scarf she sells. The materials for each scarf cost $8.39. How much does Priscilla sell each scarf for?

   Ⓐ $32.89
   Ⓑ $16.11
   Ⓒ $34.89
   Ⓓ $22.21

9. Ivan earned $300.00 doing lawn work. His profit was $266.72. How much were his expenses?

   Ⓐ $566.72
   Ⓑ $33.28
   Ⓒ $144.38
   Ⓓ $44.28

10. **Multi-Step** Wilson helped his uncle move. He spent $33.58 for gas and $24.88 for work gloves. He earned $200.00 from his uncle. What is Wilson's profit?

    Ⓐ $258.46
    Ⓑ $58.46
    Ⓒ $141.54
    Ⓓ $152.64

11. **Multi-Step** Christina sold 35 pairs of gloves for $840. Each pair cost her $6.22 to make. How much profit did Christina make?

    Ⓐ $217.70
    Ⓑ $622.30
    Ⓒ $818.30
    Ⓓ $17.78

12. **Multi-Step** Amy sells muffins for $1.35 each. The muffins cost $0.39 each to make. How much profit will Amy make if she sells 48 muffins?

    Ⓐ $46.08
    Ⓑ $69.60
    Ⓒ $18.72
    Ⓓ $64.80

Name ______________________________

18.3 Savings Options

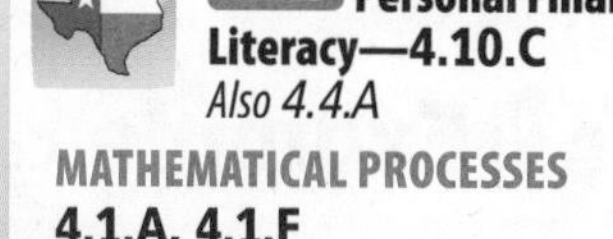

TEKS Personal Financial Literacy—4.10.C
Also 4.4.A
MATHEMATICAL PROCESSES
4.1.A, 4.1.F

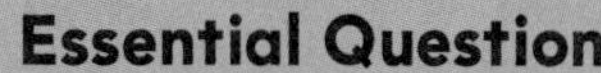

Essential Question What are the advantages and disadvantages of different savings options?

People save money for all different reasons. They also save money in different ways. You can keep your money at home or you can keep your money in a savings account at a bank. If you keep your money in a bank, you will earn **interest**, or additional money, for allowing the bank to use your money.

Unlock the Problem (Real World)

Sammie is saving her money to buy a new tablet computer. She has saved $100 so far. Sammie can either put the $100 into a savings account at her bank or keep it at home in a safe location. Help Sammie compare the advantages and disadvantages of saving her money at home or in a savings account.

Example 1 Advantages

Circle the phrases that apply.

Home:	Easy access to your money	No interest earned	Someone may take it
Savings Account:	Earn interest	Not having easy access to your money	Know where your money is

Example 2 Disadvantages

Circle the phrases that apply.

Home:	Easy access to your money	No interest earned	Someone may take it
Savings Account:	Earn interest	Not having easy access to your money	Know where your money is

- How can an advantage sometimes also be a disadvantage? **Explain.**

____

____

____

Example Compare Savings Plans

Natalie wants to buy a scooter for $100. Which bank has a better savings option?

Bank A: Put $10 a week of her allowance in a bank savings account. The interest is $3 for every $100 in the bank.

Bank B: Put $10 a week of her allowance in a bank savings account. The interest is $6 for every $100 in the bank.

After saving $10 a week for 10 weeks at Bank A, Natalie can have _____

plus $ _____ interest, or _____.

After saving $10 a week for 10 weeks at Bank B, Natalie can have _____

plus $ _____ interest, or _____.

So, _______ has a better savings option for Natalie.

Math Talk
Mathematical Processes
Explain why earning interest is an advantage.

Share and Show

1. Jacob needs $79 to buy a remote control car. Circle the advantage of Jacob saving his money in a savings account at his bank.

He can earn interest on money saved in a savings account.	He would earn no interest on money saved in a savings account.

2. Mary needs $120 to buy a new computer program. Circle the disadvantage of Mary saving her money at home.

She knows where her money is at all times.	Someone may take the money and spend it.

3. **Write Math** Give two or more reasons for saving your money in a savings account at a bank.

____

____

____

____

Name ________________________________

Problem Solving (Real World)

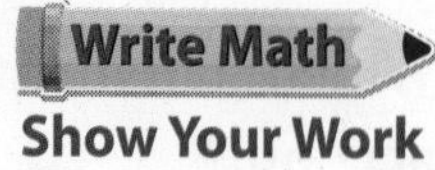

4. Connect How is a parent giving you an extra quarter every time you save $2 like earning interest in a bank savings account?

Show Your Work

5. H.O.T. John thinks of three ways he could save the $20 he needs every 4 weeks to take guitar lessons. Which plan should he choose? **Explain** an advantage and disadvantage for each plan.

He can save $5 of his allowance in a piggy bank each week.	He could save $5 of his allowance each week in a savings account at a bank.	He could earn $5 extra each week by watering people's lawns.

6. H.O.T. **Multi-Step** Marco charges $15 for every lawn he mows and $10 for every car he washes. He washes 2 cars and mows 3 lawns this week. He wants to spend $40 and put the rest in his savings account. How much money will Marco put in his savings account?

7. Apply What are some future things that you might save for by using a savings account at a bank?

Daily Assessment Task

Fill in the bubble for the correct answer choice.

8. Which statement is true about saving money in a bank savings account?

Ⓐ You may lose money.

Ⓑ You may end up with more money than the amount you deposit.

Ⓒ You can never get your money out again.

Ⓓ You have to pay the bank to keep your money there.

9. **Multi-Step** Which statement is true about the savings options below?

Option X Beth puts $6 into a bank savings account every week for a year.

Option Y Beth puts $30 into a bank savings account every month for a year.

Ⓐ She will have $52 more at the end of the year with Option Y.

Ⓑ She will have the same amount of money at the end of the year.

Ⓒ She will have $12 more at the end of the year with Option X.

Ⓓ She will have $48 more at the end of one year with Option Y.

10. Barbara puts $22 a week for 30 weeks in her savings account at the bank. If she receives $4 interest for every $100 saved, how much money will Barbara have after the 30 weeks?

Ⓐ $684 Ⓒ $660

Ⓑ $636 Ⓓ $404

TEXAS Test Prep

11. Which of the following savings options will most likely allow you to reach a savings goal of $400 the fastest?

Ⓐ Save $25 a week in a bank savings account.

Ⓑ Save $25 a week in a drawer at home.

Ⓒ Save $50 a week in a bank savings account.

Ⓓ Save $50 a week by working odd jobs in your community.

Homework and Practice

TEKS Personal Financial Literacy—4.10.C
Also 4.4.A
MATHEMATICAL PROCESSES 4.1.A, 4.1.F

Name ______________________

18.3 Savings Options

1. Leon wants to buy a new skateboard. Circle the advantage of saving money for the skateboard in a savings account at his bank.

The account will earn interest and be worth more than what Leon puts into it.	Leon can have the skateboard without waiting until the money is saved.

2. Circle the disadvantage if Leon buys the skateboard with money from his brother and then saves to pay his brother back with $4 interest for every $100.

Leon will pay more than the price of the skateboard.	Leon will have to wait to buy the skateboard.

Problem Solving Real World

3. Emmy bought a doll and then sold it for more than she paid for it. How is that like earning interest on a bank savings account?

____

____

4. Sharon's parents have 10 years to save for her college education. Give an advantage and disadvantage for each savings plan.

Plan 1	Plan 2
Make payments on a house that may be more valuable in 10 years. Then sell the house for college.	Make payments to a savings account that adds interest of $2 for each $100 in the account each year.
Advantage ______________________	Advantage ______________________
Disadvantage ______________________	Disadvantage ______________________

Lesson Check

TEXAS Test Prep

Fill in the bubble completely to show your answer.

5. **Multi-Step** Amos wants to go on a trip in 4 months. He needs $600 for the trip. Which of the following savings options is the best way for him to save $600 in 4 months (16 weeks)?

Ⓐ Save $100 a month in a bank and get $2.50 for every $100 saved.

Ⓑ Save $50 a week in a bank and get $2 for every $100 saved.

Ⓒ Save $30 a week and borrow the rest.

Ⓓ Save $40 a week and get $3 for every $100 saved.

6. Which is a disadvantage of saving your money in a secret hiding place?

Ⓐ You cannot always get to the money.

Ⓑ The money will not earn interest.

Ⓒ You will end up with more money than you saved.

Ⓓ You can save more money.

7. Vincent earned $36 on savings of $900. What interest did he earn?

Ⓐ $2 for every $100 saved

Ⓑ $4 for every $100 saved

Ⓒ $3 for every $100 saved

Ⓓ $9 for every $100 saved

8. If you save $700 and earn $3 interest for every $100, how much money will you have in all?

Ⓐ $721

Ⓑ $703

Ⓒ $730

Ⓓ $7,021

9. **Multi-Step** Mel walked 4 dogs. She earned $15 each for each dog. She earned $12 an hour for babysitting for 3 hours. If she spends $42 on shoes and saves the rest, how much money will she save?

Ⓐ $54

Ⓑ $60

Ⓒ $36

Ⓓ $96

10. **Multi-Step** Which statement is true about savings plans below?

Plan A: Save $15 in a savings account every week for 26 weeks.

Plan B: Save $50 in a savings account every month for 6 months.

Ⓐ It would be better to save at home than to use either of these savings plans.

Ⓑ At the end of the time, there will be the same amount of money using either plan.

Ⓒ There will be more money in the savings account using Plan A.

Ⓓ There will be more money in the savings account using Plan B.

Name ______________________________

18.4 Budget a Weekly Allowance

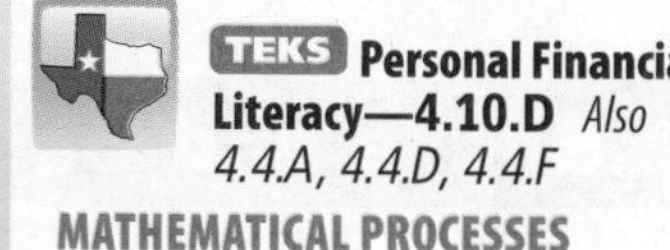

TEKS Personal Financial Literacy—4.10.D *Also 4.4.A, 4.4.D, 4.4.F*

MATHEMATICAL PROCESSES
4.1.A, 4.1.F

Essential Question How can you budget a weekly allowance?

Unlock the Problem

Luis receives an allowance of $15 each week. He wants to make a budget to show how he will use his allowance. In his budget, the expenses should not be more than his allowance.

Remember

Expenses can be fixed or variable.

A **budget** is an organized plan for spending and saving money. Help Luis budget his weekly allowance.

Find the weekly expenses.

Luis' weekly expenses are listed in the table below. Complete the table. How much will Luis save for charity?

Expenses	Daily Expense	Weekly Expense
School lunch, 3 days a week	$2.50 a lunch	_____
Snacks after school, 3 days a week	$0.75 a snack	_____
Save for college fund		$2.50
Save for special things		$2.00
Save to give to a charity		_____

Find the total for each weekly expense.

Lunch Expense: $_____ + $_____ + $_____ = $_____ a week

Snack Expense: $_____ + $_____ + $_____ = $_____ a week

Total expenses before charity expense:

$_____ + $_____ + $_____ + $_____ = $_____

To find the amount Luis will donate to charity, _________ the total expenses from his weekly allowance.

Charity Expense: $_____ − $14.25 = $_____

So, Luis will save $_____ per week to give to charity.

Math Talk Mathematical Processes

When might Luis change his budget? **Explain.**

Share and Show

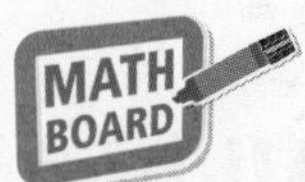

1. Since Carver goes to a school that is not near his house, he receives an allowance of $50 each week. He wants to make a budget to show how he will use his allowance. For each of 5 days, he pays $3.40 to ride the city bus, $3.60 for lunch, and $1 for snacks. He wants to save half of what money he has left each week. How much money will Carver save each week?

Complete the table.

Expenses	Per Day	Amount Per Week
Bus rides	$3.40	
Lunch	$3.60	
Snacks	$1.00	

Find the total for each expense for the week.

Bus rides: $_____ + $_____ + $_____ + $_____ + $_____ = $_____

Lunch: $_____ + $_____ + $_____ + $_____ + $_____ = $_____

Snacks: $_____ a day × _____ days = $_____

Total expenses each week: $_____ + $_____ + $_____ = $_____

Difference between allowance and expenses: $50 − $_____ = $_____

Half of the money Carver has left after expenses: $_____ ÷ 2 = $_____

So, Carver will save $_____ each week.

Use the information given to answer the question.

2. Elijah receives a weekly allowance of $25. How could he budget his allowance among spending, saving, including college, and sharing? Complete the table.

Elijah's Budget

Expenses	Amount Per Week
Spending	
Saving	
Saving for college	
Sharing	
Total	

3. Lea gets a weekly allowance. She saves $14 a week from her allowance. Each week, she puts aside $2 for charity, saves $4 for college, and $12 for fun. What is Lea's weekly allowance?

____

Name ___________________________

Problem Solving Real World

4. **H.O.T. Multi-Step** Stacy gets $15 a week allowance. She is saving for a bike that costs $321. Each week she gives $3 to charity, spends $4, and puts $5 in her college fund. If she saves the rest of her allowance for her bike, how many weeks will it take her to save enough money to buy her bike?

____

5. **Reasoning** Pero gets a weekly allowance of $10 for doing chores and $8 per hour babysitting his brother. His goal is to save $10 a week for college, give $10 a week to charity, and have $14 a week to spend. He babysits the same amount each week. How many hours does he need to babysit each week to reach his goal? **Explain.**

Write Math ▸ Show Your Work

____

____

____

____

____

6. **H.O.T. Multi-Step** Henry pays $10 per week for a gym membership, $10 a week for his cell phone, and saves $15 each week. He earns $10 for every lawn he mows. What is the least number of lawns that he needs to mow each week to cover his budgeted expenses? **Explain.**

____

____

____

____

Mathematical Processes
Model • Reason • Communicate

Daily Assessment Task

Fill in the bubble completely to show your answer.

7. Sammy is saving $5 out of his $10 allowance each week for summer science camp. He must divide the rest between his savings account, a charity of his choice, and his college fund. Sammy gives $1 per week to a local charity. He puts the same amount in his savings account as his college fund. How much does Sammy put in his college fund each week?

Ⓐ $2.00 Ⓒ $4.50

Ⓑ $2.50 Ⓓ $4.00

8. Lisa wants to buy a tablet computer that costs $300. She gets a weekly allowance of $12. If she saves $5 each week toward the cost of the tablet computer, how many weeks will it take her to save enough to buy it?

Ⓐ 300 weeks Ⓒ 60 weeks

Ⓑ 20 weeks Ⓓ 30 weeks

9. **Multi-Step** Juan is having a party to earn money for his local animal shelter. His goal is to give the shelter $250. He charges each person $5 to attend the party, and 35 people attend. If Juan saves $5 of his allowance each week for the animal shelter, how long will it take him to save the rest of the $250 for the shelter?

Ⓐ 7 weeks Ⓒ 5 weeks

Ⓑ 75 weeks Ⓓ 15 weeks

TEXAS Test Prep

10. Each week, Carol saves $24, pays $56 for her expenses, and gives $8 to the charity of her choice. If she makes $8 per hour, how many hours must she work to make enough money to meet this budget?

Ⓐ 3 hours Ⓒ 11 hours

Ⓑ 7 hours Ⓓ 10 hours

Name ______________________

18.4 Budget a Weekly Allowance

Use the information given to answer the question.

1. Carlos has a weekly allowance of $24. He spends $4 on snacks and $6 on entertainment each week. He is saving the rest for a printer that costs $224. How many weeks will it take Carlos to save enough money to buy the printer?

____

2. Brenda's weekly allowance is $15. She puts aside $5 of her weekly allowance for gifts and gives $2 to charity. She divides what's left into equal amounts for spending money and music downloads. How much spending money does Brenda have each week?

____

Problem Solving Real World

3. Darleen gets $10 a week allowance. She walks her neighbor's dog 6 days each week and earns $3 each day. She earns $7 an hour doing odd jobs. Darleen wants to save $15 a week, give $5 a week to charity, and have at least $20 each week to spend. How many hours of odd jobs does she need to do each week to earn enough money? **Explain.**

____

____

____

____

____

4. If Darleen wants to increase her spending money to $25 a week and earn an extra $12 a week for a phone plan, how many extra hours a week will she need to work doing odd jobs? **Explain.**

____

____

____

Lesson Check

TEXAS Test Prep

Fill in the bubble completely to show your answer.

5. Jim gets a weekly allowance. He keeps $8 for spending money, saves $5 and gives $2 to charity. How much is Jim's weekly allowance?

   Ⓐ $15
   Ⓑ $13
   Ⓒ $11
   Ⓓ $16

6. Gianna budgets her allowance so she uses equal amounts for spending, saving, and gifts. Her weekly allowance is $13.50. How much does Gianna save each week?

   Ⓐ $6.75
   Ⓑ $4.25
   Ⓒ $5.00
   Ⓓ $4.50

7. **Multi-Step** Lily gets $13 a week allowance. She saves $3, gives $2 a week to the soup kitchen, and divides the rest between spending money and dog treats. How much money does Lily spend each week on dog treats?

   Ⓐ $8
   Ⓑ $7
   Ⓒ $5
   Ⓓ $4

8. **Multi-Step** Hunter is saving for a cordless drill. The drill costs $160. Hunter gets a weekly allowance of $15. He keeps $8 a week for spending money and saves the rest. How many weeks will it take him to save enough money to buy the drill?

   Ⓐ 23 weeks
   Ⓑ 20 weeks
   Ⓒ 11 weeks
   Ⓓ 15 weeks

9. **Multi-Step** Wendy gets a weekly allowance of $8. She keeps $5 for spending money and divides the rest evenly into savings and giving to charity. How much does Wendy give to charity each week?

   Ⓐ $2.00
   Ⓑ $1.50
   Ⓒ $1.75
   Ⓓ $1.25

10. **Multi-Step** Dylan gets a weekly allowance of $10. He also earns $5 an hour gardening for his aunt. He wants to have $12 a week for spending money and to save at least $15 a week to buy a new guitar. How many hours will he need to work in his aunt's garden each week to reach his goal?

   Ⓐ 3 hours
   Ⓑ 2 hours
   Ⓒ 4 hours
   Ⓓ 5 hours

Name ____________________

18.5 Financial Institutions

Essential Question

What are the purposes of financial institutions?

Financial institutions, such as banks and credit card companies, are businesses. They are in the business of keeping money safe, lending money, and borrowing money.

When you open a savings account at a bank, the bank is a borrower. This has an advantage of keeping your money safe. When you take out a loan or credit card, the bank is a lender.

Unlock the Problem

Read each situation. Is the financial institution acting as lender or as borrower? Write the letters for each below.

Lending and Borrowing

Financial Institution as Lender: ____________

Financial Institution as Borrower: ____________

A Alex takes out a loan to pay for a car.	**B** Brianna is saving to take a fashion design course. Her money is in a bank savings account.	**C** Chloe uses an automatic teller machine to withdraw her money.	**D** Destiny pays off her credit card.
E Ethan deposits the check received as a gift into a bank account.	**F** Faith takes out a loan to pay for a new roof on her house.	**G** Gavin uses online banking to deposit his earnings from work.	**H** Hector uses a loan to open a business.

- Circle the situations above where money is being kept safe.

When you borrow money from a financial institution, you will pay interest on the **loan**. **Interest** is the additional money paid by a borrower to a lender in exchange for the use of the lender's money.

Example Interest

Tyler wants to buy a 4-wheeler that costs $400. Tyler doesn't have that much money. He can borrow the money from a financial institution to buy the 4-wheeler, but he will have to pay interest. How much will Tyler have to repay the bank to borrow the money?

Find the total interest on $400.

Think: How many $100 are in $400?

Interest = $_____ for every $100 borrowed × 4 = $_____

Think: Repayment of loan = loan amount + interest

Total amount paid to bank: $_____ + $_____ = $_____

Share and Show

1. Zack gets a loan for $500 from the bank. The interest rate for the loan is $11 for every $100 borrowed. How much will Zach have to repay the bank to borrow the money?

   Interest = $_____ for every $100 borrowed × _____ = $_____

   Total amount paid to bank: $_____ + $_____ = $_____

Write *borrower* or *lender*.

2. When you take out a loan from a bank, you are the __________ and the bank is the __________.

3. When you put money into a savings account at a bank, you are the __________ and the bank is the __________.

4. Circle the situations where you might use a financial institution.

   Borrowing money to buy a car.

   Letting your friend borrow $1.

   Lending your friend $5.

   Keeping $200 you earned working safe.

   Taking out a loan to buy a new house.

   Putting your monthly allowance in a safe place.

Name ______________________________

Problem Solving Real World

5. **Apply** Mrs. Artino takes out a loan from a financial institution. The loan is for $600. The total interest paid will be $6. How much is the interest per $100 borrowed?

____

6. **Write Math** ▸ When might it be better to use a bank account to save $200 by paying $20 a month than to borrow $200 using a bank loan? Use an example to explain.

____

____

____

7. **H.O.T.** **Multi-Step** Sonia takes out a loan for $700 to buy a new washing machine. The interest is $8 for every $100 borrowed. If she wants to repay the loan in 6 months, how much will she need to pay each month?

____

8. **H.O.T.** Look at the interest paid column in the table. Suppose you borrow $600. Complete the table. Which loan would you choose? **Explain** your answer.

Bank Loan Rates

	Length of Loan	Interest Paid	Total Repaid	Monthly Payment
Personal Loan	4 months	$6 for every $100 borrowed	$______ + $600 = $______	$636 ÷ 4 = $______
Personal Loan	6 months	$8 for every $100 borrowed	$______ + $600 = $______	$648 ÷ 6 = $______
Personal Loan	8 months	$12 for every $100 borrowed	$______ + $600 = $______	$672 ÷ 8 = $______

____

____

____

Daily Assessment Task

Fill in the bubble completely to show your answer.

9. Which situation shows a financial institution as a borrower?

Ⓐ Abby uses a credit card to pay for an online purchase.

Ⓑ Kevin borrows money to pay for a course as a dental assistant.

Ⓒ Luis deposits his paycheck into a savings account.

Ⓓ Hailey takes out a loan to help her buy a house.

10. Sean borrows $300 from his bank. The interest is $7 for every $100 borrowed. How much will Sean be charged in interest?

Ⓐ $21

Ⓑ $7

Ⓒ $307

Ⓓ $30

11. **Multi-Step** Casey borrows $200 from her bank. What is the total amount she will have to repay the bank?

Ⓐ $120

Ⓑ $50

Ⓒ $12

Ⓓ $212

Bank Loan Rates		
	Length of Loan	**Interest Paid**
Personal Loan	4 months	$6 for every $100 borrowed

TEXAS Test Prep

12. Which statement is NOT true about a financial institution?

Ⓐ A financial institution is a safe place to keep your money.

Ⓑ A financial institution charges a fee, called interest, on loans.

Ⓒ A financial institution can issue credit cards.

Ⓓ A financial institution is a business that never borrows money.

Homework and Practice

Name ______________________________

18.5 Financial Institutions

1. Alexia charges \$700 on her credit card. The interest on the credit card is \$18 for every \$100 borrowed. How much will Alexia have to pay back?

   Interest = \$_______ per \$100 borrowed × _______ = \$_______

   Total amount paid back = \$_______ + \$_______ = \$_______

Write *borrower* or *lender*.

2. Lucas charges \$128 on his credit card.

   ____

3. Sophia puts \$20 a week into her bank savings account.

   ____

4. Lillian has some of her pay check automatically deposited into her savings account.

   ____

5. Levi gets a loan from the bank to buy a house.

   ____

Problem Solving

6. Mathew borrows \$8,200 from the bank to buy a car. The interest on the loan is \$6 for every \$100 borrowed. How much will Mathew pay back? ______________

7. Ellie wants to buy a computer for \$900. She can save \$75 a month in a savings account and earn \$2 for every \$100 saved and buy the computer when she has enough money. Or, she can pay back \$75 a month on a bank loan for \$900 and pay interest of \$7 for every \$100 borrowed. How much will she pay for the computer for each of the 2 choices?

   ____

   ____

   ____

8. Why might Ellie save for the computer? Why might she borrow money to buy the computer? What are the advantages of each way?

   ____

   ____

   ____

   ____

   ____

Lesson Check

TEXAS Test Prep

Fill in the bubble completely to show your answer.

9. Which situation shows a financial institution as borrower?

   Ⓐ a business takes out a loan to buy equipment

   Ⓑ a shopper uses a credit card to buy a coat

   Ⓒ a student borrows money to go to college

   Ⓓ a customer makes a deposit into a savings account

10. Emma borrows $1,300 from her bank. The interest fees are $5 for every $100 borrowed. How much will Emma be charged in interest fees?

    Ⓐ $75

    Ⓑ $130

    Ⓒ $65

    Ⓓ $50

11. Which statement describes what a financial institution does with the money a customer deposits into a savings account?

    Ⓐ It makes loans to other customers.

    Ⓑ It donates the money to charity.

    Ⓒ It pays the employees of the bank.

    Ⓓ It pays back loans made to other customers.

12. Freddie borrowed $600 from a bank to buy a new table saw. The interest payment will be $30. What is the interest for each $100 borrowed?

    Ⓐ $3

    Ⓑ $6

    Ⓒ $5

    Ⓓ $18

13. **Multi-Step** Sophie borrows $500 for 4 months. She will pay $4 interest for every $100 she borrows. What are her monthly payments?

    Ⓐ $125

    Ⓑ $130

    Ⓒ $129

    Ⓓ $520

14. **Multi-Step** Roger charges $800 on his credit card. He is charged interest of $16 for every $100 borrowed. How much will Roger pay back?

    Ⓐ $928

    Ⓑ $960

    Ⓒ $128

    Ⓓ $816

Name ______________________________

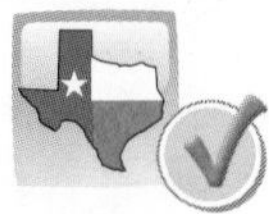

Unit 6 Assessment

Vocabulary

Choose the best term from the box.

Vocabulary
budget
financial institution
fixed expenses
interest
loan
profit
variable expenses

1. ______________________ are expenses that occur regularly and the amount does not change. (p. 641)

2. __________________ is the amount left after all the expenses are subtracted from the amount of money received from selling an item or service. (p. 647)

3. A ______________________ is a business, like a bank, that collects money, keeps it safe, and provides money for people and businesses to borrow. (p. 665)

4. The money that is lent by a bank or other financial institutions is called a ____________. (p. 665)

5. A __________________ is an organized plan for spending and saving money. (p. 659)

6. ______________________ are expenses in which the amount does change based on need or choice. (p. 641)

7. The additional money paid by a borrower to a lender in exchange for the use of the lender's money is called __________________. (p. 665)

Concepts and Skills

8. Amber receives a weekly allowance of $35. How could she budget her allowance among spending, saving, including college, and sharing? Complete the table. TEKS 4.10.D

Amber's Budget	
Expenses	**Amount Per Week**
Spending	
Saving	
Saving for college	
Sharing	
Total	

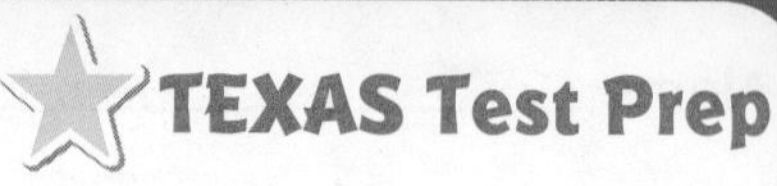

9. Describe the similarities and differences of fixed and variable expenses. Give an example of each type of expense and explain why you think the expense is the type of expense that it is. TEKS 4.10.A

10. Explain why you pay back more than you borrow when you make a loan from a financial institution. TEKS 4.10.E

11. What are some advantages and disadvantages of saving your money in a bank rather than at home in a piggy bank? TEKS 4.10.C

Fill in the bubble completely to show your answer.

TEXAS Test Prep

Use the table for 12–13.

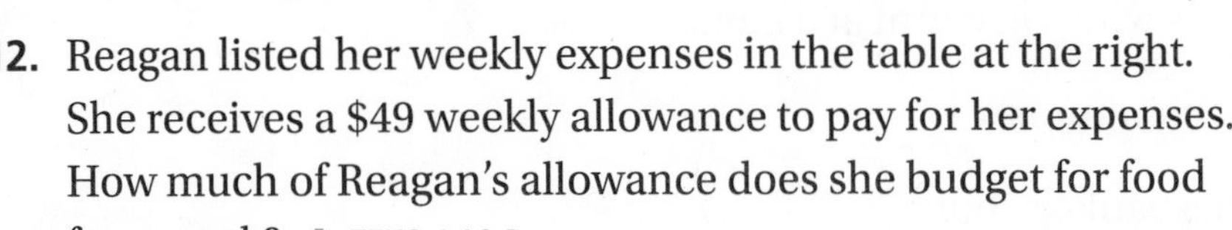

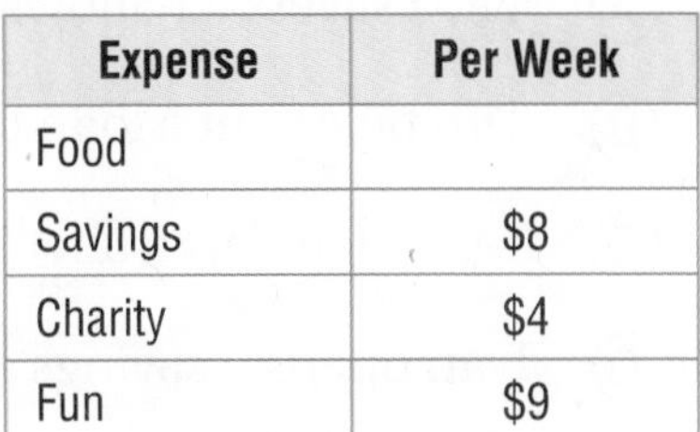

Expense	Per Week
Food	
Savings	$8
Charity	$4
Fun	$9

12. Reagan listed her weekly expenses in the table at the right. She receives a $49 weekly allowance to pay for her expenses. How much of Reagan's allowance does she budget for food for a week? TEKS 4.10.D

Ⓐ $42
Ⓑ $38
Ⓒ $28
Ⓓ $27

13. Which statement is true when budgeting a weekly allowance among spending, saving, including for college, and sharing? TEKS 4.10.D

Ⓐ The amount budgeted for spending is always the same as the amount budgeted for sharing.

Ⓑ The total amount for all expenses must not be more than the weekly allowance.

Ⓒ The amount budgeted for savings is always half the amount of the weekly allowance.

Ⓓ The total amount for all expenses can be more than the weekly allowance.

14. Arlen has several variable expenses that he pays every month. Which of the following is a variable expense? TEKS 4.10.A

Ⓐ rent
Ⓑ gas bill
Ⓒ car payment
Ⓓ loan repayment

15. Which is not the purpose of a financial institution? TEKS 4.10.E

Ⓐ keeping money safe
Ⓑ lending money
Ⓒ borrowing money
Ⓓ buying gas for your car

16. Susan wants to save her money to buy a new computer that costs $800. She is considering the advantages and disadvantages of saving her money at home or in a savings account at a bank. Which is an advantage of Susan saving her money in a savings account at a bank rather than at home? TEKS 4.10.C

Ⓐ Susan would earn interest.

Ⓑ Susan would not earn any interest.

Ⓒ Susan could use the money to buy something else.

Ⓓ Susan's money may be lost.

TEXAS Test Prep

17. Which situation shows a financial institution as a lender? TEKS 4.10.E

Ⓐ Vicki saves her allowance in a savings account at a bank.

Ⓑ Tim takes out a loan to buy a computer.

Ⓒ Terry deposits a check into his bank account.

Ⓓ Ivan opens a savings account at a bank.

18. Neil deposits $3,500 into his savings account at a financial instituion. Which is the purpose of the financial institution in this situation? TEKS 4.10.E

Ⓐ loaning Neil money

Ⓑ keeping Neil's money safe

Ⓒ letting Neil pay off his credit card

Ⓓ letting Neil buy a car

19. In a table, Maxine kept track of her expenses for the month. Which is a fixed expense? TEKS 4.10.A

Ⓐ Lunches

Ⓑ Gas Bill

Ⓒ Electric Bill

Ⓓ Rent

Maxine's Expenses

Bill	Cost
Grocery bill	$321
Gas bill	$125
Electric bill	$75
Rent	$750
Lunches	$48

20. Imid had a savings account at a bank. The account paid interest of $3.50 per $100. If Imid had $400 in the account, how much interest would he receive? TEKS 4.10.C

Ⓐ $11.50

Ⓑ $14.00

Ⓒ $12.50

Ⓓ $3.50

21. Mark sold three video games for $37.50 each. He bought the three games for $17.95 each. What was Mark's profit from selling the three video games? TEKS 4.10.B

Ⓐ $58.65

Ⓑ $85.56

Ⓒ $58.56

Ⓓ $85.65

Glossary

Pronunciation Key

a	add, map	f	fit, half	n	nice, tin	p	pit, stop	yo͞o	fuse, few
ā	ace, rate	g	go, log	ng	ring, song	r	run, poor	v	vain, eve
â(r)	care, air	h	hope, hate	o	odd, hot	s	see, pass	w	win, away
ä	palm, father	i	it, give	ō	open, so	sh	sure, rush	y	yet, yearn
b	bat, rub	ī	ice, write	ô	order, jaw	t	talk, sit	z	zest, muse
ch	check, catch	j	joy, ledge	oi	oil, boy	th	thin, both	zh	vision, pleasure
d	dog, rod	k	cool, take	ou	pout, now	t͟h	this, bathe		
e	end, pet	l	look, rule	o͝o	took, full	u	up, done		
ē	equal, tree	m	move, seem	o͞o	pool, food	û(r)	burn, term		

ə the schwa, an unstressed vowel representing the sound spelled a in above, e in sicken, i in possible, o in melon, u in circus

Other symbols:
- • separates words into syllables
- ′ indicates stress on a syllable

acute angle [ə•kyo͞ot′ ang′gəl] **ángulo agudo** An angle that measures greater than 0° and less than 90° (p. 450)
Example:

acute triangle [ə•kyo͞ot′ trī′ang•gəl] **triángulo acutángulo** A triangle with three acute angles (p. 456)
Example:

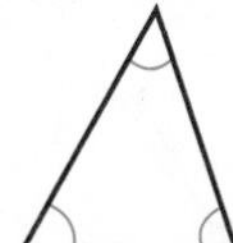

addend [a′dend] **sumando** A number that is added to another in an addition problem
Example: 2 + 4 = 6;
2 and 4 are addends.

addition [ə•di′shən] **suma** The process of finding the total number of items when two or more groups of items are joined; the opposite operation of subtraction

A.M. [ā•em′] **a. m.** The times after midnight and before noon

analog clock [anəl• ôg kläk] **reloj analógico** A tool for measuring time, in which hands move around a circle to show hours, minutes, and sometimes seconds
Example:

angle [ang′gəl] **ángulo** A shape formed by two line segments or rays that share the same endpoint (p. 450)
Example:

area [âr′ē•ə] **área** The number of unit squares needed to cover a flat surface (p. 427)
Example:

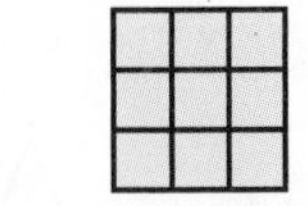

area = 9 square units

array [ə•rā′] **matriz** An arrangement of objects in rows and columns
Example:

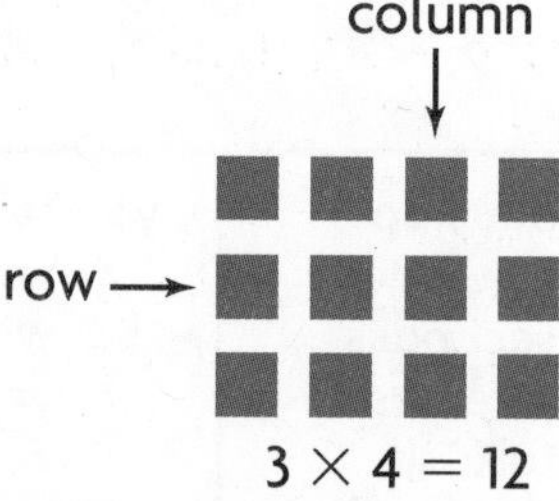

Associative Property of Addition [ə•sō′shē•āt•iv präp′ər•tē əv ə•dish′ən] **propiedad asociativa de la suma** The property that states that you can group addends in different ways and still get the same sum
Example: $3 + (8 + 5) = (3 + 8) + 5$

Associative Property of Multiplication [ə•sō′shē•ə•tiv präp′ər•tē əv mul•tə•pli•kā′shən] **propiedad asociativa de la multiplicación** The property that states that you can group factors in different ways and still get the same product
Example: $3 \times (4 \times 2) = (3 \times 4) \times 2$

bar graph [bär graf] **gráfica de barras** A graph that uses bars to show data
Example:

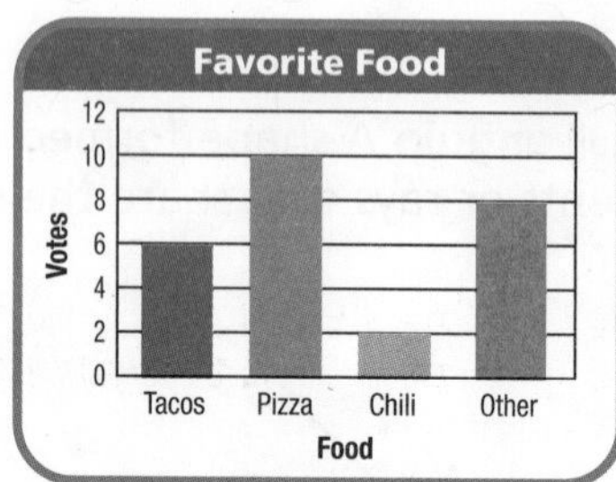

base [bās] **base** A polygon's side or a two-dimensional shape, usually a polygon or circle, by which a three-dimensional shape is measured or named
Examples:

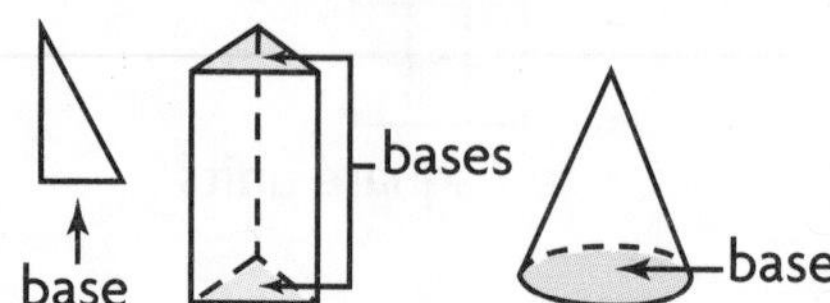

benchmark [bench′märk] **punto de referencia** A known size or amount that helps you understand a different size or amount (p. 113)

budget [bŭj′ĭt] **presupuesto** An organized plan for spending and saving money (p. 659)

calendar [kal′ən•dər] **calendario** A table that shows the days, weeks, and months of a year

capacity [kə•pas′ĭ•tē] **capacidad** The amount a container can hold when filled

Celsius (°C) [sel′sē•əs] **Celsius** A metric scale for measuring temperature

centimeter (cm) [sen′tə•mēt•ər] **centímetro (cm)** A metric unit for measuring length or distance
1 meter = 100 centimeters
Example:

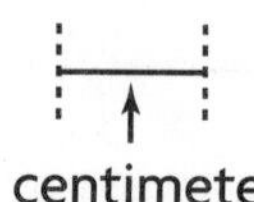

cent sign (¢) [sent sīn] **símbolo de centavo (¢)** A symbol that stands for *cent* or *cents*
Example: 53¢

clockwise [kläk′wīz] **en el sentido de las manecillas del reloj** In the same direction in which the hands of a clock move (p. 488)

closed shape [klōzd shāp] **figura cerrada** A two-dimensional shape that begins and ends at the same point
Examples:

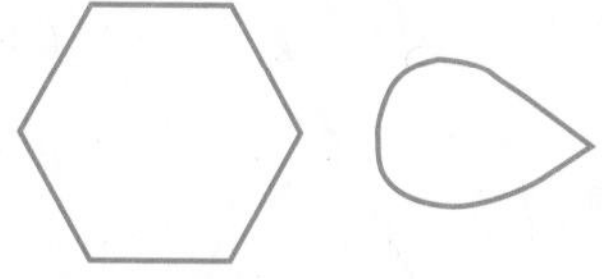

common denominator [käm′ən dē•näm′ə•nāt•ər] **denominador común** A common multiple of two or more denominators
Example: Some common denominators for $\frac{1}{4}$ and $\frac{5}{6}$ are 12, 24, and 36.

common factor [käm′ən fak′tər] **factor común** A number that is a factor of two or more numbers

common multiple [käm′ən mul′tə•pəl] **múltiplo común** A number that is a multiple of two or more numbers

Commutative Property of Addition [kə•myo͞ot′ə•tiv präp′ər•tē əv ə•dish′ən] **propiedad conmutativa de la suma** The property that states that when the order of two addends is changed, the sum is the same
Example: 4 + 5 = 5 + 4

Commutative Property of Multiplication [kə•myo͞ot′ə•tiv präp′ər•tē əv mul•tə•pli•kā′shən] **propiedad conmutativa de la multiplicación** The property that states that when the order of two factors is changed, the product is the same
Example: 4 × 5 = 5 × 4

compare [kəm•pâr′] **comparar** To describe whether numbers are equal to, less than, or greater than each other

compatible numbers [kəm•pat′ə•bəl num′bərz] **números compatibles** Numbers that are easy to compute mentally (p. 273)

composite number [kəm•päz′it num′bər] **número compuesto** A number having more than two factors
Example: 6 is a composite number, since its factors are 1, 2, 3, and 6.

corner [kôr′nər] **vértice** See *vertex*.

counterclockwise [kount•er•kläk′wīz] **en el sentido contrario de las manecillas del reloj** In the opposite direction in which the hands of a clock move (p. 487)

counting number [kount′ing num′bər] **número positivo** A whole number that can be used to count a set of objects (1, 2, 3, 4, . . .)

cube [kyo͞ob] **cubo** A three-dimensional shape with six square faces of the same size
Example:

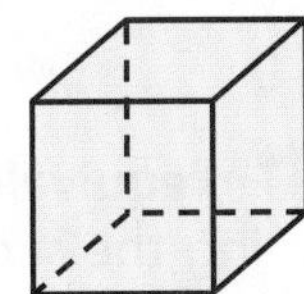

cup (c) [kup] **taza (tz)** A customary unit used to measure capacity and liquid volume (p. 537)
1 cup = 8 ounces

data [dāt′ə] **datos** Information collected about people or things

decagon [dek′ə•gän] **decágono** A polygon with ten sides and ten angles

decimal [des′ə•məl] **número decimal** A number with one or more digits to the right of the decimal point (p. 31)

decimal point [des′ə•məl point] **punto decimal** A symbol used to separate dollars from cents in money amounts, and to separate the ones and the tenths places in a decimal (p. 31)
Example: 6.4
↑ decimal point

decimeter (dm) [des′i•mēt•ər] **decímetro (dm)** A metric unit for measuring length or distance (p. 549)
1 meter = 10 decimeters

degree (°) [di•grē′] **grado (°)** The unit used for measuring angles and temperatures (p. 493)

denominator [dē•näm′ə•nāt•ər] **denominador** The number below the bar in a fraction that tells how many equal parts are in the whole or in the group
Example: $\frac{3}{4}$ ← denominator

diagonal [dī•ag′ə•nəl] **diagonal** A line segment that connects two vertices of a polygon that are not next to each other
Example:

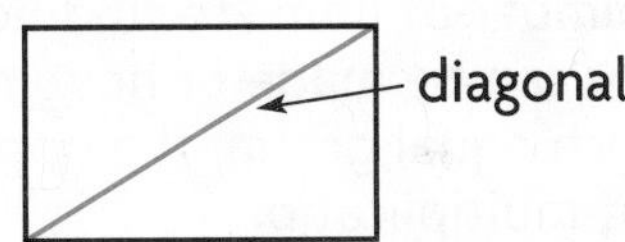

difference [dif′ər•əns] **diferencia** The answer to a subtraction problem

digit [dij′it] **dígito** Any one of the ten symbols 0, 1, 2, 3, 4, 5, 6, 7, 8, or 9 used to write numbers

digital clock [dij′i•təl kläk] **reloj digital** A clock that shows time to the minute, using digits
Example:

dime [dīm] **moneda de 10¢** A coin worth 10 cents and with a value equal to that of 10 pennies; 10¢
Example:

dimension [də•men′shən] **dimensión** A measure in one direction

Distributive Property [di•strib′yo͞o•tiv präp′ər•tē] **propiedad distributiva** The property that states that multiplying a sum by a number is the same as multiplying each addend by the number and then adding the products (p. 229)
Example: $5 \times (10 + 6) = (5 \times 10) + (5 \times 6)$

divide [də•vīd′] **dividir** To separate into equal groups; the opposite operation of multiplication

dividend [dəv′ə•dend] **dividendo** The number that is to be divided in a division problem
Example: $36 \div 6$; $6\overline{)36}$; the dividend is 36.

divisible [də•viz′ə•bəl] **divisible** A number is divisible by another number if the quotient is a counting number and the remainder is zero
Example: 18 is divisible by 3.

division [də•vi′zhən] **división** The process of sharing a number of items to find how many equal groups can be made or how many items will be in each equal group; the opposite operation of multiplication

divisor [də•vī′zər] **divisor** The number that divides the dividend
Example: $15 \div 3$; $3\overline{)15}$; the divisor is 3.

dollar [däl′ər] **dólar** Paper money worth 100 cents and equal to 100 pennies; $1.00
Example:

dot plot [dät plöt] **diagrama de puntos** A graph that records each piece of data on a number line (p. 609)
Example:

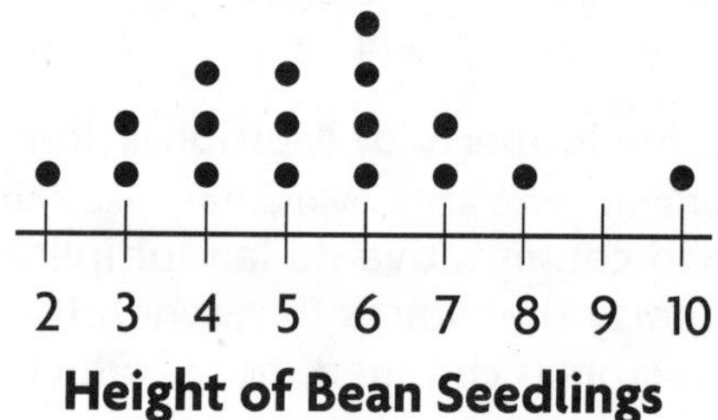

elapsed time [ē•lapst′ tīm] **tiempo transcurrido** The time that passes from the start of an activity to the end of that activity

endpoint [end′point] **extremo** The point at either end of a line segment or the starting point of a ray

equal groups [ē′kwəl gro͞opz] **grupos iguales** Groups that have the same number of objects

equal parts [ē′kwəl pärts] **partes iguales** Parts that are exactly the same size

equal sign (=) [ē′kwəl sīn] **signo de igualdad (=)** A symbol used to show that two numbers have the same value
Example: $384 = 384$

equal to [ē′kwəl to͞o] **igual a** Having the same value
Example: $4 + 4$ is equal to $3 + 5$.

equation [ē•kwā′zhən] **ecuación** A number sentence which shows that two quantities are equal
Example: $4 + 5 = 9$

equivalent [ē•kwiv′ə•lənt] **equivalente** Having the same value or naming the same amount

equivalent decimals [ē•kwiv′ə•lənt des′ə•məlz] **decimales equivalentes** Two or more decimals that name the same amount

equivalent fractions [ē•kwiv'ə•lənt frak'shənz] **fracciones equivalentes** Two or more fractions that name the same amount (p. 75)
Example: $\frac{3}{4}$ and $\frac{6}{8}$ name the same amount.

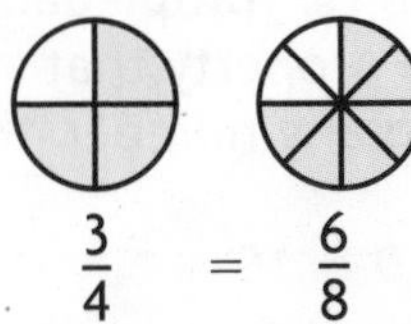

$\frac{3}{4} = \frac{6}{8}$

estimate [es'tə•māt] *verb* **estimar** To find an answer that is close to the exact amount

estimate [es'tə•mit] *noun* **estimación** A number that is close to the exact amount (p. 23)

even [ē'vən] **par** A whole number that has a 0, 2, 4, 6, or 8 in the ones place

expanded form [ek•span'did fôrm] **forma desarrollada** A way to write numbers by showing the value of each digit (p. 11)
Example: 253 = 200 + 50 + 3

expression [ek•spresh'ən] **expresión** A part of a number sentence that has numbers and operation signs but does not have an equal sign

fact family [fakt fam'ə•lē] **familia de operaciones** A set of related multiplication and division equations, or addition and subtraction equations
Example: 7 × 8 = 56 8 × 7 = 56
56 ÷ 7 = 8 56 ÷ 8 = 7

factor [fak'tər] **factor** A number that is multiplied by another number to find a product

Fahrenheit (°F) [fâr'ən•hīt] **Fahrenheit (°F)** A customary scale for measuring temperature

financial institution [fə•năn'shəl ĭn•stĭ•too'shən] **institución financiera** A business, like a bank, that collects money, keeps it safe, and provides money for people and businesses to borrow (p. 665)

fixed expense [fĭkst ĭk•spĕns'] **gastos regulares** Expenses that occur regularly and the amount does not change (p. 641)

fluid ounce (fl oz) [floo'id ouns] **onza fluida (oz fl)** A customary unit used to measure liquid capacity and liquid volume (p. 537)
1 cup = 8 fluid ounces

foot (ft) [fo͝ot] **pie (ft)** A customary unit used for measuring length or distance
1 foot = 12 inches

formula [fôr'myoo•lə] **fórmula** A set of symbols that expresses a mathematical rule (p. 422)
Example: Area = length × width, or $A = l \times w$

fraction [frak'shən] **fracción** A number that names a part of a whole or part of a group
Example:

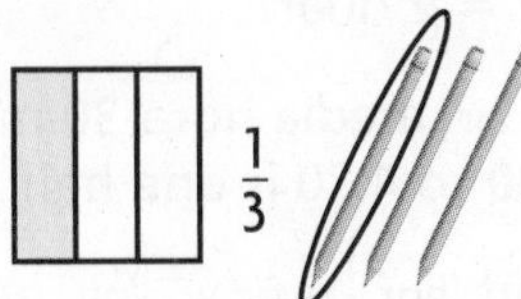

fraction greater than 1 [frak'shən grāt'ər *th*an wun] **fracción mayor que 1** A number which has a numerator that is greater than its denominator

frequency [frē'kwən•sē] **frecuencia** The number of times the data occurs. (p. 597)

frequency table [frē'kwən•sē tā'bəl] **tabla de frecuencia** A table that uses numbers to record data about how often something happens (p. 597)
Example:

Favorite Color	
Color	**Frequency**
Blue	10
Red	7
Green	5
Other	3

gallon (gal) [gal'ən] **galón (gal)** A customary unit for measuring capacity and liquid volume (p. 537)
1 gallon = 4 quarts

gram (g) [gram] **gramo (g)** A metric unit for measuring mass
1 kilogram = 1,000 grams

greater than sign (>) [grāt′ər t͟han sīn] **signo de mayor que (>)** A symbol used to compare two quantities, with the greater quantity given first
Example: $6 > 4$

grid [grid] **cuadrícula** Evenly divided and equally spaced squares on a shape or flat surface

half gallon [haf gal′ən] **medio galón** A customary unit for measuring capacity and liquid volume (p. 537)
1 half gallon = 2 quarts

half hour [haf our] **media hora** 30 minutes
Example: 4:00 to 4:30 is one half hour.

half-square unit [haf skwâr yo͞o′nit] **media unidad cuadrada** Half of a unit of area with dimensions of 1 unit × 1 unit

height [hīt] **altura** The measure of a perpendicular from the base to the top of a two-dimensional shape

hexagon [hek′sə•gän] **hexágono** A polygon with six sides and six angles
Examples:

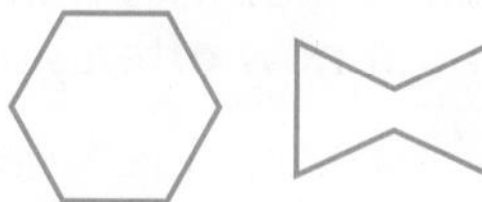

horizontal [hôr•i•zänt′l] **horizontal** In the direction from left to right

hour (hr) [our] **hora (h)** A unit used to measure time
1 hour = 60 minutes

hundredth [hun′drədth] **centésimo** One of one hundred equal parts (p. 31)
Example:

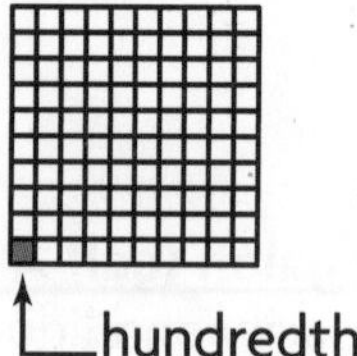

Identity Property of Addition [ī•den′tə•tē präp′ər•tē əv ə•dish′ən] **propiedad de identidad de la suma** The property that states that when you add zero to any number, the sum is that number
Example: $16 + 0 = 16$

Identity Property of Multiplication [ī•den′tə•tē präp′ər•tē əv mul•tə•pli•kā′shən] **propiedad de identidad de la multiplicación** The property that states that the product of any number and 1 is that number
Example: $9 \times 1 = 9$

inch (in.) [inch] **pulgada (pulg)** A customary unit used for measuring length or distance
Example:

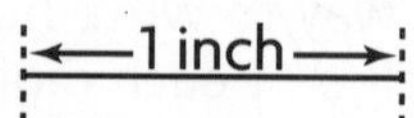

input/output table [ĭn′po͝ot/out′po͝ot tā′bəl] **tabla de entrada y salida** A table that matches each input value with an output value, where the output values are determined by the pattern, or function (p. 415)

interest [ĭn′trĭst] **interés** The additional money paid by a borrower to a lender in exchange for the use of the lender's money. For example, you earn interest from a bank if you have a savings account. (p. 653)

intersecting lines [in•tər•sekt′ing līnz] **líneas intersecantes** Lines that cross each other at exactly one point (p. 461)
Example:

inverse operations [in′vûrs äp•ə•rā′shənz] **operaciones inversas** Operations that undo each other, such as addition and subtraction or multiplication and division
Example: $6 \times 8 = 48$ and $48 \div 6 = 8$

key [kē] **clave** The part of a map or graph that explains the symbols

kilogram (kg) [kil′ō•gram] **kilogramo (kg)** A metric unit for measuring mass
1 kilogram = 1,000 grams

kilometer (km) [kə•läm′ət•ər] **kilómetro (km)** A metric unit for measuring length or distance (p. 520)
1 kilometer = 1,000 meters

length [lengkth] **longitud** The measurement of the distance between two points

less than sign (<) [les t͟han sīn] **signo de menor que (<)** A symbol used to compare two quantities, with the lesser quantity given first
Example: $3 < 7$

line [līn] **línea** A straight path of points in a plane that continues without end in both directions with no endpoints (p. 449)
Example:

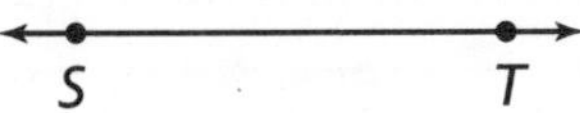

line graph [līn graf] **gráfica lineal** A graph that uses line segments to show how data change over time

line of symmetry [līn əv sim′ə•trē] **eje de simetría** An imaginary line on a shape about which the shape can be folded so that its two parts match exactly (p. 473)
Example:

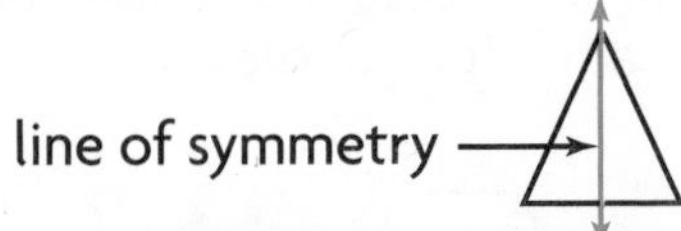

line segment [līn seg′mənt] **segmento** A part of a line that includes two points called endpoints and all the points between them (p. 449)
Example:

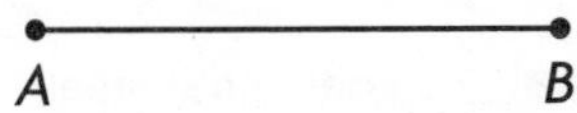

line symmetry [līn sim′ə•trē] **simetría axial** What a shape has if it can be folded about a line so that its two parts match exactly (p. 473)

linear units [lin′ē•ər yo͞o′nits] **unidades lineales** Units that measure length, width, height, or distance

liquid volume [lik′wid väl′yo͞om] **volumen de un líquido** The measure of the space a liquid occupies (p. 537)

liter (L) [lēt′ər] **litro (L)** A metric unit for measuring capacity and liquid volume
1 liter = 1,000 milliliters

loan [lōn] **préstamo** The money that is lent by a bank or other financial institution (p. 665)

mass [mas] **masa** The amount of matter in an object

meter (m) [mēt′ər] **metro (m)** A metric unit for measuring length or distance
1 meter = 100 centimeters

midnight [mid′nīt] **medianoche** 12:00 at night

mile (mi) [mīl] **milla (mi)** A customary unit for measuring length or distance (p. 519)
1 mile = 5,280 feet

milliliter (mL) [mil′i•lēt•ər] **mililitro (ml)** A metric unit for measuring capacity and liquid volume (p. 555)
1 liter = 1,000 milliliters

millimeter (mm) [mil′i•mēt•ər] **milímetro (mm)** A metric unit for measuring length or distance (p. 549)
1 centimeter = 10 millimeters

million [mil′yən] **millón** The counting number after 999,999; 1,000 thousands; written as 1,000,000

millions [mil′yənz] **millones** The period after thousands

minute (min) [min′it] **minuto (min)** A unit used to measure short amounts of time
1 minute = 60 seconds

mixed number [mikst num′bər] **número mixto** An amount given as a whole number and a fraction (p.105)

multiple [mul′tə•pəl] **múltiplo** The product of a number and a counting number is called a multiple of the number
Example:

$$\begin{array}{r} 3 \\ \times 1 \\ \hline 3 \end{array} \quad \begin{array}{r} 3 \\ \times 2 \\ \hline 6 \end{array} \quad \begin{array}{r} 3 \\ \times 3 \\ \hline 9 \end{array} \quad \begin{array}{r} 3 \\ \times 4 \\ \hline 12 \end{array} \quad \begin{array}{l} \\ \leftarrow \text{counting numbers} \\ \leftarrow \text{multiples of 3} \end{array}$$

multiplication [mul•tə•pli•kā′shən] **multiplicación** A process to find the total number of items in equal-sized groups, or to find the total number of items in a given number of groups when each group contains the same number of items; multiplication is the inverse of division

multiply [mul′tə•plī] **multiplicar** To combine equal groups to find how many in all; the opposite operation of division

nickel [nik′əl] **moneda de 5¢** A coin worth 5 cents and with a value equal to that of 5 pennies; 5¢
Example:

noon [no͞on] **mediodía** 12:00 in the day

not equal to sign (≠) [not ē′kwəl to͞o sīn] **signo de no igual a** A symbol that indicates one quantity is not equal to another
Example: $12 \times 3 \neq 38$

number line [num′bər līn] **recta numérica** A line on which numbers can be located
Example:

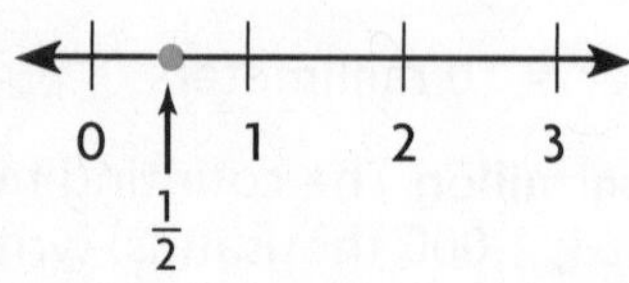

number sentence [num′bər sent′ns] **oración numérica** A sentence that includes numbers, operation symbols, and a greater than or less than symbol or an equal sign
Example: $5 + 3 = 8$

numerator [no͞o′mər•āt•ər] **numerador** The number above the bar in a fraction that tells how many parts of the whole or group are being considered

Example: $\frac{2}{3}$ ← numerator

obtuse angle [äb•to͞os′ ang′gəl] **ángulo obtuso** An angle that measures greater than 90° and less than 180° (p. 450)
Example:

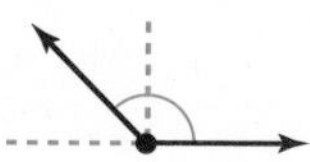

Word History

The Latin prefix ***ob-*** means "against." When combined with ***-tusus***, meaning "beaten," the Latin word ***obtusus***, from which we get ***obtuse***, means "beaten against." This makes sense when you look at an obtuse angle, because the angle is not sharp or acute. The angle looks as if it has been beaten against and become blunt and rounded.

obtuse triangle [äb•to͞os′ trī′ang•gəl] **triángulo obtusángulo** A triangle with one obtuse angle (p. 456)
Example:

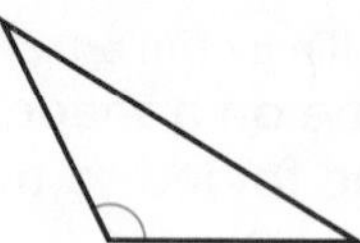

octagon [äk′tə•gän] **octágono** A polygon with eight sides and eight angles
Examples:

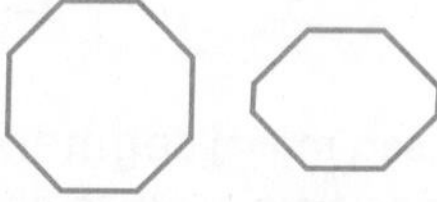

odd [od] **impar** A whole number that has a 1, 3, 5, 7, or 9 in the ones place

one-dimensional [wun də•men′shə•nəl] **unidimensional** Measured in only one direction, such as length
Examples:

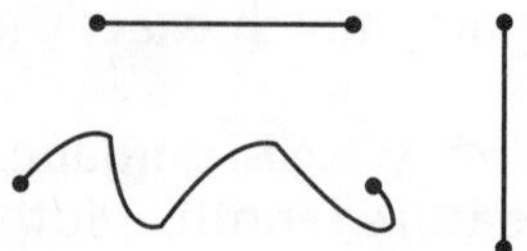

open shape [ō′pən shāp] **figura abierta** A shape that does not begin and end at the same point
Examples:

order [ôr′dər] **orden** A particular arrangement or placement of things one after the other

order of operations [ôr′dər əv äp•ə•rā′shənz] **orden de las operaciones** A special set of rules which gives the order in which calculations are done

ounce (oz) [ouns] **onza (oz)** A customary unit for measuring weight (p. 531)
1 pound = 16 ounces

parallel lines [pâr′ə•lel līnz] **líneas paralelas** Lines in the same plane that never intersect and are always the same distance apart (p. 461)
Example:

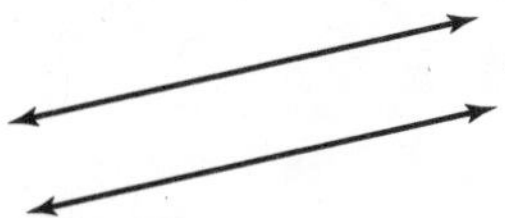

Word History

Euclid, an early Greek mathematician, was one of the first to explore the idea of parallel lines. The prefix ***para-*** means "beside or alongside." This prefix helps you understand the meaning of the word ***parallel***.

parallelogram [pâr•ə•lel′ə•gram] **paralelogramo** A quadrilateral whose opposite sides are parallel and of equal length (p. 467)
Example:

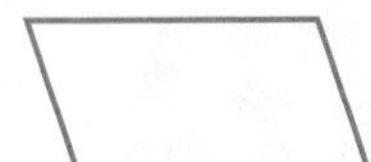

parentheses [pə•ren′thə•sēz] **paréntesis** The symbols used to show which operation or operations in an expression should be done first

partial product [pär′shəl präd′əkt] **producto parcial** A method of multiplying in which the ones, tens, hundreds, and so on are multiplied separately and then the products are added together (p. 230)

partial quotient [pär′shəl kwō′shənt] **cociente parcial** A method of dividing in which multiples of the divisor are subtracted from the dividend and then the quotients are added together (p. 349)

pattern [pat′ərn] **patrón** An ordered set of numbers or objects; the order helps you predict what will come next (p. 409)
Examples: 2, 4, 6, 8, 10

pattern unit [pat′ərn yo͞o′nit] **unidad de patrón** The part of a pattern that repeats
Example:

pentagon [pen′tə•gän] **pentágono** A polygon with five sides and five angles
Examples:

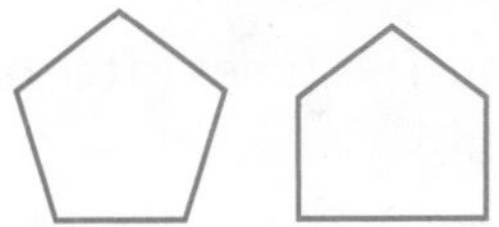

perimeter [pə•rim′ə•tər] **perímetro** The distance around a figure (p. 421)

period [pir′ē•əd] **período** Each group of three digits in a multi-digit number; periods are usually separated by commas or spaces. (p. 11)
Example: 85,643,900 has three periods.

perpendicular lines [pər•pən•dik′yo͞o•lər līnz] **líneas perpendiculares** Two lines that intersect to form four right angles (p. 461)
Example:

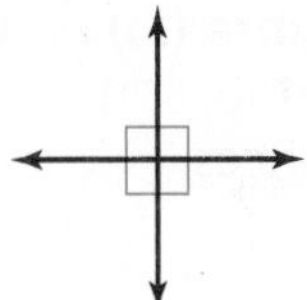

pictograph [pĭk'tə·grăf′] **pictografía** A graph that uses symbols to show and compare information
Example:

How We Get To School	
Walk	❋ ❋ ❋
Ride a Bike	❋ ❋ ❋ ❋
Ride a Bus	❋ ❋ ❋ ❋ ❋ ❋
Ride in a Car	❋ ❋

Key: Each ❋ = 10 students.

pint (pt) [pīnt] **pinta (pt)** A customary unit for measuring capacity and liquid volume (p. 537)
1 pint = 2 cups

place value [plās val′yōō] **valor posicional** The value of a digit in a number, based on the location of the digit

plane [plān] **plano** A flat surface that extends without end in all directions
Example:

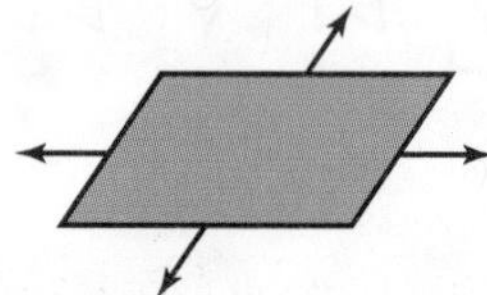

plane shape [plān shāp] **figura plana** See *two-dimensional shape.*

P.M. [pē•em] **p. m.** The times after noon and before midnight

point [point] **punto** An exact location in space (p. 449)

polygon [päl′i•gän] **polígono** A closed two-dimensional shape formed by three or more straight sides that are line segments
Examples:

Polygons

Not Polygons

pound (lb) [pound] **libra (lb)** A customary unit for measuring weight (p. 531)
1 pound = 16 ounces

prime number [prīm num′bər] **número primo** A number that has exactly two factors: 1 and itself
Examples: 2, 3, 5, 7, 11, 13, 17, and 19 are prime numbers. 1 is not a prime number.

prism [priz′əm] **prisma** A solid figure that has two same size, same polygon-shaped bases, and other faces that are all rectangles
Examples:

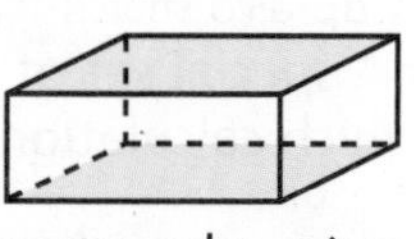

rectangular prism

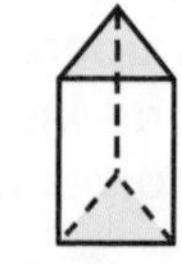

triangular prism

product [präd′əkt] **producto** The answer to a multiplication problem

profit [prŏf′ĭt] **ganancia** The amount left after all the expenses are subtracted from the amount of money received from selling an item or service (p. 647)

protractor [prō′trak•tər] **transportador** A tool for measuring the size of an angle (p. 499)

quadrilateral [kwä•dri•lat′ər•əl] **cuadrilátero** A polygon with four sides and four angles

quart (qt) [kwôrt] **cuarto (ct)** A customary unit for measuring capacity and liquid volume (p. 537)
1 quart = 2 pints

quarter hour [kwôrt′ər our] **cuarto de hora** 15 minutes
Example: 4:00 to 4:15 is one quarter hour

quotient [kwō′shənt] **cociente** The number, not including the remainder, that results from dividing
Example: 8 ÷ 4 = 2; 2 is the quotient.

ray [rā] **semirrecta** A part of a line; it has one endpoint and continues without end in one direction (p. 449)
Example:

rectangle [rek′tang•gəl] **rectángulo** A quadrilateral with two pairs of parallel sides, two pairs of sides of equal length, and four right angles (p. 467)
Example:

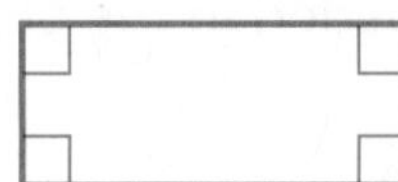

rectangular prism [rek•tang′gyə•lər priz′əm] **prisma rectangular** A three-dimensional shape in which all six faces are rectangles
Example:

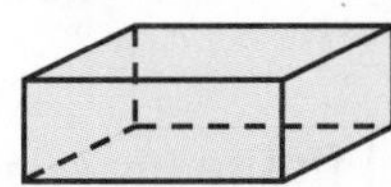

regroup [rē•grōōp′] **reagrupar** To exchange amounts of equal value to rename a number
Example: 5 + 8 = 13 ones or 1 ten 3 ones

regular polygon [reg′yə•lər päl′i•gän] **polígono regular** A polygon that has all sides that are equal in length and all angles equal in measure
Examples:

related facts [ri•lāt′id fakts] **operaciones relacionadas** A set of related addition and subtraction, or multiplication and division, number sentences
Examples: 4 × 7 = 28   28 ÷ 4 = 7
7 × 4 = 28   28 ÷ 7 = 4

remainder [ri•mān′dər] **residuo** The amount left over when a number cannot be divided equally (p. 312)

rhombus [räm′bəs] **rombo** A quadrilateral with two pairs of parallel sides and four sides of equal length (p. 467)
Example:

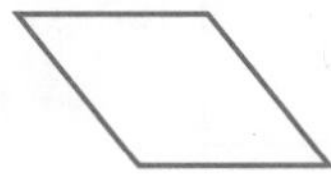

right angle [rīt ang′gəl] **ángulo recto** An angle that forms a square corner (p. 450)
Example:

right triangle [rīt trī′ang•gəl] **triángulo rectángulo** A triangle with one right angle (p. 456)
Example:

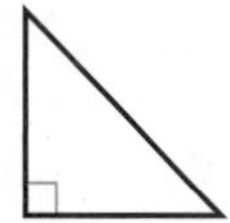

round [round] **redondear** To replace a number with another number that tells about how many or how much (p. 23)

rule [rōōl] **regla** A procedure (usually involving arithmetic operations) to determine an output value from an input value

scale [skāl] **escala** A series of numbers placed at fixed distances on a graph to help label the graph

second (sec) [sek′ənd] **segundo (s)** A small unit of time (p. 563)
1 minute = 60 seconds

simplest form [sim′pləst fôrm] **mínima expresión** A fraction is in simplest form when the numerator and denominator have only 1 as a common factor (p. 88)

solid shape [sä′lid shāp] **cuerpo geométrico** See *three-dimensional figure.*

square [skwâr] **cuadrado** A quadrilateral with two pairs of parallel sides, four sides of equal length, and four right angles (p. 467)
Example:

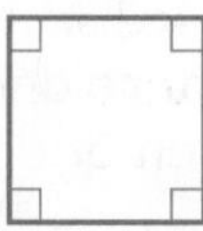

square unit [skwâr yōō′nit] **unidad cuadrada** A unit used to measure area such as square foot, square meter, and so on (p. 427)

standard form [stan′dərd fôrm] **forma normal** A way to write numbers by using the digits 0–9, with each digit having a place value (p. 11)
Example: 3,540 ← standard form

stem-and-leaf plot [stĕm ənd lēf plŏt] **diagrama de tallo y hojas** A graph that shows groups of data arranged by place value (p. 621)

straight angle [strāt ang′gəl] **ángulo llano** An angle whose measure is 180° (p. 450)
Example:

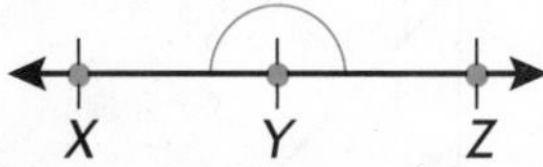

subtraction [səb•trak′shən] **resta** The process of finding how many are left when a number of items are taken away from a group of items; the process of finding the difference when two groups are compared; the opposite operation of addition

sum [sum] **suma o total** The answer to an addition problem

survey [sûr′vā] **encuesta** A method of gathering information

tally table [tal′ē tā′bəl] **tabla de conteo** A table that uses tally marks to record data

> **Word History**
>
> Some people keep score in card games by making marks on paper (IIII). These marks are known as tally marks. The word ***tally*** is related to ***tailor***, from the Latin ***talea***, meaning "twig." In early times, a method of keeping count was by cutting marks into a piece of wood or bone.

temperature [tem′pər•ə•chər] **temperatura** The degree of hotness or coldness usually measured in degrees Fahrenheit or degrees Celsius

tenth [tenth] **décimo** One of ten equal parts (p. 31)
Example:

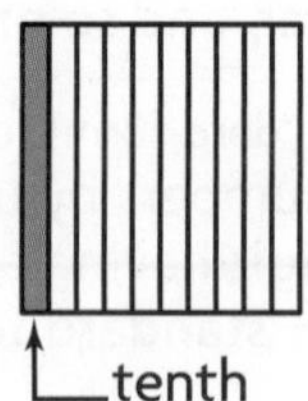

term [tûrm] **término** A number or object in a pattern (p. 409)

thousands [thou′zəndz] **millares** The period after the ones period in the base-ten number system

three-dimensional [thrē də•men′shə•nəl] **tres dimensiones** Measured in three directions, such as length, width, and height
Example:

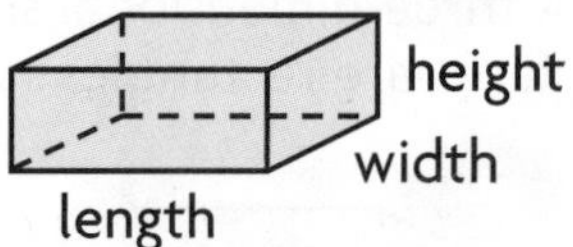

three-dimensional figure [thrē də•men′shə•nəl fig′yər] **figura de tres dimensiones** A figure having length, width, and height

ton (T) [tun] **tonelada (t)** A customary unit used to measure weight (p. 532)
1 ton = 2,000 pounds

trapezoid [trap′i•zoid] **trapecio** A quadrilateral with exactly one pair of parallel sides (p. 467)
Examples:

triangle [trī′ang•gəl] **triángulo** A polygon with three sides and three angles
Examples:

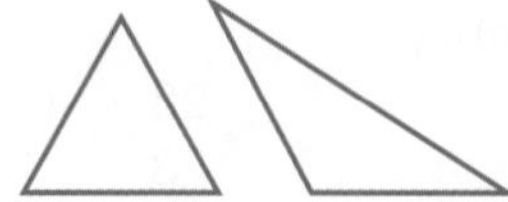

two-dimensional [to͞o də•men′shə•nəl] **dos dimensiones** Measured in two directions, such as length and width
Example:

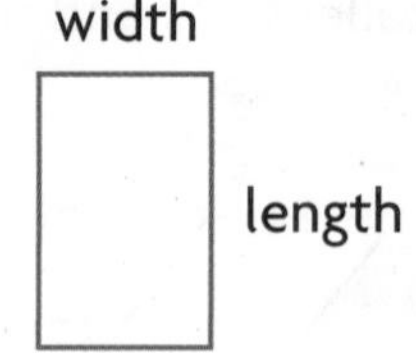

two-dimensional figure [to͞o də•men′shə•nəl fig′yər] **figura de dos dimensiones** A figure that lies in a plane; a shape having length and width

unit fraction [yōō′nit frak′shən] **fracción unitaria** A fraction that has a numerator of one (p. 99)

unit square [yōō′nit skwâr] **cuadrado de una unidad** a square that is 1 unit long and 1 unit wide (p. 427)

variable [vâr′ē•ə•bəl] **variable** A letter or symbol that stands for a number or numbers

variable expense [vâr'ē•ə•bəl ĭk•spĕns'] **gastos variables** Expenses in which the amount does change based on need or choice (p. 641)

Venn diagram [ven dī′ə•gram] **diagrama de Venn** A diagram that shows relationships among sets of things
Example:

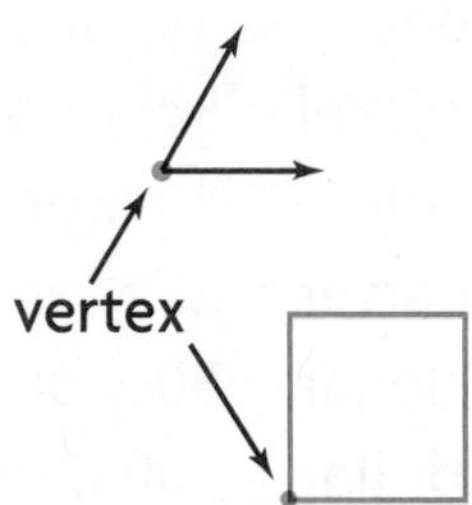

vertex [vûr′teks] **vértice** The point at which two rays of an angle meet or two (or more) line segments meet in a two-dimensional shape
Examples:

vertex

vertical [vûr′ti•kəl] **vertical** In the direction from top to bottom

weight [wāt] **peso** How heavy an object is

whole [hōl] **entero** All of the parts of a shape or group

word form [wûrd fôrm] **en palabras** A way to write numbers by using words
Example: Four hundred fifty-three thousand, two hundred twelve

yard (yd) [yärd] **yarda (yd)** A customary unit for measuring length or distance
1 yard = 3 feet

Zero Property of Multiplication [zē′rō präp′ər•tē əv mul•tə•pli•kā′shən] **propiedad del cero de la multiplicación** The property that states that the product of 0 and any number is 0
Example: $0 \times 8 = 0$

Table of Measures

METRIC	CUSTOMARY
Length	
1 centimeter (cm) = 10 millimeters (mm)	1 foot (ft) = 12 inches (in.)
1 meter (m) = 1,000 millimeters	1 yard (yd) = 3 feet, or 36 inches
1 meter = 100 centimeters	1 mile (mi) = 1,760 yards, or 5,280 feet
1 meter = 10 decimeters (dm)	
1 kilometer (km) = 1,000 meters	
Capacity and Liquid Volume	
1 liter (L) = 1,000 milliliters (mL)	1 cup (c) = 8 fluid ounces (fl oz)
	1 pint (pt) = 2 cups
	1 quart (qt) = 2 pints, or 4 cups
	1 half gallon = 2 quarts
	1 gallon (gal) = 2 half gallons, or 4 quarts
Mass/Weight	
1 kilogram (kg) = 1,000 grams (g)	1 pound (lb) = 16 ounces (oz)
	1 ton (T) = 2,000 pounds

TIME
1 minute (min) = 60 seconds (sec)
1 half hour = 30 minutes
1 hour (hr) = 60 minutes
1 day (d) = 24 hours
1 week (wk) = 7 days
1 year (yr) = 12 months (mo), or about 52 weeks
1 year = 365 days
1 leap year = 366 days
1 decade = 10 years
1 century = 100 years

MONEY
1 penny = 1¢, or \$0.01
1 nickel = 5¢, or \$0.05
1 dime = 10¢, or \$0.10
1 quarter = 25¢, or \$0.25
1 half dollar = 50¢, or \$0.50
1 dollar = 100¢, or \$1.00

Table of Measures

SYMBOLS

Symbol	Meaning	Symbol	Meaning
$<$	is less than	$\perp$	is perpendicular to
$>$	is greater than	$\parallel$	is parallel to
$=$	is equal to	$\overleftrightarrow{AB}$	line *AB*
$\neq$	is not equal to	$\overrightarrow{AB}$	ray *AB*
¢	cent or cents	$\overline{AB}$	line segment *AB*
$	dollar or dollars	$\angle ABC$	angle *ABC* or angle *B*
°	degree or degrees	$\triangle ABC$	triangle *ABC*

FORMULAS

Perimeter		Area	
Polygon	$P =$ sum of the lengths of sides	Rectangle	$A = l \times w$
Rectangle	$P = (2 \times l) + (2 \times w)$ or $P = 2 \times (l + w)$		
Square	$P = 4 \times s$